Quantitative
Methods
in Law

Quantitative Methods in Law

*Studies in the Application
of Mathematical Probability and
Statistics to Legal Problems*

Michael O. Finkelstein

THE FREE PRESS
A Division of Macmillan Publishing Co., Inc.
NEW YORK

Collier Macmillan Publishers
LONDON

This book was prepared with the support of NSF Grant SOC 76-22375. However, any opinions, findings, conclusions, or recommendations herein are those of the author and do not necessarily reflect the views of the National Science Foundation.

The Free Press
A Division of Macmillan Publishing Co., Inc.
866 Third Avenue, New York, N.Y. 10022

Collier Macmillan Canada, Ltd.

Library of Congress Catalog Card Number: 77-94081

Printed in the United States of America

printing number

1 2 3 4 5 6 7 8 9 10

Library of Congress Cataloging in Publication Data

Finkelstein, Michael O
    Quantitative methods in law.

    Includes indexes.
    1. Law--Methodology. 2. Law--Mathematical models.
I. Title.
K212.F5   340.1'82   77-94081
ISBN 0-02-910260-X

For
Claire Oakes
and
Katherine Eban

CONTENTS

PREFACE AND ACKNOWLEDGMENTS

THE STUDIES IN THIS BOOK were written over approximately twelve years, during which time I was (as I still am) a lawyer engaged primarily in private practice. The original impulse was a problem in jury discrimination that I believed the Supreme Court had resolved incorrectly due to a failure to understand the significance of certain statistical proof. Almost simultaneously I saw problems in antitrust and evidence that seemed amenable to a mathematical approach. This swift unfolding of ideas led me to think that mathematics might offer new insights for a broad range of legal questions of which I had glimpsed only a few examples. While still unraveling the first problems, I decided to attempt a series of essays demonstrating the possibilities and diversity of a mathematical approach. This book is the fruit of that effort.

The choice of subjects deserves a word of explanation. My method probably is best descibed as persistent haphazard selection, for the principal research tool was simply to look in a new way at the flow of problems and judicial opinions that crossed my desk. The topics drawn from this source thus represent a personal encounter with the law over a period of time rather than a census of important legal problems susceptible to a mathematical approach. Very large and important areas which seem potentially interesting from a quantitative point of view—such as environmental law—are not touched here.

When I began publishing these studies, statistical methods in the law were in their infancy and the techniques seemed arcane. Today they are more advanced: there are courses in statistics for lawyers at the major law schools, and legal journals are devoted to the subject. However, the progress of application has been slower than one might have hoped. Most attempts to use quantitative methods in litigated disputes have encountered strong legal and technical objections. Clearly the effort is not worth making unless mathematical findings are a significant aid to legal judgment. The purpose of this book is to show that this is indeed the case in diverse fields of law.

Except for the introductory chapter, the essays appear here in approximately the order in which they were written. They begin with probability and end with statistics; fortuitously this is the order of most elementary courses on statistics. However, each is self-contained and may be read separately.

To a significant extent, this book represents a collaboration with mathematicians. I thank them all for their generous participation in the studies that originally appeared as co-authored writings, and for their assistance in the others that appeared under my name alone. William B. Fairley, formerly a professor of statistics at Harvard University, over many years has been a valued mentor in mathematics and is the co-author of certain portions of Chapter 3 on evidence, and of the Appendix, which originally appeared in the *Harvard Law Review* (1970). Herbert Robbins, Professor of Mathematical Statistics at Columbia University, is the author of the mathematical appendix to Chapter 4 on voting which originally appeared as part of an article in the *Columbia Law Review* (1973). I thank him for his interest in legal applications of probability and for his unfailing willingness to elucidate mathematical theory for me. Richard M. Friedberg, a professor of physics at Columbia University, is the co-author of Chapter 5 on economic concentration, which originally appeared in the *Yale Law Journal* (1967). He also contributed key mathematical ideas in a number of other essays; I am deeply grateful for our friendship and for his help. Gerald J. Glasser, Professor of Business Statistics at New York University, and Patricia Pickrel, a practicing lawyer, are the co-authors of Chapter 8 on wrongful death, which originally appeared in the *Columbia Law Review* (1975). In various projects together over the years, Professor Glasser has given me the benefit of his craftsmanship in working out the problems of practical studies.

In addition to the chapters mentioned above, Chapter 2 on jury discrimination is an updated and revised version of an article that originally appeared in the *Harvard Law Review*

(1966); Chapter 6 on insurance company reserves appeared in the *University of Pennsylvania Law Review* (1971); Chapter 7 on regression models appeared in the *Harvard Law Review* (1973); and Chapter 9 on guilty plea practices is a corrected version of an article published in the *Harvard Law Review* (1975). I thank the publishers of the various law reviews for permission to reprint these and the articles mentioned in the preceding paragraph.

Frederick Mosteller, Professor of Statistics at Harvard University, read and made mathematical corrections to certain portions of the manuscript. I appreciate the time and trouble he took to do this. I am also indebted to David Baldus, Abigail Davis, John Endicott, Lisa Horowitz, Martin F. Richman, Marvin E. Frankel, and Jack B. Weinstein for various contributions, comments, and suggestions.

My secretary, Elizabeth Bell, was indefatigable in typing the manuscript and in preparing data. The book could not have been written without her.

Certain of the research for the book was supported by grants from the George H. and Edythe F. Heyman Family Foundation and from the Walter E. Meyer Foundation. Publication was supported by a grant from the National Science Foundation.

During the writing of this book, I frequently discussed the theory of the enterprise and its problems with my wife, Elinor Fuchs. She knew nothing of mathematical statistics and little of law. But she brought wonderful powers of intellect to her taste for a deep pursuit, mastered the themes of these studies, and was able repeatedly to suggest improvements and new lines of inquiry. I hope this book contributes to the humane values that she cherishes!

Quantitative Methods in Law

Chapter 1

INTRODUCTION TO QUANTITATIVE METHODS

LEGAL THOUGHT IS threaded with assessments of probability and descriptions of a statistical nature, but the data underlying these ideas seldom are collected and rarely are used for other than general impressions. Even far-reaching and debatable questions of fact are decided on a thoroughly subjective basis and in panoramic terms that are congenial to moral or political judgment. The pressures of decision thus have created two levels of discourse. While we recognize the "sociological" principle that a rule should be tested by its consequences, the way those consequences are determined remains less rational than the theory that summons their consideration.

This impressionism in legal fact finding is not without exception. There are efforts in diverse fields of law—perhaps no more than eddies in the main current—to deal with facts on a more systematic and objective basis. It is natural that these efforts to make law more "scientific" should involve mathematics. Since much of our knowledge in social and economic matters is expressed in numbers, analysis of data becomes necessary whenever legal rules require relatively precise findings based on such evidence. If decisions in these contexts are to be rational, we need correct methods for assembling the data and systematic techniques for analyzing them. It is for these purposes that we turn to mathematical probability and statistics.

1

I

In professional matters involving experiences of ordinary life, intuition about probability is comfortable for most lawyers. They have no reason to doubt their intuition and no occasion to test their perceptions against the mathematics of probability. Even the idea of such a test is unlikely to suggest itself since legal probability seems far removed from its mathematical counterpart. While the notion of probability is used in law to express uncertainty, only the broadest use is made of probabilistic conceptions, and for such purposes common sense, without mathematics, is perceived as adequate.

Moreover, in formulating legal rules, most lawyers regard themselves as rather good probabilists in the sense that they act with discrimination in the face of doubt. This view appears in the work of G. W. Leibniz, who was the first lawyer to look at probability in legal thought from a mathematical point of view. Writing to John Bernoulli in 1710, Leibniz pointed out that lawyers used concepts such as "conjecture," "indication," and "presumption" and that these corresponded to levels of probability which he expressed as "not full," "half full," and "full." Such shadings of meaning led him to conclude that "Jurists have practiced best of all mankind the art of logic in regard to contingencies, as have mathematicians in regard to necessities." To develop the subject, he planned (but never executed) a work in which lawyers would be presented as models of probability logic in "contingent" questions.[1] More than two centuries later, in his classic work on probability, John Maynard Keynes analyzed several English law cases in which the judges

---

[1]COUTURAT, LA LOGIQUE DE LEIBNIZ 240–41 (1961). The quoted phrase is from a fragment of an introduction to this projected work, the only part extant. It appears in COUTURAT, OPUSCULES ET FRAGMENTS INÉDITS DE LEIBNIZ 210 (1961).

One of the earliest applications of the new calculus of probability to a legal question was an essay by Nicolas Bernoulli published in Basle in 1709. Bernoulli examined various questions relating to human affairs, among them the time at the end of which a missing person might be deemed dead, the value of annuities, marine insurance, the probability of the truth of testimony, and the probability of innocence of an accused person. TODHUNTER, HISTORY OF THE MATHEMATICAL THEORY OF PROBABILITY 194–96 (1865). Some of these themes were picked up by later investigators. See, e.g., LAPLACE, A PHILOSOPHICAL ESSAY ON PROBABILITIES (1819).

had wrestled with the problem of drawing a line between an estimate of damages based on probabilities (which would be allowed) and a claim of a totally problematic character (which would not). He echoed Leibniz: lawyers were indeed subtle probabilists.[2]

But agreeing with Leibniz and Keynes that legal rules reflect degrees of probability does not mean that judges and juries are immune to certain persistent biases in estimation that distort intuitive judgment. Studies have demonstrated the nature of these biases. Did man X die in an accident? Did suspect Y leave this telltale trace? Such statements are of the form: What is the probability that the object (e.g., man X's cause of death) belongs to the class (deaths from accident)? The answers require a comparison of the object's characteristics with those of known class members. It is useful to divide these characteristics into those described in general terms that form the evidentiary "background" (the deceased was a male of certain age), and those described in sufficient detail to make them more particular to the object (the detailed circumstances of the deceased's death). Obviously there is no bright line between these types of evidence.

One important bias arises because persons tend to underestimate the probative force of the background; this distorts the perceived value of more particular evidence. For example, the judicial refusal to accept identity of blood type as affirmative proof of paternity is a rule precluding particular evidence that could not be justified if the significance of the background were understood.[3] A jurisprudence that recognized such biases would insist on an appraisal of the background (quantified where possible) and evidentiary rules based on a logically correct view of the combined force of both types of proof.

Another important bias arises from the tendency of persons to underestimate the significance of differences between the object and those of the class. The characteristics of the trace do not perfectly match those of the accused; the reported circumstances of death do not agree perfectly with those generally associated with suicide. In theory these are issues of random sampling. How probable is it that random selection from the

[2]KEYNES, TREATISE ON PROBABILITY 25 (3d ed. 1973).

[3]See chapter 3 *infra* at pp. 74–78 for a discussion of this example.

class would produce an object with the observed traits? In answering such questions, people tend to overestimate the probability that random selection would produce a sample with characteristics that differ from the average selection. Test yourself: In a random sample of twenty-four balls picked without replacement from an urn containing fifty white and fifty black balls, the expected number of white balls is twelve. What is the probability that there will be no more than five? The correct answer is much smaller than the intuitive estimate generally given.[4] This natural bias has distorted judgment in cases involving alleged discrimination in the selection of jurors[5] and in various other legal contexts in which chance selection from a population is an accepted legal model.[6]

Probability calculations are also important when accuracy is necessary and the probabilistic process is foreign to common experience. No sensible administrative law judge would accept pure subjective appraisal of the risk of a catastrophic spill of liquefied natural gas in a crowded port if he had access to more objective information.[7] Nor should an insurance commissioner be content to guess at the reserves required of insurance companies to protect them from random fluctuations in claims.[8]

The need for calculation in technical contexts is most generally recognized in the field of sampling. Appraising sample statistics requires probabilistic statements about sampling variation, a process that common experience recognizes only in terms that are too broad to be very useful. Objective calculation of such variation is the basic aim of scientific sampling and is usually required in legal presentations. For example, an antitrust consent decree required the defendant to conduct "a scientific sample of the performances of the compositions of its members," with a court-appointed independent person to "examine the design and conduct of the survey, make estimates of

---

[4] The probability is approximately one in a thousand.

[5] See chapter 2 *infra*.

[6] Random selection models may sometimes be presumed to be appropriate in the absence of contrary evidence. See chapter 4 *infra* at 120–28 for an example.

[7] See Fairley, *Evaluating the "Small" Probability of a Catastrophic Accident from the Marine Transportation of Liquified Natural Gas*, in STATISTICS AND PUBLIC POLICY (FAIRLEY & MOSTELLER EDS. 1977).

[8] See chapter 6 *infra*.

the accuracy of the samples, and report thereon to the Court and the parties."[9] This mandate can be met only if the sample is drawn in accordance with rigorous procedures that control the methods used and determine the limits of permissible inference.

The size of the sample is a particularly important issue in experimental design. The ideal design involves reasoning "backward" from the precision of the sample estimate to the size of the experiment necessary to achieve it. In theory at least, an experiment larger than this is unwarranted and undesirable. Since legal studies frequently involve relatively large statistical differences, mathematical theory teaches that sufficient precision is obtainable from much smaller samples than are used when the design is not analytically determined. An admirable experiment in personal-injury litigation used a sample of some 3,000 cases to demonstrate that, contrary to accepted opinion, a mandatory pretrial conference did not increase rates of settlement. The sample appeared substantially larger than was necessary to determine whether mandatory pretrial produced sufficiently higher rates of settlement to make it worth judicial time.[10]

Achieving the right size for experiments affects important issues of cost and control over nonsampling errors. It is of special importance in official legal experiments in which the state subjects persons chosen at random to some new procedure designed to achieve a benefit (perhaps of efficiency or economy) to the legal system. Experiments of this kind may be justified if it is anticipated that the reform will not adversely affect either the individual or society.[11] But ethical and constitutional concerns dictate that no more than the minimum number

[9]United States v. American Society of Composers, Authors & Publishers, [1960] TRADE CASES (CCH) ¶ 69, 612 at 76, 468–69 (S.D.N.Y. 1960). Federal agencies frequently require standard error estimates to be presented with sample data. See, e.g., Interstate Commerce Commission, *Guidelines for the Presentation of The Results of Sample Studies*, § D(3) (1968).

[10]The study is described in ROSENBERG, THE PRETRIAL CONFERENCE AND EFFECTIVE JUSTICE (1964). The large sample of 3,000 cases produced an estimate of the difference in settlement rates with a standard error of approximately 1.5 percentage points. A sample one-fifth as large would have produced an estimate with a standard error of 3.4 percentage points, and a sample one-tenth as large an estimate with a standard error of 4.8 percentage points.

[11]*Cf.* Aguayo v. Richardson, 473 F. 2d 1090 (2d Cir. 1973).

needed to obtain the necessary information ought to be involved, and that the study ought to stop whenever it is known
that, contrary to expectations, the proposed reform does have an
adverse impact. The ethical goals of such "stopping rules" can
be achieved only with the analytic methods of mathematical
probability.[12]

While it is still unusual to find probabilities computed in
legal cases, elementary statistical methods have established
considerably more than a foothold. Statistical indices of central
tendency, such as the mean or the median, have long been accepted. More recently, attention has turned to measures based
on correlation. In constitutional challenges to the property tax
financing of public schools, the courts have looked at Pear-
sonian correlation coefficients to measure the association between wealth of school districts and their per pupil expenditures.[13] "Beta" coefficients that reflect the correlation between
the return on portfolio securities and the average return for
market securities have been used to fix insurance company
rates,[14] and to assess the performance of portfolio managers.[15]
Tests for employment that disqualify disproportionate
numbers of minority groups must be validated by correlation
of test scores with employment success.[16]

[12]For example, suppose a state wishes to experiment with small (six-person) juries in criminal trials, and to adopt such juries if they do not appreciably
disadvantage defendants. An experiment based on a sample of fixed size
would be undesirable because it would continue until the requisite number
of cases had been tried, even though the interim results might show that
smaller juries produced unacceptably lower acquittal rates. Under the method
known as sequential analysis, the experiment would terminate whenever sufficient evidence of a significant difference appeared, thus avoiding further
trials with small juries after they were known to have undesired consequences. See generally WALD, SEQUENTIAL ANALYSIS (1947).

[13]See, e.g., San Antonio School District v. Rodriguez, 411 U.S. 1, 15, 25–27
(opinion of the Court per Powell, J.); 95 n. 56 (dissenting opinion of Marshall,
J. with Douglas, J. concurring); Northshore School District v. Kunnear, 84
Wash. 2d 685, 530 P.2d 178 (1974).

[14]See Opinion, Findings, and Decision on 1978 Automobile Insurance
Rates (Mass. Ins. Comm., Dec. 28, 1977).

[15]2 S.E.C., *Institutional Investor Study Report* 263–65, 400–10 (1971).
Market studies using beta coefficients abound. See, e.g., CAMPANELLA, THE
MEASUREMENT OF PORTFOLIO RISK EXPOSURE (1972).

[16]If an employment test produces a disparate pass rate for a cognizable
group, Federal Equal Employment Opportunity Commission guidelines
require that the relationship between the test and at least one relevant crite-

Statistical models are also used to infer causal relations from patterns in data. In such contexts, statistical findings may correct false impressions and provide assessments when there is no other basis for judgment. Errors in intuitive perception of cause range from vagaries in judgment to fundamental misconceptions.

The former may be illustrated by judgments about the future conduct of persons—a job applicant, a student seeking admission, a defendant awaiting sentence, or an inmate applying for bail or parole. The traditional clinical prediction is assumed to be reasonably accurate, and the administrators fortify themselves with a conviction of correctness. For example, the District of Columbia's pretrial detention law authorizes judicial officers to detain arrested persons whose release would, in their opinion, pose a threat to the community. Unfortunately, statistical study has demonstrated convincingly that the identification of those committing future crimes will be more often wrong than right, regardless of the numbers detained.[17] Nor is this an atypical result. The clinical prediction of infrequent human behavior appears largely unreliable, and the clinician's conviction has come to be regarded as an illusion of validity.

In an effort to improve its evaluations, the U.S. Board of Parole now relies on a statistical measuring device to estimate the probability of an inmate's parole violation if released. In

---

rion of employment success be statistically valid, i.e., "the relationship must be sufficiently high as to have a probability of no more than 1 in 20 to have occurred by chance." 29 C.F.R. § 1607.5(c) (1) (1975). A measure of significance is thus used as a surrogate for the degree of association. This is inappropriate because a low level of association may coexist with a high level of significance if the numbers of employees are large; the opposite is true, and close association may lack significance, if the numbers are small. Since even a test that correlates fairly well with employment experience will not necessarily satisfy this criterion if very few employees are involved, the guideline may strike down tests before the evidence is in. The small numbers of employees involved, rather than a lack of intrinsic correlation, may account for the "odd patchwork of results" noted by the Supreme Court in Albermarle Paper Company v. Moody, 422 U.S. 405 (1975), its first case involving this guideline.

[17]See Note, *Preventive Detention: An Empirical Analysis*, 6 HARV. C. R. - C. L. L. REV. 289 (1971). The Harvard study showed that the best predictive use of the statutory criteria in the District of Columbia preventive-detention law would cause more nonrecidivists than recidivists to be detained—regardless of the cutoff point for detention. *Id.* at 324–30.

this method, the probability of violation is predicted from inmates' personal factors that have been found to correlate with violations. Parole-release guidelines are then based in part on the statistical estimate. The Board's method has been upheld by the courts as an acceptable way of fulfilling its statutory duty to determine whether the inmate "will live and remain at liberty without violating the laws."[18]

Actuarial methods are advantageous in parole because the decisions are based on objective and consistent evaluations of predictive factors. By eliminating idiosyncracy and bias, statistical appraisal has demonstrated a predictive power that appears superior to traditional clinical judgment, although the point has been disputed.[19] The superiority of statistical methods in the long run seems assured, since the selection of relatively few objectively defined factors has enabled investigators to experiment with various combinations, to refine methods, and to record progress.

However, statistical studies have shown that the best predictors are prior criminal activity and selected facts from personal history, such as education and employment. This raises the thorny question whether release is properly postponed on the basis of factors antedating the offense, which in effect punish an inmate for his social status.[20] And behind this discrimination is the inexorable quality of the statistical verdict with its rejection of individual character and will. The empirical evidence generated by statistical methods reveals a clash of values reaching deeply into the theory of parole and individual responsibility in the criminal law.

Much larger intuitive misconceptions about cause flow from the common belief that the world conforms to simple a priori conceptions. If it seems logical, reasonable, or morally satisfy-

---

[18]18 U.S.C. § 4203(a) (1969); see, *e.g.*, Lupo v. Norton, 371 F. Supp. 156 (D. Conn. 1974); Battle v. Norton, 365 F. Supp. 926 (D. Conn. 1973). The current statute has a new criterion. 18 U.S.C. § 4206 (Supp. 1978).

[19]See generally MEEHL, CLINICAL VS. STATISTICAL PREDICTION (1954). To be sure, the Board's device is not impressively accurate. For example, approximately 55% of those whom the Board classifies as "poor" risks - and retains for more than a year on that basis - do not have reported unfavorable results when released. Hoffman & Beck, *Parole Decision-Making: A Salient Factor Score*, 2 J. CRIM. JUST. 195, 202 (1974).

[20]The factors currently used by the Board were selected as the best predictors from some 66 candidates. See Hoffman & Beck, *supra* n. 19.

ing to infer that *A* causes *B*, judges (and lesser beings) forget that *A* may be only an imperfect or partial cause of *B*, or that complicating factors may obscure or destroy the connection suggested by theory. In approving the constitutionality of plea bargaining, the Supreme Court assumed that those yielding to the pressure would in any event be convicted. This assumption diminishes the constitutional concern over pressures to plead. However, an observed negative correlation between guilty pleas and defendants not convicted in various federal district courts suggests that many defendants are being induced to plead who would not otherwise be convicted. Evidently, prosecution for crime is a less predictable process for those entering pleas than the Court has recognized.[21]

Another seemingly reasonable notion is that juries are more arbitrary in awarding damages than judges, who are trained to apply the law strictly. Again the truth is more complex. Analysis of awards in wrongful death cases involving children shows that damage recoveries vary less in states that allow juries to award compensation for emotional distress than they do in states that formally refuse to allow such recovery. The reason appears to be that the strict rule is relaxed or abandoned by judge and jury under the pressure of equities in compelling cases.[22]

These statistical findings are not paradoxical. Indeed, when the facts are thoughtfully examined, they seem to provide important new insights. They disclose a reality less neat, less morally unequivocal, and more interesting than the smooth world of legal theory. But the logic of these situations is not so compelling that any particular point of view could be accepted without investigation.

Frequently, a variable of legal interest is recognized to be dependent on a number of causal factors and a legal issue turns on an analysis of the relationship. To quantify such complex situations, statisticians commonly use a technique known as multiple regression, in which numerical codes for the explanatory factors are weighted so as to maximize their correlation with the dependent variable. This technique is of particular value in the law since it is not usually possible to dissect complex real-life situations using controlled experiments.

[21]See chapter 9 *infra*.
[22]See chapter 8 *infra*.

Does pretrial detention adversely affect the ability of those charged with a crime to defend themselves? Those detained suffer a higher conviction rate than those released on bail, but detention per se may not be the cause, since factors that lead to high bail (e.g., a prior criminal record) may also increase the probability of conviction. To determine the separate effect of pretrial detention, the Legal Aid Society of New York subjected data for sample groups of defendants to multiple regression analysis in which the probability of conviction was represented as the weighted sum of numerical codes for pretrial status and other relevant factors, such as type of crime, drug use, and criminal record. The multiple regression weight for pretrial status showed that pretrial detention increased the conviction rate by about one third, making it the single most important influence on probability of conviction.[23]

Multiple regression has also proved useful in employment discrimination cases to isolate the effect of race or sex apart from correlated variables that might justify inferior employment status. In a recent challenge to practices at the *Reader's Digest*, plaintiffs' multiple regression analysis showed significant discrimination against women after controlling for variables of age, experience, and education. Confronted with this evidence, the defendant agreed to an award of back pay and to mend its ways.[24]

Regulatory agencies frequently face questions susceptible to multiple regression when they attempt to gauge the effect that changes in prices or rates will have on regulated industries. The staff of the U.S. Civil Aeronautics Board has used regression studies to show the effect that increases in fares set by the Board would have on the demand for air travel.[25] Without such

[23]For a detailed description of the study, see Plaintiff's Memorandum on the Merits, Roballo v. The Judges, No. 74-2113 (S.D.N.Y., filed May 16, 1974). An earlier study which used a similar technique and reached similar conclusions is described in Brief for Plaintiff at 13–29, A36–40, Bellamy v. the Judges, 41 App. Div.2d 196, 342 N.Y.S.2d 137 (1973), *aff'd without opinion*, 32 N.Y.2d 886, 346 N.Y.S.2d 812 (1973).

[24]Smith v. The Reader's Digest Association, 73 Civ. 4883 (S.D.N.Y., filed Nov. 14, 1973). For a discussion of this type of application see Note, *Beyond the Prima Facie Case in Employment Discrimination Law: Statistical Proof and Rebuttal*, 89 HARV. L. REV. 387 (1975).

[25]Domestic Passenger Fare Investigation Phase 7, No. 21866-7 (C.A.B., Apr. 7, 1971) discussed in chapter 7 *infra* at pp. 240–45.

analysis the price elasticity of this demand could not be estimated. Regression models have also been used to set rates of return for regulated industries by providing projections of the returns investors would require if such industries were in the unregulated, competitive sector of the economy.[26]

II

The uninformed view is that errors in mathematical analysis are like those of the tailor of Laputa, who took measurements in a seemingly scientific way with quadrants, rules, and compasses but produced clothes "very ill made" and "quite out of shape" by mistaking a figure in the calculation. Simplistic errors like this do occur, but are not very interesting. The more important questions involve the validity of the assumptions. A mathematical model cannot reflect all elements of reality and need not do so to produce usable estimates. However, modeling involves drastic simplifications, and care is needed to avoid conclusions that are wide of the mark. In particular, there is a tendency—which must be scrutinized in each case—to sweep away complexity to permit mathematical accessibility. This drive for quantification sometimes tempts the mathematician to ignore or reject complicating factors that are nonetheless essential to the legal picture.[27] The lawyer may be an unwitting ac-

[26]Protocols designed to maximize the usefulness of such studies are developed in chapter 7 *infra*.

[27]In his seminal work on probability theory, Poisson calculated that, in the early nineteenth century, 47 percent of the criminally accused in France were not guilty, and that individual jurors erred in one third of their verdicts. His calculation was based on the assumption that each juror had the same probability of being in error and that this probability was unaffected by the votes (and presumably the deliberations) of other jurors. Briefly, Poisson proceeded as follows. He wrote two equations in which the probability of conviction was expressed as the sum of (i) the product of the probability that the accused was guilty and the jurors were not mistaken in their verdict, and (ii) the probability that the accused was not guilty and the jurors were mistaken. The first equation used the probability of conviction by a simple majority (seven votes out of twelve), which was then allowed under French law; the second equation used the probability of a conviction by eight or more votes. This breakdown took advantage of the fact that available data showed the proportions of convictions by seven votes and by eight or more votes, respectively, and these were used

complice in this process if he limits his role to a passive understanding of his expert's work, and fails to pursue a critical evaluation from a carefully focused legal point of view. The
records of judicial and administrative proceedings are already
strewn with the disasters that this uncritical acceptance sometimes allows.

When constitutional challenges to capital punishment
reached the U.S. Supreme Court, the Solicitor General submitted a then unpublished regression study purporting to show
that the risk of execution deterred murder.[28] The conclusion
depended on a negative correlation in recent years between the
rate of executions per conviction (which had declined) and the
murder rate (which had increased). But these trends were
probably coincidental rather than related since the increase in
murder was part of a general increase in violent crime.[29]
Spurious correlations are a particular problem in models based
on time-series data, since an observed relationship may always represent a parallel movement over time rather than a
causal sequence.

In a proceeding to set minimum wellhead prices for natural
gas, the staff of the Federal Power Commission sponsored a

-----

as estimates of the conviction probabilities. The probability of a jury mistake
was represented as the cumulative binomial probability of mistakes by the
requisite numbers of jurors based on the probability of error by an individual
juror. Solving the two equations simultaneously yielded estimates for the two
unknowns—the probability of guilt and the probability of error by a juror.
POISSON, RECHERCHES, SUR LA PROBABILITÉ DES JUGEMENTS EN MATIÈRE
CRIMINELLE ET EN MATIÈRE CIVILE 373 (1837). Unfortunately, it is easy to
agree with John Stuart Mill, who complained that calculations of this type
were "misapplications of the calculus of probabilities which have made it the
real opprobium of mathematics." Mill, *A System of Logic*, Bk. III, Ch. XV in
PHILOSOPHY OF SCIENTIFIC METHOD 283 (1950). Mill's deeper objection was
that "even when the probabilities are derived from observation and experiment a very slight improvement in the data, by better observations, or by taking into full consideration the special circumstances of the case, is of more use
than the most elaborate application of the calculus of probabilities founded on
the data in their previous state of inferiority." *Id.* This point of view sometimes surfaces in judicial pronouncements.

[28]The study, prepared by Professor Isaac Ehrlich, was submitted with the
Solicitor General's Brief for the United States as Amicus Curiae, Fowler v.
North Carolina, 428 U.S. 904 (1976).

[29]Investigators before and after Ehrlich have found no statistical evidence
of deterrence. See, e.g., Passell, *The Deterrent Effect of the Death Penalty*,
28 STAN. L. REV. 61 (1975).

regression model to demonstrate that an increase in prices would decrease exploration because the decline in demand would outweigh the price-increase incentive. The crucial regression equation was successfully attacked because it failed to include profitability as an explanatory factor. This omission was fatal to the staff's position since, if profitability had been included, the inverse relationship between price and exploration displayed by the model would have been reversed, and a positive relationship shown.[30]

In a tax case, a television station used a mathematical model to compute a life expectancy table for its network affiliation agreement on the assumption that the risk of termination remained unchanged by the length of association between the station and the network. The average life estimated on this theory was rejected for depreciation purposes because the judges deemed it implausible that the termination probability would not decline as the relationship between the station and the network solidified.[31]

With the benefits of distance and reflection the inappropriateness of these models seems obvious, or nearly so. But even major defects are not always apparent at closer range. A reduction of reality is essential to any mathematical model, and indeed to any thought about a complex problem, so that simplification is not objectionable per se. Although mathematical technique has been elaborated to provide tests of models, the large assumptions usually depend on judgments that cannot be objectively confirmed or refuted. Frequently, not enough is known to settle matters unequivocally, so that when the storm of conflicting testimony subsides, the judges may still be left in doubt.

At least when important public issues are involved, one might expect that a received body of professional opinion would help determine the factual aspects of the dispute. Unfortunately, this seldom happens. The difficulties of statistical proof only epitomize the larger problem. There is no important tradition for empirical testing of legal doctrine and the issues

---

[30]The use of econometric testimony in this case is discussed in chapter 7 *infra*, at pp. 228–30.

[31]Commissioner of Internal Revenue v. Indiana Broadcasting Co., 350 F.2d 580 (7th Cir. 1965), *cert. denied*, 382 U.S. 1027 (1966).

may be of insufficient general interest to attract investigators
from other disciplines. Even when questions of broader import
are involved, the knowledge of experts from other fields is seldom decisive. Legal issues of public or general importance
have a life cycle; there is a point of ripeness, and a decision
may be pressing before the process of investigation is sufficiently advanced. Moreover, a sociological or economic investigation frequently will deal with much larger (or sometimes simply different) aspects of the subject, leaving it
unclear what learning would dictate at the narrow point of
legally relevant effects. Racial prejudice was much studied
when segregation in public schools was held unconstitutional
in 1954, but the Supreme Court's proposition that segregated
schools were inherently inferior could not be supported by
deep investigation directed to that question.[32] More recently,
when the constitutionality of six-person juries was challenged,
there was no firm evidence demonstrating the impact of size
reduction on jury deliberations, despite the fact that the in-
teractions within small groups had been the subject of extensive psychological study.[33] In this instance, an important
decision was needed to arouse scholarly interest in the legal
aspect of the subject.[34] One may rail at judicial fact finding in
such cases, but those who see the apparent inadequacies as
failings of particular courts or judges underestimate the depth
of the problem.

III

Confronted with statistical evidence of uncertain validity,
judges tend to avoid the uncongenial and exposed task of evaluation in favor of intuitive appraisals that cannot be as readily
attacked or a simple refusal to make any finding. The first is al-

[32]Brown v. Board of Education of Topeka, 347 U.S. 483, 494 n.11 (1954).
[33]Williams v. Florida, 399 U.S. 78 at 102 nn. 48–49 (1970).
[34]The Supreme Court decision in Williams v. Florida, 399 U.S. 78 (1970),
which approved six-person juries, stirred scholarly investigation of the subject of jury size which in turn influenced the Court in subsequently refusing
to sanction five-person juries. Ballew v. Georgia, 46 U.S.L.W. 4217 (U.S.
March 21, 1978) (No. 76–761).

most always indefensible; whether the second is acceptable depends on the legal issue.

When the Legal Aid Society's initial pretrial detention study was attacked on slender grounds, the judges took the first tack simply by rejecting its findings without explanation in favor of their unvalidated personal view that detention per se had no effect on the chance for acquittal.[35] This conclusion should have been unacceptable because objective analysis contradicted it. In the natural gas proceedings, the Federal Power Commission took the second tack by declining to make any estimate of the relationship between prices and exploration for gas. For this it was criticized and the decision reversed by the Court of Appeals.[36] In the debate on the deterrent effect of capital punishment, the opinion of three Supreme Court justices took both tacks: they found that the empirical studies were inconclusive, but that for "many potential murderers" contemplation of the penalty may enter into "the cold calculus that precedes the decision to act."[37]

The refusal to take account of seemingly relevant information is frequently cited by experts in other disciplines as evidence that the law is an ignoramus. But since any result in a litigated case determines rights, relief cannot always be denied when the factual picture is uncertain. Instead, decision makers may legitimately react by defining a narrower inquiry in which the results turn on selected salient points, and complications that might be relevant in science are consigned to rebuttal, collateral significance, or irrelevance. If their definition is sound, the scope of the legal universe will reflect some ethically satisfying accommodation of the conflicting values that are at work in the dispute. To say that the law omits some factually significant matter is not necessarily a reproach; the issue is whether the treatment of that matter is consistent with legal purposes.

This judicial technique, which is essential to the growth of

[35]Bellamy v. The Judges, 41 App. Div. 2d 196, 202, 342 N.Y.S.2d 137, 144 (1973), *affd without opinion*, 32 N.Y.2d 886, 346 N.Y.S.2d 812 (1973).

[36]Southern Louisiana Area Rate Cases, 428 F.2d 407, 436 n.91 (5th Cir.), *cert. denied*, 400 U.S. 950 (1970).

[37]Gregg v. Georgia, 428 U.S. 184–87 (1976) (opinion of Stewart, Powell, and Stevens, JJ.). A more detailed attempt to deal with the issues appears in the dissenting opinion of Justice Marshall, 428 U.S. 153, 233–38.

the law, opens a door to statistical evidence. Over a broad spectrum of legal problems the restricted universe of relevance makes it possible to construct more manageable mathematical models than those deemed necessary in full-fledged scientific pursuits of the same subject. For example, no one disputes that the actual significance of an individual's vote depends on many demographic or political factors in his district. But with certain exceptions, the Supreme Court has implemented constitutional policy by insisting only that election districts include equal numbers of persons. This position can be formalized as an express mathematical model of voting power that may in turn be applied to test more complex reapportionment schemes involving weighted voting or multimember districts.[38] The courts should respect findings based on such models, for while factual complications justifiably may be omitted, there is no justification for drawing ill-founded inferences from admittedly relevant data.

When mathematical models are used in this way, the effect of analysis is to produce formal findings by which questions of statistical inference are detached from those of law. The separation frequently discloses that significant legal issues have been obscured by misconceptions of evidence or by ambiguities in the intuitive formulations of statistical ideas. This is a leitmotif of the studies in this book. Whether the issue is the evaluation of jury discrimination, election irregularities, rules relating to wrongful death, or plea-bargaining practices, it repeatedly appears that mathematical analysis of evidence changes impressions of the underlying factual context, and by that process suggests that the issues for legal judgment are rather different from those seemingly presented when the decision maker accepted the horizons of his intuitive view. Even when data are not available, the mathematical way of thinking may reveal aspects of rules that have not been recognized because intuitive formulations were sufficiently vague to cover the alternatives without directing attention to important distinctions.

The original interest in mathematical analysis of social or moral questions was Cartesian. Having dramatically used arithmetic to conquer geometry, Descartes at the beginning of the

[38]See chapter 4 *infra* at pp. 105–20.

seventeenth century proposed a universal mathematics to express all knowledge, including ethics and metaphysics. His dream of a universal calculus was given more definite form by Leibniz, who imagined a mathematical symbolism—*Characteristica Universalis*—by which all thinking could be replaced with calculation. "If we had it," he wrote, "we should be able to reason in metaphysics and morals in much the same way as in geometry and analysis.... If controversies were to arise, there would be no more need of disputation between two philosophers than between two accountants. For it would suffice to take their pencils in their hands, to sit down to their slates, and to say to each other (with a friend as witness, if they liked): Let us calculate."

In dreams of this sort, inexorable mathematics is imagined to offer a comforting path through the thicket of moral, political, and historical questions that surround most important legal problems. The virtues of such solutions perennially have attracted those who are weary of the endless disputes and would like to settle things on a clean, unanswerable basis. The modern Cartesians propose such things as mathematical prediction of court decisions or the mechanical parsing of statutes. They have their adherents, but the principal effect of their proposals has been to discredit more sophisticated mathematical treatment of legal questions by reinforcing the false notion that exact science in law necessarily implies a formal or mechanical deduction of legal consequences. What mathematics offers is not a deus ex machina for legal problems but only the opportunity for new insight into values based on a deeper knowledge of the facts. It is not the less worth pursuing for that. The resolving power of a mathematical approach is very high, and it brings into focus our inchoate ideas and purposes, just as we gain perspectives of a different sort from the study of foreign codes or historical processes.

Chapter 2

JURY DISCRIMINATION

THE EVOLUTION OF STATISTICAL METHODS in cases involving charges of discrimination in the selection of jurors is a process not yet completed. In a decade of decisions, the courts have only begun to accept what is to be learned from statistical evidence. I tell the story here from its beginnings to the present way station. Part I traces the implicit use of probabilistic ideas by the Supreme Court before mathematical methods appeared in analysis; Part II describes those methods; Part III demonstrates their application to several cases; Part IV discusses the Supreme Court's reaction to statistical evidence when it began to be introduced in the more recent cases, and the issues that remain.

I

For more than eighty-five years it has been the law that a conviction in a state court violates the equal-protection clause of the Fourteenth Amendment if it is based on an indictment of a grand jury or a verdict of a petit jury from which blacks were excluded because of their race.[1] Discrimination must of course

---

[1] The seminal cases are Strauder v. West Virginia, 100 U.S. 303 (1880), and Neal v. Delaware, 103 U.S. 370 (1880).

be proved.[2] In the initial cases in which the principle emerged, problems of proof did not arise because the fact of discrimination was never put in issue. Blacks were excluded by statute;[3] the fact of exclusion was uncontested;[4] or the principle was tested solely on the pleadings.[5] In three early cases, discrimination was denied by the state, but the defendants failed to produce evidence to support their claims.[6]

The current type of case appeared in 1934 with the Supreme Court decision in *Norris* v. *Alabama*.[7] There the Court for the first time faced disputed issues of discrimination in the selection of grand and petit jurors and a record containing evidence purporting to bear on the issue. The evidence on the motion to quash the indictment was that although blacks comprised 7.5 percent of the total adult male population of Jackson County, where the petitioners were indicted, no blacks in the recollection of witnesses had ever served on any grand or petit jury. This single fact, the Court held, made out a *"prima facie* case of the denial of the equal protection which the Constitution guarantees."[8] The prima facie case was "supplemented," the Court noted, by evidence of the presence of at least thirty qualified blacks in the county and by the testimony of the jury commissioners that blacks had not been included on the jury roll because their names were "never discussed."

The evidence on the motion to quash the trial venire was that although blacks comprised about 18 percent of the adult male population in Morgan County, where the petitioners were tried,[9] and although many were qualified, no black within the memory of witnesses had ever served on a jury or been called for service. The county sheriff was unable to identify any names of blacks on the jury roll. The Court held the general denials of discrimination by a member of the jury board insufficient "to

[2]Tarrance v. Florida, 188 U.S. 519 (1903).

[3]Bush v. Kentucky, 107 U.S. 110 (1883).

[4]Neal v. Delaware, 103 U.S. 370 (1881).

[5]Carter v. Texas, 177 U.S. 442 (1900).

[6]Martin v. Texas, 200 U.S. 316 (1906); Brownfield v. South Carolina, 189 U.S. 426 (1903); Smith v. Mississippi, 162 U.S. 592 (1896).

[7]294 U.S. 587 (1935).

[8]*Id.* at 591.

[9]The trial was transferred to Morgan County because of asserted prejudice against the defendants in Jackson County.

rebut the strong *prima facie* case which the defendant had made."[10]

The issue in *Norris* was whether the particular grand and petit juries which indicted and convicted the petitioners were selected without discrimination. No testimony was introduced pertaining specifically to the selection of either jury; instead, discrimination was proved from the racial statistics of jury selection over a number of years. Statistical evidence of this type can be relevant in different ways to the existence of discrimination in the choice of a particular venire. The absence of blacks from other venires selected from the same jury roll may be evidence that there are no blacks on that roll. The practice of the jury commissioners in excluding blacks from other venires may be evidence of their intent to exclude blacks from the venire in question.[11] The unvarying failure of different groups of commissioners to select any blacks may be evidence of a governing custom of discrimination. Whatever the relevant inference, the deduction of discrimination rests on the idea that when blacks constitute a substantial segment of the population, their absence from the jury roll or from jury venires is evidence of racial exclusion somewhere in the selection process.

The facts in *Norris* made it easy for the Court to accept this idea. The absence of blacks from juries, jury venires, and the jury roll, and the direct testimony of the commissioners that blacks were never considered, combined to present a clear case of discrimination. The facts in other cases in which the Court has granted relief have been equally extreme.[12] But since, on the Court's reasoning, the Constitution prohibits *any* discrimination in selection, it was inevitable that the idea used by the Court in *Norris* would be tested in cases where the evidence was less blatant. Challenges were made in cases where blacks had appeared on juries, although in proportions smaller than their proportion in the population. In such underrepresenta-

[10]294 U.S. at 598.

[11]In Brown v. Allen, 344 U.S. 443, 479 (1953), the Court noted that "past practice is evidence of past attitude of mind." It found such evidence not decisive because there had been a purge and refilling of the jury box before the jury in question was selected.

[12]E.g., Arnold v. North Carolina, 376 U.S. 773 (1964) (one black served on a grand jury in twenty-four years); Hill v. Texas, 316 U.S. 400 (1942) (no blacks served on a grand jury for at least sixteen years).

tion, the Supreme Court has yet to hold squarely that a statistical disparity alone is sufficient to make out a prima facie case of discrimination.[13]

The Court has already considered a substantial number of such underrepresentation cases, and because blacks still appear to be grossly underrepresented on state juries, there is the prospect of many more.[14] In addition to a larger flow of cases involving criminal defendants, an increasing number of class actions has been brought on behalf of blacks to secure the right to serve on juries.[15] The plaintiffs in these cases do not seek to set aside a conviction but to restructure the selection system. Inasmuch as the claims in these cases involve many juries, the proof by necessity is statistical. The statistics usually show underrepresentation rather than exclusion, thus testing the principles of the exclusion cases in an important institutional setting.[16]

Dallas County, Texas, was the site of the first two underrepresentation cases. The stage was set in 1942 when the Supreme Court, in *Hill* v. *Texas*,[17] reversed the murder conviction of a black because blacks had been totally excluded from grand juries, including the grand jury which indicted him. Following this decision, a black appeared on each of the next two grand-jury lists, and one served on the grand jury which indicted Robert Akins, a black, for the rape of a white woman. Akins appealed his conviction to the Supreme Court, claiming that the number of blacks serving on the grand jury which indicted him had been limited by design to one. In *Akins* v. *Texas*,[18] the Court rejected this claim. It computed that "on the strictly mathematical basis of population, a grand jury of twelve

[13]True when written in 1965. For later cases see pp. 53–58 *infra*.

[14]See, e.g., Michael, Mullin, O'Reilly & Rowan, *Challenges to Jury Composition in North Carolina*, 7 NORTH CAROLINA CENTRAL L.J. 1 (1975).

[15]E.g., Carter v. Jury Commission of Greene County, 396 U.S. 320 (1970); White v. Crook, 251 F.Supp. 401 (M.D. Ala. 1966) (jury box required to be emptied and refilled).

[16]See, e.g., Mitchell v. Johnson, 250 F.Supp. 117 (M.D. Ala. 1966), where the number of white persons on the jury roll represented 55 percent of the eligible white population and the number of blacks represented only 9 percent of the black population. The court held that this evidence demonstrates "wide disproportions" and that this, "without more, requires an inference of systematic exclusion on racial grounds . . . ."

[17]316 U.S. 400 (1942).

[18]325 U.S. 398 (1945).

would have 1.8552 black members on the average," apparently deriving this figure by multiplying the black percentage of the population by the number of jurors. Since there had been one black member on each jury list, and since one served on the jury that indicted Akins, the Court concluded that "we cannot say that the omission from each of the two lists of all but one of the members of a race which composed some fifteen percent of the population alone proved racial discrimination."[19]

During the five and one-half years after *Hill*, twenty-one grand juries were convened in Dallas County. It is consistent with the implied invitation in *Akins* that one black each appeared on seventeen grand juries, and none on the remaining four. These statistics were scrutinized by the Supreme Court in *Cassell* v. *Texas*,[20] the third of the Dallas County cases. Cassell, a black convicted of murder, charged discrimination and relied on the above statistics and on the testimony of the jury commissioners to prove it. Since there had been only seventeen blacks among the 252 members on the twenty-one grand juries, only 6.7 percent of the jurors were blacks. The Court observed, however, that the discrepancy between this figure and the 15.5 percent black population was explicable, because blacks constituted only 6.5 percent of the county poll-tax payers, and payment of the poll tax was a prerequisite for jury service. Since 6.7 percent was the ratio of blacks actually sitting on the juries, the Court concluded that "without more it cannot be said that negroes had been left off the grand jury panels to such a degree as to establish a prima facie case of discrimination."[21]

The *distribution* of blacks presented, in the Court's view, a different question. If it was true that the jury commissioners had limited their number to one per jury, this action would have been unconstitutional since "jurymen should be selected as individuals . . . and not as members of a race."[22] But Mr. Justice

[19]*Id.* at 405–06. Apart from the superficiality of the mathematical argument, the decision might not have caused confusion, but the Court added a caveat to its opinion, one wholly inexplicable in the light of former rulings that race may not be considered in the selection process: "This conclusion makes it unnecessary to decide whether a purposeful limitation of jurors by race to the approximate proportion that the eligible jurymen of the race so limited bears to the total eligibles is invalid under the Fourteenth Amendment." *Id.* at 407.

[20]339 U.S. 282 (1950).

[21]*Id.* at 285–86.

[22]339 U.S. at 286.

Reed's opinion for the Court, concurred in by three other Justices, avoided resting decision on the ground that the appearance of a single black on each of seventeen juries was evidence of limitation; instead, it reversed because the commissioners testified that they took only people they knew and admitted they did not know any blacks. "When the Commissioners were appointed as judicial administrative officials, it was their duty to familiarize themselves fairly with the qualifications of the eligible jurors of the county without regard to race and color. They did not do so here, and the result has been racial discrimination."[23]

Although the decision in *Cassell* was based on other grounds, the case was the first in which the Court accepted an explanation for a disproportionately small black representation on juries. The issue reappeared a few years later in two cases reported together from North Carolina, *Brown* v. *Allen* and *Speller* v. *Allen*.[24] The Court then proved willing to accept such explanations. In North Carolina, two blacks, Brown and Speller, were convicted of rape and sentenced to death. Their challenges to the grand and petit juries were based solely on statistical evidence. In Brown's case this showed that although blacks comprised 33.5 percent of the adult population of the county, in the year of his indictment and the previous year only 7–10 percent of those chosen for grand-jury service were blacks; in the year he was indicted, the percentage of blacks on petit jury panels ranged from 9–17 percent. The Court stated that "variations in proportions of Negroes and whites on jury lists from racial proportions in the population have not been considered violative of the Constitution where they are explained and not long continued."[25] It concluded that the disparity had been explained. The names of prospective jurors were drawn from poll- and property-tax lists, and blacks appeared to constitute a much smaller percentage of such lists than of the general population—although how much smaller a percentage did not appear from the evidence. The decision below was affirmed.

In Speller's case, jurors were selected from the tax lists. Thirty-eight percent of the taxpayers were blacks, but only 7

[23]*Id.* at 289.
[24]344 U.S. 443 (1953).
[25]*Id.* at 471.

percent of those selected for the jury box were blacks. The Court held, however, that the discrepancy could be explained by the testimony of the clerk that he took those with "the most property." It concluded that "evidence of discrimination based solely on race in the selection actually made is lacking."[26]

The apparent reluctance of the Court to consider under-representation as evidence of discrimination was confirmed by two subsequent cases. In the first case, *Swain* v. *Alabama*,[27] Swain, a black, was convicted of rape in Talladega County, Alabama, and sentenced to death. The Supreme Court summarized the evidence on the panels as follows: "While Negro males over 21 constitute 26% of all males in the county in this age group, only 10 to 15% of the grand and petit jury panels drawn from the jury box since 1952 have been Negroes, there having been only one case in which the percentage was as high as 23%."[28] In Swain's case there were four or five blacks on the panel of thirty-five from which his grand jury was selected, and eight blacks on the panel of one hundred from which his petit jury was selected. The Court held that these statistics did not constitute prima facie evidence of discrimination: "We cannot say that purposeful discrimination based on race alone is satisfactorily proved by showing that an identifiable group in a community is underrepresented by as much as 10% .... The overall percentage disparity has been small, and reflects no studied attempt to include or exclude a specified number of Negroes."[29] As I shall demonstrate, this result is inconsistent with the announced principles governing these cases.

Swain also attacked the petit jury which had convicted him, claiming that the prosecution had used its peremptory strikes to exclude blacks. The evidence showed that the six blacks available for service in Swain's case had been struck by the prosecution. The Court, three Justices dissenting, rejected the

[26]*Id.* at 481.

[27]380 U.S. 202 (1965).

[28]*Id.* at 205.

[29]*Id.* at 208–09. The deceptiveness of this statement was called to the Court's attention. Brief of the American Civil Liberties Union as Amicus Curiae in Support of Petition for Rehearing at 10–11. If 90 percent of the population and 80 percent of the average panel are black, the "10 percent disparity" may be insignificant. This is not so if 10 percent of the population but *no* panelists are black.

claim. It held that in any given case it is presumed that the prosecution has used its peremptory challenges to secure an impartial jury, and that this presumption is not overcome by allegations that "in the case at hand all Negroes were removed . . . because they were Negroes."[30] In the Court's view the case would have been different, and the Fourteenth Amendment claim would have taken on added significance, if defendant had shown that the prosecutor "in case after case, whatever the circumstances, whatever the crime and whoever the defendant or the victim may be, is responsible for the removal of Negroes who have been selected as qualified jurors by the jury commissioners and who have survived challenges for cause . . . ."[31] But although blacks had never served on petit juries in Talladega County, Swain had failed to prove his case, because he had not shown that the prosecution had been responsible in each case for striking them.

The Court has thus drawn a line between a peremptory strike based on a belief that a black juror would be biased in a particular case and the systematic use of peremptory strikes to keep blacks off juries. The first is permitted, the second is unconstitutional.[32]

In the other case, *State* v. *Barksdale*,[33] a black was convicted of rape and sentenced to death. The evidence showed that blacks in Orleans Parish comprised about 33 percent of the adult male population, but only 10–16 percent of the grand jury venires, and 11–19 percent of the petit jury venires. From May, 1958, when the Supreme Court reversed a murder conviction in the parish on the ground of exclusion of blacks from the grand jury,[34] until September, 1962, when Barksdale was indicted, nine grand juries had been selected. Eight of these contained two blacks each, and one black served on the ninth.[35] On this evidence the Supreme Court of Louisiana affirmed, holding that the smaller proportion of blacks serving on grand juries was adequately explained by their deficiencies in education (which

[30]380 U.S. at 222.
[31]*Id*. at 223.
[32]See Note, *Fair Jury Selection Procedures*, 75 YALE L.J. 322 (1965).
[33]247 La. 198, 179 So. 2d 374 (1964), *cert. denied*, 382 U.S. 921 (1965).
[34]Eubanks v. Louisiana, 356 U.S. 584 (1958).
[35]247 La. at 223, 170 So.2d at 383.

resulted in the qualification of fewer blacks) and income (which led more blacks to request hardship excuses).[36] The Supreme Court denied certiorari. The denial, of course, does not mean that the Court approved the state court's holding. I shall try to show that, when put to a mathematical test, the facts in *Barksdale* point to a contrary decision.

The opinions of the Court in underrepresentation cases leave little doubt that disparity between the proportion of blacks on venires and in the population generally is evidence of discriminatory selection if it is large, continuing, and unexplained. But it is also clear that a defendant is not entitled to a venire or a jury on which members of his race are proportionately represented, and efforts to create proportional representation by systematically including blacks have been held unconstitutional.[37] Consequently, not every disparity in proportions is constitutionally fatal. "The mere fact of inequality in the number selected does not in itself show discrimination."[38]

The refusal of the Court to grant relief in *Swain* throws into sharp relief the problem of drawing a line between significant and insignificant disparities. Counsel in *Swain* asserted flatly that "the State must surely offer some explanation of why the proportion of Negroes on grand and petit jury venires averages at most one-half the proportion of eligible Negroes in the population."[39] But neither Court nor counsel offered a rational way of determining which disparities were large enough to be considered evidence of design. As a result, counsel could do little more than assert, without reasoned support, that the statistics required a finding of discrimination. And when the Court reached a contrary conclusion in *Swain*, the basis for its decision remained equally Delphic.

In the exclusion cases the Court has consistently refused to countenance the explanation that blacks were omitted from juries because they were unqualified. The explanation arose again in the underrepresentation cases, this time in more compelling form, since all that had to be asserted was that some but

---

[36]*Id.* at 223–24, 170 So.2d at 384.

[37]E.g., Collins v. Walker, 329 F.2d 100, *aff'd on rehearing*, 335 F.2d 417 (5th Cir.), *cert. denied*, 379 U.S. 901 (1964).

[38]Akins v. Texas, 325 U.S. 398, 403 (1945).

[39]Brief for Petitioner at 19.

not all blacks were unqualified. In *Cassell, Brown,* and *Speller,* the Court accepted such assertions, refusing to find discrimination on the basis of disparities in percentages. In *Cassell,* the evidence showed that the average proportion of blacks on grand juries was at least approximately equal to their proportion on the tax rolls; but in *Brown* and *Speller,* the evidence showed only that the number of eligible blacks was to some undetermined extent smaller than their number in the adult male population. On what theory the Court found these nonquantitative explanations sufficient does not appear.

The failure of the Court to articulate a rationale for the underrepresentation cases is a consequence of the problem they present. In the exclusion cases the disparity is gross enough to support the intuitive conclusion that jurors were chosen on the basis of race. But the notion that *some* blacks should have been chosen is too imprecise to offer guidance once some blacks are in fact chosen. Since the judges have recognized that not every deviation from proportionate numbers is evidence of design, they are confronted with the harder problem of drawing a line between significant and insignificant variations and the related problem of determining the effect to be given to "explanations" for significant variations.

The resolution of these problems involves important questions of legal policy which the Court has never reached, because the legal and statistical issues have remained intertwined. What we need is not more tenderminded Justices or more appealing verbal formulations but an analysis of the data which will expose the true legal issues.

II

Probability theory has been found to apply to events commonly called "random" or "chance." The toss of a coin is the classic example. Theoretically, at least, we might determine the outcome of a toss in advance by calculating the forces acting on the coin. But since minute changes in some of these forces can produce a different outcome, there is for all practical purposes no way of making this calculation, and the result is treated as independent of determinable cause. It is this practical independence of cause and result that characterizes phenomena suited to the application of probability theory.[40]

It is obvious that the racial outcome of jury selection is—or rather should be—independent of the method of selection. This is true not because the selecting agent is unable to control the result, as in the coin-tossing case, but because he is not legally permitted to do so. But whether the outcome is independent because of the physical impossibility of connecting it with its causes or because of the unconstitutionality of making such a connection, the result is the same: the racial outcome is or should be random.

This is not to say that the method of selection for the jury roll must be neutral with respect to the number of whites and blacks considered. The use of qualification tests, such as literacy, or the operation of the selection machinery (e.g., voter lists) may result in the qualification or consideration of a disproportionately small number of blacks. But within the poll of eligibles, however restricted, the selections must still be made without reference to race, and this means that the racial composition of jury venires is—or should be—the result of random selection, and consequently an appropriate subject for probability theory. Using mathematically computed probabilities, a variety of tests can be constructed for the hypothesis that the number of blacks chosen for venires is consistent with random selection. Like all statistical tests, these are not infallible, but their rates of error will generally be small and are mathematically determinable. Moreover, there is judicial precedent for deciding cases with a rate of error similar to the rates of the tests I propose to use.

In holding that the persistent absence of blacks from juries is evidence of discrimination, the Supreme Court has used in principle an identical approach. Although the basis for decision usually has not been articulated, the Court has indicated at various occasions that its holdings rest on the improbability of repeated random selection of all white venires in counties with substantial black populations. Thus, in *Smith* v. *Texas*, the Court said: "Chance and accident alone could hardly have

[40]Perfect prediction is limited even in theory because of the teaching of quantum theory that certain events involving fundamental particles have no determinable cause.

brought about the listing for grand jury service of so few Negroes from among the thousands shown by the undisputed evidence to possess the legal qualifications for jury service."[41]

The mathematical test which can be used to determine the existence of discrimination is based on the probability that, as veniremen are selected, any given venireman will be a black. This probability is usually derived from the proportion of adult blacks to the total adult population. In each jury challenge case, however, it has been argued that these population figures are misleading and that the absence of blacks from venires or juries reflects a lack of literacy, integrity, or other requisite qualifications. Statistical methods can be used fruitfully here to determine the percentages of blacks and whites that one would have to assume to be disqualified in order to account for the observed numbers of blacks on venires. Whether these percentages are consistent with the education, status, and general qualifications of the black and white populations is a question the Court can approach with some confidence since it resembles other factual issues underlying constitutional claims.

The Court has taken a similar but nonquantitative approach to the qualifications issue in the cases we have discussed. In the exclusion cases, the contention that the absence of blacks from juries could be explained by their lack of qualifications was rejected because it involved the assumption (so the Court believed) that virtually the entire black population was unqualified.[42] "[A] race [cannot] be proscribed as incompetent for service."[43] Similar reasoning appears in the underrepresentation cases. In *Speller* v. *Allen*,[44] for example, the Court held that a discrepancy of thirty-one points between the percentage of blacks on venires and the percentage on tax lists from which the venires were drawn could not be explained by the clerk's disqualification of blacks for poor moral character. "It would not be assumed," the Court held, "that in Vance County there is not a much larger percentage of Negroes with qualifications of

[41]311 U.S. 128, 131 (1940); *accord*, Eubanks v. Louisiana, 346 U.S. 584, 587 (1958); Hill v. Texas, 316 U.S. 400, 404 (1942).

[42]Patton v. Mississippi, 332 U.S. 463, 468 (1947).

[43]Brown v. Allen, 344 U.S. 443, 471 (1953).

[44]344 U.S. 443 (1953).

jurymen."[45] The same method of reasoning, using mathematical techniques, will be adopted here.

In certain situations it may not be possible to determine whether the number of blacks appearing on a series of venires or juries is consistent or inconsistent with the qualifications of the black population. This may occur when there is inadequate evidence concerning qualifications, or when persons selected for service may be excused on grounds other than lack of qualifications. Those called for grand-jury service, for instance, may be excused on grounds of economic hardship. Another example is the appearance of blacks on petit juries (as distinguished from jury panels). Although in *Swain* the Supreme Court stated that the prosecution may not use peremptory strikes to exclude blacks systematically, there remains a broad area of discretion in the use of such strikes or challenges which makes it virtually impossible to determine from population statistics, however carefully refined, the probability that a black will appear on a petit jury.

While in such cases it is not possible to use a statistical analysis based on the failure to select a greater number of blacks, it is possible, at least in the case of venires and grand juries, to determine whether the pattern of black representation is consistent with randomness. To take a crude example, the appearance of a series of grand juries alternately 100 percent and 0 percent black would excite our suspicions as to the selection process whatever the probability of selecting black or white jurors. Statistical decision theory provides various measures of the extent to which a given distribution differs from the theoretical or expected random distribution and a test of the significance of such difference. Such tests indicate whether the observed distribution of blacks is so at variance with the expected distribution that the hypothesis of random selection ought to be rejected.

Although the Court has never applied this line of reasoning, the test of distribution operates on the same principles as the test based on a comparison of percentages which it has used. Perhaps the closest thing there is to judicial recognition that a skewed distribution may be evidence of discrimination is this statement of the three concurring Justices in *Cassell* v. *Texas*:[46]

---

[45]*Id.* at 481.
[46]339 U.S. 282, 294 (1950) (Frankfurter, J., concurring).

The number of Negroes both qualified and available for jury service in Dallas County precluded such uniform presence of never more than one Negro on any other basis of good faith than that the commissioners were guided by the belief that one Negro on the grand jury satisfied the prohibition against discrimination . . . .

In concluding that probability theory can usefully be applied to these problems, it has been assumed that the intuitive idea of probability used by the Court is conceptually similar to the mathematical definition used by the statisticians. Although the premises of the legal argument remain obscure, the assumption is a reasonable one, since the intuitive content of the mathematical definition is the common idea of probability. Thus the mathematical notion of an event with a probability of, say, 0.1 corresponds to the practical notion of an event that occurs on the average of once in every ten trials.[47]

III

I now apply the methods outlined above to *Swain* v. *Alabama*, *Cassell* v. *Texas*, and *Barksdale* v. *Louisiana*. The first case involves the selection of blacks for venires; the other two, their appearance on grand juries.

A.

In *Swain*, it will be recalled, there was a claim of discrimination in the selection of the grand and petit jury venires and in the selection of petit jurors. We begin our examination with a general mathematical analysis of venire selection.

The process of selecting veniremen can be treated as what is known in probability theory as a binomial model.[48] Repeated

[47]For a nontechnical discussion see Nagel, *The Meaning of Probability*, in 2 THE WORLD OF MATHEMATICS 1398 (Newman ed. 1956).

[48]Also called Bernoulli trials after Jacob Bernoulli (1654–1705), whose famous treatise on probability, ARS CONJECTANDI, appeared posthumously in 1713.

trials constitute a binomial model if (1) there are only two possible outcomes for each trial, (2) the trials are independent, (3) the probabilities for each outcome remain constant throughout the trials, and (4) the number of trials is fixed in advance. A given number of tosses of a coin may be represented by a binomial model because there are only two outcomes for each toss, heads or tails, the tosses are independent in the sense that the outcome of one does not affect the outcome of another, and the probability of tossing heads or tails remains constant throughout any series of tosses. Similarly, when veniremen are selected, there are only two possible racial results, white and nonwhite (we equate the latter with black), the result of each selection is independent of other selections, and it is reasonable to assume that the probabilities of selecting a black or a white remain constant throughout the selection process.

The last two requirements are not strictly satisfied, since each person selected is eliminated at least for a certain time from the pool of potential jurors. Theoretically, therefore, the probability of selecting a white or a black on any given trial will depend on the history of selection to the extent that the racial proportions of the available population are changed by the elimination of those already chosen. Although it is possible to take this into account in computing probabilities, it is not necessary to do so. The number of veniremen selected will in most cases change the racial proportions of the available population to an insignificant degree. Moreover, in most cases, the frequency with which whites are selected equals or exceeds their proportion of the population. In such cases, the assumption that the proportion of white and black eligibles remains constant is conservative, since the proportion of white eligibles actually declines during the selection process. The assumption that the proportion remains constant makes an improbably large percentage of white veniremen seem slightly more in accord with random selection than is really the case. It is thus reasonable to adopt the simple notion that the selection process consists of independent trials with constant probabilities applicable to each trial.

The derivation of the probabilities associated with a binomial model rests on two basic propositions. The first is the sum rule, which states that the probability of the occurrence of any one of a number of mutually exclusive events is equal to the sum of the probabilities of those events.[49] The second is the product rule, which states that the probability of the joint occurrence of a number of independent events is equal to the product of the individual probabilities.[50] Discussion of these elementary propositions may be found in textbooks on probability or statistics.[51]

Applying the product rule, if p is the probability of selecting a black venireman on one draw, the probability of selecting two black veniremen on two draws is $p \times p$, or p^2. More generally, the probability of selecting v black veniremen in v draws, where v is any number, is p^v. Similarly, if q is the probability of selecting a single white venireman,[52] then the probability of selecting w white veniremen in w draws is q^w. If $q = {}^3/_4$, as it may if whites comprise approximately three-fourths of the eligible population, and if there are thirty veniremen on a panel, the chance of picking a single panel without any blacks is, by the product rule,[53] equal to $({}^3/_4)^{30} = 0.0002$. This means that on the average only two venires in ten thousand would be all white. If every venire were all white or all black our analysis could stop here. But, since in *Swain* and in most other cases both whites and blacks were in fact chosen, some further analysis is necessary to derive the relevant probabilities.

If p is the probability of selecting a single black and q the probability of selecting a single white, pq is, by the product rule, the probability of selecting one black and one white in that

---

[49]Events are mutually exclusive if the occurrence of one precludes the occurrence of the other. For example, if we consider the selection of two veniremen and define the first event as the selection of a black on the first but not on the second trial, and the second as the selection of a black on the second but not on the first trial, then the two events are mutually exclusive, since they cannot occur in the same two drawings.

[50]Events are independent if the occurrence of one has no effect upon the occurrence of the other. Thus, whether or not a black is selected as a venireman in one drawing should have no effect upon the selection of a black as a venireman in the next drawing. The product rule is frequently used as a definition of independence.

[51]See, e.g., HOEL, INTRODUCTION TO MATHEMATICAL STATISTICS 8–12 (3d ed. 1962).

[52]Since we assume that "black" is equivalent to "nonwhite," either a white or a black must be selected. Consequently $p + q = 1$.

[53]The symbol P or Q followed by $(v = a)$ or similar expressions is used to mean the probability of selecting a venire with a blacks (or whites). Variations of this expression should be understood accordingly.

order in two selections. The order of selection, however, is unimportant. The condition of selecting a black and a white will also be satisfied by first selecting a white and then a black. The total probability of selecting a black and a white without regard to order is thus $pq + qp = 2pq$. In general, the probability of selecting a particular mixture of blacks and whites is the probability of selecting that mixture in a particular order times the number of different orders in which the mixture may be selected.[54]

If n is the number of persons on a venire, the probability of selecting v blacks is p^v and the probability of selecting $n - v$ whites is q^{n-v}. Since these events are independent, their product, $p^v q^{n-v}$, is the probability of selecting v blacks and $n - v$ whites in a particular order. Since order is unimportant, we must compute the number of ways this mixture may be selected. The number of distinguishable orderings of n objects of which v are of one class and $n - v$ of another class is:[55]

$$\binom{n}{v} = \frac{n!}{v! \, (n - v)!}$$

These two elements (the probability for each ordering and the number of distinguishable orderings) multiplied together yield the well-known "binomial distribution," which expresses the probability $P(v)$ of selecting v blacks among n veniremen:

$$P(v) = \binom{n}{v} p^v q^{n-v} \, .$$

[54]Thus if $p = \frac{1}{4}$ and $q = \frac{3}{4}$, then $pq = \frac{3}{16}$ and $2 \, pq = \frac{6}{16}$.

[55]The derivation of this formula is not difficult. If there are n distinguishable objects, the number of possible orderings is n factorial, which is written as $n! = (n)(n - 1)(n - 2) \ldots (1)$. The reader can satisfy himself that this is so by observing that there is one ordering of one object and that the addition of the nth object always multiplies the number of orderings by n, since for each previous ordering there are now n orderings corresponding to the n possible positions of the nth object when it is inserted among the $n - 1$ objects already present. Hence with the addition of the second object there are 2×1 orderings. The formula $n!$ follows immediately by induction. $0!$ is defined as equal to 1. If v of the n objects are the same, then the number of orderings must be divided by $v!$ since—given any ordering—one can arrange the v indistinguishable objects in $v!$ ways without obtaining a distinguishable ordering. In other words, one can divide the $n!$ total orderings into $n!/v!$ groups of $v!$ orderings each, and the $v!$ orderings in any group are indistinguishable, so that there are only $n!/v!$ distinguishable orderings. Consequently, if v objects are of one type and $n - v$ objects of another type, the number of distinguishable orderings is $n!/v!(n - v)!$.

The challenge to the selection system we are discussing here must be based not on the probability of selecting a particular number of blacks (which is what the above formula gives us), but on the probability of selecting not more than that number of blacks. By the sum rule, the probability of selecting not more than i blacks is the sum of the probabilities of selecting 0, 1, 2, ..., i blacks. This sum is expressed symbolically as follows:

$$P(v \leq i) \sum_{v=0}^{v=i} \binom{n}{v} p^v q^{n-v}.$$

With this preparation, we are ready to consider the grand jury venires in *Swain*. The record shows that for about ten years blacks had never accounted for more than 15 percent of the grand jury venires, with the single exception of a 23 percent black venire chosen in the summer of 1955. These venires consisted of approximately thirty persons each, and three to four were chosen every year.[56] For purposes of discussion we assume that between 1955 and 1962, thirty venires were chosen consecutively with five or fewer blacks each, and that between 1953 and 1955, five additional venires were selected, one of which had seven blacks. Thus, it is assumed that a total of 1,050 veniremen were chosen, of whom no more than 177 were black. Only males were then eligible for jury service. Census figures showed that adult black males constituted approximately 26 percent of the adult male population. Again, for purposes of discussion, we assume that black males constituted one quarter of the adult male population.

On the assumption that the probability p of selecting a black venireman is one quarter, and the probability q of selecting a white venireman is thus three quarters, the probability of selecting no more than 177 blacks out of 1,050 veniremen is given by:[57]

[56]Record at 9–12. Before excuses were granted, each venire contained sixty persons, but there was evidence that the proportions of blacks and whites were not altered by this weeding out. Record at 18. I assume thirty-person venires because some of the evidence bore on the venires' composition after weeding and because, in this context, the assumption is conservative: the smaller the panel, the more likely it is to contain a disproportionate percentage of one race.

[57]The probability here is so minute that its exact computation would strain the resources of even a computer. Statisticians frequently compute binomial probabilities from tables or by using approximations based on the Poisson or normal distributions. See FELLER, AN INTRODUCTION TO PROBABILITY THEORY AND ITS APPLICATIONS 142 (2d ed. 1957).

$$P(v \leq 177) = \sum_{v=0}^{v=177} \binom{1050}{v} (0.25)^v (0.75)^{1050-v}$$

$$= \, < 10^{-8}.$$

The probability that so few blacks would be selected at random is thus exceedingly small. If a jury venire were selected at random in Talladega County every day of the year, the daily selection would correspond to the racial results in *Swain*, on the average, on less than one day in thousands of years.[58]

Our computation of the probabilities in *Swain* was based on the assumption that the selection of veniremen corresponded to a series of binomial trials with a probability $p = \frac{1}{4}$ of selecting a black venireman. On this assumption, there was apparently only a minute probability that so few blacks would be selected. Since an event with such an apparently small probability did occur, we are led to reject the basis on which the probabilities were computed, namely, the assumption that venire selection in *Swain* is represented by a binomial model with the probability $p = \frac{1}{4}$ of selecting a black venireman. This reasoning is formalized as the following statistical test: *The assumption that the racial result of venire selection corresponds to a binomial model with probability* p $= \frac{1}{4}$ *of selecting a single black venireman is rejected whenever the probability of selecting not more than the observed number of blacks on venires is less than a certain critical value.* For purposes of illustration, the critical value selected is 0.05, the value most commonly used by statisticians.

Since the probability of selecting not more than the observed number of blacks on venires in *Swain* was vastly smaller

[58]The assumption that thirty such venires were chosen in a row receives only general support from the record, since it is not clear exactly how many were chosen. Record at 10. But our conclusions remain unaffected within a broad variation in numbers. If only twenty venires were chosen instead of thirty, the probability that all would have five or fewer blacks would also be negligible.

The petitioner in *Swain* took the position that the *average* proportion of blacks on venires was 10–15 percent. Brief for Petitioner at 19. The Court apparently did not accept this interpretation, and the weight of the evidence seems to favor the Court's understanding that 15 percent was the *maximum* proportion of blacks. See 380 U.S. at 205. Why petitioner's counsel adopted this less favorable view of the evidence is mystifying.

than 0.05, application of the test leads us to reject the hypothesis that the selection of veniremen in *Swain* corresponded to the assumed binomial model. The rejection of this hypothesis does not in itself compel a finding of discrimination in the selection process. All we know is that the assumed binomial model with $p = \frac{1}{4}$ is not consistent with the observed facts. To pursue the subject further, we must consider the alternative hypothesis that p does not equal $\frac{1}{4}$. One fourth of the adult males in Talladega County were blacks. But if—as the Court was apparently willing to believe—the jury commissioners considered a larger proportion of black adult males than white adult males to be unacceptable for jury service, p would be less than $\frac{1}{4}$. This would be unconstitutional discrimination only if the commissioners applied higher standards for blacks than for whites, if they excluded from their consideration a substantial number of qualified blacks, or otherwise failed in their duty to obtain black jurors. Since the absence of qualified blacks is the principal reason given for underrepresentation, the qualifications issue that lurked in the wings is now on stage.

The statute that governed jury selection in Talladega County was not atypical; it provided that a juror must be a male citizen, generally reputed to be honest and intelligent, esteemed in the community for integrity, good character, and sound judgment, over the age of twenty-one, not a habitual drunkard, able to read English (unless he was a freeholder), and never convicted of an offense involving moral turpitude.[59] The Court pointed out in *Swain* that the method used to find qualified jurors need not be perfect in the sense that every segment of the population receives an equally scrupulous canvass as to its qualifications.[60] The nature and range of qualifications required of jurors and the latitude allowed in searching out veniremen combine to make the qualifications issue a substantial problem.

Analysis of this problem requires changes in our former procedure. Before, the probability of observing not more than the aggregate number of blacks on the venires was calculated from an assumed probability of selecting a single black venireman. We now seek that value for the probability of selecting a

[59]ALA. CODE tit. 30, §21 (1958).
[60]380 U.S. at 208, 209.

single black venireman which would account for their observed numbers on the venires with a 0.05 probability and
would thus by our test result in the acceptance of the random
selection hypothesis. In other words, if it is contended that p is
really less than $1/_4$, we will inspect other values of p to determine how small it must become to produce results satisfying
the statistical test. Thus determined, p is the largest proportion
of eligible blacks to the total eligible population which it is
possible to assume and still obtain a probability for the observed results which is not less than the critical value 0.05.

In making this determination in *Swain,* it is useful to consider an important fact not previously taken into account: with a
single early exception, the record indicates that there were
never more than five blacks on a venire. Since the venires were
consistently not more than 15 percent black, one would intuitively recognize that blacks could not account for 25 percent of
the eligible population. In fact, if there were random selection,
the proportion of eligible blacks in the population would have
to be less than 15 percent, for otherwise some of the last thirty
venires would have shown a higher percentage. How much
less? For present purposes, it is sufficient to ask how small the
probability of selecting a single black venireman would have to
be before the probability of selecting thirty venires with no
more than five blacks each would be at least equal to 0.05. The
answer may be read from Table 1, which shows various hypothetical values for p, the probabilities of selecting a single
venire with no more than five blacks, and the probabilities of
thirty such venires:

The table shows that the value $P(v \leq 5)^{30}$ passes from less
than 0.05 to more than 0.05 as p passes from 0.11 to 0.10. Consequently, in order to obtain a value of $P(v \leq 5)$ which corresponds to a binomial model, p would have to be less than 0.11.
For simplicity it is assumed that the critical value is $p = 0.10$;
this is accurate enough for present purposes. In other words, we
cannot account for the observed number of blacks on venires
unless we assume that eligible blacks constitute $1/_{10}$ or less of
the total eligible population.

Since blacks comprise approximately 25 percent of the
adult male population, there are three times as many adult
male whites as adult male blacks. On our assumption that no

TABLE 1[61]

Probability of Selecting a Single Black Venireman p	Probability of Selecting a Single Venire of 30 with 5 or Fewer Blacks $P(v \leq 5)$	Probability of Selecting 30 Such Venires $P(v \leq 5)^{30}$
.25	.20260	4.63×10^{-21}
.20	.42751	8.48×10^{-12}
.15	.71058	3.54×10^{-5}
.12	.85692	0.0097
.11	.89509	0.0360
.10	.92681	0.1002
.05	.99672	0.9053
.02	.99997	0.9911

[61]The probabilities $P(v \leq 5)$ shown in this table were obtained from Harvard Computation Laboratory, Tables of the Cumulative Binomial Probability Distribution 137 (1955). $P(v \leq 5)^{30}$ was computed. The use of a test based on $P(v \leq 5)^{30}$ is not statistically conventional. Normally, better data would be available and the chi-square test would be used. See pp. 43–50, *infra.*

more than 10 percent of the eligibles are blacks, there must be at least nine times as many eligible whites as eligible blacks. This means that, to satisfy the statistical test established for the binomial model, it must be assumed that the proportion of adult male whites qualifying is at least three times as large as the proportion of adult male blacks qualifying. For example, if all the whites qualify, then not more than one-third of the blacks may qualify; if 75 percent of the whites qualify, then not more than 25 percent of the blacks may qualify.

Qualifications for jury service may be divided roughly into objective and subjective factors. The most important objective factor is literacy; among the subjective factors are a reputation for honesty and intelligence, community esteem, and so forth. The court should look first at census and other data to determine the impact of the objective factors. If these do not account for the three-to-one qualification rate in favor of whites, then the effect of the subjective factors must be considered.

The Census Bureau has not reported how many blacks in Talladega County have completed six years of school (and are thus presumably literate),[62] but the statewide average census figures show that approximately 48 percent of adult male blacks and 83 percent of adult male whites have had such schooling.[63] If this average applies to Talladega County, the higher rate of illiteracy among blacks cannot by itself explain their absence from the venires, since the comparative literacy ratio is not three to one but less than two to one. Assuming that literacy is the only significant objective factor,[64] the three-to-one qualification rate must be owing in part to the application of the subjective criteria.

We must now determine the proportion of the adult male literates of each race qualifying on subjective grounds. Since

[62]This is the standard for presumptive literacy used in the Voting Rights Act of 1965. 42 U.S.C. §§ 1971(c), 1973b(e) (Supp. I, 1965).

[63]DEPARTMENT OF COMMERCE, BUREAU OF CENSUS, U.S. CENSUS OF POPULATION: 1960, vol. 1, pt. 2 (Alabama). Talladega County blacks over the age of twenty-five are more literate than adult blacks in the state as a whole, since their median schooling is 6.5 years. *Id.* at 2-201, 2-224.

[64]This implies that conviction of an offense involving moral turpitude and habitual drunkenness, the two other objective factors mentioned by the Alabama statute, do not markedly affect the relative proportions of blacks and whites qualifying.

there are three times as many adult whites as adult blacks, and since 83 percent of the whites and 48 percent of the blacks are literate (using the sixth grade schooling test), the ratio of adult literate whites to adult literate blacks is

$$\frac{3 \times 83}{1 \times 48} = 5.2.$$

Thus, when adult males emerge from the literacy test, there are about five times as many whites as blacks. But we know that, after the literacy and subjective tests, there are at least nine times as many whites as blacks. We know, therefore, that whites are almost twice ($^9/_5$) as successful as blacks in getting through the subjective tests. In other words, the proportion of literate blacks qualifying on subjective grounds is $^5/_9$ of the corresponding proportion of white literates.[65]

The qualifications issue has now been refined to the point where the problems of legal policy are exposed for the Court to deal with unencumbered by subsidiary statistical questions. The principal legal question is whether a state, by imposing subjective criteria for jury service or by its method of administering the system, may cause the rate of qualification among lit-

---

[65]This line of reasoning may be expressed algebraically as follows: If *EB/LB* equals the proportion of eligible blacks in the literate black population and *EW/LW* equals the proportion of eligible whites in the literate white population, we are seeking to determine the number *a* such that *EB/LB* = (*a*)(*EW/LW*). Transposing, *a* = (*EB/EW*)(*LW/LB*). We have determined that the proportion of eligible blacks to eligible whites (*EB/EW*) must be no greater than $^1/_9$. Thus, at most, *EB/EW* = $^1/_9$. We have also determined that the proportion of literate whites to literate blacks (*LW/LB*) is approximately 5. Combining the two: $a = (EB/EW)(LW/LB) = (^1/_9)(5) = ^5/_9$, the result given in the text.

When we examined the representation of blacks on venires without considering the qualifications issue, the statistics were so extreme that it made little difference which assumptions or methods were used. This is no longer true when dealing with the qualifications issue. If twenty rather than thirty venires were assumed chosen consecutively, *p* would be closer to 0.12. The simultaneous use of other assumptions favorable to the state could raise this figure even higher. On the other hand, we have omitted information which cuts the other way, e.g., the testimony that during this period there were three or four grand juries without *any* blacks. Record on Appeal at 10. It is not necessary for our purposes to work out the numerical consequences of these possibilities. We do note that our results are sensitive to our assumptions, and that if the Court had reached the qualifications issue, it might reasonably have decided that more accurate information was essential for decision.

erate blacks to be substantially smaller (in *Swain's* case by almost half) than the rate among literate whites. Several resolutions are possible. The Court might hold such a result unconstitutional per se. It might view the result as prima facie evidence of discrimination which the defendant would be at liberty to rebut. Or it might require the petitioner to present evidence of specific malfeasance. Whatever the resolution, these alternatives present problems of basic importance to this branch of the law. The Court did not reach those problems in *Swain* because of its inability to assess the significance of statistical data without mathematical tools.

It is appropriate to consider the significance of the critical value of 0.05 in the foregoing analysis. The size of the critical value affects the probability of error. When will a test with a critical value of 0.05 lead to wrong results? In considering this question, statisticians usually divide error into two types. Type I is the error of rejecting the hypothesis of random selection when it is true. When the critical value 0.05 is used, this type of error will occur, on the average, not more than one time in twenty—on the one occasion in twenty when a series of binomial trials would yield the observed distribution. Only the state has standing to complain of type I error, since it involves a finding of discrimination when there is none.

Type II is the error of accepting the random-selection hypothesis when it is false. The extent of such error is more difficult to determine. However, only the defendant has standing to complain of type II error, since it involves a finding of nondiscrimination when in fact there is discrimination. When a court determines that discrimination is present, the only error it need consider is type I error. It is only when no discrimination is found that type II error need be considered.

It should be noted that on the facts in *Swain*, a substantially smaller critical value (and thus substantially greater accuracy) does not change the results very much. Thus, if the critical value were 0.01, p would equal about 0.12[66] and the rate of disqualification for the subjective factors would be recomputed as (6.1)/9. This is not materially different insofar as the legal issues are concerned from the $^5/_9$ rate, which was computed using the critical value 0.05.

[66]See Table 1, p. 39 *supra*.

Are a critical value of 0.05 and a type I error of one in twenty too large? This is a legal issue for which there can be no firm answer. The Court must weigh the risk of intruding on a state's selection process without cause against the risk of upholding venires which were in fact chosen discriminatorily. Where the probability line is drawn usually will not be determinative, and may vary with the facts. In *Avery* v. *Georgia*,[67] the defendant was convicted by a jury selected from a panel of sixty veniremen chosen from a box containing tickets with the names of the persons on the jury roll—yellow tickets for blacks and white tickets for whites. Five percent of the tickets in the box were yellow, but not a single yellow ticket was selected for the venire of sixty. The Court held that the all-white venire and the opportunity to discriminate presented by the yellow tickets constituted a prima facie case of discrimination. Mr. Justice Frankfurter, concurring, concentrated on the absence of blacks from the venire: "The mind of justice, not merely its eyes, would have to be blind to attribute such an occurrence to mere fortuity."[68]

The statistical case is hardly that conclusive. The probability of selecting a white is $q = 0.95$. Applying the multiplication rule, the probability that sixty whites would be selected is $(0.95)^{60} = 0.046$. This probability is enormously greater than that computed in *Swain*. The Court's conclusion in *Avery* is acceptable under our test only if a critical value of the order of 0.05 is viewed as sufficiently small. It is likely that the Court's intuitive evaluation of the probabilities was influenced by its knowledge that the colored-ticket system furnished a way to discriminate and suggested an intent to do so.

B.

I now consider the issue the Court faced in *Cassell* v. *Texas*[69] and would have faced in *Barksdale* v. *Louisiana*[70] had it granted

---

[67]345 U.S. 559 (1952).
[68]*Id.* at 564.
[69]339 U.S. 282 (1950).
[70]247 La. 198, 170 So. 2d 374 (1964), *cert. denied*, 382 U.S. 921 (1965).

certiorari, namely, whether a given distribution of blacks on grand juries is consistent with random selection.

For problems of this type statisticians frequently use a goodness-of-fit test known as the chi-square (χ^2) test.[71] In essence, the chi-square test as applied to this problem is a measure of the probability that the observed distribution of blacks on grand juries would differ to the degree it does from the distribution which would be most probable if the selection of jurors were truly random. The "distribution" referred to is the numbers of grand juries with exactly one black, exactly two blacks, exactly three blacks, and so forth. To construct the test, one must assign a measure to the difference between the observed and expected distributions and then determine the probability that a distribution with a deviation at least as large as that observed would occur by chance. If such a deviation is improbable, the assumption that the distribution occurred by chance is rejected. The theory of the chi-square test is simple, although actual computation of the probabilities leads to some technical problems.

If $P(v)$ is the probability that a jury with v blacks would be chosen at random, and if N juries are chosen, the "expected" number of juries with v blacks is $NP(v)$, which is abbreviated as $E(v)$. This is the single most probable result of random selection, although the probability of that particular result may be quite small.

We are interested in the difference between the observed and expected numbers of juries for each possible proportion of blacks. This difference is $O(v) - E(v)$, where the observed number of juries with v blacks is $O(v)$ and the expected number of such juries is $E(v)$. If, for example, the probability of selecting a jury with two blacks is $P(v = 2) = {}^1/_4$ and four juries were chosen, we would expect one of the juries to have two blacks, since $E(v = 2) = 4 \times {}^1/_4 = 1$. If in an actual drawing of four juries none had two blacks, then the difference between the number observed and the number expected would be $(0 - 1) = -1$.

[71]Discussions of χ^2 may be found in most statistics texts. See, e.g., SNEDE-COR and COCHRAN, STATISTICAL METHODS, 20–27 (6th ed. 1967). For a non-technical explanation of χ^2 see HODGES and LEHMANN, BASIC CONCEPTS OF PROBABILITY AND STATISTICS 285–88 (1964). See also Robinson, *Bias, Probability, and Trial by Jury*, 15 AM. SOCIOLOGICAL REV. 72 (1950).

In order to obtain a measure for the total deviation from the expected number of blacks on juries, the difference between the observed and expected values is summed up for each v from $v = 0$ to $v = 12$ (the size of each jury). In other words, we compare the difference between the observed and expected numbers of juries with 0, 1, 2, ... 12 blacks, add these differences, and obtain a single number which measures the totality of the differences. Since the observed values may be greater or less than the expected values, these differences would in some cases be negative (as in the example), and thus reduce the sum. This would be misleading, because in this context it is irrelevant which is greater, the expected or observed frequencies; the only significant fact is that they are different. For this reason, mathematicians usually consider the square of each difference, which is always positive. Finally, each squared difference is divided by its associated expected frequency, which makes the value of the differences proportional to the expected frequencies.[72] We thus obtain the following expression for χ^2 as the sum of the squares of the differences between the observed and expected frequencies divided by the expected frequency:

$$\chi^2 = \sum \frac{(O(v) - E(v))^2}{E(v)} \, .$$

Note that χ^2 increases as the difference between the observed and expected frequencies increases, and decreases to zero as the sum of the squared differences between the observed and expected frequencies diminishes.

Given a particular distribution of blacks on juries, the issue presented is: What is the probability of obtaining a distribution which deviates to this or a greater extent from the expected distribution? This is equivalent to asking the probability that χ^2 would have a value that would equal or exceed the χ^2 value of the observed distribution. It is a remarkable (and exceedingly useful) fact that the probability distribution of χ^2 is substantially independent of the probability distribution of the random vari-

---

[72]If, for a particular v, $O(v) = 231$ and $E(v) = 230$, the squared difference between them would be 1. But this is a much better agreement between observation and expectation than if $O(v) = 2$ and $E(v) = 1$. Dividing by $E(v)$ brings out this proportionality factor. Thus, in the first example $\chi^2 = \frac{1}{230}$, but in the second $\chi^2 = 1$.

able itself, so that a single standardized table showing probabilities for χ^2 may be used for a wide variety of problems.[73]

The χ^2 test differs in an important respect from the previous
test. Since we previously sought to determine the probability of
so few blacks being chosen, it was always possible to find a
value for p small enough to account for the observed racial composition of the venires. If very few blacks appeared on venires,
p would have to be assumed to be very small, and thus inconsistent with the actual qualifications of the black community. Still,
in every case some value of p could be found which made the
observations consistent with the hypothesis of randomness. But
since, in dealing with the χ^2 test, we are determining the probability of the appearance of a particular *distribution* and not just
a maximum number of blacks, we cannot in all cases account for
the observations merely by reducing the value of p. The value
of p which maximizes the χ^2 probability may still lead to a value
too small to be consistent with the binomial model.

This property becomes important since it enables us to
apply the χ^2 test to distributions when p is unknown. In such
cases we assume that value for p represented by the aggregate
number of blacks on all the juries divides by the aggregate
number of juries; this maximizes the binomial probability. If χ^2
so computed is still too large to be consistent with the binomial
hypothesis, then that hypothesis should be rejected since the χ^2
test indicates that the data are a poor fit. For example no matter
what we are willing to assume about black qualifications, if we
find, say, that every grand jury contains one black, neither more
nor less, we may be able to conclude that selection has not been
random.

These observations may be formalized as the following test:
*The assumption that the racial result of grand jury selection
corresponds to a series of binomial trials is rejected whenever a
distribution appears for which the calculated χ^2 probability is
less than a selected critical value.* For purposes of illustration,
the critical value 0.05 is selected. The analysis of type I and II
error used in the previous analysis may also be applied to the
χ^2 test.

It is instructive to apply these methods to *Cassell* v. *Texas*,[74]

[73]Tables of χ^2 are given in most statistical texts. See, e.g., SNEDECOR and
COCHRAN, STATISTICAL METHODS Table A5 at 550 (6th ed. 1967).

[74]339 U.S. 282 (1950).

where information concerning the grand juries was more precise than in *Swain*. Of the twenty-one grand juries considered in *Cassell*, a single black appeared on seventeen, and none on the remaining four. Blacks comprised 6.5 percent of the eligible population. The Court held that these statistics did not constitute evidence of discrimination, since the average number of blacks on the juries when considered as a group was 6.7 percent, and this did not appear to differ significantly from their proportion in the population of eligibles. On the assumption that $p = 0.067$ and $q = 0.933$, which maximizes the binomial probability, the formulas previously derived show that $P(v = 0) = 0.435$, $P(v = 1) = 0.375$, and $P(v > 1) = 0.190$. The expected numbers of grand juries with zero, one black, and more than one black are 9.14, 7.87 and 3.99, respectively. The value of χ^2 for this distribution is thus

$$\chi^2 = \frac{(4 - 9.14)^2}{9.14} + \frac{(17 - 7.88)^2}{7.18} + \frac{(0 - 3.99)^2}{3.99} = 17.47.$$

The probability of obtaining this large a value of χ^2 is far less than 0.05, so that one would have to reject the hypothesis that blacks were included on the basis of random selection, regardless of their proportion in the eligible population.[75] This result supports Justices Frankfurter, Burton, and Minton, who grounded their concurrence on the improbability that no more than one black would ever appear on a venire.

I now apply the χ^2 test to the statistics presented to the Court in petition for certiorari in *Barksdale*. In Orleans Parish nine grand juries were selected between September, 1958, and September, 1962, when the grand jury which indicted Barksdale was impaneled. Each grand jury had twelve members. There were two blacks on eight of these juries and one on the ninth. Although blacks comprised one third of the adult male population of the parish, the Supreme Court of Louisiana held that the smaller number of blacks on grand juries was explained by their lower level of literacy and by the fact that more blacks than whites requested to be excused because of economic hardship. There was no evidence as to the number of blacks and whites

---

[75]See SNEDECOR and COCHRAN, STATISTICAL METHODS Table A5 at 550–51 (6th ed. 1967). Omitted from our calculation is the refinement of the correction for continuity, which would slightly reduce the value of χ^2 but would not affect our conclusions.

requesting excuses. For this reason it is assumed that p is some unknown value less than $^1/_3$.

Blacks thus constituted $^{17}/_{108} = 0.157$ of the juries, and whites 0.843. Using these figures as the probabilities of selecting single jurors, the relevant probabilities are $P(v = 0) = 0.1288$; $P(v = 1) = 0.2879$; $P(v = 2) = 0.2949$ and $P(v > 2) = 0.2885$. The expected numbers of juries with these numbers of blacks are 1.1592, 2.5908, 2.6538, and 2.5962, respectively. In order to use the standard χ^2 table (which is an approximation), it is necessary to combine the second and third groups so that the expected numbers of juries in those categories would be at least one.[76] With that combination, χ^2 is calculated as

$$\frac{(0 - 1.1592)}{1.1592} + \frac{(8 - 2.5908)}{2.5908} + \frac{(0 - 2.5962)}{2.5962} = 16.08.$$

Since the probability that χ^2 would have a value this large is far less than 0.05, one would have to conclude that a binomial process of random selection would not have produced a distribution of seventeen blacks on twelve grand juries with as small a variation as that observed.

The significance of this rejection must now be considered. Rejection of the binomial model of the selection process implies the existence of discrimination only if this model would accurately reflect the racial results of jury selection in a system free from discrimination. Whether this is so is an empirical question. It can be resolved only by charting the results of a system which is free from discrimination but which otherwise operates in precisely the same way as the system under experimentation. But although scientific verification is lacking, the assumption we have used seems plausible.

If the observations are of venires, rejection of the binomial hypothesis implies that p must vary from venire to venire, or from the selection of one venireman to the next. Since, within each system now in use, the method of selection is supposed to remain the same for each venire and venireman, the only reason

---

[76]See SNEDECOR and COCHRAN, *supra* at 235. Some authorities require larger numbers. When the numbers are too small for the χ^2 test, Fisher's exact test must be used. *Id.*

for variation would seem to be intentional intervention: when the officials charged with selecting veniremen choose to exclude blacks, $p = 0$ and $q = 1$. It is this reasoning which makes plausible the assumption that an honest selection process consists of a series of binomial trials and that a nonbinomial process is discriminatory.

Does this also apply to the grand jury? In *Barksdale* it was claimed by the state that the relative absence of blacks from grand juries could be explained, inter alia, by their more frequent requests to be excused because of economic hardship. Assuming such requests were made, can it be said that selecting grand jurors is, in the absence of discrimination, a series of binomial trials? There appears no reason to treat the selection of grand jurors differently from the selection of veniremen. The existence of an excuse based on economic grounds might affect the number of available blacks, but within the pool of eligibles the selection of grand jurors must still be made without consideration of race. Poverty might explain why only one-sixth as many blacks as whites are left in the pool, but not why precisely one-sixth of almost every grand jury selected is black. Since economic hardship and illiteracy operate in similar ways as barriers to jury service, it appears reasonable to extend the assumption that the selection of venires is binomial to the grand jury.

Whether this assumption may be extended to the petit jury is more doubtful. If it is constitutionally permissible for the prosecutor to strike any black from the jury in a capital case in which the defendant is black, or to adopt similar racial restrictions, the selection process for the petit jury clearly is not binomial. On the other hand, if exclusionary rules are not constitutionally permissible and each juror must be considered on his merits, the case for the binomial hypothesis is stronger, since the determination to strike a juror must be more particularized and less dependent on race. However, it is still possible that p will be smaller in any case where the prosecutor might reasonably expect a greater possibility of bias on the part of a black juror. If that is so, the selection of petit jurors for a series of juries would not consist of Bernoulli trials. In short, it seems fair to extend the logic of the Court's decisions in the venire cases to grand juries, but it is doubtful that the same methods can be applied to petit juries.

Cassell and *Barksdale* involved grand juries, so the binomial hypothesis should apply. Yet we have seen that, even assuming that the proportion of blacks on grand juries was the same as their proportion in the population of eligibles, the fact that it was almost unvaryingly so makes the distribution inconsistent with the hypothesis of random selection. Since on the assumption most favorable to the state the distribution test leads to a rejection of the hypothesis of random selection, we must conclude that no argument based on the presence or absence of qualifications in the black community will explain the observed distribution. It is overwhelmingly unlikely that the *Cassell* or *Barksdale* facts could have resulted from the evenhanded use of selection criteria unfavorable to blacks or from sloppy, haphazard administration. Within the confidence limits of the test, the conclusion seems inescapable that in both cases race was considered in selecting grand jurors.

C.

"The Civil War Amendments," Mr. Justice Frankfurter wrote, concurring in *Cassell* v. *Texas*, "did not turn matters that are inherently incommensurable into mere matters of arithmetic."[77] To the reader who has faithfully threaded his way through the foregoing analysis it should be apparent that the mathematical methods developed here do not supplant the necessity for legal judgments. The purpose and effect of the mathematics is to draw implications from the data on which judgment must be founded. If the consequence is a legal decision that discrimination exists where uninformed intuition would have reached a different conclusion, the decision was compelled by the consistent application of legal principles to new information.

A basic legal principle in the jury discrimination cases holds that the selection of an improbably small number of blacks is evidence of discrimination. This principle, which links a finding of discrimination to a determination of probabilities, opens the door to the use of statistical analysis in these cases. The mathematical methods described here have been used to calculate the probabilities which the law has established as relevant for determining the existence of discrimination.

[77]339 U.S. 282, 291 (1950).

A second legal principle controlling these cases holds that a disparity between the proportion of blacks on venires and in the population generally is evidence of the improbability of random selection. Using this assumption, we have applied a statistical test for randomness to the number of blacks appearing on the jury venires described by the record in *Swain* v. *Alabama*. The test led to the conclusion that the selection process was not random with respect to race if the entire adult male population of both races was considered eligible. The results could not be justified by any lack of qualifications for jury service among blacks unless it was assumed that the rate of black qualification with respect to such subjective factors as lack of integrity was little more than half the rate of white qualification.

The failure to select a greater number of blacks for venires is not the only fact relevant to a claim of discrimination. A skewed distribution may also constitute such evidence. In order to test for skewness we used the chi-square goodness-of-fit test to analyze the distribution of blacks on grand juries in *Cassell* v. *Texas* and *Barksdale* v. *Louisiana* and concluded that in both cases race was a consideration in selecting grand jurors.

The particular statistical tests that produced these results are by no means the only possible tests of these matters. Other tests with different characteristics have been used in treating cognate problems. Unfortunately, an adequate discussion of the criteria for choosing tests would lead into the vasty deep, and the reader may feel that the waters here are already deep enough. It must suffice to say that the choice of tests depends on the nature of the suspected discrimination, and consequently presents a delicately mixed problem of mathematics, fact, and law.

It may be felt, however, that all mathematical tests are inappropriate for jury discrimination problems because such methods are too technical, elaborate, and fine-grained. Perhaps judicial intuition is sufficient to decide what the Constitution requires and only the intuitively obvious cases should be deemed appropriate for judicial correction. This view may be supported by the observation that the Court has never required jury selection to be mathematically perfect in the sense that every potential venireman receives an exactly equal chance for service; consequently, it may be said that the proposed mathematical technique is misleading because it applies exact methods to an inexact system. This charge is worth considering, because it can be leveled at many attempts, to apply scientific methods to legal problems: in each case the legal rules will invariably reflect the human imperfections of our institutions, but the methods used to analyze them will not, seemingly, allow for such imperfections.

In the present context, the need for such allowance does not appear to be a significant problem. Any statistical method of analyzing data tells us the attributes of the system under examination, but it does not tell us the causes of those attributes, though it may be able to rule out some conceivable ones. Thus in *Swain* we found that in order to sustain the observations it must be assumed that the rate of qualification of blacks for jury service was substantially smaller than that for whites. We assumed that this occurred because the commissioners disqualified a proportionately greater number of blacks, but it may be that the commissioners only innocently canvassed proportionately fewer literate blacks than literate whites.

In this and other cases, however, the cause of the result may be legally irrelevant. The Supreme Court has held that an innocent failure to canvass any blacks at all was not an acceptable excuse for a result which was, in effect, the equivalent of discriminatory selection.[78] In at least some cases, then, a system whose results appear to be discriminatory may be treated as such even though the commissioners convincingly profess good faith. Statistical techniques can be used to identify such cases. Even when a case is not extreme, so that the courts are willing to hear a defense of good faith, mathematical methods may be able, as in the *Barksdale* case, to provide a test of that defense.

The acceptance of mathematical methods undoubtedly implies a certain yielding by judges of their freedom of decision. In *Swain*, the mathematical case appears overwhelming, and it leads to a conclusion contrary to that reached by the Court. This consequence may be a source of judicial reluctance to entrust decisions to mathematical methods and may tempt the Court to continue a familiar practice of casting legal rules in broad discretionary terms which ensure that legal principles will not embarrass with results that run against the grain of judicial intuition.

[78]Cassell v. Texas, 339 U.S. 282, 287–90 (1950).

In the developing stages of a legal rule, a reservation of discretion may be the better part of judicial valor, but where principles have become established over a long period, the desire to reserve an unmeasured power over their consequences is not an appealing motive for rejecting objective methods. In the sensitive area of the law we have been considering, where cases carry the freight of broad social conflicts, the authority of decisions will not be enhanced by methods which depend unnecessarily on personal and intuitive judgments. As Learned Hand wrote, the authority and immunity of a judge rest "upon the assumption that he speaks with the mouth of others."[79] The novelty of the methods suggested here may make them seem strange to the lawyer or the judge, but, in the long run, the analysis provided by statistical theory should make the decisions in the jury discrimination cases a more natural and inevitable consequence of the data which determine them. The importance of objectivity and consistency should persuade us to follow legal principles in these cases even when their logic leads to ground made less certain by the absence of the assurance—and it is sometimes a false assurance—that intuition brings to judgment.

IV

Shortly after the preceding analysis was published in December, 1966,[80] the Supreme Court decided *Whitus* v. *Georgia*.[81] Under Georgia law, commissioners appointed by the Superior Court were to select as jurors "upright and intelligent citizens" from the lists of the tax receiver. These lists were kept on a segregated basis, with the designation (c) appearing after the names of blacks. In the county in which Whitus was tried, 27 percent of the tax digest was black. However, blacks comprised only 9.1 percent of Whitus' grand jury venire supposedly selected without discrimination from this list, and only

---

[79]Hand, *Mr. Justice Cardozo*, 52 HARV. L. REV. 361 (1939).

[80]Finkelstein, *The Application of Statistical Decision Theory to the Jury Discrimination Cases*, 80 HARV. L. REV. 338 (1966).

[81]385 U.S. 545 (1967).

7.8 percent of the petit jury venire selected from the same source.

The Court found that the segregated lists gave the commissioners an "opportunity for discrimination" and that the disparity in percentages "strongly pointed" to the conclusion that discrimination had been practiced. In support of the latter conclusion, the Court noted that, although unnecessary to its disposition of the case, the probability that only seven blacks would be included in a venire of ninety selected at random from a tax digest which was 27 percent black was 0.000006.[82]

The inclusion of statistical analysis in this observation led to the introduction of similar analyses in many jury challenges, and to some judicial acceptance of such evidence by the lower federal courts.[83] But *Whitus* left open the question whether the same conclusion would have been reached on the statistical evidence alone, without the opportunity to discriminate indicated by the segregated tax lists.

After *Whitus*, unsegregated voter lists were used in Georgia in place of the tax lists. In *Turner* v. *Fouche*,[84] the commissioners chose a jury list from this source after eliminating many names. In holding their method of selection unconstitutional, the Court focused on two statistical facts: a disproportionately large number of blacks had been eliminated as "unintelligent" or not "upright," and a substantial number of other voters not known to the white commissioners was also eliminated. Blacks accounted for only 37 percent of the pared-down list although constituting 60 percent of the county population. This "substantial disparity," which "originated, at least in part, at the one point in the selection process where the jury commissioners invoked their subjective judgment,"[85] was held to make out a prima facie case of jury discrimination.

After *Fouche*, one might have thought that statistical evidence alone could be sufficient for a prima facie case. But *Alex-*

---

[82]385 U.S. at 552 n.2. The Court apparently took judicial notice of this probability, for no statistician had testified and no probabilistic calculation had been advanced in the briefs.

[83]See, e.g., Smith v. Yeager, 465 F.2d 272 (3d Cir. 1972), *cert. denied*, 409 U.S. 1076 (1972).

[84]396 U.S. 346 (1970).

[85]*Id.* at 360.

ander v. *Louisiana*[86] demonstrated that the Court was not yet willing to go that far.

In *Alexander* Louisiana parish commissioners sent jury questionnaires to lists of persons compiled from various sources. The questionnaires included a space to indicate race. The adult population of the parish was 21 percent black, but only 13.8 percent of the questionnaires returned were from blacks. This was a first reduction in their representation. The commissioners then eliminated 5,000 questionnaires, ostensibly on the ground that these persons were either not qualified or exempt. A second reduction in black representation must have occurred at this stage, because a random sample of 400 names from the remaining questionnaires included only 6.8 percent blacks. Further reductions occurred when only one black was included in petitioner's grand jury venire of twenty selected from this list, and none was on the grand jury selected from the venire.

The petitioner argued that elementary principles of probability made it extremely unlikely that at each stage a random selection process would have so consistently reduced the proportion of blacks. The Court took note of the argument, and specifically cited petitioner's calculation that the chances that only twenty-seven blacks would have been included in the 400 name jury list drawn at random from the questionnaires was one in 20,000. As in *Whitus*, statistical analysis was thus approved. But although the Court found "striking" the progressive decimation of black jurors, it expressly declined to rest its decision on the statistics alone. Instead, it referred specifically to the fact that the racial designation on the questionnaires had made "the selection process not racially neutral." Thus the issue left open in *Whitus* remained to be resolved.

The step which the Court was unwilling to take in *Alexander* it finally took in *Castaneda* v. *Partida*.[87] In *Castaneda*, the Court again had occasion to scrutinize the Texas "key man" system for selecting jurors, this time the charge being discrimination against Mexican-Americans. The respondent Partida was indicted and convicted of burglary with intent to commit rape

[86]405 U.S. 625 (1972).
[87]430 U.S. 482 (1977).

in Hidalgo County, Texas. Hidalgo is one of the border counties of southern Texas, and the 1970 Census showed that persons speaking Spanish or with Spanish surnames constituted 79.1 percent of the population. In the period 1962–72, of the 870 persons summoned to serve as grand jurors in the county, only 339, or 39 percent, had Spanish surnames. A closely divided Court held that this alone made out a prima facie case of discrimination. Writing for the majority, Justice Blackmun pointed out that the 40 percentage point difference was greater than, or within the range of, differences in other cases in which discrimination had been found. He buttressed this comparison with a lengthy footnote expressly adopting the binomial model of jury selection and using the normal approximation to compute the very small probability of obtaining a disparity that large by random selection from the population.[88] The Court thus squarely held for the first time that statistics demonstrating underrepresentation were in themselves sufficient for a prima facie case.

The sheriff's principal rebuttal was that since three of the five jury commissioners who selected the jurors had Spanish surnames, as did the sheriff of the county and the trial judge, the "governing majority" of the county was Mexican-American and could not be presumed to discriminate against itself. The Court, however, rejected this argument as speculative, pointing out that the commissioners had failed to testify in defense of their selection practices. The Court also rejected the sheriff's argument that disproportionate numbers of Mexican-Americans were not qualified. It held that these matters also should have been the subject of rebuttal testimony. The decision emphasizes that proof—not mere argumentative speculation—is necessary to dispel the inference of discrimination raised by statistical disparities.

In support of its conclusion that *Partida* had established a prima facie case, the Court noted that the Texas "key man" system of selecting jurors was "highly subjective" and "susceptible to abuse as applied." Should the principle of *Castaneda* be

---

[88]The Court's calculation showed that the observed results were twelve standard deviations from the result expected on the basis of random selection. It noted that the probability of a departure that large is less than one in 10^{140} (430 U.S. 496, n.17).

applied where the method of jury selection is more systematic and perhaps less susceptible to abuse? The question is important since in most large urban systems, jurors are chosen from the voting lists after being screened by the clerks, but the results may nevertheless show a gross underrepresentation of blacks or other groups.[89] The Court has yet to deal with the issues presented by such systems.

It is hard to see why the *Castaneda* principle should not also extend to more sophisticated urban jury systems. If bad faith of the officials is the test, there is usually an opportunity to discriminate in the sending out of notices or in a personal interview, and a white clerk in a large urban jury office cannot be presumed to be less likely to discriminate against blacks than the Mexican-American jury commissioners against Mexican-Americans in Hidalgo county. But the larger point is that bad faith should not be the test. The injury is the discriminatory system, and the issue presented by such a system is the extent to which officials must take affirmative steps to produce non-discriminatory results. Regardless of intent, if the officials administer a system which has the effect of excluding dispropor-

[89]The importance of the issues is illustrated by the decision of the New York Court of Appeals in People v. Chestnut, 26 N.Y.2d 481, 260 N.E.2d 501, 311 N.Y.S.2d 853 (1970), which approved jury selection in New York County. The decision in *Chestnut* is of particular significance because the principal features and results of the system in New York County appear to be typical of Northern urban jury selection.

According to the record in *Chestnut*, grand jurors in New York County were selected on a voluntary basis—principally from those who had served as petit jurors—but also from those recommended by judges, the County Grand Jury Association, and other informal sources. Replacements were added as needed to maintain a jury list of some two thousand names. Those responding were personally interviewed by the clerks, who eliminated applicants lacking the statutory requirements. These included the highly subjective test of "honesty and intelligence." (The clerks also imposed certain other requirements without statutory authorization which were challenged but need not concern us here.) In the year 1964, some 41 percent of new applicants for grand jury service (144 out of 344) were rejected by the clerks after this examination; but no records were kept of the race of those rejected.

The process produced grossly disproportionate racial results. For example, of the 1,999 persons on the 1964 grand jury list, only 33, or 1.6 percent, were black, despite the fact that 24 percent of the adult population of New York County was black. Current statistics show improvement, particularly with respect to the representation of women, but New York still retains its highly subjective qualifications for jurors.

tionate numbers of blacks or other groups from jury service, they should be chargeable if that result could have been avoided by means that lie within their legal duty. The scope of that duty, not the presumed intent of the officials, should be the central inquiry in these discrimination cases.

The most effective use of statistics in this context is not to test the hypothesis of perfect random selection, but to estimate the degree to which the underrepresented group has been disfavored in the selection process apart from random fluctuation. When the statistics show that some cause other than chance significantly restricted the representation of the disfavored group, there is obviously the risk that the officials pursued "a course of conduct in the administration of their office which operated to discriminate in the selection of jurors . . . ."[90] If there is a constitutionally acceptable answer, the officials themselves can best provide it. But an inquiring challenger is likely to be met with bland assertions of good faith or a simple absence of records or information unless the officials must produce more than this to save the system from constitutional attack.

[90] Hill v. Texas, 316 U.S. 400, 404 (1942). Quoted with approval in Alexander v. Louisiana, 405 U.S. 625, 632 (1972). This is the rule with respect to federal juries, where the officials appear to have an affirmative duty to obtain a "fair cross-section" of the community. See, e.g., Rabinowitz v. United States, 366 F.2d 34 (5th Cir. 1966). In *Rabinowitz*, the Fifth Circuit held that "[t]he Constitution and laws of the United States place an affirmative duty on the county clerk and the jury commissioner to develop and use a system that will probably result in a fair cross-section of the community being placed on the jury rolls." "If a fair cross-section is consistently lacking, then, without more, it is established that the commissioners have failed in their duty." 366 F.2d at 57–58. In the celebrated trial of Dr. Benjamin Spock, it was disclosed that only 30 percent of those on the jury rolls were women and that a venire of one hundred selected from this roll for Dr. Spock's trial included the names of only nine women. As a result of this progressive decimation, and the prosecution's use of peremptory challenges, Dr. Spock was tried by an all-male jury. See Zeisel, *Dr. Spock and the Case of the Vanishing Woman Jurors*, 37 U. CHI. L. REV. 1 (1969). Federal jury selection undoubtedly has been improved by the Jury Selection and Service Act of 1968, 28 U.S.C. §§ 1861 et seq. (Supp. 1978). See Boxer, *Uniform Jury Selection & Service Act*, 8 HARV. J. LEGIS. 280 (1971).

Chapter 3

TWO CASES IN EVIDENCE

THE PURPOSE OF THIS CHAPTER is to pursue the discussion of mathematical probability in the law of evidence by examining the ramifications of two famous cases. The first, *Sargent v. Massachusetts Accident Company*,[1] involves the definition of proof by a preponderance of evidence, the general standard in civil cases. The second, *People* v. *Collins*,[2] deals with problems of statistical evidence in criminal cases in which proof beyond a reasonable doubt is required. In both these cases, evidence based on mathematical probability was said to be insufficient for the proponent's burden of proof. The results in both are generally accepted as correct, but the opinions leave a whiff of paradox, because the asserted insufficiency of mathematical probability is not reconciled with the recognized probabilistic character of all proof. I propose to treat this inconsistency as something more than a mere lapse of thought or a failure to understand numerical evidence. Rather, it suggests that the familiar standards by which evidence is judged are influenced by certain unexamined and incorrect intuitive assumptions about probability and proof. These become exposed when there is numerical evidence or when the relation between probability and proof is approached from a mathematical point of view. I

[1]307 Mass. 246, 29 N.E.2d 825 (1940).
[2]68 Cal.2d 319, 438 P.2d 33, 66 Cal. Rptr. 497 (1968) (en banc).

analyze these implicit ideas by discussing three problems raised in the *Sargent* and *Collins* line of cases. These relate, first, to the meaning of probability as it applies to unique past events; second, to the probabilistic standard implied by the requirement of preponderance of evidence; and, third, to the estimation of probabilities based on the joint evaluation of quantitative and qualitative evidence.

I

Upham Sargent, a resourceful and athletic young man of twenty-one accustomed to hazardous voyages, intended to run down the Nottoway River to James Bay in his kayak. The headwaters of the Nottoway form dangerous rapids amid large boulders, and even the best canoeists would find passage hazardous. The country drained by the river is devoid of portages, roads, trails, or paths, but fish and blueberries are plentiful and there are ducks and rabbits.

Sargent was last seen leaving Lake Mattagami in northern Canada at the beginning of September, 1934. An Indian subsequently found his paddle on the bank of the river, on the fringe of a whirlpool, fifty or sixty miles from the mouth. The next spring another Indian found another part of his kayak under some rocks in the river, forty miles from the mouth.

In a suit on an accident insurance policy covering Sargent's life, the trial court directed a verdict for the defendant because the proof of accident (which was summarized in the preceding statement) was insufficient. On appeal, the Supreme Judicial Court of Massachusetts reversed, holding that there was sufficient evidence from which a jury could find by a preponderance of evidence that Sargent met death by drowning (which would be an accident within the policy) rather than by starvation (which would not). In reaching this conclusion, Lummus, J. defined the proof required for preponderance of evidence in a passage that has been frequently cited and discussed:

> It has been held not enough that mathematically the chances somewhat favor a proposition to be proved; for example, the

fact that colored automobiles made in the current year out-
number black ones would not warrant a finding that an un-
described automobile of the current year is colored and not
black, nor would the fact that only a minority of men die of
cancer warrant a finding that a particular man did not die of
cancer. [Citing authority.] The weight or preponderance of evidence is its power to convince the tribunal which has the determination of the fact of the actual truth of the proposition to
be proved. After the evidence has been weighed, that proposition is proved by a preponderance of the evidence if it is
made to appear more likely or probable in the sense that actual belief in its truth, derived from the evidence, exists in the
mind or minds of the tribunal notwithstanding any doubts
that may still linger there. [Citing authority.]

Upon the evidence, in the opinion of a majority of the court,
a jury could find, not merely that there was a greater chance
that the insured met his death by accident falling within the
policy than that he met a different fate, but that death by accident within the policy was in fact indicated by a preponderance of the evidence.[3]

This homily on mathematical probability was gratuitous,
since there was no numerical evidence in the case, and since
the Court concluded that the jury might have found that Sargent
had died by drowning.

The significance of Lummus's statement was not tested until
Smith v. *Rapid Transit, Inc.*,[4] where the plaintiff was forced
into a collision with a parked car by an unidentified bus. Defendant had the only bus line authorized to operate on the street
on which the accident occurred, but this did not preclude a
private or chartered bus from using the street. The Court found
that "the most that can be said of the evidence in the instant
case is that perhaps the mathematical chances somewhat favor
the proposition that a bus of the defendant caused the accident."[5] But this was not enough, since on the authority of
Sargent "actual belief," not mere mathematical preponderance,
is required for the plaintiff's case.

[3]307 Mass. at 250–51, 29 N.E.2d at 827.
[4]317 Mass. 469, N.E.2d 754 (1945).
[5]*Id.* at 470, 58 N.E.2d at 755.

A.

The rejection of mathematical chances as probative evidence in *Sargent* and *Smith* appears to spring at least in part from the notion that mathematical probability is simply inapplicable to unique past events. This is a commonly held idea. After all, a particular event either did or did not occur, and it seems artificial and perhaps unacceptable to attach a probability to the occurrence, or at least to draw any implications from such an artificial idea, even though there may be uncertainty as to the truth.

This view appears explicitly in *Day* v. *Boston & Marine R. R.*[6] which was cited in *Sargent*. In *Day,* the court gave the following example to demonstrate that mathematical probability was not probative of a particular past event:

> Of course, it is possible that he noticed the handcar. Indeed, it may be quantitatively probable that he did. Quantitative probability, however, is only the greater chance. It is not proof, nor even probative evidence, of the proposition to be proved. That in one throw of dice there is a quantitative probability, or greater chance, that a less number of spots than sixes will fall uppermost is no evidence whatever that in a given throw such was the actual result. Without something more, the actual result of the throw would still be utterly unknown. The slightest real evidence that sixes did in fact fall uppermost would outweigh all the probability otherwise. Granting, therefore, the chances to be more numerous that the plaintiff's intestate did notice the handcar than that he did not, we still have only the doctrine of chances. We are still without evidence tending to actual proof.[7]

The same point of view appears in *People* v. *Risley,*[8] where the New York Court of Appeals, rejecting a probabilistic computation, distinguished the accepted use of life-expectancy tables with the observation that "the fact to be established in this case was not the probability of a future event, but whether an occurrence asserted by the people to have happened had actually taken place."[9]

[6]96 Me. 207, 52 A. 771 (1902).
[7]*Id.* at 217–18, 52 A. at 774.
[8]214 N.Y. 75, 86, 108 N.E. 200 (1915).
[9]*Id.* at 86, 108 N.E. at 203.

The view of the *Day* and *Risley* courts that mathematical probability is inapplicable to unique past events reflects a lack of familiarity with statistical inference. The difference between the future and the past is not significant to mathematical probability. A probabilistic analysis of the selection of a lottery ticket does not change when the ticket is drawn, but only when the results are known. Probability concepts are in fact routinely applied by statisticians to express uncertainties in measuring facts concerning a population.[10] Insofar as the distinction between the future and the past is concerned, there is no reason why uncertainties associated with an event in a lawsuit could not be subjected to an analysis based on the principles of mathematical probability.

The problem of attributing a probability to unique events has been more widely debated. The concept of probability is usually defined in terms of relative frequencies. When we say that the probability of tossing heads with a coin is one-half, we mean, roughly speaking, that over a run of tosses heads will "tend" to come up half the time.[11] It seems artificial to apply a similar concept to the probability of death by accident on a particular trip. To do so would involve the assumption that the trip was repeated many times, with the probability of an accident being represented by the relative frequency of accidents in such repeated trips.

But this artificiality clearly does not in theory preclude an application of mathematical probability to an event which is normally viewed as unique, since any event can be conceived as recurrent. To make the concept more palatable, some probabilists have argued that statements such as "there is a 50 percent chance that the person died by accident" imply only a

[10]A statistician estimating the average height of a population based on a sample with an average height of 5′6″ might express his conclusions as follows: the average height of the population lies in the range of 5′2″ to 5′10″ with a 95 percent probability. This statement does not imply that average height is a future event, but it does make a kind of prediction about the distribution of average heights in other such samples. The prediction is that if repeated samples were taken from this population and intervals constructed in the same way around the average height of each, we would expect that ninety-five out of one hundred of the intervals would include the actual average height of the population.

[11]More precisely: the probability of tossing heads on a single trial is one-half if the probability of tossing any other given proportion of heads in a sequence of trials may be indefinitely reduced by sufficiently increasing the number of trials.

degree of belief in the proposition asserted and need not be interpreted as expressing an artificial frequency. These kinds of estimates are said to express a "subjective," "intuitive," or "personal" probability. They have been defined in terms of the odds that a rational person acting after reflection and consistency would regard as fair in betting on the proposition. And it has been shown that probabilities so estimated can be used in probability calculus in the same way as probabilities defined in terms of relative frequencies.[12]

There is in fact no significant difference between the subjective definition of probability applied to unique events and the classical definition based on relative frequency. At the molecular level two tosses of a coin are dissimiliar events, yet they are treated as similar for probabilistic purposes because of our subjective belief that the chance of throwing heads is the same both times. And so, seemingly unique events may be grouped together with respect to the degree of belief they inspire, and the probability of the uncertain event in each case expressed as the relative frequency of such events over all cases in the class. This is perhaps a more precise statement of the intuitive content of the notion that the evidence in a particular case has met a certain standard of probability or persuasion. Thus, the statement that Upham Sargent was more likely to have died in an accident than by another cause implies that if we affirmed a proposition (any proposition) when we had a similar degree of belief, we would be right more than half the time.

Since probability concepts may validly be applied to unique past events, the insistence in *Sargent* on proof which induces "actual belief" about such an event is not necessarily opposed to probabilistic or mathematical analysis. What was rejected was the sufficiency of an estimate based on overall average frequency when that lies in the middle range. This seems reasonable, at least on the surface, since the factual context of the disappearances will induce varying beliefs about them, so that the likelihood of an accident will be appraised differently in each case. It is this likelihood rather than the average frequency of fatal accidents in cases of disappearance which is felt to be

---

[12]For discussion and citations to statistical literature see Tribe, *Trial by Mathematics: Precision and Ritual in the Legal Process*, 84 HARV. L. REV. 1329, 1346–50 (1971).

the proper determinant of the decision, whatever the standard of persuasion.

As we shall see later, this point of view is thoroughly justifiable in terms of the purposes of proof. Here it is sufficient to make two points. First, as the preceding discussion indicated, probability estimates based on more particularized evidence than overall statistics are an appropriate subject for analysis; if the "actual belief" standard is interpreted as requiring such evidence, it is consistent with an analytic approach. Second, a requirement of particularized evidence does not necessarily involve a higher standard of persuasion than that indicated by a preponderance of probability. The particularity of the evidence on which the estimate is made is, in theory at least, quite independent of the degree of persuasion produced by that evidence. However, these two ideas frequently are not distinguished, so that it becomes appropriate to consider whether a higher standard of persuasion could be justified, if the *Sargent* court also had that in mind when it required proof that establishes "actual belief."

B.

The passage quoted from Lummus's opinion in *Sargent* has been interpreted by some commentators as meaning that preponderance of evidence requires a degree of belief in a proposition greater than that associated with a preponderance of probabilities. This interpretation would find support from Lummus's rejection of "chances which *somewhat* favor a proposition" and from the conclusion that a jury must find "not merely that there was a greater chance," but that death by accident "was in fact indicated by a preponderance of evidence." In this respect, however, *Sargent* is generally regarded as an aberration, at least insofar as nonquantitative evidence is involved. A majority of courts and all commentators agree that preponderance of evidence means, as McCormick puts it, "proof which leads the jury to find that the existence of the contested fact is more probable than its non-existence."[13]

This interpretation of preponderance of evidence has been

[13]MCCORMICK, Evidence §339 at 794 (2d ed. 1972).

accepted without question, perhaps because it seems so reasonable, or even inevitable. A higher standard would cast a disproportionate burden on the proponents and would be arbitrary, because there would seem no rationale for selecting any particular decision probability above 0.50. Finally, it has been said that to require a higher standard before a proposition may be judicially accepted would ignore the probabilistic nature of all proof[14] and would encroach on the standard of "clear, strong, and convincing" evidence that has been required only in exceptional civil cases.[15]

The degree of proof or of probability required to satisfy the preponderance-of-evidence standard ought to be deduced from the purpose of that standard. Perhaps because its purpose seems so obvious, there has been virtually no analysis of the rule from this point of view. In the only discussion I know of this question, Professor V. C. Ball argues that preponderance of evidence is designed to minimize errors:

> In ordinary actions, the law ignores all the costs and utilities which might be consequences of the judgment except the benefit and loss represented by the sum of money or the property awarded or refused. This means that the cost or value of the decision is the same to each party, and the standard should therefore be the one which causes the smallest number of mistakes.[16]

If this is the purpose, it is clear that the majority of courts and commentators are correct and that a preponderance of probabilities must be used.

For reasons that will appear, let us illustrate this simple proposition with a hypothetical distribution. Suppose that cases in which the occurrence of an accident in a mysterious disappearance is the contested fact are distributed over a range of probabilities in accordance with Table 2. The two groups of cases which are closest to either side of the 0.50 line have 0.45 and 0.55 probabilities of accident, respectively. If the decision line is moved from 0.50 to 0.40, the only change will be that

[14]McBain, *Burden of Proof: Degrees of Belief*, 32 CAL. L. REV. 242, 250 (1944).

[15]McCORMICK, Evidence, *supra* at 795.

[16]Ball, *The Moment of Truth: Probability Theory and Standards of Proof*, 14 VAND. L. REV. 807, 817 (1961).

TABLE 2.   Disputed Sargent-Type Cases

Percentage of Cases	20	5	5	10	30	30
Probability of Accident	0.40	0.45	0.55	0.60	0.80	0.90

the 0.45 cases which previously were rejected will now be decided for the proponents. This clearly will increase the rate of error, since the decisions will be wrong 0.55 of the time, whereas under the previous decision rule, in which the 0.45 cases were rejected, the decisions were wrong 0.45 of the time. The same reasoning applies if the decision probability is raised above the 0.50 level. Since any change in the 0.50 rule would increase the error rate, it follows that this rule leads to minimum errors. The same conclusion follows regardless of the shape of the distribution.

There would be little more to say on this subject if it were clear that minimization of errors were the purpose of the preponderance-of-evidence standard. But there is another plausible purpose, which leads to quite different results. Its importance is indicated by the fact that it is properly derived from the reason given by Professor Ball for minimizing errors. He said, in substance, that since the burden of an error is deemed to be the same for both parties, there should be as few errors as possible. The premise is clearly correct—at least with respect to most types of civil cases—but the conclusion does not follow from it. If the burden of errors is deemed to be the same for both parties, the aim should be equal rates of errors for both parties over some assumed class of cases. Unfortunately, the policy that minimizes errors usually will not also serve the purpose of equalizing them.

For example, in the distribution previously given, a 0.50 decision rule would not achieve an equal distribution of errors. Under that rule, the cases in the first two groups would be decided against the proponents, while those in the remaining groups would be decided for them. These decisions would yield errors against the proponents (erroneous findings against the proponents) in 10.25 percent of the cases (0.40 × 20 percent for the first group; +0.45 × 5 percent for the second group), while the decisions with respect to the remaining four groups would yield errors for the proponents (erroneous findings for the proponents) in 15.25 percent of the cases($[1.00 - 0.55] \times 5$ percent for the third group; $+[1.00-0.60] \times 10$ percent for the fourth group; $+[1.00-0.80] \times 30$ percent for the fifth group; $+[1.00-0.90] \times 30$ percent for the sixth group). On these facts, the preponderance-of-probabilities rule is quite unequal in its impact: it favors the proponents by erroneously finding for them at a rate 50 percent greater than the rate at which errors are committed against them.

Inspection indicates that to equalize errors in this example the decision probability should be between 0.55 and 0.60; in that case, the rate of errors would be 13 percent for each group. It should be noted that with this cutoff, 70 percent of the cases would be decided for the proponents, which is the correct percentage, since they are entitled to prevail in that percentage of cases.

It is not difficult to prove that this result is an instance of the general proposition that to equalize errors a decision rule must produce the correct proportion of decisions for the proponents. Imagine that proponents are entitled to prevail in a certain proportion of cases, and that a decision rule is used which produces that proportion of decisions for them. If all decisions were correct there would be no errors. If there is an erroneous finding for a proponent, it must be matched by an erroneous finding against a proponent, for otherwise the number of cases in which proponents are in fact entitled to prevail would be reduced and the decision rule would have produced too many decisions for them. Thus, if the decision rule produces the correct total number of decisions for the proponents, the types of errors must come in pairs and be equal in number.

Which of these policies is to be preferred? A minimization policy would clearly be justified if the effect of shifting from minimization to equalization were merely to increase the number of erroneous decisions against the previously favored group. In that situation, the disfavored group would have no valid interest in securing a larger number of erroneous decisions in its favor. But, generally, a shift to equalization would also reduce the number of errors against the disfavored group, and this would give that group the basis for a claim that the preponderance-of-probabilities rule unfairly imposed an undue risk of error on them. If equalization of errors is the proper goal, the foregoing analysis indicates that a preponderance of probability will be the level necessary to establish a contested fact by a preponderance of evidence only in that special situation in which a 0.50 decision rule would yield the correct proportion of decisions for the proponents. From the point of view of equalizing errors, it is the 0.50 decision rule which is arbitrary, while some other figure would be the "natural" choice.

Is it fair to increase the rate of errors to equalize their impact? Should not each case be decided "simply" on the preponderance of probabilities demonstrated by the evidence, and let total error fall where it may? The initial answer is that it is not "simple" to decide cases on a preponderance of probabilities by weighing the evidence. In fact, we shall see in the next section, there is reason to believe that decision makers purporting to resolve cases on this basis may in certain situations adopt decision rules which effectively result in higher rates of error and serve the equalizing principle. The more basic answer is that the maximization of correct results is a strong policy, but one not invariably to be preferred when others conflict with it. The law of evidence (and all law for that matter) frequently imposes rules that sacrifice some measure of correctness for decisions which in the large serve other goals. Exclusionary rules are of this character. Whether equalization of errors is the goal in any given context ought to depend on the extent to which total error would be increased by the pursuit of the equality, the degree of inequality if minimum error is achieved, and the relative importance of the competing policies. In the next section, we discuss a specific numerical example. Here it is sufficient to observe that in an assumed class of cases in which plaintiffs are entitled to prevail substantially more than half the time, the decision rule which equalizes errors will usually involve a level of probability substantially in excess of a mere preponderance. Consequently, the rejection of statistical evidence which establishes a proposition by a preponderance of probabilities is not necessarily inconsistent with the preponderance of evidence standard, since that standard may involve a higher level of proof if the decision maker seeks to equalize errors.

C.

If a proponent is required to produce particular evidence in addition to statistical data to create "actual belief," the question arises how the two types of evidence are to be related. The court in *Day* v. *Boston & Marine R. R.* dealt with this question explicitly when it observed, in the passage previously quoted, that the slightest "real evidence" "would outweigh all the probability otherwise." Since *Day* was cited in *Sargent*, the same view of the relative probative force of statistical and particular evidence may underlie the *Sargent* court's view of the inadequacy of mathematical proof.

This is a common but logically incorrect idea which is a source of bias in estimation. To use an illustration from *Sargent*, suppose 10 percent of men in a particular group die of cancer and the fact finder wants to estimate the probability that a particular man in that group died of cancer. There is evidence (e.g., a description of symptoms) from which it might be inferred that the man died of cancer. Given the evidentiary facts concerning the proportion of men who die of cancer and the particular evidence of the symptoms, the fact finder must estimate the odds that the man had died of cancer.

Contrary to the opinion in *Day*, the particular symptom evidence does not deprive the general statistical evidence of probative force. Mathematical probability tells us that the odds of the man having died of cancer are equal to the odds created by the statistical evidence times the "likelihood ratio" associated with the symptom evidence.[17] In the example given, the odds are the probability that a man selected at random from the group would die of cancer divided by the probability that he would not. On the facts given, this would be 1/9. The likelihood ratio describes the probative force of the symptom evidence. It is equal to the probability of observing the symptoms if the man died of cancer divided by the probability of observing the symptoms if he did not. If the evidence of the symptoms is very strong, i.e., the symptoms are far more likely to be observed if the subject had had cancer than if not, the likelihood ratio would be large. If the symptoms were only weakly associated with cancer, they could occur with only slight unequal probability under either hypothesis, and the likelihood ratio would be near one. But whatever the degree of proof represented by

[17]This is a form of Bayes's theorem. For a discussion, see Kaplan, *Decision Theory and the Factfinding Process*, 20 STAN. L.REV. 1065, 1084–85 (1968). A derivation of another form of the same theorem is given *infra* at 87–89.

the likelihood ratio, its value would be deflated by the factor of 1/9, representing the effect of the statistical information expressed in the odds ratio. Thus, if the symptoms are nine times more likely to be observed in cases of cancer than in other cases (which would seem to be strong evidence), the odds of death from cancer are no more than even, because of the deflating effect of the background. The deflation can safely be ignored only when the likelihood ratio derived from the particular evidence is strong enough relative to the odds to make the deflation unimportant. This mathematical result demonstrates that statistical evidence does not cease to have probative force in light of particular evidence, but that particular evidence may be sufficient to overwhelm it.

The likelihood ratio derived from the particular evidence would equal the odds that the subject had died of cancer, given the evidence, only if the information outside the symptom evidence is neutral, i.e., that the odds ratio is 1. If the statistical evidence is not introduced so that the fact finder takes no account of it, his estimate based solely on the likelihood ratio would be systematically biased, since it would ignore the contribution of background or prior probability represented by the statistical evidence. In the cancer problem, the probabilistic background can be made explicit on an objective basis. This is unusual but unimportant. Every case has a similar background, which usually cannot be so definitely quantified, but the principles described above are equally applicable whether or not an objective basis exists for an estimate of background probability.

It will be thought that fact finders take background or prior probability into account either because statistics are introduced in evidence or through a commonsensical appraisal of the general plausibility of evidence. This may be true when the background evidence generates very high or very low probabilities; we do not credit evidence that defies the laws of nature.[18] But where such evidence is less than conclusive, psycholog-

---

[18]"Suppose a number of witnesses testify that they saw a man thrust his hand into a bucket of water, and on taking it out a hole remained in the water where the man's hand had been. It matters not how positive and direct such testimony was, no sane jury would accept it. Why? Because their past experience, based upon circumstances, teaches them that it is contrary to the laws of nature. . . ." Ex Parte Jefferies, 7 Okla. Crim. 544, 546, 124 P. 924, 925 (1912).

ical studies have shown rather strikingly that people ignore or reject the evidence of background probability in favor of what they view as particular evidence.[19]

For example, in one experiment, subjects were shown brief personality descriptions of several individuals reportedly selected at random from among a group of one hundred professionals—engineers and lawyers. The subjects were asked to assess the probability that a given description was that of an engineer or a lawyer. One group of subjects was told that the group from which the random selection was made consisted of seventy engineers and thirty lawyers. The other group was told that there were thirty engineers and seventy lawyers. Obviously the first group should estimate higher odds for engineers than the second, but in fact both groups produced essentially the same probability judgments. The same result followed even when the description was designed to convey no information that could prove useful in the choice between engineers and lawyers. It appeared that only when no evidence was given did the subjects correctly evaluate the impact of statistical probabilities. The tendency to focus exclusively on particular evidence illustrated by this experiment is probably magnified by the setting of a lawsuit, where the proposition to be proved is presented as an issue between two parties and the fact finder is supposed to resolve that issue on the basis of adduced evidence.

The overweighting of particular evidence disclosed by such studies has been implicitly recognized as a phenomenon by those rules of evidence that require certain issues in civil cases to be proved by "clear, strong, and convincing evidence," or by some similar guideline connoting a standard higher than a preponderance.

For example, it has been held that higher standards are required to prove fraud, to establish a parole or constructive trust, to prove an oral contract as a basis for specific performance, to impeach a notary's certificate, to establish a prior anticipatory use of an invention, or to prove an agreement to hold a deed absolute as a mortgage.[20] In most such cases, there is an

---

[19]See Tversky & Kahneman, *Decisions under Uncertainty: Heuristics & Biases,* 185 SCIENCE 1124 (1974).

[20]See 9 WIGMORE, EVIDENCE §2498(3) (3rd ed. 1940).

aura of improbability about the claim, because the proponent engages in some collateral attack on an instrument or transaction that appears regular on its face. The odds associated with the background are less than one, and the probative effect of particular evidence relating to the transaction should be deflated to that extent. If a fact finder ignores the background probability, his overweighting of particular evidence may be corrected by requiring him to have greater or more persuasive particular evidence. That arguably is a justification for the "clear, strong, and convincing" formulation. Its use recognizes the underestimation of the negative probative effect of the background, for if this effect were properly recognized there would be no justification for a stronger formulation to cover improbable claims.

When background probability is ignored, an estimate of preponderance of probabilities is really an estimate of whether the particular contested event is more or less likely to have occurred than in the average case of the same assumed class. Thus, in the cancer problem, a fact finder would tend to conclude that a subject was more likely than not to have died of cancer if the particular evidence indicates that he was more likely than men in that group to have died of cancer, even though the probability of death by cancer was still less than one-half, due to the deflating effect of the background.

There are consequently three possible standards associated with preponderance of evidence. First, there is a preponderance-of-probabilities standard, which may be the formal rule but is unlikely to be followed by decision makers. Second, there is an average case rule, which is likely to be used by decision makers who attempt to apply a preponderance-of-probabilities standard but who ignore the probabilistic background. Third, there is the decision rule which will equalize errors, which is unknown and in most cases unknowable. To examine the relation between these rules, we draw on certain statistical results developed by H. Steinhaus[21] and applied by J. Lukaszewicz[22] with respect to samples of Polish paternity cases from the early 1950s.

[21]*The Establishment of Paternity*, PRACE WROCLAWSKIEGO TOWARZYSTWA NAUKOWEGO, ser. A., No. 32, at 5 (1954).

[22]*O Dochodzeniu Ojcostwa* [*On Proving Paternity*], 2 ZASTOSOWANIA METEMATYKI 349 (1955).

D.

Under Polish family law, an accused is presumed to be the father of a child once it is proved that he is "the man who had sexual intercourse with the child's mother in the period from the 300th to the 180th day before its birth."[23] If such intercourse is established, the burden of proving nonpaternity shifts to the defendant. If the child has a blood type not shared by the mother, it could only have come from the father. In such a case, the defendant will be tested. If he does not have the type in question he is exonerated; if he does, the probability of guilt is increased although the possibility of innocence obviously is not foreclosed. These facts have made blood-type evidence admissible in American courts solely for the purpose of exonerating the accused.[24]

The background or prior probability computed by Steinhaus was the probability that the accused was the father after intercourse had been established but before the serological test. The posterior probability was the probability of paternity after the test. A significant aspect of Steinhaus's procedure was his use of population statistics to calculate an estimate of the proportion of guilty fathers among those who were designated for the test even though no individuals (except those who were subsequently exonerated by the test) could be identified as guilty or innocent. For the sake of clarifying the theory of his procedure, I shall simplify it slightly.

Different blood types occur with different frequency in the population. Let the type in question be called "A" and have the frequency f; the frequency of those who do not have this type is $1 - f$. Consider the group of accused fathers who take a serological test because the child has the blood type "A," one not shared by the mother. If the mothers' accusations were always right, the serological test would show every member of this group to have type "A" blood (although the converse of course is not true). If the mothers' accusations were always wrong, the members of this group would be a random sample from the population, and the expected frequency of those with other than type "A" blood would be $1 - f$. The difference be-

[23]Quoted at *id.* n.21.
[24]1 WIGMORE, EVIDENCE § 165a (3d ed. 1940 & Supp. 1975).

tween the actual rate of "A" blood in this accused group and the population rate can be used to measure the accuracy of the accusations as a group. The more "A" blood, the more correct the accusations.[25]

Using the results of some 1,515 Polish paternity cases in which serological tests had been made, Steinhaus concluded that the prior probability of a true accusation in these cases was about 70 percent. (With perhaps less than complete fairness, this factor has been called "the veracity measure of women.") This 70 percent figure may be regarded as the background probability in paternity cases. It was computed from a special subgroup or sample of paternity cases because it included only those cases in which the child did not share the blood type of the mother, and hence a serological test was required. But it seems fair to test the attributes of various decision rules by this subgroup because it is probably a random sample with respect to the fact of paternity, or at least there are not more paternities among the defendants in this group than in the larger group.

There are currently three sets of blood systems for which identifications can be performed: A, B, and 0; M and N; and Rh. Each of these operates independently. After a serological test is performed it is possible to make more particularized estimates of the probability of paternity based on the coincidence of these factors among the mother, the putative father, and the child. Using a different group of paternity cases in which serological tests had been made, and the three systems, Lukaszewicz derived a frequency table by calculating the probability of paternity in each case based on the results of the test and counting the number of cases at each level of probability. He showed that of 1,000 cases, 119 had a zero probability of paternity (exclusions), five a probability of paternity between 0.300 and 0.349, etc. In the highest probability category there were forty-five

[25]Let p be the proportion of the accused group who are the fathers. Then $1 - p$ is the proportion of innocents and $(1 - p)(1 - f)$ is the expected proportion of those accused who will be exonerated by the test. The ratio of the expected proportion of the accused group who will be exonerated to the proportion of those in the general population who do not have the blood type in question is $(1 - p)(1 - f)/(1 - f)$. This ratio, however, is simply $1 - p$, the prior probability of a false accusation. The key fact is that both numerator and denominator of the foregoing ratio can be estimated from objective sample and population statistics.

TABLE 3.   Paternity Probabilities Obtained for 1000 Tests

Paternity Probability	Number of Tests
0.000	119
0.300 ≤ 0.349	5
0.350 ≤ 0.399	3
0.400 ≤ 0.449	5
0.450 ≤ 0.499	19
0.500 ≤ 0.549	15
0.550 ≤ 0.599	25
0.600 ≤ 0.649	45
0.650 ≤ 0.699	70
0.700 ≤ 0.749	88
0.750 ≤ 0.799	126
0.800 ≤ 0.849	131
0.850 ≤ 0.899	154
0.900 ≤ 0.949	153
0.950 ≤ 1.000	42

cases with a probability between 0.950 and 1.000. The full distribution is as shown in Table 3.

The first important result of this table is that very high probabilities of paternity are obtainable in a substantial number of cases if blood-test evidence is used affirmatively. For example, the probability of paternity equals or exceeds 0.800 in 48 percent of the cases. There is obviously a great deal more valuable probative blood-test information than appears in the 12 percent of exclusions. This result casts doubt on the validity of the rule in most American jurisdictions that such evidence may be used only to exonerate a defendant.[26]

The table also illustrates the relation among the various decision rules previously discussed and allows us to compute their consequences. If the court used only the statistical estimate that 70 percent of those for whom a serological test was

[26]The Uniform Act on Blood Tests to Determine Paternity would open an uncertain door to affirmative use of such evidence: "If the experts conclude that the blood tests show the possibility of the alleged father's paternity, admission of this evidence is within the discretion of the court, depending upon the infrequency of the blood type." Some probability analysis would appear to be essential if a court is rationally to exercise the judgment contemplated by the Uniform Act. For a general discussion, see McCormick, Evidence, §211 at 517–23 (2d ed. 1972).

required were actual fathers, and a 0.50 decision rule, all cases would be decided for the plaintiff mothers. The total error would be 30 percent, all of it against the putative fathers. When the particular evidence is taken into account, the 0.50 decision rule produces 1.4 percent erroneous dismissals and 16.5 percent erroneous attributions of paternity. The 17.9 percent rate of total error, the least possible, represents a substantial reduction from the original 30 percent rate, thus illustrating the gain derivable from the use of particular evidence. However, the balance still strongly favors the plaintiffs, since most of the error involves mistakes in their favor. In this example, the decision rule proposed by the commentators is far from evenhanded.

To equalize errors, the fact finder would have to use a decision rule based on a probability of approximately 0.695. In that event, the rate of erroneous dismissals and erroneous attributions of paternity would each be 10.9 percent; total error would be 21.8 percent, which is slightly greater than under a preponderance-of-probabilities rule. Note that, compared with a preponderance-of-probabilities standard, the mothers would suffer under this regime, because the rate of mistakes against them would rise from 1.4 percent to 10.9 percent. If there were no other change, the putative fathers might have no basis for insisting on an equalization of errors. But the equalization standard lowers the rate of errors against them from 16.5 percent to 10.9 percent, a one-third reduction. Given this change, they may well argue that the low rate of errors against the mothers under the preponderance-of-probabilities standard has been unfairly achieved at their expense. On these facts, one might conclude that an equalization standard is to be preferred, because its implementation would involve only a relatively small increase in total error.

If fact finders ignore the 0.70 background probability which is factored into the probabilities reflected in the table, the decisions purporting to use a preponderance-of-probabilities test would be based solely on whether the probability estimate based on the serological test was greater or less than 0.70. This decision probability would be very different from preponderance of probability but virtually identical to the decision probability required to equalize errors (0.695). Thus, the decision rule which we have hypothesized would in fact be used by decision makers is virtually identical to the decision rule necessary to equalize errors, but quite different from the preponderance-of-probabilities test imposed in theory by the commentators.

There are reasons to believe that the relation between the three decision rules shown by this example is quite general. When background probability differs significantly from 0.50, the decision probability which equalizes errors is likely to be closer to the background than to 0.50. When this occurs, insistence on particular evidence should be regarded not only as a way of reducing total error, but more significantly, as a way of distributing error more equally between plaintiffs and defendants over some assumed class of cases with a common subject matter. The insistence of the *Sargent* court on such evidence may be taken as an indication that both these purposes are condensed in the standard of proof by a preponderance of evidence.

II

In *People* v. *Collins,* an elderly woman walking home in an alley in the San Pedro area of Los Angeles was assaulted from behind and robbed. The victim said that she managed to see a young woman with blond hair run from the scene. Another witness said that a Caucasian woman with dark-blond hair and a ponytail ran out of the alley and entered a yellow automobile driven by a black male with a mustache and beard. A few days later officers investigating the robbery arrested a couple on the strength of these descriptions[27] and charged them with the crime. At their trial, the prosecution called an instructor of mathematics at a state college in an attempt to establish that, assuming the robbery was committed by a Caucasian blonde with a ponytail who left the scene in a yellow car accompanied by a

[27]When defendants were arrested, the woman's hair was light, not dark blond, and the man did not have a beard. There was some evidence that the man had altered his appearance after the date on which the offense had been committed. 68 Cal.2d at 323, n.5, 438 P.2d at 35 n.5, 66 Cal. Rptr. at 499 n.5. The car was only part yellow. *Id*. at 322 n.2, 438 P.2d at 34 n.2, 66 Cal. Rptr. at 498 n.2.

black man with a beard and mustache, the probability was overwhelming that the accused were guilty because they answered to this unusual description. The witness testified to the "product rule" of elementary probability theory, which states that the probability of the joint occurrence of a number of mutually independent events equals the product of the individual probabilities. The prosecutor then had the witness assume the following individual probabilities of the relevant characteristics:

Yellow automobile	1/10
Man with mustache	1/4
Girl with ponytail	1/10
Girl with blond hair	1/3
Black man with beard	1/10
Interracial couple in car	1/1000

Applying the product rule to the assumed values, the prosecutor concluded that there would be but one chance in twelve million that a couple selected at random would possess the incriminating characteristics.[28] The jury convicted. On appeal, the Supreme Court of California reversed, holding that the trial court should not have admitted the evidence pertaining to probability.

A.

The Supreme Court objected to the expert's testimony on several grounds. First, the record was devoid of evidence to support any of the six assumed individual probabilities. This objection is clearly justified. Some evidence of those probabilities is surely required as a foundation for such testimony. However, evidence in support of a finding that the probability estimates are likely to be greater than the true values should suffice. This is significant, because it may often be possible to justify generous estimates of probabilities which cannot be determined exactly.[29]

[28]The prosecutor gratuitously added his estimation that the "chances of anyone else besides these defendants being there . . . having every similarity . . . is somewhat like one in a billion. 68 Cal.2d at 326, 438 P.2d at 37, 66 Cal. Rptr. at 501.

[29]See pp. 90–91 *infra*.

Second, the court found no proof that the six factors were statistically independent. Again the court was correct. If traits are not independent but rather tend to appear together, the multiplication of the individual probabilities of each factor will usually yield a composite probability that is far too small for the compound event, even if the individual probabilities are accurate. For example, given the hypothetical probabilities in *Collins*, if every black man with a beard also had a mustache, then the chance of a black man with a beard and mustache is one-tenth, not one-fortieth as indicated by the product rule.[30] Either the mathematical method must take correlations into account or there must be sufficient evidence of independence of the factors.[31]

A first look at *Collins* thus reveals two requirements for statistical analysis in evidence: the prosecutor must offer evidence as to the probabilities of the individual factors and of the relations among them. The court also explored two obstacles to such proof. The first, which relates to the capacity of a jury to deal with statistical evidence, will be discussed presently.[32] The second, that the court's analysis was wrong, cuts much deeper.

Writing for the court, Justice Sullivan asserted that "no mathematical equation can prove beyond a reasonable doubt . . . that only *one* couple possessing those distinctive characteristics could be found in the entire Los Angeles area."[33] He supported his conclusion with a mathematical demonstration purporting to show that even if a couple selected at random had

[30]If black men with beards seldom have mustaches, the chance of a black man with both would be smaller than one fortieth.

[31]Other courts' assumptions of independence in cases like *Collins* have been deservedly criticized. See, e.g., Kingston, *Probability and Legal Proceedings,* 57 J. CRIM. L.C. & P.S. 93, 94–95 (1966).

Whether the factors in *Collins* could, even theoretically, be independent depends on their interpretation. If the factor of "one-tenth Negro males with beards" means that one in ten black men has a beard, and the beard rate is the same for Caucasians, the joint occurrence of this factor and the factors relating to the girl could possibly be independent of the factor "interracial couple in car." Conversely, if the beard factor is interpreted as a generous estimate that one man in ten is a black with a beard, and similarly for the factors relating to the girl, the joint occurrence of the man and girl factors would of necessity be highly correlated with "interracial couple in car."

[32]Pp. 39–40 *infra.*

[33]68 Cal.2d at 331, 438 P.2d at 40, 66 Cal. Rptr. at 504.

only one chance in twelve million of bearing the incriminating characteristics, the expert witness could not conclude that the accused were probably guilty, because it was quite possible (about a 40 percent chance) that at least one other couple in the Los Angeles area had those same traits.

The court's argument is incorrect because the supporting mathematical demonstration was wrongly conceived. The court's proof begins with the probability of selecting a couple with the specified characteristics at random from the population. This is assumed, following the prosecution, to be one in twelve million. The court then proceeds to derive the probability that there are two or more such couples in the population. Because the court was dealing with an existing, finite population, the frequency with which couples with the identifying characteristics may be found in that population is identical to the probability of selecting one at random. Thus, the court's assumption that one in twelve million is a fair estimate of the probability of selecting such a couple at random necessarily implies that it is a fair estimate of the number of such couples in the population. The probability that couples with the special characteristics would appear more frequently could only have been determined by examining the precision of the estimate—an examination which neither the court nor the expert was able to make because the estimate was not the result of any statistically valid sampling procedure.[34]

[34]The formula derived in the court's appendix is

$$\frac{1 - (1 - Pr)^N - NPr(1 - Pr)^{N-1}}{1 - (1 - Pr)^N}$$

where Pr is the probability of selecting at random a couple of characteristics of the accused, and N is the total number in the population. The court first assumed the total population of suspects to be twelve million and then showed (correctly) that its conclusions would not be affected if the population were assumed to be infinite. 68 Cal.2d at 335, 438 P.2d at 42–43, 66 Cal. Rptr. at 506–07.

The court's formula generates the 40 percent probability referred to in the text because it assumes a sampling of the population with replacement of the sampled couples instead of sampling without replacement. The difference in result between these two methods frequently is not very great, because the number sampled is small relative to the whole population. But in the experiment posited by the court the number of drawings for the sample is equal to the suspect population. In this circumstance the difference between replacements and nonreplacement is critical.

To see what the court's formula leads to, assume there are twelve million

The court's formula would have been relevant if it were assumed that nothing were known about the actual population of Los Angeles and the only available information concerned some unknown process by which it had been created. If the one-in-twelve-million figure represented the probability that a couple when created would have the special characteristics, then out of all possible populations of Los Angeles that could be produced by this unknown process, 40 percent of those with at least one such couple would have at least two such couples.

The objection to this approach in *Collins* is that the one-in-twelve-million figure was intended by the prosecution and by the court to describe the actual population of Los Angeles and not as a parameter for a "generational" probability model. It is not valid to use as a generational probability an estimate intended to reflect the actual population, and then assume that since nothing was known about the actual population, the probabilities of various populations could be computed by calculating the hypothetical outcomes of the creation process. Moreover, a generational model will not usually be helpful in the problems discussed here because in most cases it will be far easier to gain knowledge of the actual population by sampling than to define in probabilistic terms the forces producing it.

The statistical problem of *Collins* is that of estimating the very figure which the court took as its assumption, namely the probability that a couple selected at random would have the characteristics of the accused. That probability represents the

---

balls in an urn, each ball standing for a couple, but only one (yellow) having the characteristics of the accused. The probability of selecting a yellow ball in a single draw from the urn is one in twelve million. A series of twelve million selections is now made; after each selection the ball is examined and thrown back into the urn from which it may be reselected. This series of twelve million selections is made repeatedly. The probability computed by the court is a fraction, the numerator of which is the number of series in which two or more yellow balls are selected and the denominator of which is the number of series in which one or more yellow balls are selected.

This statistic obviously has nothing to do with the likelihood that a couple answering the description of the accused was correctly charged. For if there was only a single ball in the urn representing a couple with the characteristics of the accused, the court's formula would still yield a substantial probability of duplication (the same ball being picked twice), although by hypothesis the accusation was made correctly.

The method developed in the appendix is similar to the analysis in 50 MINN. L. REV. 745 (1966), a discussion of *Collins* published prior to the appellate decision.

frequency of couples meeting the description of the one placed at the crime. If a sufficiently precise estimate could be made that the frequency of such couples in the Los Angeles area was one in twelve million, it would be possible to state within reasonable margins for error that there was only one such couple in the Los Angeles area.

But as a practical matter, the court was right to doubt that the prosecutor could show uniqueness. A derivation of such extraordinary small probabilities with sufficient precision would be extremely difficult. In most cases, the estimate of the population frequency of evidentiary traces (of hair or incomplete fingerprints, for example) will have to made on the basis of samples numbering at most a few thousand. As a result, probabilities of the magnitude involved in *Collins* would require an inference, based on a few thousand trials, that an event would occur once rather than more than once in millions of trials. Such an inference inevitably involves powerful assumptions which cannot be adequately supported without extensive data. Except in cases where the number of suspects is sharply limited, it will almost never be practically possible to gather enough data to sustain a conclusion of uniqueness with any confidence.[35]

The approach in *Collins* thus makes the number of suspects critical. Determining this number, however, will usually involve wholly arbitrary decisions. Shall it include only those in the same neighborhood, the same county, city, or state, or the entire country? The jury might be given a range of choices and the probability associated with each choice, but jurors cannot rationally choose when, as is usual, there is no evidence bearing on this issue. Setting a generous upper bound will usually defeat the proof: the incriminating characteristics will occur more than once in a sufficiently large population. Moreover, it is probably as difficult to decide intuitively how many "suspects" there are as to decide how many of the suspects have the incriminating characteristics.[36]

[35]Assuming independence, the probability estimates for the separate characteristics in *Collins* would have had to have been supported by a sample in the neighborhood of four hundred thousand in order to sustain the conclusion that there was only a small probability that the frequency of couples with the fatal characteristics in the population was two or more in twelve million.

[36]Another factor of considerable potential significance in this type of case (which the court did not discuss) is what can be called "selection effect." If there are, say, twenty characteristics or features which could be used for identification purposes, and the chance is one in a thousand that any given feature

We now turn to the court's second objection to the use of statistics. The court reversed the *Collins* conviction because it felt that the powerful statistics would cow a jury into overlooking the possibility that the basis for the calculations could be in error. The court was obviously right. However, correct statistical methods will usually have an effect opposite to that feared by the *Collins* court. Findings based on such statistics should generally weaken nonquantitative testimony based on the same evidence.[37] An expert's opinion that similarities between fragments (e.g., fingernails or hair) identify a defendant must rest on his limited experience with similar fragments. If to his knowledge no such similarities have been observed in fragments from different sources, he may testify flatly that the two fragments have a common origin. But proper statistical methods, by invoking an experience larger than any expert's, may well yield an estimate that a fragment occurs several times in a large population, even though the expert would conclude there were no duplicates.[38] In addition, an expert witness may base his appraisal on a multitude of details imperfectly recognized and difficult to define or catalog—just as we know a face from a multitude of features. It is impossible statistically to take all such details into account. Statistical observation concerns attributes than can be measured objectively; it cannot hope to have the richness of information involved in ordinary or educated recognition. For these reasons, the inference of identity from statistics will generally be weaker than expert judgment expressed in the usual way.

On its facts *Collins* was bizarre, and its pseudostatistics scarcely can be taken seriously. But the method used in the case

---

would match, the probability of one or more matches assuming innocence is approximately two in one hundred. A procedure by which the identifying feature is selected from a large group may thus critically affect the probabilities in these cases. Cf. People v. Trujillo, 32 Cal.2d 105, 194 P.2d 681, *cert. denied,* 335 U.S. 887 (1948), where the expert examined a large number of fibers taken from the accused's clothing and from the scene of the crime and was able to make eleven matches. Applying the product rule, he concluded that the probability was one in a billion that this many matches would have occurred by chance. A portion of the expert's testimony is reprinted in HOUTS, FROM EVIDENCE TO PROOF 325–29 (1956).

[37]The *Collins* court in fact reached such a conclusion, but, as we have seen, the method employed was erroneous.

[38]These methods are described at pp. 100–02 *infra.*

was representative of more sophisticated efforts made in earlier cases in which the experts sought to make identification (more plausibly) on the basis of similarities in typewriting, handwriting, fibers, or hairs.[39] Because of the development of new techniques for analyzing the composition of fragments,[40] evidence of this latter sort, backed with statistics, is likely to appear more frequently in future court proceedings. The *Collins* court was right when it concluded that efforts to prove uniqueness usually will be futile. Few, if any, evidentiary traces can be demonstrated by statistical analysis to be unique to a defendant. There is, however, a class of traces, potentially useful as evidence, which could be shown to appear only infrequently even though not uniquely. What is the probative significance of such nonunique traces? We propose to show that nonunique traces generally deserve substantial evidentiary weight, and that by the explicit use of mathematical theory the data can be cast in a form permitting their more effective use by the jury.

B.

Let us suppose a woman's body is found in a ditch in an urban area. There is evidence that the deceased had a violent quarrel with her boyfriend the night before. He is known to have struck her on other occasions. Investigators find the murder weapon, a knife whose handle bears a latent palm print similar to the defendant's. The information in the print is limited, so that an expert can say only that such prints appear in no more than one case in a thousand. We now ask the significance of this finding.

[39]The principal reported cases in which such statistical evidence has been presented are Miller v. State, Ark. 340, 399 S.W.2d 268 (1966); People v. Jordon, 45 Cal.2d 697, 290 P.2d 484 (1955); People v. Trujillo, 32 Cal.2d 105, 194 P.2d 681, *cert. denied*, 335 U.S. 887 (1948); State v. Sneed, 76 N.M. 349, 414 P.2d 858 (1966); People v. Risley, 214 N.Y. 75, 108 N.E. 200 (1915); See *The Howland Will Case*, 4 AM. K. REV. 625 (1870), discussing Robinson v. Mandell, 20 Fed. Cas. 1027 (No. 11959) (C.C.D. Mass. 1868).

[40]See, e.g., COLEMAN, CRIPPS, STIMSON, & SCOTT, THE DETERMINATION OF TRACE ELEMENTS IN HUMAN HAIR BY NEUTRON ACTIVATION AND THE APPLICATION TO FORENSIC SCIENCE (U.K. Atomic Energy Auth., Atomic Weapons Research Establishment Report No. 0-86/66, 1967).

Under the approach taken in *Collins* there would be little probative value to the palm-print evidence. If the number of potential suspects were as few as one hundred thousand, about one hundred persons would have such prints. This is hardly a unique identification. And yet, intuitively, the finding of such a relatively rare print matching the defendant's is telling. After all, the prosecutor may correctly argue that defendant is a thousand times more likely to have committed the crime than someone selected at random from the population. Without the print evidence, the case probably does not go to the jury. With it, the jury probably convicts. The mathematical formulation in *Collins* thus seems grossly to understate the intuitive impact of this evidence.

The difference between the two formulations lies in the unexpressed premises behind them. Proof of uniqueness was demanded in *Collins* because it was assumed as a starting point for the mathematical analysis that defendants were no more likely to have committed the offense than anyone else in the "suspect" population. The same assumption in our hypothetical case implies that the print evidence merely places defendant among a group of one hundred persons any one of whom is equally likely to be guilty. The probability of defendant's guilt remains small, though it was increased a thousandfold (from one in a hundred thousand to one in a hundred) by the print evidence.

The tacit assumption in *Collins* of no advance knowledge is inconsistent with the way we ordinarily view evidence. We tend to see a case as a whole; our appraisal of any bit of information depends on the rest of the testimony and our life experience.[41] Guilt is determined by a "cumulation of probabilities."[42] Slight additional evidence is given considerable weight, while evidence which would otherwise be highly compelling is discounted if it violates our prior beliefs.[43]

When statistics are not involved, this cumulative perspec-

---

[41]As one court put it, "Every man's experience demonstrates that his beliefs are based upon a great number of circumstances ... which, when combined together, give strength to each other...." *Ex Parte* Jeffries 7 Okla. Crim. 544, 551, 124 P. 924, 927 (1912).

[42]WHARTON, EVIDENCE IN CRIMINAL CASES 8 (11th ed. 1935).

[43]See n. 41, *infra*.

tive controls the probative significance of evidence.[44] The same perspective should be used when statistics are involved. In our hypothetical case, the analysis of the palm-print evidence should begin with the fact that defendant was far more likely to be guilty than someone selected at random. Consistent with this approach, it has been said that statistical evidence of the kind we have been considering should normally not be sufficient to support an identification unless accompanied by other evidence that would form the basis for a "prior estimate of identity."[45] This is an intuitive idea, but one that can be justified. We use Bayes's theorem for this purpose.

C.

We begin our discussion of Bayes's theorem by deriving an expression for the probability that defendant's print was on the knife, assuming that an incriminating print from a right-hand palm is found on it. In accordance with general practice, we denote this probability $P(G|H)$, where G is the event that defendant's print was on the knife and H the event that a palm print similar to defendant's is found. $P(H|G)$ is the probability of finding a print with the observed characteristics assuming there is identity. We assume for simplicity that defendant would inevitably leave such a print, so that in this instance $P(H|G) = 1$.[46] If the trace left by the accused could vary in its characteristics, $P(H|G)$ would be less than 1.[47] It is also assumed that we know $P(H|NG)$, the probability that a palm print left by someone other than defendant would have the observed characteristics. Our problem is to express $P(G|H)$ in terms of $P(H|G)$ and $P(H|NG)$. That is, we want to know the probability

[44]See People v. Trujillo, 32 Cal.2d 105, 194 P.2d 681, *cert. denied*, 335 U.S. 887 (1948). For a discussion, see REPORT OF THE PRESIDENT'S COMMISSION ON THE ASSASSINATION OF PRESIDENT KENNEDY 124 (1964).

[45]STARKIE, A PRACTICAL TREATISE OF THE LAW OF EVIDENCE 751 (9th Am. ed. 1869).

[46]Both $P(H|G)$ and $P(H|NG)$ are the probabilities that a print would have the observed characteristics, assuming that a right-hand palm print was left by the person who used the knife. It is thus assumed that the leaving of a print is not per se evidence either for or against the defendant.

[47]See pp. 95–97 *infra*.

that the print was left by the defendant, taking into account the chances that he or someone else left it.

The probability of event G conditional on the occurrence of event H is, by definition in probability theory, the probability of the joint occurrence of G and H divided by the probability of H. In symbols,

$$P(G|H) = \frac{P(G \text{ and } H)}{P(H)}.$$

This formula is intuitively reasonable because the probability of G conditional on H may be interpreted as the frequency with which G occurs out of all cases in which H occurs. [48] Applying the same definition,

$$P(H|G) = \frac{P(G \text{ and } H)}{P(G)},$$

so that $P(G + H)$ can be written as $P(H|G)P(G)$. In words, the probability of the joint occurrence of two events equals the probability of the first event times the probability of the second, conditional upon the occurrence of the first.[49]

$P(H)$, the denominator of the fraction on the right-hand side of the first equation, is the probability of finding a print with the observed characteristics. Since there is either identity or not—and since these alternatives are exhaustive—the sum of the chances of finding the print, given identity, and of finding the print if there is no identity, is the total probability of finding the print:[50]

$$P(H) = P(H \text{ and } G) + P(H \text{ and } NG).$$

Applying the definitions above for the joint occurrence of

---

[48]The numerator of the fraction given on the right-hand side above is the probability of the joint occurrence of G and H; dividing by the denominator ensures that the total probability for all the cases in which H occurs will equal unity.

[49]In the special case when G and H are independent, $P(H|G) = P(H)$ and $P(G|H) = P(G)$. The probability of neither event is affected by the occurrence of the other. The foregoing then reduces to the "product" rule used in *Collins*: $P(G \text{ and } H) = P(G)P(H)$. The whole point of our case, of course, is that G and H are not independent.

[50]This follows from the "sum rule," which states that the probability of the occurrence of either of two mutually exclusive events (in this case use and nonuse of the knife) is equal to the sum of the probabilities of those events.

identity and finding the print, and of no identity and finding the print,

$$P(H) = P(G)P(H|G) + P(NG)P(H|NG).$$

Substituting these results for the numerator and denominator in the expression for $P(G|H)$ yields Bayes's theorem:

$$P(G|H) = \frac{P(G)P(H|G)}{P(G)P(H|G) + P(NG)P(H|NG)}$$

Bayes's theorem, as previously discussed, may also be expressed in terms of odds:

$$\frac{P(G|H)}{P(NG|H)} = \frac{P(G)}{P(NG)} \cdot \frac{P(H|G)}{P(H|NG)}$$

In either form, the theorem is the desired result, because it expresses $P(G|H)$ in terms of $P(H|G)$, $P(H|NG)$, and $P(G)$.[51] A way of looking at Bayes's theorem, which is made clear by the odds formulation, is to say that we start with some idea of the probability that defendant used the knife, $P(G)$, and that our views are modified or weighted by the two probabilities associated with the print, $P(H|G)$ and $P(H|NG)$. Our final estimate of the chance that defendant used the knife is our initial or "prior" view as modified by the statistical evidence.[52] It should be observed that $P(G|H)$ does not depend on the size of the suspect population except as that factor may influence the prior probability or the frequency of the print.

Table 4 shows the values of $P(G|H)$ for various prior probabilities and statistical evidence. We assume that $P(H|G) = 1$. That is, any print left by the defendant on the knife would with

[51]Derivations of Bayes's theorem may be found in elementary texts on probability theory, for example, FREUND, MATHEMATICAL STATISTICS 52–58 (1962). An extensive discussion of Bayes's theorem appears in Edwards, Lindman & Savage, *Bayesian Statistical Inference for Psychological Research,* 70 PSYCHOLOGICAL REVIEW 193 (1963). See also GOOD, PROBABILITY AND THE WEIGHING OF EVIDENCE ch. 6 (1950).

[52]One may ask whether other "weightings" of prior probabilities and population frequency statistics would be justifiable. The answer is no. By way of illustration, if the prior probability also represented the frequency of an event, Bayes's theorem would be the only correct way of reflecting the joint effect of the two items of statistical information. And it has been shown that a subjective prior should be weighted no differently. See RAIFFA, DECISION ANALYSIS 124–27 (1968).

TABLE 4.   Posterior Probability P(G|H)

FREQUENCY OF CHARACTERISTICS P(H|NG)	PRIOR PROBABILITY $P(G)$				
	.01	*.1*	*.25*	*.50*	*.75*
.50	.019	.181	.400	.666	.857
.25	.038	.307	.571	.800	.923
.1	.091	.526	.769	.909	.967
.01	.502	.917	.970	.990	.996
.001	.909	.991	.997	.9990	.999

certainty have the characteristics observed. The probability $P(H|NG)$ is the frequency of the print in the suspect population.

The table shows that even such relatively high frequencies as one in a hundred can lead to significant posterior probabilities if the prior probability is at least one-fourth. For example, if the prior probability $P(G)$ is 0.25 and the frequency of the observed characteristic in the population $P(H|NG)$ is 0.01, then the posterior probability $P(G|H)$ is 0.970. This is significant, because evidence apart from statistics frequently will justify a fairly high prior probability of guilt. More modest probability estimates could thus be used to make telling, even decisive, cases.

For example, in *People* v. *Risley*,[53] the issue was whether defendant had altered a court document by typing in the words "the same." Defendant was a lawyer and the alteration helped his case. There was evidence tending to show that he had come to the clerk's office to examine the file (including the altered paper), then returned the next day and reexamined it. The state alleged that defendant had removed and replaced the document at these visits. This was physically possible.

Eleven defects in the typewritten letters on the court document were similar to those produced by defendant's machine. The prosecution called a professor of mathematics to testify to the chances of a random typewriter producing the defects found in the added words. The witness multiplied these component probabilities to conclude that the joint probability of all defects was one in four billion. Given the magnitude of this estimate, the court was clearly correct, when it reversed, in objecting that

[53]214 N.Y. 75, 108 N.E. 200 (1915).

the testimony was "not based upon observed data, but was simply speculative, and an attempt to make inferences deduced from a general theory in no way connected with the matter under consideration supply the usual method of proof."[54]

If the expert had adopted a Bayesian approach, he could have made good use of a justifiable probability estimate. On the evidence in *Risley*—excluding the evidence of similarity of defects—one might judge that there was at least a 25 percent chance that the alteration was typed on defendant's machine. Adding the information as to the defects, and assuming that such defects would occur in fewer than one machine in a thousand, Bayesian analysis indicates a very high probability that defendant's machine was used. This is significant because an upper-bound estimate of one in a thousand could probably have been supported—perhaps even on the basis of direct experience of the experts.[55]

D.

Bayes's theorem demonstrates that even evidentiary traces linking a defendant to a crime, a frequent occurrence, can help sustain an identification, provided there is sufficient other evidence to connect the accused with the crime. This is a modest use which merely eliminates an unwarranted distinction between the force of statistical and other types of identification evidence. A stronger, more explicit use of the theorem is also possible. An expert witness could explain to jurors that their view of the statistical evidence should depend on their view of the

[54]*Id*. at 85, 108 N.E. at 203. Apart from the problems arising from blind use of the product rule, which have already been discussed, the testimony contained a defect of a rather general character. The expert testified that the probability estimate which he computed at one in four billion was "the probability of these defects being reproduced by the work of a typewriting machine, other than the machine of defendant. . . ." *Id*. When we remember that this number represents an estimate of the frequency in the population of typewriters with the specified defects, it is clear that the statement is incorrect. Assuming the expert's figure was right, the probability of duplication depends on two additional factors (which were not discussed): (1) the number of typewriters in the suspect population, and (2) the sharpness of the estimate.

[55]One of the experts called by the prosecution testified that he had examined 20,000 machines. 214 N.Y. at 83–84, 108 N.E. at 202.

other evidence. He might then suggest a range of hypothetical prior probabilities, specifying the posterior probability associated with each prior. Each juror could then pick the prior estimate that most closely matched his own view of the evidence. In *Risley,* the expert might have testified, for example, that if the jurors believed there was a 50 percent chance that the added words were typed on defendant's machine, apart from the statistical evidence, they should believe that those chances were $^{999}/_{1000}$ if they accepted the statistical evidence. To minimize the possibility that a prosecutor would prejudice a defendant's case by choosing only highly incriminating "hypothetical" prior probabilities an expert so testifying should be required to show the posterior probabilities associated with a broad range of prior estimates. Such a procedure would also foreclose the chance that jurors would consider the expert as interjecting his own opinion as to the appropriate prior.[56]

Is there a need for some kind of explicit use? Arguably, there is. The statement that prints with particular characteristics occur with a frequency of one in a thousand persons means only that a defendant with such a print is a thousand times more likely to have left it than someone selected at random from the population. By itself, this is not a meaningful statistic for measuring probability of guilt. As we have seen, a defendant could be a thousand times more likely to be guilty than someone selected at random and still more likely to be innocent than guilty. The comparison with a random selection is irrelevant. The jury's function is not to compare a defendant with a person selected randomly but to weigh the probability of defendant's guilt against the probability that *anyone* else was responsible. Bayes's theorem translates the one-in-a-thousand statistic into a probability statement which describes the probative force of that statistic.[57]

---

[56]Also, if hypothetical specification of probabilities of guilt was believed undesirable, the expert might testify that if—and only if—the jurors thought there was a substantial probability that the words were typed on defendant's machine without the statistics, they should assume, if they believed the statistics, that it was very probable—in the neighborhood of 999 chances out of 1,000—that the words were typed on defendant's machine.

[57]To test the utility of the explicit use of Bayes's theorem. an informal survey of intuition was conducted, using the facts in the case of the murdered woman. See pp. 85–86 *supra.* The subjects (admittedly not a random sample from the population) were first given the facts, excluding the palm-print infor-

Subjective probability estimates of guilt may vary widely, depending on the person making the estimate.[58] This fact has often been raised as an objection to their use in scientific pursuits.[59] Whatever the validity of this objection in science, it does not have the same force in law. Varying judgments that reflect differing life experiences are accepted as an inevitable and even desirable aspect of the jury system. Moreover, in practice, differences among jurors who use Bayesian analysis will depend more on whether or not they believe the evidence establishing a subjective probability of guilt than on differences in the strength of their suspicions. If this evidence is disbelieved, the probability of defendant's guilt will be no stronger than that implied by defendant's belonging to the group of persons

---

mation, and asked to assess the probability of defendant's guilt. They were then given the palm-print statistics and asked for a reassessment. In all cases the prior probability was thought to be substantial in the sense we have defined it. In almost all cases the addition of the palm-print evidence was thought to raise the probability of guilt, but assessments of the weight of this evidence varied widely, and the subjects were uncertain how to treat the new information. In most cases, the assessments were not as great as they would have been if the probabilities had been computed in accordance with Bayes's theorem.

[58]In most applications of Bayesian technique, the information supplied by the prior estimate of probability tends to weaken the inference to be drawn from the statistics. This is a consequence of the fact that most prior distributions assign equal or relatively equal probabilities to the hypotheses being tested. A prior of this type is called "gentle" if the probabilities assigned are not very different, and "flat" if they are exactly equal. The exactly equal cases are sometimes equated with "no advance knowledge." If a flat prior were used in the case we have discussed, the probability of defendant's guilt would be $1/N$ where N is the total suspect population, and the Bayesian approach would reduce to the probabilities computed in the *Collins* line of cases. The proposed application is thus unusual in that a prior sufficiently ungentle to strengthen the statistical inference is a necessary step in the argument.

In their study of the disputed authorship problem in *The Federalist*, Mosteller and Wallace used the difference in rates of use of context-free words in papers of known authorship to determine odds for the papers of disputed authorship. They employed a flat or gentle prior to weaken the statistics, on the ground that a weakening was justified to allow for effect of selection of words which were apparently good as discriminators from a large pool. See Mosteller & Wallace, Inference and Disputed Authorship: The Federalist 61 (1964).

[59]For over two centuries debate has swirled about the validity of Bayesian analysis in scientific pursuits and the prior probabilities with which it begins. The issues are discussed in Joint Statistics Seminar, The Foundations of Statistical Inference (Bernard and Cox eds. 1962).

possessing the trait in question, the size of that group being determined by statistical evidence. On the other hand, if the evidence is believed, both the prior suspicion and the statistical
evidence will usually be strong enough so that, as Table 4 demonstrates, variations in the posterior probabilities will be small
relative to variations in the strength of the suspicion.

When this suggestion first appeared in print, it was objected
to by Professor Lawrence Tribe, who raised many points
against it.[60] The authors responded, and the ensuing debate is
reprinted in the appendix to this book.[61] An interesting point
that only partially emerged relates to the possible double use of
the evidence on which the juror's estimate of the prior probability is based. As in the example previously discussed, such evidence will usually relate not directly to identity, but rather to
defendant's guilt from which identity is inferred. Is it correct to
use evidence of guilt to infer identity (from which guilt itself is
then inferred), and to use the same evidence to support a direct
inference of guilt? I am frankly uncertain whether this is
proper or improper. The evidence of guilt is being used twice,
but it is not clear that double use is improper, since intuitive
appraisal frequently involves such multiple interconnections.
In any event, there is no double use with respect to the inference of identity from the similarity of traces, so that the issue
of double use would not arise when there was no real issue as
to the inference of guilt from identity. This is true in paternity
cases, in handwriting forgery, or probably in the typewriter
forgery example in *Risley*. Theoretically, a Bayesian estimate
could also be used where there was such an issue, without
raising the problem of double use. However, generally the evidence from which identity could be inferred would not be distinct from the evidence involving guilt, so that the former
could not be used without the latter to estimate a prior probability of identity.

[60]Tribe, *Trial By Mathematics: Precision and Ritual in the Legal Process*,
84 HARV. L. REV. 1329 (1971).

[61]Finkelstein, Fairley & Tribe, *The Continuing Debate Over Mathematics
in the Law of Evidence*, 84 HARV. L. REV. 1801 (1971).

E.

In Table 4 it was assumed that any right-hand palm print left by the defendant on the knife would have the characteristics of the print actually found. This was expressed as $P(H|G) = 1$. The assumption, made for simplicity, was probably reasonable as applied to fingerprints. But many other traces helpful in identification will vary because of variation within the suspected source. Thus there may be only a certain chance that the defendant would leave a hair similar to the one found at the scene of a crime. There may also be variations in reporting or measurement. In *Risley*, there were differences observed between the letters of incriminating words and those subsequently produced by defendant's machine.[62] These differences were not sufficient to rule out defendant's machine as a source, but they created some doubt, a diminished probability, that his machine produced the words. Similarly, in *Collins*, there were differences between the appearance of the defendants and the appearance of the guilty couple described by the witnesses. The statistician ignored these differences although they diminish the probability that the defendants would have been so described by the witnesses ($P(H|G)$).

Differences of the type described in *Collins* serve principally to cast some doubt on the conclusion of similarity. Usually there will be no hard data about the significance of the doubts raised, and $P(H|G)$ will have to be a guess. This might be embarrassing, except that Bayes's theorem indicates that even a substantial doubt is often insignificant to the result. Even if $P(H|G) = 1/2$ instead of 1, the posterior probabilities associated with the one-in-a-thousand statistic would deflate by a factor on the order of only $1/1000$.

But where there is significant variation within the suspected source, the doubt may well be so great as to decrease materially the likelihood of defendant's guilt. In these situations, some hard data about the variation must be used. Studies have shown, for example, that source variation is significant for hair

[62]People v. Risley, 214 N.Y. 75, 85, 108 N.E. 200, 203 (1915).

though probably not for glass.[63] Investigators analyzing the
source of hair have compared ten elements found in the hair
with the concentration of these elements in the hair of the
known source's head. They have recommended that if the composition of the incriminating hair deviates from the average
composition of a sample of defendant's hair so that such deviations would probably occur in, say, less than 1 percent of the defendant's hair, the incriminating hair should be assumed to be
not that of the defendant.[64] If the defendant's hair is "similar" to
the incriminating hair (i.e., the deviation is less than the
selected standard) the probability that someone else left such a
hair is computed by estimating the proportion of the suspect
population whose hair was "similar" (by the same standard) to
the incriminating hair.[65]

One difficulty with this procedure is its two-step approach.
By itself, a decision that defendant's hair is "similar" to the incriminating hair, by the artificial standard selected, is without
probative significance. The admission into evidence of such a
finding may be fatally prejudicial unless it is also shown that
similar hairs are not common in the population. Nor can it be
said that a finding of dissimilarity should exculpate an accused.
A hair which may be quite rare for the accused, and in this
sense unlikely to have come from him, may be still more unlikely to have come from someone else. Yet if a preliminary test of
similarity has been adopted, the hypothesis that the hair is his

---

[63]COLEMAN, CRIPPS, STIMSON, & SCOTT, *supra* note 3; COLEMAN &
WOOD, THE VALUE OF TRACE ANALYSIS IN THE COMPARISON OF GLASS
FRAGMENTS—A PRELIMINARY STUDY (U.K. Atomic Energy Auth., Atomic
Weapons Research Establishment Report No. 03/68, 1968). The extent of
source variation itself varies with the person and the element being considered. It sometimes approaches two-thirds of the variation of the element over
the population. See COLEMAN, CRIPPS, STIMSON & SCOTT, *supra*, tables
2 & 3, at 17, 18.

[64]One form of statistic used as a measure of difference is computed by taking the sum of the squared differences between the suspect's average
measurements and the crime-scene measurements divided by the standard
deviations of these differences. For a discussion of various indices of this type
see Parker, *The Mathematical Evaluation of Numerical Evidence*, 7 J. FOREN-
SIC SCI. SOC. 134 (1967); Parker & Holford, *Optimum Test Statistics with Particular Reference to a Forensic Science Problem*, 17 APPLIED STATISTICS 237
(1968).

[65]For a discussion of the foregoing procedure, see Parker, *A Statistical
Treatment of Identification Problems*, 6 J. FORENSIC SCI. SOC. 33 (1966).

would be rejected. By combining $P(H|G)$ and $P(H|NG)$ into a single formula, Bayes's theorem takes both factors into simultaneous account.

F.

Determining $P(H|NG)$ will usually require that inferences be drawn from samples taken from the general population. Complexities arise because characteristics useful for identification must be sufficiently rare so that they would appear not at all or very infrequently (usually too infrequently for reliable statistical inference) in a sample of reasonable size. Thus, the expert in *Risley* might have testified, if asked, that of the thousands of Underwoods he had inspected, he had never seen one with the same combination of defects as defendant's typewriter. We need a procedure for estimating the frequency of so rare an event.

Assume that in a random sample of size n, there are no occurrences of the trace in question. What inferences may be drawn from this fact? Since, in a criminal case, a defendant potentially identified by such a trace would not be prejudiced by too generous an estimate of its population frequency but only by one that was too small, we may compute and use an "upperbound" estimate of the true frequency: one large enough so that there is only a negligible probability that the true frequency is larger. For example, if no identifying traces were found in a sample of one thousand, we could assume without prejudice to the accused that the frequency was 10 percent, because the chances of the true frequency being larger than this would be negligible. It is possible to make this notion precise.[66] Table 5

---

[66]Let p denote the population frequency of the traces, and $q = 1 - p$ the frequency with which the traces do not appear. The probability of selecting a random sample (with replacement) of n elements none of which has the identifying trace is dependent upon q. We denote this probability as $P(n|q)$. For a given frequency, using the product rule:

$$P(n|q) = q^n$$

We seek $P(q|n)$, that is, the probability of q having a certain value given that n selections are made without finding a trace. In this way of looking at the problem, q is a random variable and n is a constant. To obtain $P(q|n)$ from

$P(n|q)$ requires Bayes's theorem, and a prior probability $P(q)$. Using a form of the theorem generalized from that previously derived (p. 89) where we assume that q takes on a sequence of values between 0 and 1, we have:

$$P(q|n) = \frac{P(q)P(nq)}{\sum\limits_{q=0}^{q=1} P(q)P(n|q)}.$$

The "prior" probability here is $P(q)$. For a given value of q, $P(q)$ is the probability that q would have this value without considering the sample results. What values shall we assign to $P(q)$? In almost all cases, larger values of q would presumably have greater probability than small values, since we are dealing with what are believed to be rare traces. Thus, choice of a flat prior (i.e., all possible values of q being deemed equally likely) is conservative in the sense that smaller values of q will be deemed more probable than they would be if a more realistic prior distribution had been used. Since an accused is favored by an estimate of q which reflects a greater probability of smaller values for q, the assumption of a flat prior should not be controversial.

We seek a value $\overline{q}$ to use as an estimate, so that the sum of the posterior probabilities $P(q|n)$ for all values of q between 0 and $\overline{q}$ is less than a critical value (e.g., .01 or .05), which we denote as x. If $\overline{q}$ meets this condition, there is only x probability that the true value of q would be less than $\overline{q}$. Using the flat prior, the value of $\overline{q}$ satisfying the condition is given by the simple expression

$$\overline{q} = x^{1/(n+1)}.$$

The mathematical derivation of this result is as follows. Assuming a flat prior and recognizing that q is a continous variate, Bayes's theorem becomes

$$P(q|n) = \frac{P(n|q)}{\int_0^1 P(n|q)dq}.$$

Substituting $P(n|q) = q^n$ and evaluating the integral, we have

$$P(q|n) = \frac{q^n}{\int_0^1 q^n dq} = (n+1)q^n.$$

Then $\qquad\qquad x = \int_0^{\overline{q}} P(q|n)dq = \int_0^{\overline{q}} (n+1)q^n dq = \overline{q}^{(n+1)}$

or $\qquad\qquad\qquad \overline{q} = x^{1/(n+1)}.$

If x is given the commonly used value .01, then, as we have determined it, q is the smallest value for q (and hence $(1 - \overline{q})$ is the largest value for p) such that there is only one chance in a hundred that q would be smaller (or p larger). Where, as here, a binomial probability distribution is involved, a beta

TABLE 5.   Upperbound Estimates for p

		SAMPLE SIZE		
100	200	500	1,000	2,000
p .05	.02	.01	.005	.002

shows approximate upper-bound estimates for the population frequency p for varying sample sizes, based on the condition that there is only one chance in a hundred that p would be larger.

The table shows, for example, that finding no trace in a sample of one thousand justifies an assumption that the frequency of the trace is no larger than approximately five in a thousand. To justify assuming a frequency of one in a thousand (a statistic we have used here) it would be necessary to take a sample of about 4,650 without finding any trace.[67]

Cases where such large samples would be feasible probably are not common. *State* v. *Sneed*,[68] however, was such a case. There was evidence that the accused on occasion had used the name "Robert Crosset," and that on the day of the murder someone by that name had purchased a handgun which, apparently, was the murder weapon. Were there two Robert Crossets? An expert witness examined telephone books in the area of the crime and found no Crosset among approximately 129 million listings. He guessed the frequency of Crosset to be about one in a million, and estimated the frequency of Robert to

---

distribution is sometimes used for the prior probability. In this form $P(q)$ is proportional to $q^s(1-q)^t$ where s and t are nonnegative real numbers. See PRATT, RAIFFA and SCHLAIFER, INTRODUCTION TO STATISTICAL DECISION THEORY ch. 11 (1965). If $P(q)$ is proportional to the beta distribution q, the estimate would be $q = x^{1/(n+s+1)}$, which is somewhat larger than the estimate given in the text. This illustrates the point previously made that the choice of a flat prior is conservative because it results in a smaller estimate for q and thus a larger estimate for p than if some other, more realistic choice, were made. Overestimation of p also results when the formulas here derived are applied to samples (taken without replacement) which are large relative to the population.

[67] With some increase in mathematical complexity, the method described here can be extended to the case in which some elements of the random sample are found to have the identifying trace.

[68] 76 N.M. 349, 414 P.2d 858 (1966).

be one in thirty. Using the product rule, he concluded the frequency of Robert Crosset to be one in 30 million. In reversing the defendant's conviction, the Supreme Court of New Mexico did not object to the product rule, but did object to the use of "a positive number . . . on the basis of the telephone books when the name Robert Crosset was not listed in those books." [69]

The expert's conclusion was not justifiable. But by using the approach adopted here, he could have treated the telephone books as a large sample of the population which arguably was not biased with respect to the frequency of Crosset in at least the general area covered by the telephone books, and estimated this frequency at less than four in a million.[70] In civil cases, where it is desirable to balance the direction of errors in estimation, it would be more appropriate to use the expected value of the frequency of the trace rather than its upper-bound value. The difference between these two methods of estimation is illustrated by the fact that the expected frequency of Crosset would be less than one in a million, or about four times smaller than the upper-bound value.[71]

G.

Where the incriminating trace consists of a number of elements which individually appear with some frequency in the sample, the information provided by these frequencies can be combined to generate even more powerful results than can be inferred from the nonappearance in the sample of the trace as a whole. In *Collins*, the probabilities of the individual elements were simply multiplied. As we have seen, the validity of this method depends on the assumption of independence. In most cases independence cannot be assumed. One must use a different technique, one that makes allowance for possible correlations among elements.

The product rule leads to a probability estimate for a com-

---

[69] *Id.* at 353, 414 P.2d at 861.

[70] $p = 1 - q = 1 - (.01)^{1/1,290,000} = .00000357$. Since "sampling" by the directories is without replacement, this result overestimates p.

[71] The expected value of q would be $\int_0^1 (n + 1) \, q^{(n+1)} dq = {}^{n+1}/_{n+2}$, and consequently the expected value of $p = 1/(n + 2)$.

pound event which is consistent with the probabilities of the elements comprising the event in the sense that the total probability for all mutually exclusive compound events in which the individual element occurs equals the probability of the individual element. For example, if we throw three dice, our estimate of the probability of three sixes should be consistent with our estimate of the probability of a six with each of the dice. This means that the sum of the probabilities for all combinations which include a six on the first die should be equal to the probability of six on that die. Similarly for each of the other dice. If the dice were thrown one hundred times, we might not see enough three sixes to be able to estimate directly the frequency of this event (other than by the upper-bound procedure already discussed), but we would see a sufficient number of sixes for each die to be able to estimate their frequencies with some confidence. We would use the product rule to obtain an estimate for the frequency of three sixes, the compound event, which was consistent in the sense described with the frequencies of the individual events, a six on each die.[72]

Similarly, if there are correlations between pairs of individual elements, we cannot use the product rule without modification, but we can look at the frequencies of all possible pairs of elements and make our estimate consistent with the frequencies of pairs, just as the product rule does with the frequencies of individual elements when there are no correlations. Estimates made in this way require a multiple iteration technique by which the solution appears as the end product of a series of successive approximations instead of a simple multiplication of individual probabilities.[73] In principle, however, the method is

[72]The difference between the upper-bound method of estimation, which makes use solely of the nonappearance of the trace, and an estimate based on the frequencies of elements of the trace may be illustrated with this dice example. If we throw three dice one hundred times without observing three sixes (a probable occurrence), our upper-bound estimate for the frequency of three sixes would be approximately $^5/_{100}$ (see Table 5). If the dice were true, our estimate using the product rule would be in the neighborhood of $^1/_{216}$, which is approximately ten times smaller than the upper-bound estimate.

[73]The method outlined here has been applied in a major study of the possibility of a causal relationship between halothane anesthesia and massive hepatic necrosis following surgery. See *Summary of the National Halothane Study*, 197 J. AM. MED. ASS'N. 775 (1966). Forensic science applications would appear to offer a good occasion for experimenting further with this technique.

the same. For example, if in *Risley* we anticipated that defects in individual letters were correlated as pairs, we would look at the frequency of each pair and estimate the probability of the occurrence of all defects in a way consistent with the frequency of the individual pairs.

The same method can be extended to higher-order correlations and, for example, to estimates made on the basis of the frequency of triplets. But the data reflecting the frequency of complex events thin out rapidly and we soon find too few cases, or perhaps none, with the requisite combinations of individual elements. The smaller the number of events, the weaker the precision of the estimate. Thus, the problem of independence of factors which the court rightly criticized in *Collins* may be pushed back but not altogether eliminated. If estimates are sought to be based on the frequencies of elements of a trace, it must be assumed that at least some higher order correlations do not exist. This assumption will appear more or less reasonable, depending upon the circumstances. It might be fairly strong in *Collins,* where the most significant effects might be correlations of pairs of attributes (i.e., beard and mustache) but much weaker in *Risley,* where the defects might be linked to the age of the typewriter.

H.

In the *Howland Will* case,[74] a mathematician, Professor Benjamin Peirce of Harvard, applied the product rule to strokes of authentic and disputed signatures and concluded that their similarities were a phenomenon which could occur only once in the number of times expressed by the thirtieth power of five. "This number," he testified, "far transcends human experience. So vast an improbability is practically an impossibility. Such evanescent shadows of probability cannot belong to actual life. They are unimaginably less than those least things the law cares not for."[75]

Numbers of this magnitude have been a consistent feature of

[74]Robinson v. Mandell, 20 Fed. Cas. 1027 (No. 11959) (C.C.D. Mass. 1868), discussed in *The Howland Will Case*, 4 Am. L. Rev. 625 (1870).

[75]*The Howland Will Case*, 4 Am. L. Rev. 625, 649 (1870).

cases like *Collins*. Unsupported, and essentially unsupportable, by data, they are likely to remain theoretical abstractions signifying little more than the expert's judgment that the event was unique. But the intrusion of such "evanescent shadows" intimidates and stultifies thought and generates legitimate skepticism in the more sophisticated. In cases like *Collins*, expert judgment will rarely be improved or better communicated by statistics, and may be distorted.

But when the event is not expected to be unique, so that the expert should say only that it is to some degree rare, there is significant value in a statistical rendering of his opinion. Rarity will mean different things to different people. Without further explanation a juror has no way of assessing the significance of the evidence. He might bring his own experience to bear when commonplace traits are involved, but he will be baffled by the technical data likely to become increasingly involved in future cases. If true judgment is to be exercised, he must know something more precise about rarity than the word alone can communicate.

There has been uncertainty in the opinions dealing with statistics about the probative significance of events not unique in the population. I have argued that it is appropriate to translate frequencies of such events into a probability statement by combining them with prior probabilities through the use of Bayes's theorem. The results confirm our intuitive notion that a trait need not be unique in the population in order to have probative significance. One need not actually inject Bayes's theorem into the courtroom to make use of this result, for it justifies the introduction of statistical evidence without explicit use of a prior to have its natural impact on the jury. I have suggested, however, making explicit use of Bayes's theorem in order to translate the data into a form congenial to scrutiny by jurors.

In rejecting unjustifiable statistics, the courts have expressed concern that, for various reasons, statistical methods might be unfair to defendants. But while abuse is of course possible, mathematics correctly used should lead to a fairer evaluation of identification evidence.

In determining the population frequency of an incriminating trace, the choice is between expertise expressed in the traditional nonquantitative way (e.g., the trace is rare), and objective studies with results reported in quantitative terms (e.g., one in a thousand). A defendant will generally be favored by the quantitative study because, as we have already observed, the conclusions are likely to be less unequivocal than those of "pure" judgment. In addition, the expert's method will be more exposed to examination and attack. It seems clear that quantitative expression of trace frequencies would not be unfair.

Bayesian analysis adds a dimension to the problem. There is a danger that in quantifying their suspicions, jurors will overstate their convictions and thus be led by the mathematics to conclude that guilt was more probable than if they had considered the same evidence without quantification. On the other hand, a juror forced to derive a quantitative measure of his suspicion on the basis of the evidence at trial is likely to consider that evidence more carefully and rationally, and to exclude impermissible elements such as appearance or popular prejudice. Moreover, Bayesian analysis would demonstrate that the evidentiary weight of an impressive figure like one in a thousand—which might otherwise exercise an undue influence —would depend on the other evidence in the case, and might well be relatively insignificant if the prior suspicion were sufficiently weak. Probably the greatest danger to a defendant from Bayesian methods is that jurors may be surprised at the strength of the inference of guilt flowing from the combination of their prior suspicions and the statistical evidence. But this, if the suspicions are correctly estimated, is no more than the evidence deserves.

Chapter 4

VOTING

THIS CHAPTER DISCUSSES two probability models that may be used to analyze statistics in voting cases. The first is a model of voting power that is relevant to test certain types of reapportionment; the second, a model of irregular ballots used in challenges to the validity of primary elections.

I

The "one person, one vote" doctrine of the federal reapportionment decisions is based on the premise that each individual's vote should count equally in the electoral process. Since all electoral districts were to be equal, and each representative was to have one vote, it seemed unnecessary at first to define precisely the attribute of voting power that required equalization. The problem of definition arose only when reapportionment plans began to be presented in which state legislative districts were of unequal size, but the inequality was intended to be cured by giving the larger districts a proportionately greater number of representatives or by giving the representatives from the larger districts a larger number of votes. These plans involved what were known respectively as "multimember" districts or "weighted" voting. A similar situation arose when reapportionment doctrine was applied to county and municipal governments. When supervisors were elected from towns of differing size, supervisors from the larger towns received a larger number of votes on the board to equalize the representational scheme.

What should the compensation be? The mathematics seemed simple enough: the votes should be distributed in proportion to the population. If, for example, a district had twice the population of another district, it would be entitled to twice the number of representatives elected at large, or to a single representative with twice as many votes. This was the rule applied by the Supreme Court in its first decisions on this question. In *Fortson* v. *Dorsey*,[1] the Court held that Georgia's multimember senatorial system was not invalid per se: "There is clearly no mathematical disparity. Fulton County, the State's largest constituency, has a population nearly seven times larger than that of a single-district constituency and for that reason elects seven senators."[2] Similarly, in *Kilgarlin* v. *Hill*,[3] the Court struck down a Texas reapportionment scheme that provided for multimember districts, observing that the addition of a single representative to two of those districts would have brought them closer to the "arithmetic ideal."[4]

In these cases the basis for the "arithmetic ideal" remained wholly unexplained and apparently unexamined. It appeared to be derived by extension from the situation in which all districts are equal. In that case, each representative with a single vote will have the same proportion of votes in the legislature as the proportion of the total population he represents. The population proportion rule simply extends this arithmetic artifact to cases in which districts are unequal. However, it is apparent that the extension cannot be automatic, since in extreme cases this rule would produce unacceptable, or at least highly dubious, results. Thus, if one district had 60 percent of the population it would surely be incorrect to give its representative 60 percent of the legislative votes, for in that case, the represen-

[1]379 U.S. 433 (1965).
[2]*Id.* at 437.
[3]386 U.S. 120 (1967).
[4]*Id.* at 125.

tatives of the remaining 40 percent of the population would never have a determining voice in the legislative process.

It may also be argued that a representative from a district which has twice the population of another district should receive twice the number of votes in the legislature, because that is the number of votes the district's representatives would have had if the district had been split into two. But this assumed equivalence overlooks the fact that if there are two legislators from separate districts, their power is diminished by the possibility of their disagreement, whereas the chance of such disagreement is diminished if both are elected at large from a single district (since both represent the same constellation of political forces), or reduced to zero if a single legislator has two votes.[5]

Perhaps these points do no more than cast some doubt on the distribution of votes in proportion to population when districts are unequal. To examine the matter more carefully it is necessary to define the nature of the voting power that must be equalized. The Court has never done this; its decisions teach only the negative fact that it is not the "actual" voting power of the individual (however that may be defined) that must be equalized to satisfy constitutional standards. A Republican in a "safe" Democratic district has no power to select his representative, but the Court has refused to look at such matters (except in the racial context)[6] and has in fact approved plans expressly designed to create "safe" districts, even though such districts deprive minorities of voting power.[7]

But if the Constitution does not require equalization of actual voting power, what is to be equalized? Presumably the relevant fact is the power of the individual to affect the choice of his representative, or the power of the legislator to affect legislation, and this power is to be determined not by reference to actual political facts but to some model of the electoral process in which the only variable is the number of votes.

[5]In the discussion that follows, it is assumed that there is no difference between the latter two situations, and multimember districts are treated as equivalent to districts whose representative has an equal number of weighted votes.

[6]E.g., Gomillion v. Lightfoot, 364 U.S. 339 (1960).

[7]Gaffney v. Cummings, 412 U.S. 735 (1973).

One model for this purpose has been suggested by Professor
J. F. Banzhaf.[8] He argued that an individual's voting power was
properly measured by his ability to cast a decisive vote either as
a voter in an election for a representative or as a legislator with
regard to a proposition. Examining the problem at the voter
level he proposed to measure this ability by computing the
total number of ways in which votes could be cast, and determining the proportion of those ways in which an individual's
vote would be decisive in the sense that he could change the
result by changing his vote. This proportion was suggested as
an index or measure of the individual's voting power. Banzhaf
originally conceived this measure to describe the effect of
changes in the size of electoral districts on the voting power of
individuals, but it was first applied to analyze the legislative
voting power of supervisors in county boards.

Under New York State county law, supervisors from the
various towns and cities in a county constitute its board of
supervisors and conduct its business by a majority vote.[9] Since
towns and cities vary in size, yet may nevertheless be
represented by a single supervisor, weighted voting of supervisors has been employed to conform to the equalization principles of the reapportionment decisions.

In *Iannucci* v. *Board of Supervisors*,[10] the New York Court of
Appeals examined weighted voting schemes for supervisors in
Washington and Saratoga counties. In Washington County, the
supervisor for a town was entitled to cast one vote for every 279
persons in the town, up to a maximum of fifteen votes; for the
larger towns additional supervisors were to be added. The largest town had three supervisors, each casting thirteen votes. The
three smallest towns had one supervisor, each casting two
votes. In Saratoga County, a similar plan led to the following
distribution: the largest town had two supervisors, each casting
fourteen votes; each of the three smallest towns had one supervisor who cast a single vote.

Under these plans, the votes of the supervisors were propor-

[8]Banzhaf, *Weighted Voting Doesn't Work: A Mathematical Analysis*, 19
RUTGERS L. REV. 317 (1965); Banzhaf, *Multi-Member Electoral Districts—Do They Violate the "One Man, One Vote" Principle*, 75 YALE L.J.
1309 (1966).

[9]N. Y. COUNTY LAW, §§150, 153 subd. 4 (McKinney 1972).

[10]20 N.Y.2d 244, 229 N.E.2d 195, 282 N.Y.S. 2d 502 (1967)(2 cases).

tional to the population they represented and so met the standard alluded to in *Fortson* and required in *Kilgarlin*. But the Court looked to voting power rather than to the number of weighted votes as the test of equality. It stated that "[t]he principle of one man–one vote is violated, however, when the power of a representative to affect the passage of legislation by his vote, rather than by influencing his colleagues, does not roughly correspond to the proportion of the population in his constituency." To estimate that power, the Court stated that a measure similar to that proposed by Banzhaf should be adopted. "Ideally, in any weighted voting plan, it should be mathematically possible for every member of the legislative body to cast the decisive vote on legislation in the same ratio which the population of his constituency bears to the total population." "A legislator's voting power, measured by the mathematical possibility of his casting a decisive vote, must approximate the power he would have in a legislative body which did not employ weighted voting."[11] The Court held that the plans for Washington and Saratoga Counties were invalid because the proponents had failed to demonstrate that the distribution of votes complied with this standard.

Following *Iannucci*, weighted voting plans based on such calculations performed by a computer were in fact approved for several counties in subsequent New York cases.[12] Perhaps the most complex plan gaining judicial approval was that for Cortland County.[13] Under it, the county was redistricted so that the larger towns were divided into several legislative districts while the smaller towns were grouped together. This achieved districts which varied in population from 2,140 to 2,716. To ac-

---

[11]*Id.* at 252, 229 N.E.2d at 199, 282 N.Y.S.2d at 508.

[12]*See, e.g.,* Franklin v. Krause, 32 N.Y.2d 234, 298 N.E.2d 68, 344 N.Y.S.2d 885 (1973), *appeal dismissed,* 415 U.S. 904 (1974). Jones v. Board of Supervisors, 46 App. Div.2d 102, 361 N.Y.S.2d 718 (3rd Dep't 1974); Slater v. Board of Supervisors, 69 Misc.2d 842, 330 N.Y.S.2d 947 (1972), *aff'd,* 42 App. Div.2d 795, 346 N.Y.S.2d 185 (3rd Dep't 1973). For a discussion of weighted voting in New York, see Johnson, *An Analysis of Weighted Voting as Used in Reapportionment of County Governments in New York State,* 34 ALBANY L. REV. 1 (1969); Imrie, *The Impact of the Weighted Vote on Representation in Municipal Governing Bodies of New York State,* 219 ANNALS N.Y. ACAD. SCI. 192 (1973).

[13]Slater v. Board of Supervisors, 69 Misc.2d 842, 330 N.Y.S.2d 947 (1972), *aff'd,* 42 App. Div.2d 795, 346 N.Y.S.2d 185 (3rd Dep't 1973).

count for these variations, weighted voting was employed, with the weights shifting, so that the same proportionate ability to cast a decisive vote would be maintained when legislation requiring three-fifths or two-thirds votes was involved.

The *Iannucci* standard required a determination of the proportion of the voting power of legislators where they do not have an equal number of votes. The idea behind Banzhaf's index was easily adapted for this purpose.[14] The measure of voting power is the ability to cast a decisive vote. Consider a particular combination of votes for a proposition. With respect to this combination, a legislator possesses a decisive vote if the result would be altered by a change in his vote alone, all other votes remaining the same. Thus, for a given combination of votes there may be no legislators with decisive votes, or one or more with such votes. The total voting power for all legislators is the total number of decisive votes for all legislators under all combinations of votes. An individual legislator's proportion of voting power is the number of his decisive votes divided by the total number of decisive votes of all legislators.

This index has the correct characteristics: When each legislator has the same number of votes, each has the same voting power because each casts the same porportion of decisive votes; a legislator with more votes than the others casts a larger proportion of decisive votes, and consequently has more power; and the sum of the voting power of all legislators is equal to one.

An example will illustrate the principal feature of this voting-power measure. Assume there are four towns in a county, three of equal size and one twice as large as the others. If the larger town were split up into two separate districts, and each were given a representative on the board, there would be five supervisors, each having 20 percent of the voting power. If the supervisor from the larger town instead receives two votes he would be able to cast a decisive vote in twelve out of the twenty-four instances in which such votes could be cast. This would give him 50 percent of the voting power, and thus would exceed the proportion of the population which he represented by some ten percentage points.

The result in this illustration is indicative of a general rule:

---

[14]The Banzhaf index has to be expressed in a form such that the total voting power of all legislators will equal one.

if a representative from a larger district is given weighted votes equal to the proportion of the population he represents, he will receive a dispproportionate share of the voting power in the legislature. The same conclusion follows with respect to multimember districts if the legislators vote together. In that event, analysis by ratios of combinations indicates that the Supreme Court's rule in *Fortson* and *Kilgarlin* required the assignment of an excessive number of legislators to multimember districts.

This conclusion is based solely on an analysis of voting power at the legislative level. It is strengthened if one uses the same type of analysis at the voter level. The question raised is whether the vote of an individual in a political district which is twice as large as other districts counts for only half, so that his representative must be twice as powerful at the legislative level. Both the Supreme Court in *Fortson* and *Kilgarlin* and the New York Court of Appeals in *Iannucci* accepted this premise.

The theory of voting power as the ability to cast a decisive vote would dictate a different conclusion. To measure how the voting power of an individual changes as the size of his district increases, Banzhaf's index may be used in its original form, and the voting power of an individual computed as the proportion of total voting combinations in which an individual may cast a decisive vote.

If there are $N + 1$ voters in a district, the number of voting combinations for two candidates is 2^{N+1}, because each voter may vote in two ways. An individual may cast a decisive vote only when all other voters are tied. Consequently, the number of combinations in which an individual casts a decisive vote is equal to twice the number of combinations in which the remaining voters are tied (for each tying combination the individual has two decisive votes, one for each candidate). The number of tying combinations for the remaining voters is

$$\frac{N!}{(N/2)!(N/2)!}$$

where $N!$ is the factorial $(N)(N-1)(N-2), \ldots, (1)$. Hence the ratio of the total number of combinations in which the individual casts the decisive vote to the total number of combinations is

$$\frac{(2)N!}{(N/2)!(N/2)!2^{N+1}}.$$

Using Stirling's approximation for the factorial, it can be shown that each individual would cast a decisive vote in approximately $1/\sqrt{2\pi N}$ proportion of combinations.[15] This means that voting power of an individual does not vary with the population but rather with the square root of the population. If one district has twice the population of another, its voters will not have half the power of those in the smaller district but $1/\sqrt{2}$, or approximately two-thirds, their power.

Thus, if the theory is right, even the *Iannucci* rule, which mandates that voting power in a legislature be distributed in proportion to population, may overstate the degree of correction required to compensate voters in the larger districts for their loss of electoral power. However by reducing the extent of the compensation, it would be closer to the mark than the rule used by the Court in *Fortson* and *Kilgarlin*.

Is the ability of a legislator or an individual voter to cast a decisive vote an appropriate test of voting power for reapportionment purposes? The question has two phases. The first asks whether the probability of casting a decisive vote is an appropriate index of voting power. If so, the second phase asks whether that probability appropriately may be computed as the simple ratios previously described.

The basic objection to the decisive-vote model as an index of voting power is that it is highly theoretical. Undoubtedly, the chance to break a tie is not a significant voting motivation. In terms of utility theory, a voter would sell that right for very little, whereas he would charge much more to give up his right to vote altogether. The chance to break a tie thus constitutes only a small part of the value of voting, and it is not clear that this chance fairly represents the comparative value of voting in multimember and single districts.

This objection is, of course, more significant at the voter level than at the legislative level, where the possibility of a tie is much greater. It seems quite reasonable to define legislative voting power in terms of the probability of casting a deciding vote, as the court did in *Iannucci,* and if that definition is adopted at the legislative level (and the method of estimation

---

[15]For the derivation of this result see Banzhaf, *Multi-Member Electoral Districts—Do They Violate the "One Man, One Vote" Principle,* 75 YALE L.J. 1309, 1323 n.28 (1966).

accepted), it becomes unnecessary to pursue the matter at the voter level to demonstrate the overcompensation caused by the population proportion rule.

However, the appropriateness of Banzhaf's index at the voter level is also not without interest. To test the conclusions of the decisive-vote model at the voter level, let us see if it is possible to derive a more general expression to describe voting power in larger and smaller districts. The problem would be insuperably difficult, except that the legal context permits certain simplifications. First, the comparison of interest is between two districts which differ only as to electoral size, so that is the only factor to be considered. Second, since combinatorial theory, at the voter level, has only been used negatively—to attack the correctness of the population proportion rule—a better index need be specified only to the extent necessary to determine whether that rule is correct. If a more inclusive model does not provide at least indicative support for allocating legislative votes in proportion to population, we should hesitate to approve multimember districts and weighted voting based on that rule as a way of compensating the larger districts for their voters' diminished power.

I give first a general summary of the chain of reasoning by which a more general index may be developed, and the conclusions to be drawn from it.

Assume two districts, one of which is twice as large as the other. A voter in the larger district feels that his vote is worth less, not because he believes he is less likely to cast a tie breaker, but because he feels that *any* result will be carried by a larger number of votes, so that his contribution will be less significant. This perception is correct: over a run of elections, the variations in numbers of votes cast (e.g., for candidates of a party) will be larger in the larger district than in the smaller one, even assuming that the two districts are identical except for the number of voters. Thus if the absolute size of the plurality determines the significance of his vote, a voter in the larger district will believe his vote to be less significant because it will more frequently be buried in larger pluralities. However, the probability of any given plurality in the larger district is not twice its value in the smaller district. Using a plausible probability model, it can be shown that the ratio of the probabilities of any given split in the small district to the large one is not 2:1, as the population rule assumes, but rather is a function dependent upon the size of the plurality. This ratio assumes a maximum value of $\sqrt{2}$:1 for the probabilities of the expected values (e.g., an even split if on the average voters are assumed to be equally likely to vote for either candidate) and diminishes as the size of the plurality departs from the expected value. Since the average ratio of these probabilities is less than $\sqrt{2}$:1, the more realistic model suggests that Banzhaf's index represents an upper bound to the true ratio. Consequently, there is no support for a higher population proportion ratio.[16]

Here is a more formal derivation of the foregoing. We assume that for any given plurality in an election, a rational voter would attach a certain value to his vote, which might be expressed as the dollar amount he would insist on being paid to give it up. This value would be greatest if his vote is the tie breaker (zero plurality without his vote) and declines as the size of the plurality increases. Obviously, the voter cares less about his vote when there is a very large majority for or against his choice than when the vote is close. The value of his vote may thus be expressed as a function of the plurality—say $g(x)$—where x is one-half the plurality (without his vote) and $g(x)$ is a numerical expression for the value of an individual's vote given that plurality (without his vote). It is further assumed that all voters (being rational) have the same $g(x)$.

Different pluralities have different probabilities prior to the election. For example, it is very unlikely that there will be an exact tie, but even more unlikely that one candidate will receive 95 percent of the votes. Let $f(x)$ be the probability that x votes will be one-half of the plurality. Following utility theory, the value of an individual's vote prior to the election could then be expressed as the value of his vote for a given plurality, multiplied by the probability of this plurality, and this product summed over all possible pluralities. Thus, the voting power of

[16]A different result follows if the fact of significance to a voter is assumed to be not the absolute but the proportional size of the plurality. A given proportionate difference is less likely in the large district than in the small one. However, this assumption would appear to be both factually and legally untenable since it would imply that an individual in a large district had more power than one in a small one. If pluralities are proportionately very large, voters might well consider both the absolute and proportionate size in weighing the significance of their votes; but pluralities this large are unlikely to be a realistic factor in the problems we are considering.

an individual (VP) in a district with N other voters may be expressed as

$$VP = \sum_{x=0}^{x=N/2} g(x)f(x).$$

I suggest that this definition corresponds quite closely to a rational individual's assessment of his voting power.

To evaluate VP in any given case requires some idea of $g(x)$ and $f(x)$. We know little about $g(x)$ except that it declines in some unspecified fashion as x increases. Arguably, we can do better for $f(x)$. We assume that each voter has a certain probability of voting for each candidate. These are not necessarily the same; some voters are far more likely than others to vote for a certain candidate. These probabilities are measured when the voters enter the booths, so that the actual votes are independent of each other. On this assumption, a fundamental theorem of probability (the central limit theorem) holds that the outcome of the votes will have what is known as a normal probability distribution.[17] Thus, if there are N persons in a district, and the average probability that a voter will vote for a certain candidate is $1/2$, the probability that half the plurality will equal x votes is

$$f_x(x) = \sqrt{\frac{2}{\pi N}} \cdot e^{-2x^2/N}.$$

If there are $2N$ persons in a district,

$$f_{2x}(x) = \sqrt{\frac{1}{\pi N}} \cdot e^{-x^2/N}.$$

Substituting the above expressions for $f_N(x)$ and $f_{2N}(x)$ in the expression previously derived for voting power yields the following:

$$VP_N = \sum_{x=0}^{x=N/2} g(x) \cdot \sqrt{\frac{2}{\pi N}} \cdot e^{-2x^2/N}$$

$$VP_{2N} = \sum_{x=0}^{x=N} g(x) \cdot \sqrt{\frac{1}{\pi N}} \cdot e^{-x^2/N}$$

[17]An empirical study of voting in Presidential elections has shown that at least in Northern states variations in plurality for the Democratic party are normally distributed. See Merrill, Citizen Voting Power under the Electoral College: A Stochastic Model Based on State Voting Patterns, at 11–13 (paper presented at the October 18–20, 1976 meeting of the Society for Industrial and Applied Mathematics).

or

$$\frac{VP_N}{VP_{2N}} = \sqrt{2}\left[\frac{\Sigma g(x) \cdot e^{-2x^2/N}}{\Sigma g(x) \cdot e^{-x^2/N}}\right].$$

Since each term in the numerator of the bracketed summation is less than the corresponding term in the denominator (except for the first terms of each, which are equal since $x = 0$), the ratio of the sum in brackets is less than 1, and consequently

$$\frac{VP_N}{VP_{2N}} < \sqrt{2}.$$

Banzhaf's result may thus be seen as a special case, in which it is assumed that $g(x)$ or $f(x)$ declines so rapidly with increasing x that terms in which $x > 0$ do not materially affect the ratio. This result supports Banzhaf's conclusion that the population rule overstates the extent to which voters in larger districts are deprived of voting power, since the more general index demonstrates that the ratio of voting power of two districts, one of which is twice the other, is even closer to unity, and thus further from the population proportion rule, than indicated by the square relation shown by Banzhaf's index.

Assuming that the ability to cast a decisive vote, or the more general expression we have derived, is an appropriate form of index of voting power, the second question is whether the models used to compute the probabilities are valid. Obviously, they are highly schematic. It was this lack of realism that led the Supreme Court in *Whitcomb* v. *Chavis*[18] to reject Banzhaf's model. Referring to the combinatorial method for computing voting power, Justice White wrote that "the position remains a theoretical one" which "knowingly avoids and does 'not take into account any political or other factors which might affect the actual voting power of the residents, which might include party affiliation, race, previous voting characteristics or any other factors which go into the entire political voting situation.'" He concluded that "[t]he real-life impact of multi-member districts on individual voting power has not been sufficiently demonstrated, at least on this record, to warrant departure from prior cases." [19]

[18]403 U.S. 124 (1971).
[19]*Id.* at 145–46.

In a separate opinion, Justice Harlan used the criticisms of the combinatorial method to illustrate his position that the Court should not have strayed into the "mathematical quagmire" of state reapportionment. He observed that Professor Banzhaf's definition of voting power was "not implausible." However, he pointed out that the probability of a voter casting a tie-breaking vote would be dramatically reduced from the estimate given by the model if voters slightly favored one candidate, or somewhat reduced if voters were committed to one candidate even though the uncommitted voters were as likely to vote for one candidate as the other.

Given these sensitivities, Justice Harlan found it not surprising that the Court declined to embrace this measure of voting power. But he correctly pointed out that the same criticism could be made with respect to the one-man, one-vote opinions of the Court, which also did not take these realistic matters into account. Since both positions were theoretical, "[t]he only relevant difference between the elementary arithmetic on which the Court relies and the elementary probability theory on which Professor Banzhaf relies is that calculations in the latter field cannot be done on one's fingers." Thus, while the Court refused to accept the combinatorial definition of voting power, "it neither suggests an alternative nor considers the consequences of its inability to measure what it purports to be equalizing."[20]

The aptness of a combinatorial model for estimating the probability of any given plurality obviously presents a substantial question. The burden of the probability estimates is that larger districts which receive a proportionately larger number of votes are overrepresented. But the model may overestimate the voting power of representatives from larger districts relative to the smaller districts, or may underestimate the depreciation in voting power inflicted on voters in larger districts. Let us consider these possibilities separately.

In using a simple ratio of combinations of votes to compute the voting power of legislators with weighted votes or of those from multimember districts, it was in effect assumed that each legislator would have an equal probability of voting for or against a measure. If this probability is not equal, and, for ex-

[20]*Id.* at 168 n.2, 169.

ample, the probability of favorable votes predominates, the probability that any legislator could cast a deciding vote would diminish. But this would apply to legislators from both larger and smaller districts. Since it is not the absolute probability of casting a decisive vote, but only the relative probability that is important in comparing the power of legislators from large and small districts, the fact that a measure may be more or less likely to pass or to fail is not likely to have significant bearing on the relative power of legislators. This is true even though, as Justice White correctly observed with respect to voters, large changes in their absolute power may be involved. In fact, as the probability of a measure's success departs from one half, the disparity in voting power between legislators from larger and smaller districts would be magnified. In that situation, voting combinations involving single-vote pluralities, which could be influenced by legislators with a single vote, would by hypothesis become less probable, while larger pluralities, which could be influenced by legislators with a larger number of votes would become more probable. Thus, at the legislative level, the lack of realism in the model is likely to produce a conservative lower-bound estimate of the degree to which the population proportion rule overcompensates legislators from the larger districts.

Of course, coalitions of forces may be imagined in which legislators from the larger districts would be consistently less powerful compared to legislators from smaller districts than the relation indicated by the ratio of combinations described here. One may equally imagine coalitions in which these relative differences would be greater than those calculated. If a probability model were to be accepted only when no state of facts could exist in which it would be incorrect, no probabilistic calculation could ever be accepted; but we know that the description of the general tendency of affairs which models provide is much more useful than such a strict rule would allow.[21]

Let us consider this question in the context of the example of the four towns previously discussed. Distribution of votes in accordance with the ratio of combinations will be correct if over the run of legislative measures all combinations or coalitions

---

[21]Certainly the answer is not given as the Court purported to do in *Whitcomb* by referring to the rule in prior cases in which the problem was not considered.

tend to emerge with equal frequency in those cases in which the vote is close enough, so that at least one legislator has the power to cast a decisive vote. This assumes that there is no consistent voting relation between the supervisor of the larger town and those of the other three towns. Distribution of votes in accordance with population proportions will be correct only if there is a reduction in the probability of those voting combinations in which the representative from the larger town is joined by one of the representatives from the smaller towns so that the representative from the larger town alone may cast a decisive vote, and a concomitant increase in the probability of those voting combinations in which the representative from the larger town is opposed by the representatives from the three other towns, so that he lacks the power to cast a decisive vote. In short, under the population proportion method, the larger town must be politically isolated and must tend to be outvoted by the smaller towns, otherwise it will have excessive voting power in the legislature.

A similar special assumption at the voter level would be required to justify the Court's approach. If the probability of casting a decisive vote is the proper test of voting power, the Court's assumption that voting power of those in larger districts would be diminished in proportion to the increase in population would be correct only if the larger districts were less evenly balanced politically than the smaller ones. In that event, the minority in such districts would suffer a further loss of voting power, which would tend to equalize the excessive voting power of their representatives. (The majority would also lose voting power in a technical sense, but they would have their way at the polls.)

Thus, either at the legislative or the voter level, the Court's insistence that votes be distributed in proportion to population requires special assumptions about the character of the political process to sustain it as a fair distribution of voting power. But it is this very type of assumption that the Court consistently has refused to accept as a justification for unequal districts. This seems correct. If reapportionment plans are to be judged by manageable standards, it seems inevitable that no reliance can be placed on the compensating effect of special political alliances or voting patterns. The consistent application of that same assumption to multimember districts and weighted voting dem-

onstrates that the population proportion method for distributing
legislative votes is not appropriate compensation for the loss of
voting power suffered by voters in larger districts.

II

Defeated candidates in primary elections sometimes challenge
the results in court and collect evidence of irregularities to support their demand for an election rerun. Frequently, this evidence consists solely of proof that a given number of persons
voted who were not qualified, with no evidence of fraud and no
indication as to how these persons voted. How large must this
group be before a new election should be ordered?

The New York Election Law provides that a new primary
election may be ordered when the "irregularities . . . render impossible a determination as to who rightfully was . . . elected."[22]
Consider a two-candidate contest in which the winner prevails
by one hundred votes out of ten thousand. If there are 150 irregular voters, it is *possible* that more than 125 of them voted for
the winner, so that their elimination would reverse the result.
Does this possibility mean that the rightful winner cannot be
determined within the meaning of the statute? The courts have
answered this question with intuitive assessments of the probability that the result would be reversed if the challenged votes
were eliminated. Thus, the New York Court of Appeals has articulated and applied the principle that the party attempting to
impeach the results must show that the "irregularities are sufficiently large in number to establish the *probability* that the
result would be changed by a shift in, or invalidation of, the
questioned votes."[23]

Two polar assessments of the relevant probabilities may be

[22]N.Y. Election Law §330(2) (McKinney 1964). There is no comparable
statutory provision for ordering a new general election. For a comprehensive
discussion of Section 330 challenges, see Note, *Primary Challenges in New
York: Caselaw Coleslaw v. Election Protection*, 73 COLUM. L. REV. 318
(1973).

[23]Ippolito v. Power, 22 N.Y.2d 594, 597–98, 241 N.E.2d 232, 233, 294
N.Y.S.2d 209, 211 (1968)(emphasis added). This standard was quoted with approval and applied in De Martini v. Power, 27 N.Y.2d 149, 151, 262 N.E.2d
857, 858, 314 N.Y.S.2d 609, 610 (1970).

illustrated by comparing *Ippolito* v. *Power*[24] with *De Martini* v. *Power*.[25] In *Ippolito,* the winner's plurality was 17 votes out of 2,827; there were 101 suspect or invalid ballots. The Court of Appeals affirmed the lower court's order for a new election. Evidently relying on intuition, the court concluded that "it does not strain the probabilities to assume a likelihood that the questioned votes produced or could produce a change in the result."[26]

In *De Martini,* out of 5,250 votes. 136 were declared irregular and invalidated, no fraud being involved. The winner's plurality was 62 votes. The lower courts and Court of Appeals differed in their estimates of the relevant probability. The Supreme Court ordered a new election bécause "it is not beyond likelihood that the small difference of 62 votes could be altered in a new election."[27] The Appellate Division unanimously affirmed. In reversing, the Court of Appeals observed that the majority of the winner would not evaporate unless at least 99 votes—i.e., at least 72.8 percent of the irregularities—had been cast in her favor. The court found this unlikely: "It takes credulity to assume that, in so close a contest, such an extreme percentage of invalid votes would be cast in one direction." It concluded that "a valid determination is not rendered impossible . . . by the remote possibility of a changed result. . . ."

Subjective estimates of the relevant probabilities have thus varied. There is, however, no reason to leave matters on a purely subjective basis. Using an assumption about the character of invalid voting which will be defensible in many cases, the relevant probabilities can be readily computed.

Consider all the votes cast in a primary election as balls placed in an urn: black balls, which predominate, are the votes cast for the winner; white balls are those for the loser. A certain number of balls representing the irregular voters are then withdrawn at random from the urn, an operation tantamount to

[24]22 N.Y.2d 594, 241 N.E.2d 232, 294 N.Y.S.2d 209 (1968).

[25]22 N.Y.2d 149, 262 N.E.2d 857, 314 N.Y.S.2d 609 (1970).

[26]22 N.Y.2d at 598, 241 N.E.2d at 233, 294 N.Y.S.2d at 211.

[27]Quoted at 27 N.Y.2d at 151, 262 N.E.2d at 857, 314 N.Y.S.2d at 610. Despite the court's casual language, the proper inquiry is whether the election result at bar was affected through irregular voting, not whether a new election would yield a different result.

their invalidation. What is the probability that, after the withdrawal, the number of black balls no longer exceeds the number of white? Note the key assumption that the balls are withdrawn at random, i.e., that each ball has the same probability of being withdrawn. In terms of the real election situation, each voter is deemed to have the same probability of casting an invalid vote. This assumption will of course be untenable if evidence of fraud or patterns of irregular voting indicate that a disproportionate number of improper votes were cast for one candidate. But in the absence of such evidence, the assumption of random distribution of the improper votes is warranted. Whether or not mathematics is used to assess the probabilities, some implicit or explicit view as to the pattern of irregular voting seems inevitable. The assumption that the probability of an improper vote being cast was equal for each voter is the only neutral and nonarbitrary view that can be taken when there is no evidence to indicate that the probabilities are not equal. Thus in *Ippolito, De Martini* and other cases,[28] where there was no evidence to disturb the assumption of randomness, the analysis depicted by the urn model is a correct expression of the intuitive probability used by the Court of Appeals in formulating the burden of proof standard for a new election.

In terms of the urn model, the mathematical probability of a reversal is simply the number of combinations in which the balls representing the invalid votes may be withdrawn from the urn so as to produce a reversal divided by the total number of combinations in which these balls may be withdrawn from the urn. If the number of votes in question was small enough, these combinations could be simply enumerated. In most practical applications however, the combinations are far too numerous for simple counting. An approximation of this probability with sufficient accuracy for legal purposes can be obtained by using the formula

$$Z = d \sqrt{\frac{s-k}{sk}}$$

where d is the winner's plurality, s the number of votes cast either for the winner or his challenger, and k the number of inval-

[28]E.g., Posner v. Power, 18 N.Y.2d 703, 220 N.E.2d 269, 273 N.Y.S.2d 480 (1966); Santucci v. Power, 25 N.Y.2d 897, 252 N.E.2d 128, 304 N.Y.S.2d 593 (1969).

TABLE 6

VALUE OF Z	PROBABILITY OF REVERSAL
0.5	.31
1.0	.16
1.5	.07
2.0	.02
3.0	.001

id votes cast either for the winner or his challenger.[29] The value of z determines the probability of reversal; as it increases, this probability declines rapidly. Table 6 gives some benchmarks.[30]

The application of this formula demonstrates a first good reason for using mathematical methods, namely, that uneducated intuition is not a reliable guide to the true probabilities. On the facts in *Ippolito*, analysis indicates about a 5 percent chance that the election would have been reversed by the removal of the irregular votes.[31] Did the court realize that the

---

[29]The derivation of this formula appears in the Appendix. The formula uses the total vote for the election, and this in general should be sufficiently accurate. If, however, votes for subdistricts are available, and if the pattern of voting varied substantially from subdistrict to subdistrict, it may be desirable to make separate computations for each subdistrict and to aggregate them as shown in the subdivision formula in the Appendix. If there are only two candidates and no other contest, k will equal the number of challenged votes. If there are more than two candidates or if there are other contests (e.g., a simultaneous primary for another party, as is frequently the case), some of the invalid votes may have been cast for the third candidate or in the other contest. To account for this effect precisely would raise mathematical complexities. Frequently, it can be demonstrated that the probability of a reversal is extremely small even if it is assumed that all the invalid votes were cast for the winner or his challenger, an assumption which clearly generates a larger probability of reversal than if a more realistic assumption were adopted. In closer cases, the probabilities fairly may be approximated by assuming that the winner and challenger combined received the same proportion of invalid votes as they did of the total vote for all candidates and contests. On this assumption k will be proportionately smaller than the total number of invalid votes. In other situations, it may be desirable to compute the probability of reversal by computer simulation (the so-called Monte Carlo method).

[30]z is simply a standard normal variate. A full table of values and associated probabilities may be found in most textbooks on statistics. See, e.g., FREUND, MATHEMATICAL STATISTICS, Table III at 366 (1962).

[31]

$$z = 17\sqrt{\frac{2827-101}{(2827)(101)}} = 1.6.$$

This is the value associated with a 5 percent probability of reversal.

chance was this small when it concluded there was a "likelihood" of reversal?[32] One cannot be sure, but 5 percent seems a
rather small probability to be termed a likelihood. If so,
Ippolito may well be wrong in the sense that the court was acting on an overestimate of the probability of reversal.[33]

In *De Martini*, although the Appellate Division found a
reversal "not beyond likelihood," the mathematical test demonstrates the contrary. The chance that the winner's plurality of
only 62 votes would be eroded to a tie or loss by the removal of
136 irregular votes was less than one in a million.[34] Thus the
Court of Appeals, reversing, was clearly correct when it
concluded that the chance of a reversal was "remote." The
court's judgment on this question may have been influenced by
a statistical analysis in appellant's brief which, using a weak
form of mathematical estimation, demonstrated that the probability of a reversal was less than 3.7 percent.[35] If the court had
this figure in mind when it characterized the probability of
removal as "remote," it evidently made a mistake in *Ippolito*
when it found that this probability was substantial although the
true figure was only 5 percent.

The court was even more clearly mistaken in *Santucci* v.
Power,[36] when it affirmed an order directing a new election on
the basis of 640 irregularities and a winner's plurality of 95

[32]No mathematical analysis was presented in the briefs for either party.

[33]In *Ippolito* the court relied on its affirmance of a new election in Nodar v.
Power, 18 N.Y.2d 697, 220 N.E.2d 267, 273 N.Y.S.2d 273 (1966), which it said
involved "almost identical facts." But the plurality in *Nodar* was twenty-
seven votes, more than 50 percent larger than in *Ippolito*. Although the
numbers in both cases were small, the difference is of some consequence. The
formula applied to the *Nodar* facts is

$$z = 27\sqrt{\frac{1417-109}{(1417)\,(109)}} = 2.4,$$

a value of z associated with a 1 percent probability of reversal. This is five
times smaller than in *Ippolito* and surely should be deemed inconsequential
for legal purposes.

[34]

$$z = 62\sqrt{\frac{5250-136}{(5250)\,(136)}} = 5.2,$$

a value of z associated with a probability of less than one in a million.

[35]Brief for Appellant, Appendix. The method used was Chebychev's inequality.

[36]25 N.Y.2d 897, 252 N.E.2d 128, 304 N.Y.S.2d 593 (1969).

votes. In citing *Ippolito*, the court evidently believed that the probability of a reversal was substantial. Mathematical analysis demonstrates, however, that it was in fact less than one in ten thousand.[37]

In assessing the probability of reversal required to order a new election, it should be recalled that this probability will be less than 0.5 regardless of the number of invalid votes removed. Consequently, the critical probability must be some not insubstantial figure, but short of a preponderance of probabilities.[38]

A second reason for using a mathematical approach is to prevent resort to misleadingly simple rules of thumb. As the formula shows, the probability of reversal depends principally upon the size of the plurality and the number of irregularities (and less sensitively on the total vote). Its results cannot, however, be expressed as a simple relation between these variables. For example, if the plurality is small enough, a substantial probability of reversal will exist if the number of irregularities is twice the plurality; but if the plurality is large, irregularities four or five times larger may be insufficient to cast even a shadow of doubt on the results.[39] Thus, the rule used in some cases that a new election will be ordered when the number of ir-

---

[37]After a proportionate reduction in the number of irregularities to account for their distribution among candidates other than the first two (in accordance with the procedure stated in note 9 *supra*) the numbers in *Santucci* were

$$z = 95 \sqrt{\frac{116,057 - 448}{(116,057)\,(448)}} = 3.8.$$

On the other hand, a defensible decision was made in Posner v. Power, 18 N.Y.2d 703, 220 N.E.2d 269, 273 N.Y.S.2d 480 (1966), where the court found 370 to 412 irregularities in a four-candidate contest in which the plurality of the winner was 24 votes. Assuming 412 irregular votes and allocating a proportionate number of irregularities to the 2 last-place candidates, the probability of a reversal was 9 percent, which would seem sufficient to justify the court's affirmance of the order directing a new election.

[38]The Court of Appeals, probably unwittingly, has sometimes sounded as if it might apply such a preponderance test. See, e.g., Ippolito v. Power, 22 N.Y.2d 594, 597–98, 241 N.E.2d 232, 233, 294 N.Y.S. 2d 209, 211 (1968) (the irregularities "would not be sufficiently large in number to establish *the probability* that the result would be changed by a shift in, or invalidation of, the questioned votes.") (Emphasis supplied.)

[39]A plurality of five votes with twice as many irregularities might justify a new election since the probability of reversal could be approximately 5 percent. On the other hand, with a plurality of one hundred votes, even four times as many irregularities would not justify a new election since the probability of reversal would be less than one in a million.

regularities exceeds a certain multiple of the plurality is incorrect as a method of intuitive estimation and misleading as a method of analyzing the precedents.[40]

A third reason for using mathematical techniques is that uncertainty over intuitive estimates of probability tends to obscure significant legal issues that arise in certain cases. An examination of *Lowenstein* v. *Larkin*, in which the Appellate Division unanimously set aside Congressman John Rooney's primary victory over Allard Lowenstein,[41] and was affirmed on the opinion below by the Court of Appeals,[42] serves to illustrate this point.

In ordering a new election, the Appellate Division purported to apply the rule of Section 330 that the election was "characterized by such . . . irregularities as to render impossible a determination as to who rightfully was nominated." If the court meant by this that the invalid votes made the result uncertain, a judicial recall of the election was not supported by the facts recited in the court's opinion.

The court found that, among other instances of misconduct, due to errors by the Board of Elections, "hundreds of persons" were turned away from the polling places to which they had been assigned, and that others were improperly permitted to vote because challenges were ignored or because their registrations should have been canceled but were not. The exact impact of these mistakes evidently was unknown, the court being able to find only that "at least" 1,920 irregular votes were cast in the election, out of a total of 29,567.

The case was removed from the ordinary run by evidence of official favoritism for Rooney. Electioneering for Rooney at polling places and ignoring the challenges of Lowenstein poll watchers were among the practices the court found to have

[40]See, e.g., Santucci v. Power, 25 N.Y.2d 897, 252 N.E.2d 128, 304 N.Y.S.2d 593 (1969) (order directing a new election affirmed when irregularities were analyzed as being "at least six and one-half times the winning margin"); Posner v. Power, 18 N.Y.2d 703, 220 N.E.2d 269, 273 N.Y.2d 480 (1966) (order directing a new election affirmed when irregularities were analyzed as being "15 to 17 times the margin of winning votes"); Merola v. Power, 60 Misc. 2d 245, 248, 303 N.Y.S.2d 229, 232 (Sup. Ct.), *aff'd mem.*, 33 App. Div.2d 514 (1st Dep't 1969) (new election ordered and prior cases analyzed on the basis that the irregularities exceeded three times the plurality.

[41]40 App. Div.2d 604, 335 N.Y.S.2d 799 (2d Dep't 1972) (*mem.*).

[42]31 N.Y.2d 654, 288 N.E.2d 133, 336 N.Y.S.2d 249 (1972) (*mem.*).

tainted the election. There was, however, nothing in the circumstances cited in the court's opinion to suggest that those improperly permitted to vote favored Rooney, while those improperly excluded or inhibited from voting favored Lowenstein. On the court's findings, one could assume no more against Rooney than that the improper voters (and those inhibited or discouraged from voting) were a random sample of the total voting population.

The number of irregularities was large—at least 1,920 votes—and the court may have believed that this was sufficient to create a substantial probability of reversal, even on a random-sample basis. Rooney's plurality, however, was also large—890 votes—and the number of irregular votes required to generate even a small probability of reversal rises very rapidly with the winner's plurality, probably much more rapidly than most statistically uneducated persons would suppose. In fact, given this large plurality, it would have taken more than 27,000 irregularities to create even a 2 percent probability of a reversal. Lowenstein did not claim irregularities on anything approaching this scale.[43]

The mathematical demonstration illuminates the nature of the specific findings of fact or legal conclusions that would have been required to justify a new election. If the court relied on the traditional standard—an appreciable probability of reversal—it would have had to conclude that the mistakes of the Board or its officials were not in fact neutral but favored Rooney, while those improperly inhibited from voting favored Lowenstein. No such findings appear in the opinion, although the evidence might have justified this conclusion.

Alternatively, the court could have taken an enlarged view of Section 330, and held that serious irregularities in procedure by Board officials, particularly deviations favoring one candidate, constitute sufficient grounds for ordering a new elec-

---

[43]In Celler v. Larkin, 71 Misc.2d 17, 335 N.Y.S.2d 791 (Sup. Ct.), *aff'd mem.*, 40 App. Div.2d 603, 335 N.Y.S.2d 801 (2d Dep't), *aff'd mem.*, 31 N.Y.2d 658, 288 N.E.2d 135, 336 N.Y.S.2d 251 (1972), Elizabeth Holtzman won the Democratic primary for Congress by some 600 out of 30,000 votes. In the trial of Celler's challenge to her victory, an expert probabilist testified that Celler would have had to show more than 16,900 irregularities out of the 30,000 votes cast to create even a one-in-a-thousand chance of a reversal. (T. at 422–23.) The courts rejected the challenge.

tion, even in cases in which it could not be shown that such errors affected, or were likely to have affected, the outcome. Since Section 330 does not seem to read this broadly, and since a liberal reading should be "confined to the subject matters plainly enumerated therein,"[44] an extension of the section to cover such cases would be a significant development in the law meriting judicial discussion.[45]

Nothing of that sort appears in the opinion of the Appellate Division. Instead, its decision appears to rest on an undifferentiated mix of disapproval for official irregularities, and hazy or mistaken intuitive notions of probability. If the method of mathematical probability had been recognized in *Lowenstein*, the attention of the courts would have been focused on the legal issues which were critical in that case and which are likely to arise in future cases: whether there was sufficient evidence to reject the assumption of random distribution of the improper votes, and if not, whether official irregularities favoring one candidate, but without demonstrable effect on the result, are a permissible statutory ground for ordering a new election.

Appendix

GLOBAL ANALYSIS OF CHALLENGED ELECTIONS

Suppose the winning candidate A has a votes and the losing candidate B has b votes, with a greater than b. Of the total of $s = a + b$ votes, k are removed at random. Let x denote the number of these k votes which are for A. There will be a *reversal* if after the removal there are at least as many votes for B as for A, *i.e.*, if

$$a - x \leqq b - (k - x),$$

---

[44]*Matter of Hyer*, 187 Misc. 946, 948, 63 N.Y.S.2d 874, 876 (Sup. Ct. 1946).

[45]Perhaps the necessary interpretation could be made by leaning heavily on the word "rightfully" in Section 330. Arguably, the winner cannot claim to be rightfully selected in an election marred by serious breaches of the rules in his favor by officials charged with maintaining neutrality.

or

$$x = (a - b + k)/2. \tag{1}$$

In a random withdrawal of k balls from $s - a + b$ balls in an urn, the number x of A balls withdrawn is a random variable with a "hypergeometric" distribution (sampling without replacement from a finite population); the mean and variance of x are given by

$$E(x) = ka/s, \qquad \text{Var}(x) = kab(s - k)/s^2(s - 1).$$

The standardized random variable

$$z = (x - E(x))/\sqrt{\text{Var}(x)}$$

is then (replacing $s - 1$ by s for simplicity) given by the formula

$$z = \frac{sx - ka}{\sqrt{kab\left(1 - \dfrac{k}{s}\right)}}.$$

z has mean 0 and variance 1. The condition (1) for reversal in terms of z is that the numerator of z be greater than or equal to $s(a - b + k)/2 - ka = (s - k)(a - b)/2$; i.e., that z be greater than or equal to the constant

$$C = \frac{(a - b)\sqrt{(s(s - k))}}{2(kab)}.$$

Now, since $a + b = s$, $ab = s^2/4$, with approximate equality when a and b are nearly equal. In any case, we see that

$$C \gtreqqless (a - b)\sqrt{\frac{1}{k} - \frac{1}{s}}. \tag{2}$$

Since z is approximately normally distributed, *the probability of a reversal is about equal to the probability that a standard normal random variable z will exceed the constant given by the right-hand side of (2).*

ANALYSIS BY SUBDISTRICTS

If k votes are removed in the ith district, an elaboration of the global analysis shows that the condition for a reversal is that an approximately standard normal random variable z will exceed the constant

$$\frac{(a - b + k) - 2\left[\text{sum over } i \text{ of } \dfrac{k_i a_i}{a_i + b_i}\right]}{2 \text{ sq. rt.}\left[\text{sum over } i \text{ of } \dfrac{k_i a_i b_i}{a_i + b_i}\right]}$$

where again $k = [\text{sum over } i \text{ of } k_i] = $ total number of votes re-moved from the $a + b$ votes.

Chapter 5

ECONOMIC CONCENTRATION

SECTION 7 OF THE CLAYTON ACT prohibits mergers whose effect "may be substantially to lessen competition, or to tend to create a monopoly" in any line of commerce.[1] In applying this act, the Supreme Court has seemed to give judicial recognition to the economic view that "the relative size distribution of firms in particular markets is an important clue, often the single most important one, to the nature of the competitive process in them."[2] Both the Court and the Federal Trade Commission have come to rely increasingly on numerical measures of concentration in appraising the competitive character of an industry.[3] A standard for measuring economic concentration has thus emerged as a requirement of a rational antimerger policy.

[1]15 U.S.C. § 18 (1964).

[2]Statement of Carl Kaysen, *Hearings before the Subcommittee on Antitrust and Monopoly of the Senate Judiciary Committee*, 89th Cong., 1st Sess., pt. 2, at 543 (1965).

[3]The leading cases are: United States v. Pabst Brewing Co., 384 U.S. 901 (1966); United States v. Von's Grocery Co., 384 U.S. 270 (1966); United States v. Continental Can Co., 378 U.S. 441 (1964); United States v. Aluminum Co. of America, 377 U.S. 271 (1964); United States v. Philadelphia National Bank, 374 U.S. 321 (1963); Brown Shoe Co. v. United States, 370 U.S. 294 (1962).

The spectrum of firm sizes in an industry has also played a key role in government reports dealing with the merger problem and the level of competition. See, e.g., NINTH REPORT OF THE ATTORNEY GENERAL ON COMPETITION IN THE SYNTHETIC RUBBER INDUSTRY (1963); FTC, ECONOMIC INQUIRY

Measures of concentration are designed to reduce figures portraying the sizes of firms in a market into a single figure summarizing the degree of concentration of that market. This compression of data inevitably results in the loss of certain information. The nature and significance of the loss depend on the type of summary, and the purpose for which the measure is used. There is, consequently, little right or wrong in the abstract about a measure of concentration; its "correctness" depends entirely on its context.[4]

In Clayton Act merger cases, lawyers and judges have generally relied on a measure of economic concentration known as the concentration ratio. The structure of this ratio is so simple and intuitively appealing that there has never been a satisfactory analysis of its utility for resolving antitrust issues. This omission has become increasingly important as the Court has come to rely more heavily on economic statistics interpreted through concentration ratios. Other measures of concentration, however, have significantly different attributes, which may impel different results. In the absence of analysis, it cannot be assumed that the concentration ratio or any other measure will rightly serve the policies of the antimerger law.

This chapter examines various methods of measuring concentration for Clayton Act purposes. It is suggested that none of the methods now in use fulfills the requirements of the law, and that a new measure of economic concentration may express more accurately the relationship between market structure and competition that is crucial to the Clayton Act merger cases. I have called this an entropy measure of concentration because it formally resembles a measure of entropy—the degree of molecular disorder in a gas—used in a branch of physics known as the kinetic theory of gases. Perhaps this formal resemblance

---

INTO FOOD MARKETING, PART II, THE FROZEN FRUIT, JUICE AND VEGETABLE INDUSTRY (1962) and PART III, THE CANNED FRUIT, JUICE AND VEGETABLE INDUSTRY (1965); FTC, ECONOMIC REPORT ON MERGERS AND VERTICAL INTEGRATION IN THE CEMENT INDUSTRY (1966).

[4] If, for example, sizes of individual firms are expressed as percentages of market, a firm that has ten customers out of a market of one hundred, and a firm that has one hundred customers out of a market of one thousand, will both be labeled 10 percent firms. There is nothing wrong with this formulation if relative size in a market is the significant fact. The percentage measure is misleading only if absolute size is more important; if it is, the second firm should be treated as ten times larger than the first rather than as its equal.

reflects some underlying similarity between molecular and economic disorder. Here, the connection with physics is viewed only as a coincidence that furnishes a name. The justification of the measure presented here in no way depends on any deeper substantive connection.

I

A.

The measure of economic concentration most frequently used by lawyers and economists in the horizontal-merger cases is the concentration ratio. This is a percentage figure representing the aggregate market share of a given number of leading firms in an industry.[5] Thus, if the first two firms control, respectively, 30 and 10 percent of the market, the two-firm concentration ratio for that market is 40 percent. Economic trends and individual mergers have been assessed in terms of these ratios and by considering changes in the number of firms in the relevant lines of commerce. The concentration ratio most commonly used by economists is the aggregate market percentage of the top four firms, although concentration ratios based on different numbers of firms are not uncommon. For purposes of illustration, we employ a four-firm ratio.

The first observation about the concentration ratio is that the value of the four-firm ratio changes only when any of the four firms grows or declines relative to any firm in the industry outside the top four. The ratio does not reflect changes in the market shares of the four leading firms when their aggregate market share remains unchanged, or changes involving

---

[5]For studies involving the application of concentration ratios to various industries, see, e.g., U.S. BUREAU OF THE CENSUS, CONCENTRATION RATIOS IN MANUFACTURING INDUSTRIES (1963); Sheperd, *Trends of Concentration in American Manufacturing Industries, 1947–1958*, 46 REV. OF ECON. & STATISTICS 200 (1964) and articles cited therein at note 2. For a discussion of some of the limitations of concentration ratios and other measures, see NATIONAL BUREAU OF ECONOMIC RESEARCH, BUSINESS CONCENTRATION AND PRICE POLICY (1955); Adelman, *The Measurement of Industrial Concentration*, 33 REV. OF ECON. & STATISTICS 269 (1951).

the market share of the remaining firms when their aggregate market share remains unchanged. Yet these changes can be of considerable economic importance. Industries *A* and *B* may show the same ratio, even though in *A*, the top four firms are of equal size, while in *B*, one huge firms dominates the second. Similarly, the remaining market may be divided among few or many firms. The competitive behavior of firms in a market with eight equal firms, usually considered an oligopoly, will probably differ greatly from that in a market with a hundred firms, even if in both cases the first four firms have a 50 percent share.

An additional defect of the concentration ratio is the complete arbitrariness of the number of included firms. A gain by firm five at the expense of firm ten would not change a four-firm ratio but would be reflected if five firms were included. But there is no reason to suppose that the fate of firm four should be given full significance and that of firm five none. Whatever number of firms included in the concentration ratio, we are led to some such unreasonable hypothesis, since there is no argument by which any particular number of firms is to be preferred. Because it thus reflects only a limited, arbitrarily chosen class of size changes, the concentration ratio is a poor method for measuring trends in concentration.

The use of a concentration ratio to measure a single change in firm sizes resulting from an acquisition presents other difficulties. First, as the Court has used it, the ratio does not accurately reflect the decrease in competition resulting from an acquisition. To illustrate this assume a line of commerce with ten competing firms, each commanding 10 percent of the market. One firm turns predator and successively acquires the other nine. How should the significance of these acquisitions be measured? The Court has approached problems of this type by computing both the absolute increase (i.e., the number of percentage points added) and the percentage increase in the ratio. In the example, if the concentration ratio is defined by the percentage share of the predator firm, then every acquisition increases the ratio by the same absolute amount—ten percentage points—which becomes a smaller percentage increase of the ratio as the size of the leading firm grows. As a result of the first acquisition, the ratio increases from 10 to 20 percent, a 100 percent increase. When the predator firm acquires its last rival, the ratio increases from 90 to 100 percent, an increase of only 11 percent.

This result, however, is inconsistent with the likely effect of these acquisitions on competition. The first acquisition, which leaves eight competitors in the field, surely hurts competition less than the last, which eliminates the final competitor. The ratio test, in effect, rewards bigness: the larger the acquiring firm the smaller the percentage change resulting from an acquisition. Whatever the economic truth may be, it is clear that the change in the concentration ratio fails to give effect to the Court's teaching in several cases that the greater the degree of concentration, the smaller the permissible increase.[6]

A second basic difficulty arises in connection with the number of firms included in the ratio. When used to reflect the result of a single acquisition, the ratio must be computed from the aggregate market share of the acquiring firm and of the firms larger than it. The acquiring firm must be included, otherwise the ratio will not change as a result of the acquisition. Firms smaller than the acquiring firm must be excluded, or an acquisition by that firm will not be distinguishable from an acquisition by one of the included smaller firms.

As a result, the number of included firms must vary from case to case, making it impossible to use a predetermined

---

[6]In United States v. Philadelphia National Bank, 374 U.S. 321 (1963), the Court invalidated a merger of the second and third largest banks in the Philadelphia area. The defendants argued that there would be no increase in concentration if consideration were restricted to the first three banks before the merger. In purportedly answering this argument, the Court established, in a footnote, an important principle:

> If this argument were valid, then once a market had become unduly concentrated, further concentration would be legally privileged. On the contrary, if concentration is already great, the importance of preventing even slight increases in concentration and so preserving the possibility of eventual deconcentration is correspondingly great.

Id. at 365 n.42.

The footnote in *Philadelphia Bank* became the basis for decision in United States v. Aluminum Company of America, 377 U.S. 271, 279 (1964). In this case the Court invalidated the acquisition by Alcoa of the stock and assets of Rome Cable, a corporation which produced various wire and cable products and accessories. The Court determined that bare and insulated aluminum conductor was the relevant line of commerce. In this market Alcoa was the leader, with a market share of 27.8 percent, while Rome was ninth, with 1.3 percent. The Court found that in this market the first two companies controlled 50 percent of the market; the first five, 76 percent; and the first nine, 95.7 percent. It thus concluded that "the line of commerce showed highly concentrated markets, dominated by a few companies but served also by a small, though diminishing group of independents." The case was then decided on the authority of the *Philadelphia Bank* footnote.

number for measuring all acquisitions. Since comparisons cannot validly be drawn between concentration ratios based on differing numbers of firms, comparability of result is destroyed,
and with it the possibility of stare decisis.[7]

The lack of comparability may affect the issues considered
by a court. In the Alcoa case, for example, two lines of commerce were asserted by the Government—insulated aluminum
conductor and a wider line of insulated and bare aluminum conductor. In the insulated line, Alcoa was third with 11.6 percent
of market. Rome, the firm it acquired, held 4.7 percent. In the
wider line of aluminum conductor, Alcoa was first with 27.8
percent of market, while Rome held 1.3 percent. In which
proposed line of commerce was the merger more significant? In
the absence of a measure leading to comparable results for both
mergers, the Supreme Court rested its decision on the effect of
the acquisition in the wider line. The merger probably appeared worse in that setting, since it involved the leader of an
industry. The Court thus assumed that insulated and bare aluminum properly constituted a single line of commerce. As the
dissenters pointed out, this was a dubious proposition for which
there was no evidence in the record. In fact, the issue was irrelevant since the merger's anticompetitive effects were probably
more significant in the narrower than in the wider market.[8]

The concentration ratio thus has fundamental defects when

---

[7]To illustrate this, assume that the leading firm in an industry holds 50 percent of the market and acquires the second firm, which holds 25 percent. The
concentration ratio measured by the leading firm has increased from 50 to 75
percent. Now assume that the first two firms hold 25 and 25 percent, respectively, and the second firm acquires a third firm, which also holds 25 percent.
In this case the two-firm concentration ratio rises from 50 to 75 percent, just as
the single-firm concentration ratio did in the first case; yet the two mergers are
statistically very different.

[8]Comparisons were also important in United States v. Manufacturers
Hanover, 240 F.Supp. 867 (S.D.N.Y. 1965), where the Government claimed
that the merger between Manufacturers Trust Co. and The Hanover Bank
should be invalidated on the basis of the statistical evidence alone in light of
Philadelphia Bank. The Court had found in *Philadelphia Bank* that the merger would result in a signifcant increase in concentration. It based this
conclusion on the fact that before the merger the first and second banks controlled 44 percent of the market, and that if the merger were permitted, the
first and second banks (the merging banks being two and three) would control
59 percent of the market. "Plainly," the Court concluded, "we think this
increase of more than 33 percent in concentration must be regarded as significant." Since the merger in *Philadelphia Bank* involved the second and third
banks in the area, the concentration ratio could consist of the aggregate shares

used to measure either economic trends or the effects of a single horizontal merger. In measuring trends, its value depends on a narrow, arbitrarily chosen class of economic changes which of necessity tell only part of the story. In measuring the effects of a single acquisition, it either overstates their significance when the market is concentrated, or understates their significance when the market is not concentrated, or both. Moreover the results must be cast in terms of such limited comparability as virtually to destroy the usefulness of the measure as a unifying index of the significance of acquisitions.

B.

Similar problems appear in measuring the significance of vertical mergers. Vertical integration may be accomplished either permanently by merger or temporarily by contract. In the first case, legality under the Clayton Act turns on the applicability of Section 7, and in the second, on the applicability of Section 3, which prohibits exclusive arrangements, such as requirements contracts, where their result "may be to substantially lessen competition or tend to create a monopoly in any line of commerce."[9]

Although Sections 3 and 7 use similar language, their governing principles are not identical. Under Section 3, as a result of the *Standard Stations* decision,[10] a determination that

---

of not more than the first two banks. In *Manufacturers Hanover*, however, the merger was between banks five and eight in the New York City area. The concentration ratio for this market would necessarily include not less than five banks. Consequently a comparison of the statistics in these cases using a concentration ratio was not possible. Instead, the district court concluded that the merger in *Philadelphia Bank* was worse than in *Manufacturers Hanover* because the relative size of the merged banks was greater in the first case than in the second. While this comparison is relevant, it does not take into account significant information from the remainder of the market.

[9]15 U.S.C. § 14 (1964).

[10]Standard Oil Co. of California v. United States, 337 U.S. 293 (1949). The quantitative substantiality approach to vertical mergers was in evidence when the FTC announced that it would attack vertical acquisitions in the cement industry where the acquired company was a ready-mixed concrete firm ranked among the first four nonintegrated producers in any metropolitan market, or was a cement consumer purchasing 50,000 or more barrels of cement annually. FTC, *Commission Enforcement Policy with Respect to Vertical Mergers in the Cement Industry*, 1 TRADE REG. REP. ¶ 4510.

a requirements contract, for example, is likely to result in a substantial lessening of competition depends primarily on the degree of market foreclosure resulting from the contract. If foreclosure is quantitatively substantial, a violation of Section 3 would be established. In *Standard Stations*, the Court found requirements contracts, which foreclosed 6.7 percent of an extemely large market, illegal.

Regardless of differences in interpretation, the percentage of foreclosure is undoubtedly relevant in determining whether there has been a substantial lessening of competition, just as the combined percentage of market of the merging firms is relevant when horizontal mergers are considered. To the extent of the foreclosure, competitive firms are cut off from customers, and vice versa. But to determine whether the foreclosure has been substantial, a court must consider the degree of concentration (and foreclosure) in the remainder of the market, a factor which the percentage foreclosure test does not take into account. In the proposed Bethlehem-Youngstown merger, one vertical aspect of the case arose from the fact that Youngstown was an independent producer of rope wire, a product used in the manufacture of wire rope by Bethlehem among others. The threatened foreclosure was approximately 10 percent. In holding this substantial, the court, in *United States* v. *Bethlehem Steel Corp.*,[11] relied on the additional fact that there were only five other independent producers of rope wire. It found the percentage foreclosure significant in light of the high degree of concentration in the remainder of the market.

There is another disadvantage to the percentage foreclosure test. In justifying its conclusion in *Philadelphia Bank* that an increase of 33 percent in concentration was substantial, the Court cited *Standard Stations* and other vertical-integration cases in which the percentage foreclosure was less than 33 percent. The comparison, however, was misplaced. The percentage foreclosure test measures the degree to which the market has shrunk for the remaining competitive firms. The change in the concentration ratio measures the growth in the size of a firm. Although in both cases results may be expressed in percentage terms, they measure different things. Thus, a 5 percent foreclosure is not analogous to a 5 percent increase in a concen-

[11]168 F.Supp. 576, 611–13 (S.D.N.Y. 1958).

tration ratio. A lack of comparability thus appears inherent in tests dependent on concentration ratios, and between such tests and percentage foreclosure tests.

It may be argued that the failure of these measures to take account of economically significant facts may be remedied by considering those facts on a separate basis. For example, if concentration ratios do not reflect changes in the number of firms, those changes can be stated independently. But this does not solve the problem. If significant matters are considered separately, there is no way of deciding how their effects should be combined and, if conflicting in their impetus, how that conflict should be resolved.[12] The solution requires a unitary measure, one combining the effect of all relevant factors and expressing that result in a form useful for the economic judgments required of a court.

C.

Some lawyers and economists have suggested that a unitary measure could be created by pruning the statistical tree to a single branch. They have proposed that a merger should be deemed prima facie unlawful if the market shares of the merged firms exceed a given percentage.[13] Few commentators, howev-

[12]A conflict of factors was present in United States v. Von's Grocery Co., 384 U.S. 270 (1966), where the district court found that concentration had decreased because the aggregate percentage of the top firms had declined, while the Supreme Court concluded *au contraire* that concentration had increased because the number of firms had declined. *Id.* at 273 n.3. Neither court attempted to reach a conclusion based on a weighing of both sets of factors.

[13]See, e.g., Bork, *The Rule of Reason and the Per Se Concept: Price Fixing and Market Division II*, 75 YALE L.J. 377 (1966); KAYSEN & TURNER, ANTITRUST POLICY 133 (1959); Stigler, *Mergers and Preventive Antitrust Policy*, 104 U. PA. L. REV. 176 (1955). Professor Stigler, for example, would establish presumptions whereby mergers which create a firm with less than 5 to 10 percent of the market would be sanctioned, while mergers which create a firm with more than 20 percent would be disapproved. In-between, legality would turn on other factors. Stigler, *supra* at 182.

The Federal Trade Commission announced that mergers by retail food chains or voluntary and cooperative groups of food retailers which create an enterprise with a sales volume in excess of $500 million raised "sufficient question regarding their legal status to warrant attention and consideration by the Commission . . . ."The Commission added, however, that lesser mergers

er, have suggested that a merger that produces a firm with less than such a percentage should be conclusively valid. The more usual opinion holds that such cases demand an examination of all factors. This reservation severely limits the usefulness of the rules, since important cases frequently involve small percentages.[14]

The critical point in rules of this type is that they consign to irrelevance most of the factors which the Court has held important in deciding Clayton Act cases. They focus instead on a single element, the size of the merged firms. Consequently, whatever the percentage selected as the determining point of illegality, it is easy to construct examples illustrating the perversity of the result that would follow the faithful application of any such rule. And it is the coup de grâce for such proposals that they afforded no way of measuring the trends in concentration which have played such a large role in these cases.

---

could also pose a threat to competition, and that such a threat would be present whenever leaders who were direct competitors in metropolitan markets sought to merge. FTC, *Commission Enforcement Policy with Respect to Mergers in Food Distribution Industries*, 1 TRADE REG. REP. ¶4520.

[14]Two Supreme Court decisions are notable examples. In United States v. Von's Grocery Company, 384 U.S. 270 (1966), the Court held that the acquisition in 1960 by Von's Grocery Company of Shopping Bag Food Stores, both large retail supermarket chains in Los Angeles, violated Section 7. Even though after the merger Von's controlled only 7.5 percent of the Los Angeles grocery market, the Court concluded that the acquisition was illegal because both Von's and Shopping Bag were successful and expanding companies and because the relevant market, though not yet concentrated, was "characterized by a long and continuous trend toward fewer and fewer competitors." The Court cited facts showing that the number of single-store owners had declined and that the share of chains had increased as a result of acquisitions which were continuing at a rapid rate. This was, the Court felt, the very sort of trend Congress had declared "must be arrested."

In the second case, United States v. Pabst Brewing Company, 384 U.S. 901 (1966), the Court reversed a dismissal of the Government's action against the acquisition by Pabst Brewing Company of Blatz' Brewing Company, holding that the Government's evidence was "amply sufficient" to show a violation of Section 7. At the opening of 1958, the year of the merger, Pabst was the tenth largest brewer in the country, and Blatz the eighteenth. The acquisition made Pabst the fifth largest brewer, with 4.49 percent of total industry sales. By 1961, three years after the merger, Pabst's share of the national beer market was still only 5.83 percent.

Under a rule such as Stigler's, see note 13 *supra*, the Court would have approved the mergers in both Von's and Pabst, since the firms resulting from both mergers had less than 10 percent of the market.

Derek Bok of Harvard has proposed a more discriminating set of rules. He has suggested that the prohibitions of Section 7 be applied to any acquisition "resulting in an appreciable increase in the superiority of the leader's size over the margin of leadership which he enjoyed in the base period," and he has urged that any increase of more than a few percentage points should be viewed as "appreciable."[15] With respect to acquisitions by a firm other than the leader, Bok offers a rule based on the concentration ratio of up to eight firms. If this ratio shows an increase of more than 7 to 8 percentage points from a base period, the merger should be prohibited, because the industry has demonstrated a tendency to oligopoly, which the statute was designed to arrest.[16]

Apart from the arbitrary nature of the particular percentages chosen, the principal problem with this set of rules is that they do not depend on the degree of economic concentration in the industry. This is important, because the greater the concentration in a market, the smaller the legally permissible increase in the leader's share or that of any number of leading firms.

Bok's reliance on the aggregate market share of the leading firms (up to eight) involves the use of the familiar concentration ratio, and is subject to the objections already discussed. He attempts to meet at least one of these objections by claiming that changes in the number of firms should not be viewed as significant, since the presence of marginal firms has little effect on competition. Clearly the Court thinks otherwise—as evidenced by the stress placed on the total number of firms in an industry in the *Von's* and *Pabst* decisions.[17] There appears no legal justification for considering less than all the available information concerning the number and relative sizes of firms in a line of commerce. The failure of Bok's concentration ratio to take such facts into account is a shortcoming reflecting the general limitations of this class of measures.

[15]See Bok, *Section 7 of the Clayton Act and the Merging of Law and Economics*, 74 HARV. L. REV. 226, 308 (1960).

[16]*Id.* at 313.

[17]See note 14 *supra*. Of course, defendants are still free to prove if they can that disappearing firms were in fact marginal, and consequently not significant for competition.

D.

In studying the distribution of wealth in a population, economists have frequently used indices based on the average difference in wealth of its members. Differing functions have dressed this fundamental variable in various related fashions.[18]

The earliest method, developed by M. O. Lorenz in 1905, measures distribution of income in a population by plotting the cumulated percentage of wealth or income of that population.[19] The resulting Lorenz curve is a straight diagonal if the distribution is equal, and becomes more bowed as concentration increases.

The curve was given a more useful, numerical expression in 1912 by Corrado Gini. Gini proposed an index of concentration based on the ratio of the area between the Lorenz curve and the diagonal line of equal distribution divided by the total area under the diagonal.[20] Thus, as the distribution of firm sizes moves from equality to inequality, the ratio moves from zero to one. This ratio, called the Gini coefficient, is a function of the average difference of market shares of every possible pair of firms in the industry. It has been widely used by economists to measure what is commonly called relative concentration—the degree to which firm sizes differ.[21] But the Gini coefficient does not measure the degree of absolute concentration—the extent to which economic power has gravitated into a few hands. It is zero, whether an industry is divided among two or a hundred firms, so long as the division is equal. In general, the coefficient will not change as a result of a change in the number of firms so long as the same percentage of firms controls the same percent-

[18]The literature on this subject is collected in Singer, *The Structure of Industrial Concentration Indexes*, 10 ANTITRUST BULL. 75 (1965).

[19]Lorenz, *Methods of Measuring the Concentration of Wealth*, 70 AM. STATISTICAL ASSOC. J. 1 (1905).

[20]GINI, VARIABILIA E MUTABILIA 19 (1912).

[21]If there are three firms, A, B, and C, the Gini coefficient would be a function of the average of the differences $(A - B)$, $(A - C)$ and $(B - C)$. WOYTINSKY, EARNINGS AND SOCIAL SECURITY IN THE UNITED STATES 251 (1943). More precisely, the Gini coefficient is equal to the sum of the differences between every pair of firms divided by two times the number of pairs of firms and this divided by the mean firm size.

age of market. This feature severely limits its usefulness as a tool for administering the antitrust laws.[22]

In fact, any measure based on some average of the size differences between firms, while appropriate for measuring inequality of wealth, is unsuitable for measuring economic concentration. Since any such measure is based on differences in firm sizes, the entry or exit of a firm causes a dramatic change in value; the smaller the firm, the greater the change. This is misleading, because the presence or absence of a firm of negligible size does not significantly alter the degree of competition in the market. The difference is that in measuring the distribution of wealth we are concerned with the economic status of each individual, while in measuring competition we care only about the contribution of each firm to the level of competitive activity in the market as a whole. A firm which is too small to change this level should be ignored.

Other measures based on the sum of the squares of firm sizes have been proposed by Herfindahl and Niehans.[23] These indi-

---

[22]There is also no reason to suppose (although the fallacy is not apparent) that the Gini coefficient will correctly reflect changes in competition when the number of firms remains constant but their relative sizes change. The coefficient, for example, would treat a market of four firms with respectively 30 percent, 30 percent, 30 percent, 10 percent shares as having the same degree of concentration as a market whose four firms have 40 percent, 20 percent, 20 percent, 20 percent shares. While this may be a correct result, there is nothing in Gini's theory to support the conclusion that these markets will probably be equally competitive.

[23]Niehans, *An Index of the Size of Industrial Establishments*, 8 INT'L ECON. PAPERS 122 (1958); Herfindahl, Concentration in the Steel Industry, 1950 (Ph. D. dissertation, Columbia University).

More recently it has been suggested that the variance be used for appraising the degree of economic concentration. This standard measure of dispersion is defined as the sum of the squares of the deviations of items (e.g., percentages of market) from the arithmetic mean item (e.g., the arithmetic mean percentage) divided by the number of items (e.g., firms). It is apparent from this definition that the variance shares the limitations of the Gini coefficient. Like the Gini coefficient it does not measure absolute concentration, it changes dramatically with the appearance or disappearance of a small firm, and its measurement of relative concentration lacks any theoretical connection with the degree of competition.

For a discussion of the use of a variance which makes the use of the logarithms of the sizes of firms see Hart & Prais, *The Analysis of Business Concentration: A Statistical Approach*, 119 J. OF THE ROYAL STATISTICAL SOC'Y ser. A, pt. I at 150 (1956); Simon & Bonini, *The Size Distribution of Business*

ces are superior to those discussed earlier in that they reflect both relative and absolute concentration and are not dramatically affected by the entry or exit of a firm of negligible size. Nevertheless, they have other attributes that limit their usefulness for the law. Discussion of these problems, however, is best deferred until the development of the entropy measure.

II

In enacting the Celler-Kefauver amendment to Section 7 of the Clayton Act, Congress expressed concern with the social and political implications of concentration as well as with its economic effects. The relationship of bigness to the social and political ills which Congress sought to avoid is too generalized to lead to any particular measure of economic concentration. The relationship, however, between economic concentration and competition provides a more informative guide. The effort here will be to construct a measure as a function of the number and sizes of competing firms which reflects the minimum competitive effort firms will believe necessary to hold their customers.

It is a discouraging but inescapable fact that economic knowledge is not sufficiently advanced to enable us to predict the degree of competitive activity in a market even if all available economic evidence is considered. A fortiori, given information concerning solely the number and relative sizes of competing firms, one cannot say that such a market will be x times more competitive than another with a different spectrum of firms. Yet the law, which presents the test of a "substantial lessening" of competition, requires that some such comparison be made.

How may the legal requirements be met within the limits of economic knowledge? There is no mathematical answer to this question. But certainly the numbers should play no more than

---

Firms, 48 AM. ECON. REV. 607 (1958). The use of the log variance grew out of an effort to describe theoretically the basis of the distribution of firm sizes in a market—a problem which does not have to be solved for purposes of the antitrust laws.

the minimum role required by legal theory: they should formulate an economic statement which so reduces the scope of judgment as to determine the economic issue in the more extreme merger cases; in the closer cases, the formulation should permit the numbers to be used as an important element together with other evidence. In addition, these economic statements should be cast in a form that permits comparisons between cases for purposes of stare decisis.

To fulfill these requirements, a measure might be used that translates any market into a market deemed to have an equivalent level of competitive activity but consisting solely of firms enjoying equal shares of market. The effect of this translation is to reduce the problem of comparing markets with differing numbers of unequal firms to the narrower problem of comparing equal-firm markets. The significance of the difference between equal-firm markets is not determined by a translation measure. Thus a market found equivalent to one with eight equal firms is not necessarily twice as competitive as a market equivalent to one with four. In fact, the meaning of the difference may vary from case to case. In closer cases, therefore, where the precise significance of the difference may become important, additional economic evidence will be essential to any decision.

The entropy measure derived here is but one of a number of possible equal-firm translation measures of the type described. Three independent derivations of the entropy measure are shown and then some alternative translation measures are examined.

A.

In the discussion that follows, it is assumed that certain activities of a firm may be defined as competitive, and that it is valid to speak of the degree to which a firm engages in such activities. Economists have described competitive activities as those which are determined by the market. In a perfectly competitive market all activities would be determined in the sense that market conditions would dictate every move. Conversely, in a perfect monopoly, the controlling firm would have perfect freedom. The total of all competitive activities in a market may be thought of as the sum total of the competitive activities of each firm. If the firms in a market are all equal in size, each will contribute equally to the total. One may quarrel with these ideas, but the legal standard—"a substantial lessening of competition"—implies some conception of levels of competitive activity.

The foregoing conceptions can be expressed symbolically in the following way. If $f(n)$ is a function that describes the degree of competitive activity in a market consisting of n equal firms, then since all are equal, the contribution of each firm to $f(n)$ is $1/_n f(n)$. If, for example, there are four equal firms in a market, then

$$f(4) = 1/_4 f(4) + 1/_4 f(4) + 1/_4 f(4) + 1/_4 f(4).$$

We now make a far-reaching assumption: the minimum competitive effort a firm will undertake to retain its customers is a function solely of its percentage share of the market. Or, putting the same thought in a different way, the total competitive threat to a firm with a given percentage of market is constant no matter how the remaining market is divided. The underlying conception on which this assumption rests is that large firms constitute a proportionately greater threat than small firms, and therefore the total competitive danger from a few large firms is equivalent to the total competitive danger from a greater number of proportionately smaller firms. This is admittedly a speculative assumption, but one which is at least not inconsistent with economic knowledge and which need only be generally and not precisely true in order to be useful.

If this assumption is accepted, then the contribution each firm makes to the total degree of competitive activity will be equal to the contribution that firm would make in a market otherwise identical but composed solely of firms equal to it in size. Thus the contribution of a 50 percent firm in any market would be $1/_2 f(2)$, the contribution of a 20 percent firm would be $1/_5 f(5)$, and in general the contribution of a firm which controlled $1/n$th of a market would be $(1/n)f(n)$. Denoting the percentage share of the first firm by $1/n_1$, the percentage share of the second firm by $1/n_2$, etc., the total degree of competitive activity in the market is

$$1/n_1 f(n_1) + 1/n_2 f(n_2) \ldots 1/n_n f(n_n).$$

Two markets are equivalent if they have the same total competitive activity. Given a market, what is the equivalent equal-firm market? The entropy measure, denoted by C, is the number of firms in this equivalent market. It follows that

$$f(C) = 1/n_1 f(n_1) + 1/n_2 f(n_2) \ldots + 1/n_n f(n_n).$$

When all firms are equal in size then

$$f(C) = f(n).$$
$$C = n$$

We now consider the problem of determining $f(n)$. This is approached by examining the way $f(n)$ should change as the market (or a fixed percentage segment of it) becomes divided among a larger number of equal firms.

What can be said about the way $f(n)$ should increase as n increases? If a single firm controls an entire market, dividing it in two will obviously increase greatly the level of competitive activity, since there will be some competition where none existed before. The increase in value of $f(n)$ should be correspondingly great. But if there are one hundred equal firms dividing a market, the addition of a single firm will obviously be far less significant for competition; consequently the increase in $f(n)$ should be correspondingly smaller. These considerations lead to the general principle that as n grows larger $f(n)$ should increase, but at a diminishing rate.

An infinite number of functions share this characteristic, and economic theory or legal principle cannot be expected to determine a unique choice; arbitrary elements are inevitable in any conclusion.

The first decision is whether $f(n)$ should increase without bound as n increases or whether there should be some upper value for $f(n)$ beyond which it never rises no matter how large n becomes. In economic terms, the question is whether competition should be deemed to increase without limit as the number of firms increases. Or, stated differently, should small firms be viewed as significant contributors to competition? An affirmative answer is suggested by the fact that in both *Von's* and *Pabst,* the Court treated the disappearance of extremely small firms (those with less than .001 percent of market) as significant for competition. In view of this, and in the absence of compelling economics to the contrary, a tentative decision is justified in favor of functions which treat small firms as significant. Thus $f(n)$ should increase without bound (although at a diminishing rate) as n increases. The opposite decision on this issue leads to an alternative measure, which is considered in Part III.

There are two important classes of functions which increase without bound at a diminishing rate. These differ in the importance they assign to small firms. In the first class are the "fractional power functions," so called because n is raised to some fractional power between 0 and 1. Thus $f(n) = n^{a/b}$. Probably the most familiar function of this type is $f(n) = n^{1/2}$ which means that $f(n)$ is equal to the square root of the number of equal firms.

The fractional power functions assign great significance to small firms. To see this, consider the effect on $f(n)$ of doubling the number of firms in a market. A doubling yields the ratio $f(2n)/f(n) = 2^{a/b}$. The importance of this result is that $2^{a/b}$ is a constant independent of n. Thus if a fractional power function is used, doubling the number of firms will have the same proportional significance for competition regardless of the number of firms with which we started.

This result indicates that the fractional power functions probably overstate the significance of an increase in the number of firms. Doubling the number of firms in a market from one to two or from two to four should lead to a greater proportional increase in competition than doubling the number of firms from one thousand to two thousand. Generally it seems probable that a doubling in the number of firms should result in a diminishing proportional increase in $f(n)$ as n increases. Since the fractional power functions assign equal significance to all doublings, we reject this class of functions as candidates for $f(n)$.

The other class consists of the logarithmic functions.[24] The

---

[24]The base 10 is used for logarithms. This means that the logarithm is defined as the power to which 10 must be raised to give the original number. In symbols, $10^{\log n} = n$. Thus, $10^2 = 100$; log $100 = 2$. $10^3 = 1000$; log $1000 = 3$. $10^1 = 10$. $10^{1.7} = 50$; log $50 = 1.7$. The last pair of equations is not exact. $10^{1.7}$ is really a trifle more than 50, and $10^{1.699}$ is closer to 50 than either $10^{1.700}$ or $10^{1.698}$. Therefore, log $50 = 1.699$, to three decimals. Tables are available giving the logarithm of any number to five decimals, but there is no advantage in the calculations which follow here to using logarithms with more than three decimals.

Certain properties of the logarithm should be kept in mind in the discus-

simplest of these is $f(n) = \log n$, which means that $f(n)$ is simply equal to the logarithm of the number of equal firms. The logarithmic functions assign less significance to an increase in the number of firms than the fractional power functions. For example, if $\log n$ is used, doubling the number of firms yields the ratio $(\log n + \log 2)/\log n$. As n increases this ratio approaches 1, which is consistent with the idea that a doubling becomes of diminished proportional significance as the number of firms increases. It is for this reason that we make a tentative choice in favor of the logarithmic functions. This choice will in many cases favor the defendants, since it assumes a slow reduction in competitive activity as the number of firms declines.[25] The problem of deciding which logarithmic function to use remains unsolved, since there are others more complex than $\log n$, such as $\log \log n$ and $(\log n)^2$, which also satisfy our requirements. But it is not at all clear which, if any, more complicated logarithmic function would be justified, and the simplicity of $\log n$ commends it as at least a leading candidate for $f(n)$. We shall see later that there are independent reasons for this choice.

Combining this result with the prior result yields the following:

$$\log C = 1/n_1 \log n_1 + 1/n_2 \log n_2$$
$$+ 1/n_3 \log n_3 \ldots + 1/n_n \log n_n$$

$$\log C = \log(n_1^{1/n_1} n_2^{1/n_2} n_3^{1/n_3} \ldots n_n^{1/n_n})$$

$$C = n_1^{1/n_1} n_2^{1/n_2} n_3^{1/n_3} \ldots n_n^{1/n_n}.$$

This expression for C is the entropy measure of concentration.

Before examining the characteristics of the entropy measure, there is some insight to be gained by considering again, in an entirely different way, the problem of measuring competition in terms of the number and sizes of firms.

---

sion which follows. First, the larger the number, the larger the logarithm. Second, as n increases, its logarithm increases more and more slowly, so that n may become very large while $\log n$ remains quite small. Thus if $n = 1,000,000$, $\log n$ is still only 6. Third, the sum of the logs of two numbers is equal to the log of their product.

[25] For a discussion of the difference in rate of increase between the logarithmic and power functions, see 1 COURANT, DIFFERENTIAL AND INTEGRAL CALCULUS 190–93 (1937).

B.

The fear of losing customers, or the hope of gaining them, is a principal motivation for competitive behavior. Where the expectation of customer change is high, firms tend to engage in those activities which are called competitive. Assuming generally rational management of firms, these expectations ought to be related to the probabilities that such customer transfers will occur. A mathematical depiction of these probabilities which takes into account all relevant factors is of course vastly beyond the reach of present econometrical and mathematical sciences. The Supreme Court, however, by focusing on the number and sizes of firms, has already suggested the limits of our inquiry. It would be consistent with the bounds of legal relevancy to derive a mathematical expression which describes, at least in a general way, the probabilities of gaining or losing customers as a function of the number and sizes of firms in a market. This suggests that the probability of customer loss (or gain) measured on this basis could be used as a measure of competition.[26]

It is a basic theorem of mathematical probability that the chance of the occurrence of an event which can happen with equal probability in different ways is equal to the probability of its happening in one way times the number of ways in which it can occur. The more such ways, the more likely the occurrence. The probability of tossing heads with a coin on both of two attempts is half the probability of tossing heads only once in two trials because the first can occur in only one way (heads on both tosses), while the second can occur in two ways (heads on either the first or second toss).

A similar principle can be applied to firms and customers. If there are only two competing firms in an industry and only two customers, one for each firm, each firm can lose a customer in only one way, and that is by transfer of its customer to the other firm. On the other hand, as the number of firms and customers increases, the number of different ways customers can move about also increases. If other things are equal, it seems reason-

[26]The use of methods drawn from the mathematical theory of probabilities is not unknown in connection with the analysis of measures of concentration. See, e.g., Statement of Professor Leonard W. Weiss, *Hearings Before the Subcommittee on Antitrust and Monopoly of the Senate Judiciary Committee,* 89th Cong., 1st Sess., pt. 2, at 728 (1965).

able to assign a greater probability of customer transfer to a market where such changes can occur in a larger number of ways. This suggests that competition be measured as a function of the number of possible customer transfers.[27]

A customer transfer can be defined most generally as a transfer of any number of customers from any number of firms to any number of firms. A transfer might involve all or part of a single customer's business and two firms or many customers and firms. Not all transfers are equally probable. The loss by the leading firm of all its customers is a possibility too remote to influence behavior. On the other hand, transfers that result in not more than minor changes in firm standing are much more probable. If there is some degree of market share stability it is arguable that the most probable transfers will be permutations—i.e., those transfers which leave market shares unchanged. An exchange of customers by two firms would be a permutation if each firm gained the same number of customers it lost (within some selected period of time). Since permutations are highly probable, we propose to use the class of permutations as representative of the entire class of transfers. In relying on the class of permutations, we are in effect using the number of ways a market can be churned around within a given spectrum of firm sizes. It is our premise that the greater the number of such ways, the greater the possibility of competitive behavior.

Obviously the validity of this derivation depends upon the assumption that customers (or separable units in which purchases are made) are either roughly equal in size, or, if different in size, are randomly distributed among all firms. While this will not always be true, it will be approximately true in a sufficient number of instances—e.g., all retail-store cases—to warrant the derivation.

In deriving the formula we begin with a simple example. Assume a market with only two firms and four customers. In the first situation firm *A* has three of the customers and firm *B* has the fourth. How many different permutations of customers are there that will preserve the three-to-one ratio? The answer is four—the one with which we started and the three resulting

[27]Evidence of customer transfer has been introduced in the merger cases. See, e.g., Brief for Appellees at 65, United States v. Aluminum Co. of America, 377 U.S. 271 (1964).

from the exchange by firm A of any one of its customers with firm B's single customer. Suppose now the customers are split evenly between A and B. The number of possible permutations is then six: the one with which we started and five additional permutations resulting from the exchange by firm A of both its customers with both of firm B's customers; or the exchange by firm A of each of its customers with one or the other of B's customers. The number of permutations thus rises as the market becomes more evenly divided. This is what one would expect if the number of permutations were a valid measure of the degree of competitive activity.

In the more general case, if there are n firms in an industry and the first firm has a_1 customers, the second firm a_2 customers, etc., the problem is to determine how many different ways these customers may be distributed among all the firms in the market. If the customers of the firms are arranged in a line, the customer of firm a_1 first, firm a_2 second, and so on, the question becomes: how many different ways can one arrange the customers in the line? The answer is, by a well-known formula, that if there are N distinguishable customers, the number of different arrangements is the product $(N)(N-1)(N-2)\ldots(1)$ which is designated with the symbol $N!$ ("N factorial"). Since the total number of customers in our example is $a_1 + a_2 + a_3 \ldots + a_n$, the number of different permutations is $(a_1 + a_2 + a_3 \ldots + a_n)!$ Not all these permutations "count," however. Those involving solely a permutation of the customers of a single firm are irrelevant. For each firm the number of such permutations is (by the same formula) $a!$ Consequently, the total number of permutations (*Perm*) involving intercompany exchanges is[28]

$$Perm = \frac{(a_1 + a_2 + a_3 \ldots + a_n)!}{a_1!\, a_2!\, a_3!\ldots a_n!}.$$

The number of permutations is thus a function both of the total number of customers in a market and their distribution among the competing firms. In most cases involving horizontal mergers the number of customers is extremely large, so large in fact that the effect on the degree of competition of a change in the number of customers is usually ignored. The only changes

---

[28]Derivations of $N!$ and this expression appear in HOEL, INTRODUCTION TO STATISTICS 17 (1965); see also p. 34 *supra*.

considered are those involving the number and relative sizes of firms. The measure should then be cast in terms which permit us to reflect either of these changes without also reflecting changes in the total number of customers. In addition, the number of permutations must be converted into the form of a translation into equal-firm markets.

To accomplish both these purposes let N equal the total number of customers, $1/n_1$ the fractional share of the first firm, $1/n_2$ the fractional share of the second firm, and so forth. Since $a_1 + a_2 + a_3 + \cdots + a_n = N$, and $N/n_1 = a_1$, etc., the expression previously derived becomes by substitution

$$Perm = \frac{N!}{(N/n_1)! \, (N/n_2)! \, (N/n_3)! \ldots (N/n_n)!}.$$

When N (or any other number for that matter) is large, there is an approximation for its factorial known as Stirling's approximation, which is[29]

$$N! \approx \frac{N^N}{e^N}.$$

Substituting this approximation for the factorial in the expression for *Perm* above and simplifying the result yields

$$Perm \approx [n_1^{1/n_i} n_2^{1/n_2} n_3^{1/n_3} \ldots n_n^{1/n_n}]^N.$$

If all firms are equal, then

$$Perm \approx n^N.$$

The number of permutations is thus a function both of the n_i and N. To eliminate this dependence on N and to set our measure equal to n for equal firm markets we let $Perm = P^N$. We then have

$$P^N \approx [n_1^{1/n_1} n_2^{1/n_2} n_3^{1/n_3} \ldots n_n^{1/nn}]^N$$

$$P \approx n_1^{1/n_1} n_2^{1/n_2} n_3^{1/n_3} \ldots n_n^{1/n}n.$$

This meets our requirements. P is dependent solely on the number and relative sizes of firms and is equal to n when all

---

[29]A derivation of Stirling's approximation appears in COURANT, *op. cit. supra* note 25 at 361.

firms are equal in size.[30] Comparing the right hand of the above
expression with the expression previously obtained for C gives
the result that the "permutations measure" which satisfies
these requirements is identical to the "competitive activities"
measure previously derived: $P = C$.

C.

There is a third, perhaps deeper approach to these problems
of measurement. Consider again the stability of customer-firm
allegiances, but this time to determine the probability that,
given a particular distribution of customers among firms, no
firm will lose a customer to any other.[31]

It is assumed that there is a probability that a firm in a
market will not lose a particular customer; this probability may
be denoted as q. If this firm has a customers, and if we assume
further that customers come and go independently, then the
total probability that this firm will not lose any customers is q^a.
Similarly, the probability $(Prob)$ that no firm in the market will
lose any customers is

$$Prob = q_1^{a_1}\, q_2^{a_2}\, q_3^{a_3} \ldots q_n^{a_n}.$$

What are the probabilities q_i? Assume for a moment that the
values q_i are given and we wish to determine what distribution
of numbers of customers among the firms is most likely to be observed. It can be shown, using calculus, that the most likely distribution occurs when the a_i are such that $q_i = a_i/N$ where N is
the total number of customers. In other words, the most likely
distribution is that in which each firm has the same fraction of
the total number of customers as its probability of holding a
single customer. This is not unreasonable. If, for example, a
firm has a 50 percent chance of holding each customer, that firm
is most likely to hold 50 percent of the total number of customers.

[30]The entire chain of this manipulation, involving permutations, factorials,
Stirling's formula, and the elimination of the exponent N, is directly analogous
to the fundamental argument in the statistical theory of gases. Mathematical
details may be found in the introductory chapters of any textbook on statistical
mechanics. See, e.g., TER HAAR, ELEMENTS OF STATISTICAL MECHANICS 22
(1954).

[31]The argument here is also analogous to an argument used in the statistical theory of gases. See TER HAAR, *op. cit. supra* note 30.

In our problem the q_i are not known but the a_i are. Since we have found that the most likely distribution occurs when the a_i are proportional to the q_i, it follows that if the a_i are given, the most likely situation is that the q_i will be proportional to the given a_i. Thus, $q_i = a_i/N$.

Let $1/n_1$ be the fraction of the market held by the first firm, etc. Then $a_1 = N/n_1$, etc., as before, and q_1, etc., $= 1/n_1$, etc., by virtue of the argument given above. Substituting these terms in the expression for *Prob* above, we have

$$Prob = [(1/n_1)^{1/n_1}(1/n_2)^{1/n_2}(1/n_3)^{1/n_3} \ldots (1/n_n)^{1/n_n}]^N$$

$$= \frac{1}{[n_1^{1/n_1} n_2^{1/n_2} n_3^{1/n_3} \ldots n_n^{1/n_n}]^N}.$$

The smaller the probability that no customer will shift firm allegiance, the greater the level of competitive activity. Thus, as *Prob* decreases, competition should increase. This suggests that the "probabilities" measure of concentration, which we denote as Q, should be constructed from the inverse of *Prob*, so that Q will increase with increasing competition. At the same time, for reasons already discussed in connection with the permutations derivation, we take the *N*th root to eliminate the variable of the number of customers. Thus,

$$Q = (1/Prob)^{1/N}$$
$$= n_1^{1/n_1} n_2^{1/n_2} n_3^{1/n_3} \ldots n_n^{1/n_n}.$$

The probabilities derivation thus leads to the same result as the competitive activities and permutations derivations.

Although economic theory is not adequate to establish the validity of any measure beyond question, theoretical arguments can lend plausibility to our choices; it is for this reason that we have given three different theoretical derivations for the entropy measure. We now consider whether the entropy measure leads to any probably wrong results such as we found in examining the concentration ratio and other measures.

D.

In order to demonstrate the characteristics of the entropy measure as applied to horizontal mergers, consider the same type of problem discussed earlier for the concentration ratios—the successive acquisition by a predator firm of its competitors. Imagine a market with one hundred equal firms. C for this market is 100. After the predator has acquired five firms, there are ninety-five left: the predator with 6 percent and ninety-four others with 1 percent each. For this market $C = 89.8$. When the next five firms are acquired, leaving a market with 90 firms, the predator has 11 percent of the market and there are eighty-nine others with 1 percent each: $C = 76.8$. The absolute decline in C as a result of the first five acquisitions was 10.2; its absolute decline after the second five acquisitions was 13.0. Since the numbers of firms were reduced, there was an even larger percentage decline. As the process continues, the absolute decline caused by the acquisition of five firms diminishes, because monopoly conditions are being approached, but the percentage decline continues to grow. Thus, when the predator firm controls 51 percent of the market, $C = 13.5$, and when it controls 56 percent, $C = 10.5$. This is an absolute decline of only 3.0 but a percentage decline of about 29 percent. These results seem more closely related to the probable changes in competition than the changes in the concentration ratio which, it may be recalled, showed identical absolute increases and diminished percentage increases as the process continued.

The entropy measure declines as the result of an acquisition because the market shares of the merging firms are combined into a single firm. If two 10 percent firms merge, their contribution to $f(C)$ declines from 2/10 log10 to 1/5 log5. Since log5 is less than log10, we have in effect said that the total competitive activity of two 10 percent firms is greater than the total of such activity on the part of a single 20 percent firm. This method of registering a change in competition resulting from a merger indicates that there is no problem here of comparability or of uniqueness of results such as we faced in dealing with concentration ratios. The effect of every horizontal merger is measured in exactly the same way, and each possible combination of percentages of the merging firms yields a quantitative reduction in the measure. The so-called "defensive merger" which improves competition is thus not recognized but must be proved as a special case. This seems consistent with judicial treatment of this defense.[32]

[32]United States v. Bethlehem Steel Corp., 168 F. Supp. 576 (S.D.N.Y. 1958).

As applied to trends in horizontal concentration, the entropy measure avoids the arbitrary determinations which characterized the concentration ratios. It takes into account both the number of firms and the percentages of market held by each firm; none are excluded from consideration. The result is that if the leading firms hold a given total percentage of market and the number of firms dividing the remainder increases, the measure will not remain fixed, as is the case with the concentration ratio, but will increase, reflecting the more competitive situation.

In extreme cases this leads to results which may at first seem paradoxical. Assume, for example, a market divided between a 90 percent and a 10 percent firm. The contribution of the 10 percent firm to the measure $f(C)$ is $1/10 \log 10$. If the 10 percent firm divides into two 5 percent firms, the total contribution of the 5 percent firms becomes $1/10 \log 20$. Repeating the splitting process so that four firms share $1/10$ of the market raises the total contribution of the four firms to $1/10 \log 40$. In general, if n firms account for $1/10$th of the market, their contribution to $f(C)$ is $1/10 \log 10n$. As n increases, the value of this expression increases without limit and, as a result, so does the value of $f(C)$. Thus, even in a market dominated by a 90 percent firm, the entropy measure may still show a highly competitive market provided the remaining 10 percent is divided among a sufficiently large number of firms.

Is this a paradoxical result? At first thought it may seem so, since it can be argued that a market dominated by a 90 percent firm should never be treated as highly competitive. This is probably true, but the reason it is so depends on a factual assumption: a firm with less than 1 percent of market cannot be an effective competitive force, and consequently a large group of firms whose share aggregates less than 10 percent cannot be effective competitors to a 90 percent firm, no matter how large their number. But if very small firms were in fact significant

[33]In the case depicted in the example it may be argued that a single 10 percent firm might be more willing to take on a 90 percent leader than would a 1 percent firm. If this were so, it could be argued that there would be less competition, not more, if the 10 percent firm were split into ten 1 percent firms. But this point of view overlooks the existence of competition among the small firms and is most likely to be true with respect to competition with the leading firm in pathological markets of the type illustrated by the example. For these reasons this possibility is treated as an exception to the measure, rather than one of its attributes.

competitors—at least among themselves—there seems no
reason to disregard their contribution to the total degree of competitive activity. Thus there is reason to believe that an increase
in their number should indeed increase the total of competitive
behavior. The theoretical issue then is not whether small firms
should be taken into account but what weight should be given
to them.

It is worthwhile noting that in practical examples the entropy measure does not give impossible results. In the 90 percent–10 percent example, if one firm controls 10 percent then
$C = 1.15$. If the 10 percent firm is split up into 1,000 equal
firms, C rises only to approximately 2.5. To bring C up to 5, these
1,000 firms would have to become one million; to bring C up to
10, they would have to become 10 billion.

The relative insensitivity of C to the presence of very small
firms makes the decision about which marginal firms to include
less important than when other measures are used.[34] Nevertheless, other examples might be cited (the facts in *Von's* perhaps
present one of them) where the value of the measure turns on
the contribution of large numbers of extremely small firms. In
such cases it may be argued that the contribution to the total
level of competitive activity of these small firms should be
given even less importance than their size would indicate, and
that the entropy measure overestimates their significance by
giving them any weight at all.

It is important to recognize that such a cutoff would introduce an entirely new principle. The contributions of large
firms would still be taken seriously, but the contributions of
small firms would be regarded as irrelevant, however much
they struggled for a share of the market. It is obviously very difficult to make the judgment this requires. The critical size
would probably have to depend on the nature of the market,
and its determination would present problems. These difficulties suggest that the issue of effectiveness of competitive activity must be determined as a factor separate from the entropy
measure. The next section considers briefly a measure that
avoids an arbitrary cutoff by treating the competitive activity of
small firms as less significant than large ones, thus providing a
"smooth" limit to the contribution of smaller firms.

[34]This problem and the not very satisfactory solution of "truncated" indexes is discussed in Singer, *supra* note 18 at 86.

In applying the entropy measure to vertical integrations (either by contract or merger) it is useful to consider the factor $1/n$ as representing the extent of competitive activities of the firm in question and $\log(n)$ as representing the intensity or degree of such activities. Thus, for a firm which controls half the customers in a market, $1/2$ represents the proportion of customers affected by its competitive activities and $\log(2)$ represents the intensity or rate of such activities.

To the extent that a firm absorbs its customers by merger or ties them with requirements contracts, competing firms find a segment of the market shut off from them. Thus, if a firm controlling half a market acquires half its customers, the firm's segment of market still open to competitors would decline from one half to one fourth. To reflect this closure, when vertical mergers or requirements contracts are involved, the factor $1/n$ should represent the proportion of the firm's *free* customers to the total number of customers in the market, while the factor $\log n$ continues to represent the degree or rate of competitive activity of the tying firm. (Since $1/n$ and $\log n$ may now vary independently, it is no longer technically correct to write them both in terms of n, because this implies a false relation between them. We continue to do so for convenience.

A reduction in the proportion of the market which remains free is not, however, the only anticompetitive consequence of vertical integration. Another possibility is that as a firm ties its customers and assures itself a market vis-à-vis these customers, the impetus for competitive activity in the free sector should diminish. Thus, when applying the entropy measure to vertical integrations, $\log n$ should be replaced by a function that decreases in value as integration increases. But what are the limits to the decrease? When a firm ties all its customers, should it be viewed as engaging in no competitive activities, and thus have the replacement function equal zero? Factually, of course, this would not be true, since most "customers" in these vertical acquisitions are distributors or processors who must compete with distributors or processors of other firms. Even a firm which has tied all of its distributor-customers must still act competitively if they are to receive goods which can compete in the market. The level of that activity will depend on a variety of factors relating to the imperfections of the market on the distributor level.

These uncertainties deepen if a specification is sought of the full shape of the curve by which the replacement function should diminish as vertical integration increases. In most situations, firms fight hard even for the last percentage points of market. For this reason, the decline in the replacement function should be negligible until a very large percentage of the market is tied. Since most integrations are not even substantially complete, and since it is difficult to postulate how the replacement function should decrease, this effect is ignored. It is thus assumed that a firm which engages in a vertical-integration program will not change its level of competitive activities, —although the entropy measure will decline, because, in appropriate cases, the effect of such activities will reach only the free customers. In considering vertical mergers, the two factors $1/n$ and $\log n$ are derived from two different values of n. In evaluating $1/n$ the market share of the firm is limited to its free customers; in evaluating $\log n$, all a firm's customers are included.

This conception is also consistent with the probability measure Q. A customer who is tied to a firm has probability 1 of not transferring to another firm. To the extent customers are tied, Q is changed proportionately in the way indicated.

Vertical integration always produces a decline in the entropy measure. If there are nine equal firms in a market and one firm ties half its customers, the measure declines from 9 to approximately 8.7. If one firm ties all its customers, the measure declines from 9 to 8.5. This is greater than C for an eight-firm market, a result consistent with the fact that the remaining firms would engage in a higher level of competitive activity to prevent depredations by the firm whose customers are completely tied. If each firm ties half its customers, the measure declines from 9 to 3. This may seem a large change, but it should be recalled that integration this extensive would be extremely unusual and that the percentage foreclosure test used by the Court would itself show at least a 50 percent reduction on these facts.

III

Two important assumptions made in deriving the entropy measure were that (1) the level of a firm's competitive activity is a function solely of its size, leading to the form of $f(c)$ as a sum, and (2) small firms should count in the sense that the measure should show an increase without limit (although at a decreasing rate) as the number of such firms increased, leading to the choice of log n. There was support for these assumptions because the same results were also produced by independent derivations. And the second assumption appeared to be necessary because of the difficulties in determining a cut-off point after which firms of less than a certain size would no longer be deemed to contribute to competition. However, the considerations which led to and support these choices do not eliminate other possibilities, and it is therefore worthwhile to consider briefly alternatives to each of these assumptions.

An alternative to the first is to assume that the level of a firm's competitive activity is determined not by its size, independent of the market, but by its place in the market independent of its size. The simplest way of doing this is to replace $f(n)$ by the rank of the firm in question. The largest firm occupies rank 1, the next, rank 2, and so forth. Two firms of equal size must nonetheless be assigned successive ranks. The rank of each firm is multiplied by its percentage share of market and the products added, as in the entropy measure. The grand total is then doubled and 1 is subtracted to obtain L, the ordinal measure of concentration. The purpose of the doubling and subtraction is to establish that if all firms are equal and there are n firms, then $L = n$, as in the case of the entropy measure.

Thus, if there are five equal firms, their ranks, market shares, and ordinal products are as listed in Table 7.

TABLE 7

Rank	Share	Ordinal Product
1	0.20	0.20
2	0.20	0.40
3	0.20	0.60
4	0.20	0.80
5	0.20	1.00
		3.00

$L = 3.00 \times 2 - 1 = 5$

TABLE 8

Rank	Share	Ordinal Product
1	0.40	0.40
2	0.20	0.40
3	0.20	0.60
4	0.20	0.80
		2.20

$$L = 2.20 \times 2 - 1 = 3.4$$

If two of these firms merge, the results are as listed in Table 8.

Algebraic calculation shows that the ordinal measure is closely related to the Lorenz curve. In fact, L is just twice the area under the curve when the vertical scale is relative and the horizontal scale absolute. That is, the total height of the graph is taken as one unit, regardless of the actual market size, but the total width is taken as equal to the number of firms, so that each firm contributes one unit of width.[35]

If G is the value of the Gini coefficient measured in the usual way and n the number of firms, then $L = (1 - G)n$. If one wishes to base a measure of economic concentration on the Lorenz curve, then L rather than G is the appropriate measure. L measures both absolute and relative concentration (G measures only changes in relative concentration), and in addition has the desirable property of changing only slightly as a result of the appearance or disappearance of an extremely small firm (whereas G changes dramatically).

Although the ordinal measure is a better index of market concentration than the Gini coefficient, there is no reason to prefer it to the entropy measure, and there are some important reasons not to. First, the entropy measure may be supported by

---

[35]The area under the Lorenz curve can be divided into horizontal slabs, each bounded on the left by a diagonal element of the curve. If the firm that corresponds to this diagonal element has a rank a and market share x, then the slab has vertical thickness x and horizontal length varying from a to $a - 1$ at the top. Therefore, the area of the slab is $(a - \frac{1}{2})x$. The total area under the graph is

$$\sum (a - \frac{1}{2})x = \sum ax - \frac{1}{2}\sum x = \sum ax - \frac{1}{2}.$$

Twice the area is $2 \sum (ax) - 1$, which by definition is equal to L.

the theoretical arguments given; there are no such arguments to sustain the ordinal measure. The only possible theoretical justification for the ordinal measure may be that it is related to the Lorenz curve familiar to economists. Second, although the ordinal measure may seem easier to compute than the entropy measure, since the rank of a firm is more easily found than the logarithm of its size, it is actually more difficult. For the labor of multiplication in computing C can be circumvented by using a ready-made table of $1/n \log (n)$, whereas no ready-made table for computing L is possible, since each firm's contribution depends on two quantities—its rank and size—which can vary separately. Third, the ordinal measure appears to give excessive weight to small firms. In the 90 percent—10 percent example given earlier $L = 1.10$ when the 10 percent firm is undivided; $L = 6.00$ when the 10 percent firm splits into 99 equal firms; and $L = 51.0$ when these 99 become 999. According to the ordinal measure, it is thus possible to have a low degree of concentration in a market dominated by a 90 percent firm. As we have seen, this is not practically possible if the entropy measure is used.

In the second assumption, the degree of competition increases without limit as the number of small firms increases. An alternative to this is a measure which never increases beyond a fixed limit, no matter how large n becomes for a segment of the market. The simplest such function which satisfies the requirement $f(1) = 0$ and which also increases at a decreasing rate as n increases is

$$f(n) - 1 - 1/n.$$

This function leads to the remainder measure, so called because the function $f(n)$ for each firm is the fraction of the market which it does *not* control. Denoting this measure by R, we have

$$f(R) = \sum 1/n f(n)$$
$$= \sum 1/n(1 - 1/n)$$
$$= \sum (1/n - 1/n^2).$$

Since $\sum 1/n = 1$, this yields

$$f(R) = 1 - \sum 1/n^2.$$

Since $f(n) = 1 - 1/n$, then $f(R) = 1 - 1/R$. Substituting in the expression for $f(R)$, we have

$$1 - 1/R = 1 - \sum 1/n^2$$
$$1/R = \sum 1/n^2.$$

R is thus easy to compute. If all the firms are equal, then $1/R = (n)(1/n^2) = 1/n$, or $R = n$, as we required. If there are four firms in the market of the sizes 40 percent, 20 percent, 20 percent, 20 percent, then $1/R = 0.40^2 + 0.20^2 + 0.20^2 + 0.20^2 = 0.28$; $R = 3.57$. (This may be compared with $C = 3.78$ and $L = 3.40$.)

Returning to the small-firm problem, which was the reason for considering R, in the 90 percent—10 percent example considered earlier, $R = 1/0.82 = 1.22$ if there are only two firms. If the 10 percent firm is split up into many small firms, R never grows larger than $1/0.81 = 1.23$, no matter how many small firms there are. R is thus extremely insensitive to small firms. This is a major objection to its use as a measure of trends in concentration. (Since R is the reciprocal of the Herfindahl index [see p. 143 *supra*], the objections to R would also apply to the Herfindahl index.)

When all firms are equal in size, the measures C, L, and R all equal the number of firms. The concentration ratio is usually not expressed in this way, although it obviously can be, and the remaining measures were defined to produce this result. When firms differ in size only slightly, the measures differ only slightly. Usually C is the largest and L the smallest. But as the number of small firms starts to grow the situation changes. Then, in order of increasing sensitivity to small firms, we have: the concentration ratio, which remains unchanged; the remainder measure R, which increases but never by more than a small fixed amount; the entropy measure C, which may increase indefinitely in theory but only a little in practice; and lastly the ordinal measure L, which may become very large both in theory and practice.

In the applications that follow, we consider principally the entropy measure, since it is supported by theoretical considerations that the others lack and since the values produced do not lead to obviously erroneous results. But these other measures also merit consideration, and some comparative calculations are given for them in footnotes.

IV

In applying the entropy measure it is not unusual to find that
the record affords an inadequate basis for an exact computation.
Frequently, basic statistical information is incomplete even in
antitrust records comprising thousands of pages. A method of
dealing with such gaps is to assume a state of facts adverse to
the Government since it carries the burden of proof. A few examples are selected to demonstrate the method of computation
and the information which the entropy measure makes available.

In the *Alcoa* case, the Court found that two lines of commerce could be differentiated: insulated aluminum conductors
and a broader line of insulated and bare aluminum conductors.[36] The significance of the merger was not the same in these
lines, and this difference turns out to be meaningful for the
choice-of-line problem.

Prior to the merger, the total contribution by Alcoa and
Rome to $f(C)$ in the broader line was 0.179. After the merger,
Alcoa's contribution became 0.156, decreasing $f(C)$ from 0.891
to 0.868. Thus C declined from 7.7 to 7.35 as a result of the
merger.[37] This indicates a rather small increase in a highly concentrated line of commerce.

[36]United States v. Aluminum Co. of America, 377 U.S. 271 (1964).

[37]In 1958, shortly before the merger, the shares of the firms in the
aluminum-conductor line and the corresponding values of $1/n \, f(n)$ were as
follows:

ALUMINUM CONDUCTOR (BARE AND INSULATED)

FIRM	1958 PERCENTAGE SHARE	$1/n \, f(n)$
Alcoa	27.8	0.155
Rome	1.3	0.025
Anaconda	15.8	0.127
Kaiser	23.1	0.147
Bristol	4.5	0.061
Reynolds	10.4	0.102
General Cable	6.0	0.073
Essex Wire	4.5	0.061
Hendrix	0.2	0.005
Southwire	2.3	0.038
Nehring	0.5	0.012
Walker	0.1	0.003
Western	0.1	0.003
8 Other Firms	3.3	0.079
21 Firms	99.9	0.891

Plaintiff's Exhibit 434, Record on Appeal at 2713–14.

TABLE 9.   The Entropy Measure

	PREMERGER	POSTMERGER
Insulated & Bare Aluminum	7.7	7.35
Insulated Aluminum	10.6	9.6

In the line of insulated aluminum conductors, the total contribution of Alcoa and Rome to $f(C)$ prior to the merger was
0.171. After the merger, Alcoa's contribution became 0.128,
decreasing $f(C)$ from 1.025 to 0.982. Thus C declined from 10.6
to 9.6 as a result of the merger.[38] These findings are summarized
in Table 9.

We are now in a position to compare the effects of merger in
the two lines of commerce in a way not open to the litigants.
The entropy measure indicates that the wider line of aluminum
conductor was more concentrated than the line of insulated aluminum conductor, although both were highly concentrated. It
also shows that the merger was probably more significant, both
absolutely and proportionately, in the insulated line than in the
wider line. This suggests that the case could and should have
been disposed of solely on the basis of the effect on the
insulated line. The Court's reliance on the dubious broader line
was unnecessary in light of the finding of the entropy measure
that the merger in the insulated line was probably of greater significance.[39]

Manufacturers Hanover[40] illustrates the use of the entropy
measure in resolving problems of stare decisis. The District
Court had held that the decision in *Philadelphia Bank* afforded
no basis for concluding that the *Manufacturers Hanover* merger
should also be held prima facie unlawful. The court gave two
reasons for its conclusion: first, the share of the merged firms
was 30 percent in *Philadelphia Bank* and only 14 percent in
Manufacturers Hanover, and second, if the merger were con-
summated, the merging banks in Philadephia would have had a
significantly larger share of market than their nearest competitors, while in *Manufacturers Hanover* the merged banks would
have been only third in the New York metropolitan area.

These considerations are obviously relevant but not exhaustive. The entropy measure provides a more systematic basis for comparison.

Prior to the merger in *Philadelphia Bank*, $f(C) = 1.049$; $C = 12.73$. The merger of Philadelphia National Bank and Girard Trust Company reduced their contribution to $f(C)$ by

[38]In the line of insulated aluminum conductor the figures are as follows:

ALUMINUM CABLE (INSULATED)

Firm	1958 percentage share	$1/n\,f(n)$
Alcoa	11.6	0.109
Rome	4.7	0.062
Kaiser	26.8	0.153
Anaconda	16.9	0.131
General Cable	9.5	0.097
Essex	6.1	0.074
Olin Mathieson	5.3	0.068
Reynolds	4.8	0.063
Southwire	2.5	0.040
Firms 10–19	11.8	0.228
19 Firms	100.0	1.025

Plaintiff's Exhibit 436, Record on Appeal at 2517–18.

[39]As applied to this case the ordinal measure L and the remainder measure R are shown in this table.

Measure	C		L		R	
LINE OF COMMERCE	BROAD	NARROW	BROAD	NARROW	BROAD	NARROW
Before Merger	7.7	10.6	5.846	8.168	5.72	7.38
After Merger	7.35	9.6	5.558	7.412	5.50	6.84
Absolute Decrease	0.35	1.0	0.288	0.756	0.22	0.54
Percent Decrease	4.6%	9.4%	4.9%	9.2%	3.8%	7.3%

The significance of the merger was "probably" greater in the narrow line because the exact meaning of the change in C poses an economic question which the measure does not purport to answer.

[40]*See* note 8 *supra*.

TABLE 10.   The Entropy Measure

	PREMERGER	POSTMERGER
Philadelphia National Bank	12.7	8.8
Manufacturers Hanover	13.8	12.9

0.105. Thus, as a result of the merger, C declined from 12.73 to 8.79.[41]

Prior to the merger in *Manufacturers Hanover*, $f(C)$ = 1.140; $C = 13.8$. The merger of Manufacturers Trust Co. and The Hanover Bank reduced their contribution to $f(C)$ by 0.044. Thus, as a result of the merger, C declined from 13.8 to 12.9.[42] These findings are summarized in Table 10.

The entropy measure indicates that the *Philadelphia Bank* market was slightly more concentrated than the *Manufacturers*

[41]The statistics in United States v. Philadelphia National Bank, 374 U.S. 321 (1963), are as follows:

DEPOSITS IN COMMERCIAL BANKS PHILADELPHIA METRO-POLITAN AREA

BANK	PERCENT OF TOTAL DEPOSITS OF 4 COUNTIES	$1/n\ f(n)$
The Philadelphia National Bank	21.3	.143
Girard Trust Corn Exchange Bank	14.5	.122
	35.8	.160
First Pennsylvania Banking	22.1	.145
Provident Tradesmens Bank	9.9	.100
Fidelity-Philadelphia Trust Co.	9.3	.096
Central-Penn National Bank	5.2	.067
Broad Street Trust Co.	2.9	.044
Liberty Real Estate Bank	2.0	.034
Montgomery Co. Bank & Trust Co.	1.8	
Nine other commercial banks with head offices in Phila.	3.2	.078
Fifteen other commercial banks with head offices in Montgomery Co.	4.1	.105
Delaware County National Bank	1.6	.029
Nine commercial banks with head offices in Bucks Co.	2.1	.055
Total	100.0	1.049

See Table 2, Record on Appeal at 2349. The table reflects the more elaborate data from the record rather than the abbreviated data cited by the court.

Hanover market and that the merger in *Philadelphia Bank* appears more significant than in *Manufacturers Hanover*. These results sustain the Court's conclusion that *Manufacturers Hanover* cannot be deemed a prima facie case solely on the basis of the decision in *Philadelphia Bank*.

The facts in the *Von's* case[43] can be used to illustrate the application of the entropy measure to trends in concentration. In *Von's*, the decision apparently depended on two factors: (1) the reduction in the number of firms in the periods prior to and following the merger, and (2) the increase in size of the merging firms.

---

[42]The statistics in *Manufacturers Hanover* are as follows:

DEPOSITS IN COMMERCIAL BANKS: NEW YORK METROPOLITAN AREA

BANKS RANKED BY SIZE OF ASSETS	PERCENT TOTAL DEPOSITS	$1/n \, f(n)$
Chase Manhattan Bank	20.01	.140
First National City Bank	17.59	.133
Chemical Bank New York Trust Co.	10.16	.101
Morgan Guaranty Trust Co.	9.12	.095
Manufacturers Hanover Trust Co.	9.24	.096
Bankers Trust Co.	7.81	.089
Irving Trust Co.	5.33	.068
Hanover Bank	4.64	.062
Franklin National Bank	1.93	.033
Marine Midland Trust Co.	1.81	.032
Bank of New York	1.62	.029
Meadow Brook National Bank	1.42	.026
County Trust Co.	1.29	.024
Savings Bank Trust Co.	0.54	.012
Empire Trust Co.	0.52	.012
Grace National Bank	0.55	.012
United States Trust Co. of New York	0.50	.012
National Bank of Westchester	0.57	.013
Federation Bank & Trust Co.	0.53	.012
Commercial Bank of North America	0.45	.012
Sterling National Bank & Trust Co.	0.40	.009
First National City Trust Co.	0.32	.008
Trade Bank & Trust Co.	0.30	.008
Long Island Trust Co.	0.26	.007
Subtotal	97.05	.095
Total 48 Remaining Banks	2.95	.095
Total All Banks	100.00	1.140

[43]384 U.S. 270 (1966). See note 14.

The Government did not introduce any evidence of the size breakdown of individual firms in 1948, ten years before the merger, but it did introduce evidence of percentage shares of groups of firms. Assuming a distribution most favorable to the defendants, namely, that the firms in each group were equal, for the year 1948, $C = 985$.[44] The principal contribution was from very small firms. By any standards, this is a highly competitive market.

For the year 1958 the Government put in more detailed statistics. Since in making comparisons it would be misleading to use the more general figures for 1948 and the more specific figures for 1958, we use the more general figures for 1958 as well.[45] Using these for the year 1958, $C = 364$. Although the decline over the decade was evidently substantial, the market, in 1958, was still highly competitive.

In order to determine the effect of the merger of Von's and Shopping Bag it is necessary to compute the shares of the individual firms. This computation, based on the detailed breakdown, shows that before the merger $f(C) = 2.564$; $C = 367$. The merger reduced C from 367 to 340 equal firms. Thus, both before and after the merger, the market remained highly competitive. By giving significant weight to large numbers of small firms, the entropy measure leads to results which do not sustain the Government's claim that the market in *Von's* had become so highly concentrated that it "was approaching oligopoly."[46] If the evidence of the entropy measure is accepted, *Von's* is an "incipiency" case with a vengeance.[47]

[44] GROCERY FIRMS IN LOS ANGELES—1948

NUMBER OF FIRMS	AGGREGATE SHARE	$1/n\, f(n)$
Firms 1–4	25.9	.308
Firms 5–8	7.8	.136
Firms 9–12	5.1	.133
Firms 13–16	2.8	.060
Firms 17–20	2.1	.048
Firms 21–6221	57.2	2.308
6221	99.9	2.993

See Record on Appeal at 2331.

[45] GROCERY FIRMS IN LOS ANGELES—1958

Number of Firms	Aggregate Share	$1/n\,f(n)$
Firms 1–4	24.4	0.296
Firms 5–8	16.5	0.229
Firms 9–12	7.9	0.135
Firms 13–16	4.6	0.089
Firms 17–20	3.5	0.072
Firms 21–4741	43.1	1.741
4741	100.0	2.562

See Record at 2324, 2331. The figure for total firms is as of the end of 1960, the only figure available.

DETAILED BREAKDOWN: GROCERY FIRMS IN LOS ANGELES—1958

Firm	Percentage Share	$1/n\,f(n)$
Safeway	8.0	.088
Ralph's	6.4	.076
Von's	4.7	.062
Market Basket	4.4	.060
Thriftimart	4.4	.060
Shopping Bag	4.2	.058
Food Giant	3.6	.052
Alpha Beta	3.1	.047
Fox Markets	2.8	.043
Mayfair	2.0	.034
Firms 11–12	5.2	.082
Firms 13–16	4.6	.089
Firms 17–20	3.5	.072
Firms 21–4741	43.1	1.741
4741	100.0	2.564

See Record at 2329, 2331.

The result here is, as one would expect, close to the estimate based on the more general data. The fact that C is larger than if computed on the more general data is due to discrepancies between the general and particular data for 1958.

[46]Brief for the United States at 28.

The three measures yield very different results when applied to the facts in *Von's*. From the individual firm sizes we obtain $L = 1750$ before the merger, and $L = 1748$ after; $R = 40.4$ before, and 34.9 after. The measures differ substantially because they attach different relative importance to large and small firms. The merger affects only the larger firms, and therefore has little effect on L, which is large because of the large total number of firms. But it has a strong effect on R, which depends almost exclusively on the larger firms.

The effect of this merger may be compared with that of an imaginary one in which roughly 400 of the small firms are absorbed by the larger ones. This would also reduce C from 367 to roughly 340. But R would fall only to 40.0, remaining almost unchanged. L, however, would drop by about 100. These examples demonstrate that C is intermediate between L and R in its weighting of small firms.

[47]United States v. Pabst Brewing Co., 384 U.S. 901 (1966), also appears to be an incipiency case—although less extreme than *Von's*. The record in *Pabst*

V

By holding that evidence of the number and sizes of firms in a market is sometimes alone sufficient for the Government's case, the Court has assigned a crucial role to such evidence and shifted the battle over the use of statistics in Section 7 proceedings. Judges must now decide not *whether* but *when* to rely solely on statistical evidence. It has been the thesis of this chapter that the methods presently used to measure economic concentration—principally concentration ratios—are not well suited to resolve this and other issues which the Court's rule has made prominent.

In cases arising under the amended Section 7, the Court has repeatedly relied in its analysis of statistics on the results in prior cases. Since comparisons of this sort are a primary analytic tool, the method used to express the degree of concentration should facilitate them. But as we have seen, there are only limited factual situations in which concentration ratios permit valid and adequate comparisons. In *Manufacturers Hanover*, comparison was not possible, while in *Von's* and *Pabst*, the change in the concentration ratio reflected a particular, and relatively less important, aspect of market changes. Comparability may be improved by relying on a single factor, such as the sizes of merging firms, but only at the cost of disregarding potentially highly relevant market data. And the use of such artificially limited measures emphasizes the economic unreality of the Court's reliance on statistics.

The lack of comparability is but the prelude to a deeper problem. When comparisons with statistics from other industries are sought, or where stare decisis does not dictate the an-

---

was uniquely complete. It showed the market share percentage of every firm down to .001 for the years 1958 through 1961. Record on Appeal at 170–84. On the basis of these statistics, the Court found that the three-year period immediately following the merger had been marked by a continuing trend toward concentration. The calculations of the entropy measure are too long for reproduction here, but they show that in 1958 C declined from 66 to 64 as a result of the merger; and that the trend to concentration relied on by the Court, by 1961, reduced C to 51. This would appear to be a substantial decline, although the market is evidently still highly competitive. For a discussion of Pabst's market share before and after the merger, see note 14 *supra*.

swer, a court must make a decision concerning the economic significance of the statistics. Since the economic problem is complex, some simplification or reduction is essential. But concentration ratios are of little help in this regard because the reduction they effect is purely statistical. It is because no theory of competitive behavior underlies the concentration ratio that the Court, in the leading Section 7 cases, has been unable to supply a reasoned connection between its economic judgments and the statistical basis on which they rest.

A measure in the form of a translation into equal-firm markets would be better suited to implement the Court's view. A translation measure simplifies the economic problem by making an economic statement: the level of competitive activities of the market under consideration is equivalent to that of a market with a certain number of equal firms. This would seem to be a better form in which to make the ultimate economic judgment, even though the results of the measure cannot determine that judgment. A court must still determine the degree of competition to be anticipated for the equivalent equal-firm markets before and after the merger and decide whether the change should be viewed as substantial. But expressing the statistics in terms of equal-firm markets may simplify a court's task. It also seems more reasonable to conclude, as the Court has done without using this measure, that the greater the change in the equal-firm measure occasioned by a merger, the less relevant other economic information becomes, until, finally, the statistical evidence alone is sufficient for a prima facie case. Once the statistics are cast in the form of an economic statement, the role of other economic evidence becomes—logically as well as legally—complementary to this primary evidence.

The foregoing assumes that the translation measure embodies an economic truth. What assurance do we have that a given market has the same degree of competitive activity as a market consisting of n equal firms? The general problem is that economic theory "cannot yet sustain reliable predictions concerning the impact on market behavior of any but the most sweeping mergers."[48] The most that can be said is that if a

---

[48] Bok, *Section 7 of the Clayton Act and the Merging of Law and Economics*, 74 HARV. L. REV. 226, 244 (1960).

measure is egregiously wrong, a majority of economists would believe its statements false; but even then there is probably no empirical or theoretical test of these opinions.

The absence of provability is not fatal to the usefulness of a translation measure. Any measure on which comparisons rest depends on some equally unprovable assumptions. The simple decision to consider solely the sizes of the merging firms depends on the unverifiable hypothesis that the rest of the market is irrelevant. So the choice is not whether to use unprovable assumptions, but which ones to use. The assumptions used in deriving the entropy measure have certain arbitrary elements, but they seem to be within a range of reasonableness, and they or some equally unprovable alternatives are necessary to construct any translation measure.

With respect to the "competitive activities" derivation, the choice of the logarithmic functions seems preferable to its rivals, but the choice of $\log(n)$ over the logarithmic functions is necessarily arbitrary. $\text{Log}(n)$ was chosen because this is the simplest of the log functions and there is no economic basis for a different, more complicated, choice. The log function also turns out to be consistent with the results of other derivations. The independence hypothesis—the assumption that a firm's level of competitive activity is a function solely of its size—was again a choice based on considerations of simplicity. For no way appears to resolve the complex choices involved in the contrary assumption that the rate of competitive activity is dependent on the shape of the entire market or a part of it.

With respect to the "permutations" derivation, the assumption that customer permutation is a valid measure of competition is undoubtedly novel. The probability of customer transfer would seem related to competitive activity, and permutations are of importance if transfers are considered in terms of their probability. The fact that the number of permutations is inversely proportional to the probability (as computed) that no customer would change allegiance lends support to the use of the number of permutations as a measure of the probability of customer transfer. The "probability" derivation itself rests on the independence hypothesis and on our determination that a firm's probability of holding its customers is most likely to be proportional to its size.

The test of these assumptions is whether plausible alternatives leading to essentially different results can be framed. The testing process has been illustrated by examining alternatives to the independence hypothesis and the choice of the log function. These yield results which seem less in accord with economic ideas than the entropy measure. Other choices may yield better results.

The problems of constructing a measure reflect the larger fact that the law has established a test involving prediction which in most cases will remain beyond the reach of economic science. These uncertainties will deepen if the Government extends its antitrust enforcement program to the full range apparently sanctioned by the Court's decisions. A more inclusive program of this type will present the enforcing agencies and the court with much closer questions than those with which they have dealt so far. More than ever, the weaknesses, gaps, and inadequacies of economic prediction will reveal the problems inherent in applying the statutory standard, and more than ever, the Court will have to take refuge in the fact that Congress was dealing "with probabilities and not certainties" and that "mergers with a probable anticompetitive effect were to be proscribed by this Act."

Even within the permissive standard of probabilities, it is obvious that the entropy measure itself is not an end to the problem of measuring concentration for the Clayton Act, any more than a mercator or polar projection is an end to map making. Factors may be added—such as the degree of stability of market structure—which would perhaps lead to greater refinement. The entropy measure is proposed not to give a complete answer to these problems, but to demonstrate the first result of an approach which seeks to coordinate the problems of measurement with the purposes of the law.

Chapter 6

SOLVENCY CONTROLS

THE GAP BETWEEN the teaching of mathematical theory and regulatory practice is probably nowhere more significant than in the field of insurance, where protection of solvency is a prime purpose of regulation. A vast mathematical literature on the theoretical aspects of solvency control has developed in the past fifty years, but insurance authorities in the United States have remained impervious to its teachings, and solvency controls continue to be set here by a generalized appeal to experience and intuition. In addition to protecting the public from failure of insurance companies, solvency controls influence both the degree of competition and the extent to which insured risks are redistributed by reinsurance with other insurers in the nonlife insurance industry. Minimum-reserve rules also effect the extent to which a company can use free surplus in different lines of business, to distribute to stockholders, or to pledge for borrowings. The stringency of controls will thus influence not only dividends but also the growth of insurance holding companies and conglomerates.

In Finland, insurance authorities have drawn on the mathematical theory of solvency control in creating their regulations. Beginning in 1952, the Finnish Department of Insurance, concerned that inflation might be eroding company solvency, began to evolve minimum-capital and -reserve rules based on sophisticated mathematical techniques drawn from the branch

176

of mathematical probability known as risk theory.[1] Under this theory, the total amount of claims against an insurance company becomes a variable which may, with determinable probabilities, assume different values, instead of being a set quantity as in classical actuarial science. The future financial position of a company is thus estimated on a probabilistic basis from mathematical models for distributions of numbers and sizes of claims, an approach which is needed for nonlife companies because total claim amounts fluctuate from year to year.[2] Risk-theoretic methods articulate the variables relevant to solvency and the interrelationships among various types of controls, and furnish an estimate of the degree of risk entailed in any particular choice. Of course, solvency controls cannot be determined on a purely technical basis. Determining the acceptable level of risk of insolvency requires a weighing of that risk against the costs and anticompetitive effects of high reserve requirements and controls on premiums. In making this policy judgment, however, technical methods are useful, because the risk side of the policy equation cannot be appraised without them.

This chapter will examine the evolution of the Finnish solvency controls and compare them with the rules used in New York State, the single most important American insurance regulatory jurisdiction. The Finnish methods are instructive because they suggest that the intuitive controls used in the United States could be relaxed, without endangering solvency, to promote competition among domestic companies and to eliminate unnecessary reinsurance costs, thereby permitting reductions in premium rates. Reduction in reinsurance would also reduce or eliminate a U.S. dollar drain caused by payments of reinsurance premiums abroad. Apart from its immediate application to insurance, the Finnish method is worth understanding because it represents an apparently successful effort to handle analytically a subject that traditionally had been treated intuitively by regulators in this country.

---

[1] There is a huge literature on risk theory. The most readable current book is BEARD, PENTIKAINEN & PESONEN, RISK THEORY (1969), which also contains a good bibliography.

[2] Risk-theoretic techniques are not needed for life insurance because the force of mortality is relatively constant and predictable.

I

Protection against insurance company insolvency begins with statutory requirements for minimum initial surplus and capital. In the United States, statutes usually prescribe fixed dollar amounts for minimum paid-in capital which must be maintained at all times, and separate requirements for initial surplus, which may be expended. New York has the highest and most elaborate minimum-capital requirements of any state, and since its statute applies to any insurance company doing business in New York[3] it has broad extraterritorial reach.

The theory underlying the New York statute is that separate, fixed amounts of minimum capital should be required for each line of insurance and that additional initial surplus should equal 50 or 100 percent of this mimimum capital.[4] The amounts currently required in New York are essentially unchanged from the 1939 revision of the insurance law, when they were almost doubled at the behest of the Department of Insurance, reflecting, it was said, the experience of the Depression.[5] Today, a

---

[3]N.Y. INS. LAW §40 (McKinney 1966).

[4]Capital, for present purposes, is defined as "the aggregate par value of all classes of shares of capital stock issued and outstanding." N.Y. INS. LAW §4(8) (McKinney 1966). Additionally required "initial surplus" is defined merely as an amount at least equal to a specified percentage of minimum paid-in capital: 50 percent for the kinds of business set forth in §311, and 100 percent for the kinds set forth in §341 (fire and marine). *Id.* §§311(1), 341(1).

The kinds of insurance authorized in New York are divided into twenty-three classifications, *id.* §46, and requirements for minimum paid-in capital are established separately for each kind of insurance. See *id.* §§311 (1)(a) − (e), (i), 341(1). When a company engages in more than one line of insurance the requirements are cumulative, though mitigated by (1), for some classes, a flat $50,000 reduction in minimum capital for each class except the first, *id.* §311(1)(f), and (2) overlapping requirements for fire, marine, and associated insurance, *id.* §341.

[5]"The capital requirements for casualty insurance and surety companies have been substantially increased. This has been done by subdividing the insuring powers with regard to the amount of capital deemed requisite for the particular power. Due consideration has been given to the experiences of the recent depression and to the records of the Liquidation Bureau of the Insurance Department." N.Y. STATE INS. DEP'T INSURANCE LAW REVISION OF THE STATE OF NEW YORK, TENTATIVE DRAFT 1937 ix. The provisions of the *Tentative Draft* were adopted in 1939 virtually without change and have since been amended principally to reflect the allowance of multiple-line powers.

New York stock casualty company[6] desiring to write all types of casualty and surety business must have a total minimum paid-in capital and initial surplus[7] of $2.7 million,[8] $1.8 million of which must be maintained.[9] If fire and marine lines are added, total minimum paid-in capital and initial surplus rises by $1 million, and minimum capital that must be maintained rises by $500,000, subject to certain minor adjustments.[10] A company engaged in all permitted lines of casualty, surety, fire, and marine insurance would thus need total minimum paid-in capital and initial surplus of $3.55 million, of which $2.2 million must be maintained.[11]

[6]A stock casualty insurance company organized as a stock insurance company, N.Y. INS. LAW §48, and given power to do any of the kinds of business incorporated in §310 by reference to §46.

[7]The required amount of capital and surplus, see note 4 *supra*, must have been paid to the company before a license to do any business may be issued. *Id.* §48(8)(2).

[8]See *id.* §311(1). A calculation deriving this result may be found in N.Y. STATE INS. DEP'T, 2 EXAMINATION OF INSURANCE COMPANIES 75 (1953) (table 2).

The statutes of other states are in general form similar to those of New York. See, e.g., CAL. INS. CODE §§700.01, 700.02 (West Supp. 1971) (Minimum paid-in capital is the lesser of $1 million or the aggregate of a schedule of amounts ranging from $50,000 to $250,000 each for designated classes of insurance; surplus must equal 50 percent of minimum capital for insurers in business more than five years, and 100 percent for others); ILL. ANN. STAT. ch. 73, §625 (Smith-Hurd Supp. 1971) (Minimum paid-up capital is $400,000 for fire and marine companies, and either $400,000 or $600,000 for casualty companies, depending on whether more than one type of casualty business is authorized; initial surplus is 50 percent of minimum capital for new companies while permanent surplus is required only for vehicle insurance); PA. STAT. tit. 40, §386 (Supp. 1971) (Minimum paid-up capital is $100,000 to $300,000 for fire and marine companies, depending on the range of activities, $100,000 to $300,000 for casualty companies, depending on the range of activities, with certain exceptions for which higher amounts are required. A casualty company may transact all types of business with $1 million. Minimum paid-in surplus is 50 percent of the subscribed total stock.); TEX. INS. CODE ANN. art. 2.02(4) (1963) (Minimum paid-in capital of $100,000 and surplus of $50,000 for fire and marine insurers; $15,000 capital and $75,000 surplus for fidelity and casualty insurance; $200,000 capital and $100,000 surplus for all classes combined).

[9]See N.Y. STATE INS. DEP'T., 2 EXAMINATION OF INSURANCE COMPANIES 75 (1953) (table 2).

[10]See N.Y. INS. LAW §§311, 341 (McKinney 1966); note 4 *supra*.

[11]This calculation may be found in N.Y. STATE INS. DEP'T, 2 EXAMINATION OF INSURANCE COMPANIES 77 (1953) (table 5).

These requirements are supplemented by a statutory rule limiting the size of any single risk, and by administrative guides against which unimpaired reserves are tested annually on the basis of statements filed with the New York Insurance Department. The statutory rule provides that a company's maximum single net retained risk[12] may not exceed 10 percent of its policyholders' surplus.[13] As we shall see, this is a critical element in the pattern of controls, although it has never attracted much attention and has been carried forward from the 1939 law without change or discussion. The basic administrative guide is an unwritten two-to-one rule to the effect that net written premiums (written premiums remaining after deduction of premiums paid to reinsurers) in all lines of insurance except fire and marine may not exceed twice the policyholders' surplus.[14] Put another way, the New York Insurance Department requires a minimum policyholders' surplus equal to 50 percent of net written premiums. For fire and marine insurance a special one-to-one rule requires a surplus equal to 100 percent of written premiums, reflecting the possibility of greater claim fluctuations in these lines. In describing these rules, the Department stresses that these limitations are only benchmarks and that higher multiples are permitted if a company has shown a history of profitable underwritings.[15]

The two-to-one and one-to-one administrative guides were based on the observation of a former New York Commissioner of Insurance that companies with greater ratios tended to get into trouble during the 1930s and that the companies them-

[12]N.Y. INS. LAW §47 (McKinney 1966). Risks may be passed on or "reinsured" with an "assuming insurer." *Id.* §47.

[13]*Id.* §47. "Surplus to policyholders" is a term keyed to the ongoing liquidity of the company's reserves and is thus to be distinguished from initial surplus. While initial surplus refers only to initially required funds in excess of minimum capital, "surplus to policyholders" is defined as the excess of "admitted" or qualifying assets, see *id.* §70, over the liabilities of the company. *Id.* §4(34). This is alternatively defined as "the sum of all capital and surplus accounts minus any impairment thereof." *Id.* For purposes of determining the maximum allowable risk, surplus to policyholders explicitly includes "any voluntary reserves." *Id.* §47(a).

[14]See N.Y. STATE INS. DEP'T REPORT OF THE SPECIAL COMMITTEE ON INSURANCE HOLDING COMPANIES 46 (1968).

[15]Interview with William Gould, New York State Insurance Commissioner, June 1971.

selves have since followed these rules.[16] A statutory requirement to this effect was included in a draft of the 1939 recodification of the New York Insurance Law as a restriction on dividend payments, but was deleted to avoid controversy.[17]

The insurance law also currently provides that aggregate dividends within any twelve-month period may not exceed 10 percent of surplus to policyholders or 100 percent of investment income (whichever is greater) unless the Superintendent has previously found that the insurer will retain sufficient surplus to support its obligations and writings.[18] This limitation may usefully identify questionable distributions but does not, in itself, constitute a substantive control, since smaller distributions may imperil solvency, and the statute does not specify which larger ones involve peril.

Insurance regulators in the United States have generally accepted this arrangement: statutory minimum-capital requirements are fixed dollar amounts, and administrative controls are multiples of net written premiums. Discussion of the rules has focused on the amounts of minimum capital and the multiple of net written premiums. In relatively recent years, a number of states have amended their statutes to increase minimum required capital and policyholders' surplus, thus bringing their requirements closer to those of New York.[19] On the other hand, New York's two-to-one rule has been criticized as "surely too stringent when used as a test of solidity,"[20] and the National As-

[16]See N.Y. STATE INS. DEP'T, REPORT OF THE SPECIAL COMMITTEE ON INSURANCE HOLDING COMPANIES 46 (1968).

[17]Section 91.5 of the *Tentative Draft* of 1937 provided that a stock company could not pay a cash dividend unless its surplus to policyholders after the payment would be at least 50 percent of its net premiums written during the preceding year. The Department's comment on this provision was that, "[t]he limitations placed upon such companies in this section are no more severe than those observed by the more conservative casualty and surety companies." N.Y. STATE INS. DEP'T, INSURANCE LAW REVISION OF THE STATE OF NEW YORK, TENTATIVE DRAFT 1937, at 291.

[18]See N.Y. INS. LAW §§313 (casualty and surety companies), 343 (fire and marine insurance companies) (McKinney Supp. 1970–71).

[19]See *Hearings on the Insurance Industry Before the Subcomm. on Antitrust and Monopoly of the Senate Comm. on the Judiciary*, 91st Cong., 1st Sess., pt. 15, at 9026–27 (1969) (testimony of D. Pack).

[20]N.Y. STATE INS. DEP'T, REPORT OF THE SPECIAL COMMITTEE ON INSURANCE HOLDING COMPANIES 46 (1968).

sociation of Insurance Commissioners is reported to consider three-to-one a conservative ratio.[21]

II

When a new insurance law was enacted in Finland in 1952, the Department of Insurance was headed by Teivo Pentikainen, a mathematician who had written some basic papers on applications of risk theory. Pentikainen and others persuaded the Finnish Government to accept risk-theoretic considerations in framing statutory minimum-capital rules and to write into the law express authority to use risk theory in connection with the equalization reserve.[22] The role of these methods expanded in 1965, when the Department of Insurance, under Erkki Pesonen (also a mathematician), refined some of the earlier techniques and established new rules for judging insurance company solvency.

A.

The Finnish statutory minimum-capital rule derives from the principle that minimum capital should be large enough to leave only a small specified probability (on the order of 0.01 or less) that claims against a company would exceed the aggregate of net premium income and working capital.[23] Since net premium income (that is, net earned[24] premiums less administrative expenses) is computed to cover expected claims, the

[21]Kaplan, *Regulation for Insolvency in Hearings on the Insurance Industry before the Subcomm. on Antitrust & Monopoly of the Senate Comm. on the Judiciary*, 91st Cong., 1st Sess., pt. 15, at 8962, 8966 (1969).

[22]See text accompanying note 47 *infra*.

[23]The description in the text of the derivation of the rules contained in §5 of the Finnish Insurance Companies Act of 1952 draws principally on an unpublished, undated memorandum of the Finnish Department of Insurance entitled "A Short Summary Concerning the System of Security Margin, Stabilization Reserve and Net Retention Applied by the Finnish Supervisory Office."

[24]Earned premiums rather than written premiums reflect the risks carried. See text following note 84 *infra*.

function of working capital is to supply a reserve against years in which losses exceed the amounts expected.

The amount of working capital needed to cover claims in excess of those expected requires complex calculations which depend on the number and sizes of the policies in a company's portfolio. For purposes of a statutory minimum-capital rule, it was necessary to make simplifying assumptions. The Finnish Supervisory Service assumed that net premium income was just adequate to cover expected losses; it thus assumed no profit. If, however, minimum-capital requirements were simply based directly on net premium income, a company could always meet the statutory standards by increasing its reinsurance, since net premium income excludes premiums paid to reinsurers. To prevent this practice—which might tempt undercapitalized companies to carry excessive reinsurance—the Finnish statutory rule assumes net premium income to be one half of gross earned premiums.[25]

The degree to which actual claims may exceed expected claims is expressed in terms of the standard deviation, which is a measure of the spread or dispersion of a random variable about its mean or expected value.[26] Thus, if the total amount claimed is normally distributed,[27] there is a 0.01 chance that it

---

[25]Finnish Dep't of Insurance, *A Short Summary Concerning the System of Security Margin, Stabilization Reserve and Net Retention Applied by the Finnish Supervisory Office 2*. In marine insurance and received reinsurance, where the need for reinsurance is greater than in other lines, calculations are based on the premium after deducting the reinsurer's share. There is, however, a proviso that this premium figure after reinsurance shall be at least 50 percent of the gross figure. Finnish Ins. Companies Act of 1952, §5(3), translated in 1964 INS. IN FINLAND, No. 2, at 3. The combined effect of these rules is to permit net premium income for marine and received reinsurance to be as low as 25 percent of gross premiums, instead of 50 percent as in other lines.

[26]The standard deviation provides a quantitative measure of the variability of random variables which may differ even though they have the same expected value (mean). For example, assume the expected amount of claims against an insurer is $500 in a given year. This could mean that most years will show between $400 and $600 in claims. Alternatively, it could mean that some years are very good for the company and result in over $800 in claims. The latter case would require more stringent solvency controls. The standard deviation, as defined above, distinguishes between these situations. The standard deviation squared (the variance) is defined as the expected value of the squared difference between the variable and its mean value.

[27]For a discussion of the validity of assuming a normal distribution, see note 33 *infra*.

will be more than 2.3 standard deviations above the expected amount,[28] and only a 0.0001 chance that the departure will be more than 3.7 standard deviations above the expected amount.[29] In the present context, the standard deviation can be shown to be approximately equal to $\sqrt{KpM}$, where p is the total net earned premiums and M the maximum realistically possible single claim. K is a factor reflecting the variation in amounts claimed under individual policies, which increases as this variation diminishes and equals a maximum of 1.0 when individual claims are all equal to the maximum.[30] Based on empirical studies of variations in claims, it was known that K usually ranges between 0.2 and 0.6.[31] Since larger values of K lead to larger capital requirements, the Supervisory Service had reason to believe it was acting conservatively in setting K equal to 0.67.

Using these assumptions, minimum capital, U, may be written as

$$U = y\,\sqrt{0.67pM}$$

where y is the number of standard deviation units from the expected claim amount sufficient to secure whatever degree of safety is required as a matter of policy, and $\sqrt{0.67pM}$ is the standard deviation.[32] The Supervisory Service decided that a risk of insolvency of 0.0001 would be permitted, which, assuming the total amount of claims to be normally distributed,[33] is

---

[28] 1 FELLER, AN INTRODUCTION TO PROBABILITY THEORY AND ITS APPLICATIONS 167 (2d ed. 1957).

[29] *Id.*

[30] See BEARD, PENTIKAINEN & PESONEN, RISK THEORY 58 (1969). On the assumption that claims occur randomly and independently, the standard deviation of total claims amount is $\sqrt{a_2 n}$ where a_2 is the second moment of the distribution of individual claim amounts and n the expected number of claims. For a derivation, see *id.* 22–23.

Setting $p = nm$, where m is the mean amount of a single claim, and $K = a^2/mM$ yields the result given in the text. *Id.* 58–59.

[31] *Id.* 58.

[32] The total resource of a company with which to pay claims is $U + p$, where U is the working capital and p the net premium income. Since p must equal the expected amount of claims, U must be an additional amount large enough to cover claim fluctuations within the specified degree of safety. Thus $U + p = p + y\sqrt{0.67pM}$, or $U = y\sqrt{0.67pM}$, as stated in the text.

[33] There is a theoretical warrant for this assumption, because the total amount of claims against a company is the sum of many small independent claims and the central limit theorem of probability states that, under general

equivalent to 3.7 standard deviations.[34] Thus y was set equal to 3.7, p was assumed equal to one half of gross earned premiums for the reasons already given,[35] and M was estimated at 1 percent of gross earned premiums. When these values are inserted in the above equation, minimum capital equals about 20 percent of gross earned premiums. This formulation assumes, however, that M increases in a linear fashion with gross premiums, an overstatement that causes capital requirements to rise too steeply as business increases. To correct this, a separate segment was added: the additions to capital for gross earned premiums over 4 million Finnish marks (Fmk)[36] are at the rate of 10 instead of 20 percent of gross earned premiums.[37]

This rule does not make allowance for the costs of starting or winding up a company. For these purposes, the Finnish act requires a fixed initial capital, which may be expended, and a fixed permanent working capital in addition to the amount determined on the basis of gross premiums. An insurance company is entitled to a license to do business if it has initial capital of at least Fmk 1 million ($238,100) for fire and marine insurance, or at least Fmk 500,000 ($119,050) for other kinds of nonlife insurance.[38] The issuance of a license is discretionary if initial capital is at least half the amounts specified.[39] The fixed part of the permanent working capital is Fmk 200,000 ($47,620),

---

conditions, the sum of a large number of independent random variables will be approximately normally distributed. See, e.g., FREUND, MATHEMATICAL STATISTICS 185 (1962). In fact, however, the choice of a normal distribution is not conservative because it understates the probability of large claims. This assumption was not used by the Supervisory Service in its subsequent development of more detailed reserve rules.

[34] 1 FELLER, *supra* note 28, at 167.

[35] Text accompanying note 25 *supra*.

[36] At the time of this writing the Finnish mark (Fmk) converted at about 4.2 to the dollar. 1 THE EUROPA YEARBOOK 1970, at 616.

[37] Finnish Ins. Companies Act of 1952, §5, translated in 1964 INS. IN FINLAND, No. 2, at 2–3. The amount was raised to Fmk 4 million to account for inflation. If M were assumed to equal 10 percent of surplus, the legal maximum in New York, but the assumptions of the Finnish method were otherwise accepted, the minimum capital required would be 45 percent of gross premiums—close to New York's administrative two-to-one rule.

[38] Finnish Ins. Companies Act of 1952, §4, translated in 1964 INS. IN FINLAND, No. 2, at 2. These figures include recent increases to account for inflation.

[39] Finnish Ins. Companies Act of 1952, §4, translated in 1964 INS. IN FINLAND, No. 2, at 2.

which covers all types of nonlife insurance. Thus the current rule specifies that fixed minimum working capital must equal Fmk 200,000 plus about 20 percent of average gross earned premiums over the preceding three years up to Fmk 4 million, and 10 percent on average gross earned premiums in excess of this amount.[40] A similar rule obtains in England.[41]

Use of the 10 percent segment of the rule, which lacks statistical support, and reliance on approximations instead of calculations for individual cases, make it uncertain that all companies will be protected within the stated margin of safety by this capital rule. The choice of that margin was itself a significant policy decision since the required reserves would be on the order of 15–20 percent less if a safety margin based on a ruin probability of 0.001 instead of 0.0001 had been used. While changes in the approximating assumptions or in the safety margin would change the parameters of the rule, the significant fact is that minimum working capital is linked to premium volume, and the magnitude of the link has been defined by solvency considerations. Finnish companies are thus required to maintain sufficient surplus to cover claim fluctuations but are not unnecessarily burdened, as United States companies may be, by minimum-capital requirements when premium volume is small.

B.

Statutory minimum-capital requirements, which provide continuously applicable, rough limits, are supplemented by ad-

---

[40]*Id.* §5, translated in 1964 INS. IN FINLAND, No. 2, at 2–3. The amount was recently increased to account for inflation.

To prevent companies from being wound up due to insufficient capital and free surplus, the Finnish law provides a further cushion: a company whose policyholders' surplus and reserves are less than twice the required minimum shall transfer each year to such surplus at least 10 percent of its business profit. Finnish Ins. Companies Act of 1952, §28, translated in 1964 INS. IN FINLAND, No. 2, at 10.

[41]Under English statutes, a nonlife insurer must have a surplus of at least £50,000 if the general premium income of the company in the previous year did not exceed £250,000, one-fifth of that income if it exceeded £250,000 but not £2.5 million, or the aggregate of £500,000 and one-tenth of the amount by which that income exceeded £2.5 million. Companies Act 1967, c. 81, §62(2). Note that the use of a stair step and the percentages of gross premiums are similar to those of Finnish law.

ministrative rules against which reserves are tested more precisely at the close of each year. These rules, based on risk-theoretic considerations,[42] were originally introduced in Finland in a context not directly connected with solvency.

Prior to 1952, because of high corporate tax rates, Finnish insurance companies found it more profitable to pay reinsurance premiums, which were deductible expenses, than to accumulate reserves from after-tax funds. Reinsurance was frequently carried with foreign companies, and the funds flowing out of Finland had adverse effects on the balance of payments and were lost for domestic investment. To encourage retention of funds, the insurance law was amended in 1952 to provide for a new "equalization reserve" as a source of funds for years when claims exceed the amounts expected.[43]

In agreeing to permit tax-deductible transfers to the equalization reserve, the Ministry of Finance insisted that changes in the reserve follow a definite formula. Accordingly, Supervisory Service regulations provide that in years in which the actual amount of incurred claims exceeds the expected amount, the equalization reserve is decreased by that difference, which for accounting and tax purposes is treated as income. In years in which the actual claims are lower than expected, the difference is added to the equalization reserve and deducted from income.[44] The equalization reserve thus acts both to smooth out variations in taxable income and as a reserve in lieu of reinsurance to cover fluctuations in claims.[45]

---

[42]General descriptions of the risk-theoretic method may be found in Pentikainen, *Fluctuation Reserve: A Technique to Take into Account the Fluctuation of the Risk Business When Calculating the Technical Reserves of Insurance Companies,* 1970 INS. IN FINLAND, No. 1, at 2; and in Pesonen, *Technical Reserves and Solvency,* 1965 INS. IN FINLAND, No. 2, at 5. A technical description appears in Porn, *A Study in Risk Theory and Its Application to the Computation of the Fluctuation Reserve Used in Finland,* reprinted from SKANDINAVISK AKTUARIETIDSKRIFT 1 (1968).

[43]Finnish Ins. Companies Act of 1952, §46, translated in 1964 INS. IN FINLAND, No. 2, at 14.

[44]See MINISTRY FOR SOCIAL AFFAIRS, GENERAL LETTER TO CASUALTY INSURANCE COMPANIES ON THE BASIS OF THE EQUALIZATION RESERVE 3–5 (May 31, 1965) [hereinafter cited as GENERAL LETTER].

[45]See Porn, *supra* note 42, at 2. New companies initially have a zero reserve. When the equalization reserve system was introduced, each company was permitted to establish an initial reserve, principally from a revaluation of surplus and secondarily by transfers from other technical reserves. As a company grows, it needs an absolutely larger (although proportionately smaller)

In permitting a tax deduction, the Ministry of Finance also insisted that the equalization reserve could not grow indefinitely without taxation, and exempted it only to the extent it could be regarded as cover for potential claim liability.[46] The law authorizing an equalization reserve expressly endorsed a risk-theoretic approach to the limit problem by providing that the reserve would be "calculated according to risk theory, to provide for years with unusually heavy losses."[47] In implementing this statute, the Supervisory Service decided that the equalization reserve would not be excessive as long as there was at least a 0.01 probability that claims higher than those expected would exceed the amount reserved. A supplementary rule, however, provides that the reserve may grow to at least twice the company's maximum single net retained risk.[48] These rules lead to amounts substantially larger than those needed to protect solvency, because other company assets available for the payments are not considered. Because other assets are always available, it is in a sense artificial to view the maximum permitted reserve as necessary to cover fluctuations in claims, but the rule does at least put a cap on the equalization reserve.

American companies are currently in a position comparable to Finnish companies of the pre-1952 era, because no tax deduction is allowed for additions to a reserve for claims not yet incurred.[49] Since much reinsurance is carried abroad—there being a substantial net outflow from premiums paid by American companies to foreign companies[50]—balance-of-payment

---

reserve to cover fluctuations in claims. To allow for growth, the Supervisory Service permits companies to assign an arbitrary percentage not exceeding 15 percent to the amount computed each year as expected claims in the formula governing changes to the reserve. GENERAL LETTER, *supra* note 44, at 3–5. The result is a growth in the reserve at the average rate of the selected percentage. This percentage must be fixed in advance and may not be changed without a demonstration of necessity. *Id.*

[46]See Pesonen, *supra* note 42, at 7.

[47]Finnish Ins. Companies Act of 1952, §46, translated in 1964 INS. IN FINLAND, No. 2, at 14. In making the necessary computations, primary consideration must be given to protecting policyholders. *Id.* §70, translated in 1964 INS. IN FINLAND, No. 2, at 21.

[48]GENERAL LETTER, *supra* note 44, at 3.

[49]INT. REV. CODE of 1954, §§831, 832. But see *id.* §832(e) (mortgage guaranty insurance losses resulting from adverse economic cycles).

[50]The dollar drain from these payments has been of sufficient concern for the Department of Commerce to collect statistics. In 1968, United States in-

considerations suggest that a similar tax rule might be desirable here.

In 1965, the Supervisory Service refined the calculation of the maximum limitation.[51] More importantly, it extended risk-theoretic techniques to govern determination of total minimum working capital consistent with solvency. Several considerations led to this step. First, officials of the Service had been relying on intuitive judgment in assessing company financial condition, and they believed that impartiality would be furthered by objective rules. Second, the Service had only six examiners, and the lack of manpower argued for a simpler, mechanistic method for making the necessary determinations. Third, risk-theoretic rules generate, in effect, an index of financial strength that can be used for advance warning of financial trouble. The Service regarded this as important, because it is empowered to stop company operations if solvency is threatened and thus effectively force a merger as an alternative to liquidation.[52]

The approach adopted was similar in theory to that already described in connection with the minimum-capital rules.[53] The

surance companies paid $407.9 million to insurance companies resident abroad and received $170.6 million on reinsurance assumed from abroad. Counting losses recovered from abroad on ceded reinsurance ($291 million) and losses paid abroad on assumed reinsurance ($151.6 million) there was a net outflow in 1968 of $97.9 million, the highest in the twenty years since the survey was started. INSURANCE ADVOCATE, Nov. 29, 1969, at 5 (U.S. Dep't of Commerce figures).

[51]The principle adopted was that the equalization reserve would not be excessive if there were a 0.01 probability that claims higher than those expected would exceed the reserve at least once in a five-year period. The assumption is made that during the five years business remains at its current level. The principal component of this probability is represented by the chance that the reserve will be depleted by a series of bad years in which losses exceed expectations, the company completely exhausting its reserve in the fifth year. Because the probability of exhaustion is much greater in the fifth year, the Service accepts calculation of the 0.01 probability based solely on the chance of exhaustion in that year. See CENTRAL ASSOCIATION OF FINNISH INSURANCE COMPANIES, COMPUTATION OF THE LIMITS OF THE EQUALIZATION RESERVE 9–11 (1967) [hereinafter cited as COMPUTATION MANUAL].

[52]Finnish Ins. Companies Act of 1952, §81, translated in 1964 INS. IN FINLAND, No. 2, at 22.

[53]The description in the text is drawn from the GENERAL LETTER, *supra* note 44, the COMPUTATION MANUAL, *supra* note 56, and from interviews with Dr. Erkki Pesonen, Director of the Department of Insurance, and Kalevi Loimaranta, head of the Statistical Center for Nonlife Insurance.

minimum equalization reserve is that amount which together with the other working capital of the company and net premium income is large enough so that there is only a small specified probability that losses will exceed total reserves and net premium income in the coming year. A supplemental restriction requires reserves at least equal to the maximum single risk retained by the company. This prohibits the writing of a single policy larger than total reserves, regardless of the likelihood of a claim under such a policy.

C.

An exact computation of the reserves required by the theoretical statement of the objectives of these rules would not be simple. Most Finnish companies, however, find that their reserves are within authorized safe approximations (safe bound computations) for the minimum and maximum, which are extremely simple to compute, and thus are spared the more complicated computation.[54] For purposes of these computations, premiums in the various lines of insurance are aggregated and treated as a single line.

The approximation for minimum required reserves is computed using a hypothetical company for which individual claims vary in number as in the normal case, but are all equal in size to the largest realistically possible claim against the real company. The expected number of claims against the hypothetical company is deemed to be sufficiently smaller so that the expected total claim against the hypothetical company is equal to the expected total against the real company. The Supervisory Service assumes that the hypothetical company, which is subject to much larger but fewer claims, has a greater probability of being required to pay any given integral multiple of the maximum net retained risk than the real company. For this reason, the approximation is regarded as "safe."[55] While this assump-

[54]A technical description of the safe-bound method appears in Pesonen, *Magnitude Control of Technical Reserves in Finland*, 4 THE ASTIN BULLETIN 248, 250 (1967).

[55]To avoid the possibility that the rough, step-function form of the distribution of the total-claims amount for the hypothetical company would cause a miss of the last catastrophic claim, an amount equal to one claim of the stated constant size is added to the final result. Porn, *supra* note 42, at 2 (equation 1'); COMPUTATION MANUAL, *supra* note 51, at 8.

tion has been rigorously proved only for a special case, it appears true for all realistic situations,[56] and the Service acts on that assumption. Use of the maximum net retained risk is as a practical matter an appropriate solvency control, because companies frequently extend themselves in competing for the largest policies. Since, under the Finnish solvency rules, the maximum net retained risk is already taken into account in computing the required reserves, there is no need for a special limitation as under New York law. Accordingly, Section 6 of the Finnish act simply provides:

> The insurance company shall, by reinsurance or in some other way, carry on its business in such a manner that the interests of the insured are safeguarded by a sound relationship between the probable fluctuation of the company's loss costs and its working capital.[57]

The expected amount of claims is computed from the average loss ratio (incurred losses to earned premiums) for at least five preceding years, multiplied by earned premiums in the year just closed. The expected number of claims against the hypothetical company in the next year is computed by dividing the amount of expected claims in the year just closed by the maximum realistically possible single claim. If a trend in losses or premiums is noticed in any line of insurance, its influence may be taken into account by linear projections from the data of up to five preceding years.[58]

Claims in excess of those expected may be viewed as arising in two ways. First, the basic probabilities associated with the risk may increase due to some temporary change in conditions or as part of a long-term trend. Thus, an exceptionally dry summer will create a heightened risk of fire and change for a time the basic probabilities associated with that risk. Second, changes may arise from simple random fluctuation in the number and amount of claims. In formulating the statutory minimum-capital rule, the Service in effect took both classes of risk into account simply by requiring a safety factor of 0.0001. In its administrative rules, these risks are considered separately, "Bad years" are accounted for by multiplying expected claims

---

[56]Porn, *supra* note 42, at 15.

[57]Finnish Ins. Companies Act of 1952, §6, translated in 1964 INS. IN FINLAND, No. 2, at 3.

[58]COMPUTATION MANUAL, *supra* note 56, at 19.

by a factor intended to increase those amounts to the level of a bad year. The factors required by the Supervisory Service are for the most part between 20 and 40 percent, depending on the class of insurance.[59] They were determined by examining variations in claims statistics for the various lines of insurance over a period of years, excluding extremely abnormal situations such as those produced by major depressions or war, and determining the proportion of the variation which could not within a 0.01 probability be attributed to chance fluctuations, and so might be said to represent a change in the basic probabilities. The Supervisory Service believes the present estimates are somewhat overstated and intends to revise them as further data accumulate. Even though firm conclusions as to the proper magnitudes of these factors are not yet possible, their use protects against trouble for a large number of companies in a bad year, which would make rescue operations by merger extremely difficult, particularly in a small country such as Finland.

Random fluctuations are those variations that would occur even assuming basic probabilities remained unchanged. Protection against such variations is provided by estimating from the expected total amount of claims (strengthened as previously described) an amount sufficiently large so that only a 0.01 probability remains that the actual claims amount would exceed the estimate.

Determining this 0.01 point requires a probability distribution for the number of claims. For this purpose, the Supervisory Service uses the Poisson distribution, which has been employed in mathematical descriptions of a wide variety of phenomena in which discrete events occur randomly and independently.[60] As applied to claims, the Poisson distribution defines the probability of the occurrence of any given number of claims on the assumption that the occurrence or nonoccurrence of claims up to a certain point does not alter the probability that

[59]GENERAL LETTER, *supra* note 44 (appendix 2). For example, liability insurance has a 0.20 factor, fire insurance a 0.40 factor, and forest insurance is in a class by itself with a 6.00 factor. After applying these factors to net premium income for each line, the amounts are aggregated and treated as a single line. *Id.*

[60]The distribution of telephone calls coming into a switchboard is a frequently used example. See 1 FELLER, AN INTRODUCTION TO PROBABILITY THEORY AND ITS APPLICATIONS 413–21 (2d ed. 1957).

additional claims will be made thereafter. One may object that this assumption is not realistic in the insurance context because the occurrence of claims in the beginning of a year may indicate a greater probability that more of the same type are to follow. A model could be constructed on this basis,[61] but the Service prefers to use the Poisson distribution and to account for a "contagion" of claims as a change in the basic probabilities by the method previously described.[62] To simplify computations, a table for applying the Poisson model is furnished by the Supervisory Service.

The consequences of the safe-bound formula may be summarized as follows: There is somewhat less than a 0.01 chance that underlying conditions affecting claims in any line of insurance would so change that the expected claims in that line would exceed the expected amount for a bad year. The probability that all lines would simultaneously have such a bad year is far less than 0.01. In the extraordinary year which is simultaneously bad in all lines, the chance that claims would exceed the required reserves is less than 0.01. The 0.01 probability is based on the assumption that claims in the various lines are independent; to the extent that they are correlated, the probability of excess claims in the extraordinary bad year would be greater than 0.01. Thus, the model is not so precise or statistically so fully supported that the degree of risk can be appraised with certainty. It does, however, offer some benchmarks for this risk, and one can say with some conviction that it is very small.

[61]The Polya model. See Porn, *supra* note 42, at 4–17.

[62]In these computations, earned premiums are premium payments plus (or minus) the net change in the reserve for unearned premiums. Similarly, incurred losses are losses paid plus (or minus) the net change in the reserve for unpaid losses. The premiums received and the losses paid are assumed to have been received and paid evenly throughout the year. The changes in the reserves are computed as if they occurred at midyear, and an annual interest factor of 5 percent is applied to bring them to that point. (This is done by multiplying the reserve at the close of the preceding year by $\sqrt{1.05}$ and the reserve at the close of the year by $1/\sqrt{1.05}$. See COMPUTATION MANUAL, *supra* note 51, at 8–9.) The 5 percent figure was chosen as a conservative estimate of a company's earnings on its investments. Since the net earned premium and the reserve requirements are thus both computed as of the middle of the year, both these quantities are multiplied by an interest factor $(1/\sqrt{1.05})$ to give the amounts required for the beginning of the year. Thus, at the beginning of a year, reserves must not be less than $(1/\sqrt{1.05})(My[v] - p)$, where the symbols have the meaning given in note 72 *infra*.

D.

When reserves lie outside the safe bound limits, a company must either increase its reinsurance if reserves are inadequate or write additional policies or reduce reinsurance if reserves are excessive. But before the former becomes necessary a company may make more exact computations to determine whether the theoretical requirements have been met. The method of computation has not been prescribed by the Supervisory Service, but a manual written by the Central Association of Finnish Insurance Companies describes methods informally approved by the Service.[63]

Since claims may be made in any amount within policy limits, each claim size has a certain probability associated with it. In the more exact computations, these probabilities are determined from historical statistics of the distribution of claim sizes in the same line of insurance. The Finnish Statistical Center for Nonlife Insurance has collected such statistics from a variety of sources, and from them computed the probabilities of various claim amounts for different lines on an industrywide basis. For example, in private accident insurance, these statistics show that there is about a 0.50 probability that a claim will be $10 or less, and a 0.99 probability that it will be approximately $887 or less.[64]

In computing these probabilities, the basic difficulty encountered was that no very large claims were made, thus making it impossible on the basis of experience to determine their probability. The Statistical Center observed, however, that when probability was graphed against claim size on logarithmic paper, the lines were almost straight. It therefore argued that in the absence of other evidence the probabilities for larger claims could be estimated graphically by extending the lines. The Supervisory Service accepts this method of estimation because it appears reasonable and attributes a greater probability to large claims than almost any other plausible assumption involving the hypothesis that the probability of a claim decreases as its size increases. In fact, although this assumption is important in theoretical calculations, it is less significant in practice,

[63]COMPUTATION MANUAL, *supra* note 51.
[64]*Id.* (appendix 2).

because reinsurance cuts off most of these very large potential claims.[65] The Supervisory Service will accept a company's calculations based on the industrywide probability distributions of a single claim unless substantial reasons exist for believing that the shape of the claim distribution of the company is significantly different from that of the industry. This might occur if a company accepted groups of risks uniformly more dangerous or larger compared to its mean risk than was common in the industry.

Determining the probability distribution of total claims in all lines of insurance based on the probability distribution of individual claims presents a formidable calculation problem arising from the fact that any given total can result from a huge number of combinations of single claims. If there were ten thousand individual claims—not an unreasonable figure for a significant company—the required computations would be unwieldy and uneconomic even for modern computers.

Fortunately, ways of approximating these probabilities are known. In 1965, at the time the requirements for a minimum equalization reserve were established, companies making the exact calculation used the so-called Monte Carlo technique.[66] In this method, a computer, using an input of random numbers and the probability distribution of a single claim, simulates the occurrence of claims and computes the total amount of claims a large number of times. The 0.01 probability point is then determined from the sample total. More recently, the Supervisory

---

[65]When safe-bound computations are made, reinsurance of this type (excess of loss) is accounted for by considering only the maximum risk retained by the company. COMPUTATION MANUAL, *supra* note 51, at 6, 20. When exact methods are used, the problem of accounting for such reinsurance is slightly more difficult, because the values of the components of the formulas depend on the probability distribution of a single claim and they change when the probability distribution is changed by the elimination of large claims. To facilitate computation, the *Computation Manual* provides practical tables giving values of the formula components for a broad range of net retentions. *Id.* (appendix 3).

Particular difficulties arise in the case of quota-share reinsurance when the proportion of the policies insured varies. Some companies have assumed, when computing the minimum required reserves, that the reinsurance level is uniformly equal to the minimum proportion reinsured, and have made the converse assumption in computing the maximum permitted reserves. Less draconian solutions to these complexities are still being explored.

[66]*Id.* 4.

Service has approved an extremely simple formula known as the normal power approximation, which is sufficiently accurate unless the company has a disproportionate number of high-risk policies.[67] The Service permits the normal power approximation to be used if the maximum single retained risk is less than twice the standard deviation of the total amount of claims.[68] In only one instance has a company failed to meet this criterion.[69] As in the case of the safe-bound approximation, this method assumes that claims in the various lines are independent; to the extent they are correlated, the risk of insolvency will be larger than that computed.

[67]A derivation of the normal power approximation may be found in BEARD, PENTIKAINEN & PESONEN, RISK THEORY 43–47 (1969). Its accuracy is discussed and numerical examples given in Pesonen, *NP-Approximation of Risk Processes*, SKANDINAVISK AKTUARIETIDSKRIFT 158 (1968). Instructions for using this approximation, which have the informal approval of the Supervisory Service, may be found in COMPUTATION MANUAL, *supra* note 51, at 5–9. A published, slightly different version appears in Hovinen, *Procedures and Basic Statistics to be Used in Magnitude Control of Equalization Reserves in Finland*, 5 THE ASTIN BULLETIN 227 (1969).

Using the normal power approximation as in the *Computation Manual*, the minimum working capital required under the Finnish rules at the beginning of a year is given by

$$U = \frac{1}{\sqrt{1.05}} \left[qp + y\sigma + \frac{1}{6} \frac{\mu^3}{\sigma^2} (y^2 - 1) \right].$$

Substituting the values for $y_{0.01}$, we have

$$U = .976 qp + 2.27\sigma + 7.17 \frac{\mu^3}{\sigma^2}.$$

See COMPUTATION MANUAL, *supra* note 51, at 9. Each term of this expression is the sum of the indicated quantity for all lines of insurance. The first term, qp, represents the excess of expected losses in a bad year over those in a normal year. The second term, $y\sigma$, represents the number of standard deviations necessary to provide a safety margin (here 0.01). The third term adds an amount to account for the fact that the distribution does not die away symmetrically in both tails but has greater area, or probability, in the right tail. The factor μ^3/σ^2 is a measure of the skewness multiplied by the standard deviation of that distribution.

[68]COMPUTATION MANUAL, *supra* note 51, at 7. The technical condition is that the measure of skewness referred to in the preceding note must be less than 2.0.

[69]Interview with Dr. Erkki Pesonen, Director of the Dep't of Insurance, Finnish Ministry for Social Affairs, in Helsinki, June 1970.

III

Solvency controls represent a balancing of risks of insolvency against the cost burdens and anticompetitive effects of required reserves. Every control, explicitly or implicitly, embodies some risk policy. This section uses the Finnish methods to appraise the risk policies implicit in New York's statutory minimum-capital requirements and in its two-to-one and one-to-one administrative rules.

Following the Finnish model, we may view a regulatory authority as making separate policy decisions concerning, respectively, the scope and the degree of protection from risk. The scope of protection is the extent to which provision is made for changes in basic conditions affecting risks. In the Finnish model, questions of this sort were resolved by making a bad-year allowance for each line of insurance, determined from past statistics of abnormal variations of claims in that line.[70] A 20 percent allowance for a line means that in a bad year expected claims would be 20 percent greater than in the current year. In determining these bad-year factors, the Service omitted extremely abnormal years, such as those involving major wars or economic depressions, on the ground that protection from such abnormalities was not worth the cost. Presumably, bad-year factors based on domestic statistics would be different from the Finnish factors, and the difference might be substantial if regulatory authorities here adopted different policies with respect to the remoteness of the risks considered.[71]

The second policy decision is the degree of protection from fluctuation in claims that occurs under the conditions assumed to exist. In the Finnish model, the Supervisory Service assumed the conditions of the hypothetical bad year and permitted a fluctuation risk[72] of 0.01, thus allowing a risk of one in a

---

[70]An abnormal fluctuation was defined as one that would not occur within a 0.01 probability, assuming that current premium rates represented expected losses. The allowance is the percentage by which current expected losses would have to be increased so that losses in the bad year could have occurred within a 0.01 probability.

[71]Other things being equal, one might expect bad-year factors to be smaller for United States companies due to their much greater size and diversity.

[72]The fluctuation risk is the probability that the total claims amount will exceed the amounts reserved.

hundred that in such a year claims would exceed the amounts reserved. Obviously, the 0.01 choice was arbitrary, probably more reflective of a cutoff point commonly used by statisticians in testing hypotheses than a special choice relating to insurance. The risk that claims will in fact exceed the reserves is far smaller than 0.01, since there is only a small probability that the bad-year situation would be realized in any line, and a much smaller probability that it would be simultaneously realized in all lines.

The use of separate bad-year and fluctuation risk factors in effect divides variations in claims into two components. Mathematically, any given reserve could be the result of different combinations of bad-year and fluctuation risk factors which work in opposite directions: the greater the allowance for bad years, the smaller the allowance for the fluctuation risk, and conversely. Since the New York rules do not specify either risk factor, we must relate each rule to pairs of values, each pair being equivalent in total risk to the rule being tested.

In computing these effective policies, the "exact" method of the Finnish system cannot be used, since it depends on the probability distribution of claims derived from Finnish statistics, and we have no assurance that the probability distribution of domestic claims would be similar. The safe bound approximation, however, does not depend upon any particular situation or characteristic of Finnish companies, but only on the general assumption that claims are random and, to a degree, independent events. There is no reason to believe that the claims process on this basic level is different in the United States. Table 11 is based on the safe-bound approximation as applied to established companies—those not experiencing significant growth—whose earned premiums may be taken to equal their written premiums. It pairs the values for the bad-year factors and the fluctuation risks that would lead to the same reserves as the two-to-one rule, assuming a maximum single net retention equal to the New York limit, 10 percent of policyholders' surplus.

For established companies whose largest single risk is equal to the legal maximun, Table 11 shows that the two-to-one rule is equivalent, at one extreme, to the assumption of no change in basic conditions in a bad year and a fluctuation risk of 0.002. At the other extreme, expected claims in a bad year are assumed to

TABLE 11. Risk Equivalents of the Two-to-One Rule (Established Companies)[73]

Bad-year factors	0	0.20	0.40	0.50
Fluctuation risk[74]	0.002	0.01	0.05	0.08

[73]The probabilities shown in Table 11 are from MOLINA, POISSON'S EX-PONENTIAL BINOMIAL LIMIT (1942) (table II). A 50 percent loss ratio (losses to earned premiums) has been assumed.

A sample calculation is set out below. Let

p = net premium income carried during the year = expected claims amount for the year (by assumption),

M = maximum single net retained risk,

q = bad year factor,

U = surplus to policyholders at the beginning of the year, and

$y_a[v]$ = the number of claims, such that, assuming a Poisson process with v as the expected number of claims, there is an a probability that the number of claims will equal or exceed this number.

In the Finnish system,

$$v = \frac{(1 + q)p}{M} \tag{1}$$

(GENERAL LETTER, *supra* note 49, at 2). v is rounded upwards to the next number appearing in tabulations of the Poisson distribution.

The Finnish safe-bound rule is

$$U \geq Max\left\{0, \frac{1}{\sqrt{1.05}} (My_a[v] - p)\right\}.$$

See Porn, *supra* note 42, at 15. The minimum permissible U is defined by the equality portion of the equation, yielding

$$U = \frac{1}{\sqrt{1.05}} (My_a[v] - p),$$

or

$$U + .976p = .976My_a[v].$$

Using (1),

$$U + .976p = .976 \, My_a\left[\frac{(1 + q)p}{M}\right]. \tag{2}$$

In New York, the two-to-one rule dictates that net written premiums shall not exceed twice policyholders' surplus (U). Assuming that during the year net premium income (p) is one-half of net written premiums, as previously stated, and that written premiums are equal to earned premiums, we have $U = p$. Assuming that the maximum permitted single net retained risk is insured, $M = 0.1U = 0.1p$. Therefore,

$$1.976p = .976(0.1p)y_a\left[\frac{(1 + q)p}{0.1p}\right], \tag{3}$$

TABLE 12.   Risk Equivalents of the One-to-One
Rule (Established Companies)[75]

Bad-year factors	0	0.20	0.40	0.70
Fluctuation risk	0.00007	0.0005	0.002	0.01

increase by 50 percent, and the two-to-one rule is equivalent to
a 0.08 fluctuation risk. If the 0.01 fluctuation risk used in
Finland is accepted, the table shows that the two-to-one rule in
effect assumes that expected claims in a bad year would
increase by about 20 percent, a value at the bottom of the range
actually computed by the Finns. This suggests that for an established company with a maximum net retention equal to the
legal maximum, the two-to-one rule would probably be consistent with reasonable values for both parameters.

The one-to-one rule was adopted for fire insurance because
of the possibility of greater fluctuations of claims in that line.
The Finnish method provides a way of appraising this choice
(see Table 12).

The shift in policy on claim fluctuations represented by the
one-to-one rule may be analyzed by comparing the bad-year allowances in Tables 11 and 12 for the same fluctuation risk. Thus
a 0.01 risk under the two-to-one rule has about a 20 percent bad-
year allowance associated with it, while the same risk under the
one-to-one rule corresponds to about a 70 percent allowance.
The one-to-one rule for fire insurance thus embodies the assumption that fluctuations in fire claims arising from changes in
basic conditions are about three and one-half times greater than
plausible average bad-year allowances for other lines.[76]

Although data are lacking for the United States, the Finnish

---

or, $20.24 = y_a \, [10(1 + q)]$. Assume $q = .20$, and the result is $20.24 = y_a \, [12]$.
Using tables of the Poisson distribution for an expected value of 12, we find
that the probability of twenty-one or more claims (the point of ruin) is 0.012 as
shown in the table (rounded to 0.01).

[74]Fluctuation risk is defined in note 72 *supra*.

[75]Same source and assumption as in Table II. See note 73 *supra*. The figures in Table 12 may be derived from the sample calculation given for Table
11 by setting $U = 2p$ in equation (3) of note 73 *supra*.

[76]The multiple would be larger for smaller values of q, and smaller for
larger values, although in the latter case, the assumed q value for the fire line
would have to become so large as to be unreasonable.

studies indicate that fire claim fluctuation is much closer to fluctuation in other lines than is indicated by this relation between
the New York rules; probably it is not twice the average for
other lines.[77] Even assuming it to be twice this average, a 0.01
fluctuation risk would lead to approximately a three-to-two rule
for fire insurance—a one-third reduction in the amounts currently required.

Although the two-to-one rule may be defensible for established companies insuring the legal maximum single risk, it
represents a much more stringent policy for companies electing
not to compete for the largest contracts. This is because the
rules are not correlated with the size distribution of potential
claims, but only with their total amount as reflected in written
premiums. In the safe-bound method, the largest single risk is
used as a surrogate for the probability distribution of claim
sizes, and so the risk policy represented by the two-to-one rule
changes with the size of that risk.

**TABLE 13. Risk Equivalents of the Two-to-One Rule (Es-
tablished Companies)[78]**

BAD-YEAR FACTORS	0	0.20	0.40	0.50
Fluctuation risks when MNR* equals:				
1%[79]	0[80]	0	0.000003	0.00002
5%	0.00003	0.001	0.01	0.03
10%	0.002	0.01	0.05	0.08

*Maximum single net retained risk as percent of surplus to policyholders.

[77]The bad-year factor for fire insurance is 0.40 in the Finnish system, while
the smallest factor is 0.20. GENERAL LETTER, *supra* note 44, at 12.

[78]Same source and assumption as in Table 11. See note 73 *supra*. The 10
percent line of Table 13 is taken directly from Table 11. The 5 percent line
may be derived by setting $M = 0.05p$ in equation (3) of note 73 *supra*. The 1
percent line may be derived by setting $M = 0.01p$ in equation (3) of note 73
supra.

[79]These entries were calculated using the normal approximation to the
Poisson distribution. For large expected values, the Poisson distribution
approaches the normal distribution. The figures are from NAT'L BUREAU OF
STANDARDS, TABLES OF NORMAL PROBABILITY FUNCTIONS (1953).

[80]Zero entries indicate a probability of less than 0.000001.

Table 13 shows, for example, that allowing 20 percent for a bad year, a company with a legal maximum single risk (10 percent of policyholders' surplus) has a fluctuation risk of about 0.01; if the largest single risk is half the maximum, the fluctuation risk is about 0.001; if one tenth the maximum, the fluctuation risk is less than one in a million. Similar disparities appear in the full range of bad-year factors.

The lack of consistency means that the two-to-one rule, or any rule based solely on a multiple of premiums, cannot be sustained in general as a reasonable accommodation between the risk of insolvency and the burden of reserves. If the rule is correct for companies at the legal limit for their largest single risk, it must be excessive as to others, and for some vastly so.[81] If it is correct for those companies with smaller maximum single risks, it is inadequate for those insuring the legal maximum.

Probably the most important consequence of the New York rules is the burden they impose on entering and growing companies. New York's statutory fixed minimum-capital requirements have their principal effect on entering companies, because the administrative rules will require reserves greater than the statutory reserves as a company's premium writings grow much above $4 million.[82] Beneath this premium level, statutory reserves will usually lie between $1 million and $2 million, and this will exceed the amounts required even under the one-to-one rule for companies with less than $1 million in written premiums. This distinct treatment of smaller companies—requiring reserves which bear a larger proportion to written premiums—may be justified on the ground that smaller companies are likely to be subject to greater claim fluctuations than larger companies. To test the extent to which proportionately larger reserves could be justified on this basis, consider the situation if $1 million is required as permanent capital. Expendable capital for start-up costs and permanent capital-

[81]The theoretical conclusions that the two-to-one rule requires excessive resources is supported by a recent statistical study showing that for most lines of insurance, the industrywide average of claims is less than 50 percent of the average net premium writings. Hofflander, *Minimum Capital and Surplus Requirements for Multiple Line Insurance Companies: A New Approach*, in INSURANCE, GOVERNMENT AND SOCIAL POLICY: STUDIES IN INSURANCE REGULATION 69, 82–86 (Kimball & Denenberg eds. 1969, table 2).

[82]See text accompanying notes 19–11 *supra*.

TABLE 14. Fluctuation Risks Assuming $1 Million in Required Surplus[83]

BAD-YEAR FACTOR:	0	0.20	0.40	0.50
Fluctuation risk when net written premiums equal (in $1,000s):				
100[84]	0	0	0	0
250	0	0	0	0
500	0.000002	0.00002	0.00008	0.0002
750	0.00005	0.0003	0.001	0.002
1,000	0.00007	0.0005	0.002	0.005

liquidation expenses are deemed covered by separate amounts. Using the safe bound approximation, and assuming that the maximum single-net retained risk is 10 percent of surplus, the fluctuation risks are given in Table 14.

Table 14 shows that for companies with written premiums up to $1 million, the risk of the total claims amount exceeding the statutorily required reserves is far smaller than under the two-to-one rule if that were applied solely to a larger company. Thus, for entering and small companies, the statutory rules represent a significantly more stringent risk policy, which cannot be justified by reference to the possibility of greater fluctuations in claims.

As a company grows, it needs a greater absolute reserve due to increased expected losses. These losses for the coming year are generally estimated by multiplying the earned premiums for the preceding year (the portion of the written premium allocated to that year) by an average loss ratio (losses to earned premiums averaged over a number of recent years). Clearly the written premium, if different from the earned premium, would not be correct in this computation. Since the New York rules use written premiums, and since for a growing company written premiums exceed earned premiums, these rules overstate the

[83]Same source and assumption as in Table 11. See note 73 *supra*. For the first entry of Table 14, set $p = 0.1U$ in equation (3) of note 73 *supra*. Then $p = 0.05U$ and $M = 2p$ in the same equation. These figures are then used in equation (3) of note 73 *supra*. Similar calculations yield the rest of Table 14.

[84]Zero entries indicate a probability of less than 0.000001.

TABLE 15.   Increase in Safe Bound Reserves as
a Percentage of Increase in Two-to-One Reserves

BAD-YEAR FACTORS	0	0.20	0.40	0.50
Percentage relationship	22	40	57	65

increase in reserves required to cover growth. We measure the
overstatement by comparing the reserves a growing company is
required to add under the safe bound rules as a percentage of
the required additions under the two-to-one rule. To make the
comparison, we assume a maximum net retention of 10 percent
of surplus and that the increase in earned premium is one-third
the increase in written premiums. Setting 0.01 as a reasonable
fluctuation risk, Table 15 shows the percentage relationships.

The table indicates that additions to reserves at the rate of
between one-fifth and two-thirds the rate required by the two-
to-one rule would preserve a consistent margin of safety in a
growth situation; looking at the matter another way, under one
set of assumptions, if the fluctuation risk under the two-to-one
rule for an established company is 0.01, the risk for a company
whose written premiums have increased by 30 percent over the
preceding year would be 0.008; if the increase were 150 percent, risk would be 0.001.[85] Written premium rules thus impose
an excessive burden on growing companies, the extent of which
depends on the rate of growth.

The burden of the requirements on growing companies is
compounded by the method of accounting for unearned premiums. Assume that the expenses of writing an additional $100
in premiums are $40, that expected loss claims over three years
are $50, and that a third of the written premium is earned in the
current year and the balance deferred by crediting the unearned premium reserve. Under current accounting practice,
the company deducts the entire $40 as a current expense and
$17 in loss claims, and carries the unearned premium reserve as
a liability. The difference between the net increase in assets
($43) and the increase in liabilities ($67) reduces policyholders'

---

[85]To separate out effects it has been assumed in the above figures that the
maximum single net retention grows with the company, always remaining at
the legal maximum. If this were not true, disparities between growth and established companies would be substantially greater than stated.

surplus $24. This depletion would be reversed in subsequent years, when the balance of the premium is earned without additional charge. But since growing companies have a disproportionate number of first-year policies, they continually drain policyholders' surplus in building up a prepaid expense equity in unearned premiums, a process which continues until the rate of growth declines. Meanwhile, the requirements of the administrative rules must be satisfied. Thus, in the above example, an additional policyholders' surplus of $74 would be required to fund the increase of $100 in premium writings ($50 to cover the $100 increase in written premiums and $24 to cover depletion of surplus).

Since most rapidly growing companies do not have sufficient surplus to meet the requirements of the New York rules, they use reinsurance to finance premium growth. The company pays to the reinsurer the proportion of the gross premium equal to the reinsurer's proportion of the risk assumed; the reinsurer pays to the company a commission in an amount such that the net premium retained by the reinsurer is sufficient to cover its portion of the expected loss claim plus expenses and a profit. The company's net written premium is thus reduced, while its surplus benefits from substituting a current commission, which increases surplus, for later-accruing premiums, which are carried as a liability. By reinsurance, the company in effect borrows policyholders' surplus against its prepaid expense equity in unearned premiums.[86]

If the company in the above example reinsures half the $100 policy, it would give up half the earned and unearned premiums in return for, say, a $21 commission from the reinsurer and the reinsurer's assumption of half the claim loss. During the first year, the company's financial statement would show $50 in net written premiums and $21 in commission income, against $40 in expenses, $8 in loss claims, and a $33 increase in unearned premium liability, for a net decrease in surplus of $10. Reserves required to finance this $100 growth would thus be $35 ($25 to cover the $50 increase in net written premiums and $10 to cover depletion of surplus). Under risk-theoretic rules, assuming the risk standards of the two-to-one rule set

[86]For a discussion, see 1 MUNICH REINSURANCE CO., REINSURANCE AND REASSURANCE 3–8 (1963).

forth in Table 11, the required reserves would be only slightly larger—some $41—and the company would not have the net $4 cost of reinsurance ($29 reinsurance premium less $25 loss claim assumed by the reinsurer). The example illustrates that by reducing the reserves required for growth, even safe bound risk-theoretic methods should permit substantial savings in reinsurance premiums.

IV

Risk-theoretic analysis reveals significant defects in New York's solvency-control rules. The New York statutes impose unnecessary burdens on entering and small companies because they require fixed dollar amounts of capital without reference to premium income or other measures of expected losses. The Department of Insurance's administrative rules, based on written premiums, discriminate against companies not competing for the largest policies and against those in rapid growth: the first because the rules ignore the size distributions of retained risks, and the second because they make no allowance for the lag between earned and written premiums. Entering companies are also at a disadvantage compared to established companies because of the Department's previously mentioned policy of relaxing the administrative rules in favor of companies with a history of profitable operations.[87] While this may be justifiable in terms of solvency protection, the discrimination against new entrants emphasizes that the stated rules should be no stricter than solvency considerations would dictate when underwriting skill has yet to be established. The special burden of the present rules on entering and growing companies may have an unnecessary chilling effect on competition and on expansion of industry capacity.

This much is deducible from, or at least suggested by, theoretical considerations without reference to empirical data. If some reasonable assumptions are made concerning claim statistics, it appears that the two-to-one rule may not be overly stringent in all situations, but that the one-to-one rule probably represents an extreme view of the extent of fluctuation in fire and

---

[87]Text accompanying note 15 *supra*.

marine claims. A definitive judgment as to the acceptability of these rules, however, would have to await study of claim materials and decision on risk policies.

If the Finnish experience is a fair guide, the introduction of risk-theoretic rules should affect reinsurance practices most significantly. By reducing reserve requirements, total reinsurance should be reduced. In Finland, reinsurance declined from about 50 percent when the equalization reserve was introduced in 1953 to about 33 percent in 1957; the figures for transport insurance were about 70 percent and 58 percent, respectively.[88] Further declines may occur as the full impact of the changes made in 1965 is realized. Under rating systems commonly used in the United States, the cost of reinsurance is passed on to the consumer in the form of higher premium rates.[89] Consequently, if comparable reductions in reinsurance were effected here, there should be substantial savings for consumers, particularly in the case of rapidly growing companies.

In defining more precisely and persuasively the reserves actually required for solvency, risk-theoretic methods should throw into sharp relief the propriety of present practices by which policyholders bear the total cost of reinsurance. This issue has not arisen in Finland probably because Finnish companies lack the extensive resources of American companies. But since free reserves of companies are extensive and are frequently used in acquisition programs through conglomerates—to the benefit of stockholders—it seems reasonable for policyholders to carry only that portion of reinsurance costs needed to protect solvency, while reinsurance costs above that level should not be considered in setting premium rates.[90]

[88]See Pentikainen, *Fluctuation Reserve: A Technique to Take into Account the Fluctuation of the Risk Business When Calculating the Technical Reserves of Insurance Companies*, 1970 INS. IN FINLAND, No. 1, at 3, 7.

[89]Reinsurance premiums paid by a company will normally exceed the losses paid by the reinsurer. As a result, a reinsurance program will increase the loss ratio (the ratio of net losses paid by the company to net premiums retained by the company after deduction of payments to reinsurers). Since overall premium rates are commonly set so that, after deduction of expenses and an allowance for profit, the remaining proportion of premium dollar equals the loss ratio (averaged over several recent years), an increase in the loss ratio leads directly to an increase in rates.

[90]Cf. *Hearings on Leasco Data Processing Corp. Before the House Antitrust Subcomm. of the House Comm. on the Judiciary*, 91st Cong., 2d Sess., ser., 23, pt. 2, at 32 (1970)(remarks of Representative Celler).

When mathematical methods are used in the law, the fear is sometimes expressed that with some mathematical twist or seemingly innocent shift in input, the cognoscenti can manipulate the techniques for their benefit. In constructing their regulations, the Finns were concerned with the problem of technicality, but from a different point of view. The regulators promoted risk-theoretic methods but, to facilitate compliance, sought techniques that could easily be applied, even by those who did not understand them. In fact, the essence of the Finnish method is not the application of computer techniques to the problem of solvency control but the distillation of very simple rules from a highly complicated and technical branch of probability theory.

The safe-bound methods applicable to the great majority of companies are so simple, and their basis so clearly revealed, that manipulation is difficult to envision short of simple fraud in reporting, a risk under any system. When "exact" methods are required, companies will usually use the normal power approximation; this would require a computer, except that prepared tables reduce the computation to a trivial matter of substitution in a formula. In the exceptional cases governed by neither the safe-bound rules nor the normal power approximation, the computation is more complex. The failure, however, to satisfy requirements of more simple methods means that the company is much closer to danger and its status deserves more careful consideration. By sharpening the focus of regulatory concern, risk-theoretic methods should reduce the opportunities for manipulation, even in the exceptional case where the level of technicality is substantial.

It may be objected that the Finnish method does not yield an accurate measure of the fluctuation risk and does not in fact even purport to do so. This is true. The use of safe-bound assumptions at several points means that the computed risk is overstated, but the degree of overstatement cannot be estimated without complicated effort. Moreover, as we have observed, making allowances for bad years precludes a precise specification of risk, even assuming no overstatement in the methods of approximation. Greater precision is attainable in theory but would require more data and more complex calculations.

The Finns in fact made a decision common in the law: they traded precision of result for certainty and simplicity in application. It should be noted, however, that the formal regulations merely require that mathematical methods be used to compute reserves sufficient to keep the fluctuation risk under 0.01. The technique by which this is done is left open, and a company may use methods different from those suggested if it can demonstrate that accuracy would be improved by the substitution. Thus the basic regulatory decision was to require a mathematical approach to the problem of solvency and a specification of the degree of acceptable risk. Within this framework, the methods of computation can become as accurate as the companies undertake to make them. Meanwhile, the public interest is protected by "safe" methods.

The fluctuation risk is not of course the only threat to solvency. There are many others, but probably the most frequently discussed is the danger of investment losses from declines in the securities markets. This problem is less visible in Finland, where insurance companies invest principally in debt and do not have the common-stock portfolios held by American companies which are subject to much greater fluctuations in value.

But this problem was recognized in Finland, and by omitting it from mathematical consideration the Finns in effect treated market fluctuation as a problem distinct from claims fluctuation. This seems correct: the extent of market risk depends on the nature of the investment portfolio and other factors comparatively unrelated to claims risk.[91] To squeeze both market and claims risks under a single written premium rule implies that regulation cannot in any realistic sense rest on an informed judgment as to the degree of danger from each source. It is generally accepted that protection from investment losses calls for a conservative valuation of portfolio securities, and there would be no conflict between the use of a conservative rule in this valuation and the simultaneous use of risk-theoretic methods to estimate the fluctuation risk.[92]

[91]A study has shown that claims losses and return on investment are in fact independent phenomena. See Lambert & Hofflander, *The Impact of New Multiple Line Underwriting on Investment Portfolios of Property-Liability Insurers*, 33 J. RISK & INS. 209–33 (1966).

[92]An appropriate rule could be built on statistics of variations in securities prices. See Hofflander, *Minimum Capital and Surplus Requirements for Multiple Line Insurance Companies: A New Approach*, in INSURANCE, GOVERNMENT AND SOCIAL POLICY: STUDIES IN INSURANCE REGULATION 69 (Kimball & Denenberg eds. 1969). A theoretical development appears in ARTHUR D. LITTLE, INC., PRICES AND PROFITS IN THE PROPERTY AND LIABILITY INSURANCE INDUSTRY E-8 (1967) (a report to the American Insurance Association).

To what extent does the Finnish method depend on particular conditions not likely to be duplicated in a different regulatory setting? The exact method depends on the probability distribution of claim sizes, and this must reflect claim statistics. It is, however, a mathematical fact that differences in the shapes of these distributions within the range encountered in practice will not change the results very much. And, as previously noted, the safe-bound methods applicable to most companies use the maximum claim as a safe approximation for the distribution function of claim sizes, and thus are not to any extent dependent on the shape of those distributions or on the parochial claim experiences underlying them. Of course, bad-year factors must be set, and the policy decisions there involved should be predicated upon the experience of variations in claims. But because the factors being measured are to reflect abnormalities, a frequent updating of the experience would not seem necessary; and requiring the regulatory authority to take systematic cognizance of its experience from time to time is not unduly onerous. Indeed, the present two-to-one and one-to-one rules represent just such an intuitive appreciation of experience in the 1930s.

If it had been necessary to compute exact probabilities of ruin in Finland, the objective of simplicity could not have been achieved. But this was not necessary; to avoid complexities which might introduce errors, the model builders chose safe approximations as simplifying assumptions at various points in the method. No one knows how much was denied to accuracy in these choices. It is nevertheless striking that despite compromises with perfection, the results read so strongly on rules formed by educated intuition.

Chapter 7

REGRESSION MODELS IN ADMINISTRATIVE PROCEEDINGS

I

THE TERM "regression," as it is used here, refers to a certain technique for estimating a mathematical relationship between factors on the basis of numerical data. The use of regression has become firmly established as the standard method of analysis in econometric (mathematical economic) models used by both public and private decision makers in formulating and examining policies.[1] The same techniques are now beginning to be used in dealing with important issues in sharply contested regulatory proceedings; in these contexts the precision, reliability, and usefulness of regression methodology have become a special province and concern of lawyers.

---

[1]Several well-known models of the United States economy are used by government departments and agencies in formulating policies. The best known of these are the Wharton School Model and the Brookings Institution Model. See, e.g., EVANS & KLEIN, THE WHARTON ECONOMETRIC FORECASTING MODEL (1968); THE BROOKINGS QUARTERLY ECONOMETRIC MODEL OF THE UNITED STATES (Dusenberry ed. 1965). A number of departments and agencies make use of these models for long-range planning. Regression analysis has also been used by groups appearing before congressional committees. See, e.g., *Hearings on Competition in the Pharmaceutical Industry before the*

Regression studies have been introduced in proceedings before the Commodity Exchange Authority,[2] the Federal Power Commission,[3] the Securities and Exchange Commission,[4] the Civil Aeronautics Board,[5] the Federal Communications Commission,[6] the Postal Rate Commission,[7] and various state

---

Subcomm. on Monopoly of the Senate Select Comm. on Small Business, 90th Cong., 1st & 2d Sess., pt. 5, at 1746 (1968) (study sponsored by the Pharmaceutical Manufacturing Association); *id.* at 2120 (reply study introduced by the Federal Trade Commission).

For a discussion of the use of regression models by private decision makers, see, e.g., HEWARD & STEELE, BUSINESS CONTROL THROUGH MULTIPLE REGRESSION ANALYSIS (1972).

Other uses of regression have a statutory basis. For example, §9 of the Federal Aid Highway Act of 1962 requires that the Secretary of Transportation shall not approve transportation projects in any urban area of more than fifty thousand persons "unless he finds that such projects are based on a continuing comprehensive transportation planning process...." Federal-Aid Highway Act of 1962, 23 U.S.C. §134 (1970). The Federal Highway Administration interpreted the statute as requiring "that estimates be made of the future demands for all modes of transportation both public and private for both persons and goods," and set forth requirements for those estimates which appear to contemplate econometric techniques. Federal Highway Administration, Policy and Procedure Memorandum No. 50–9, at 2 (Nov. 24, 1969). One of the techniques used was a mathematical regression in which the percentage of trips by mass or by automobile was estimated from the ratio of mass-transit travel time to automobile travel time, family income, population density, automobile ownership, parking costs, employment density, accessibility to the population of each form of transit, and accessibility of employment from each form of transit. U.S. DEPARTMENT OF TRANSP., MODAL SPLIT: DOCUMENTATION OF NINE METHODS FOR ESTIMATING TRANSIT USAGE 94–95 (1966). Common sense suggests that an increase in speed of mass transit will lure patrons away from their automobiles; the regression equation purports to give quantitative assessments of this and similar defects.

For introductory discussions of regression techniques, see WONNACOTT & WONNACOTT, ECONOMETRICS (1970) [hereinafter cited as WONNACOTT]; EZEKIEL & FOX, METHODS OF CORRELATION AND REGRESSION ANALYSIS (3d ed. 1967) [hereinafter cited as EZEKIEL & FOX]. More technical and difficult is the standard JOHNSTON, ECONOMETRIC METHODS (1963) [hereinafter cited as JOHNSTON]. See also, DRAPER & SMITH, APPLIED REGRESSION ANALYSIS (1967); RAO & MILLER, APPLIED ECONOMETRICS (1971) [hereinafter cited as RAO & MILLER]; SMILLIE, AN INTRODUCTION TO REGRESSION AND CORRELATION (1966).

[2]See pp. 224–26 *infra.*

[3]See pp. 226–32 *infra.*

[4]See pp. 235–37 *infra.*

[5]See pp. 240–44 *infra.*

[6]See pp. 215–24 *infra.*

[7]See p. 247 & note 131 *infra.*

public-utility commissions.[8] The regression models introduced in most of these proceedings purport to furnish estimates of the economic effect of changes in the factor subject to regulatory control on the assumption that other economic factors and conditions either remain unchanged or change in specified ways. Since this is precisely the type of judgment frequently made by administrative agencies, proponents of econometric studies have presented regression methodology as a tool of considerable regulatory value.

Despite this theoretical promise, the proponents of regression studies have not been particularly successful in practice. Mathematical formulation thoroughly exposes the assumptions and methods of deduction by which the expert econometrician makes statistical projections. Those assumptions and methods are relatively easy to criticize; in simplifying reality, as it must, any mathematical model is open to the charge that some important element has been omitted or imperfectly represented. Parties adversely affected by econometric results have seized the opportunity afforded by cross-examination and rebuttal to loosen barrages of criticism and to introduce alternative models yielding significantly different conclusions. Confronted with the welter of objections and conflicting technical points, decision makers have often retreated to safe ground and either rejected econometrics outright or emphasized that their decisions did not depend on the mathematical results even when consistent with them.

The unfamiliarity of regression techniques has undoubtedly impeded their acceptance. But the conflicting views of the experts in adversary proceedings have also disclosed certain difficulties arising from the complexity of phenomena sought to be described, from the baffling clash of objections, and from some uncertainty on the part of decision makers as to the proper use of econometric estimates. A closer examination of these difficulties in the context of several proceedings involving regression models suggests that certain protocols should be observed when econometric studies are introduced in evidence, and particularly when they are used as a basis for economic prediction. The purpose of this article is to develop these protocols. I begin by presenting basic regression concepts and methodology

[8]See, e.g., note 45 *infra*.

through a discussion of one hypothetical example and two actual cases, the first before the Federal Communications Commission, the second before the Commodity Exchange Authority.

II

Suppose one seeks to determine the relationship between the heights of fathers and their sons as part of a study of the genetic transmission of stature. A range will be observed in the heights of the sons whose fathers are at any given level of height. Thus, no general mathematical relationship between the height of a son and that of his father can be formulated. However, a mathematical expression can describe the relationship between the average (mean) height of sons and of fathers at each given level of height. This is known as a regression relation, in which the dependent variable (average height of sons) is regressed on the explanatory or independent variable (height of fathers), which is the regressor.[9] The graphic description of this relation is a regression line or curve, and its mathematical description is a regression equation. If one wishes to include other influences on the dependent variable, such as the height of the mother, these may be added as regressors. In the regression equation, a number (its coefficient[10]) determining its "weight" in the estimate of the dependent variable is associated with each explanatory variable.

The coefficients of the explanatory variable are computed so as to minimize the sum of the squared differences between each

[9]The term "regression" is used to describe this technique of analysis because, in terms of the example, the height of sons of exceptionally short or exceptionally tall fathers will be closer to or "regressed" toward the average height of all sons in the sample. This is so because the impact of other influences, such as the height of the mother, will tend on the average to make less exceptional the stature of children of exceptional fathers. See WONNACOTT 122 & n. 7.

[10]In addition, a separate constant term, also estimated from the data, is frequently included in the equation.

[11]Ideally, one would estimate the regression equation on the basis of the entire population of data. However, because the population is generally unknown, computations must be performed on the basis of a sample. The regres-

of the observed values of the dependent variable[11] and the values computed on the basis of the regression equation.[12] This procedure is known as the "least squares" method of estimation, and the widespread use of packaged computer programs makes the computations of the equations relatively easy. In some contexts, the value of these coefficients is the point of primary concern to the investigator, while in others, the focus of attention is on the computed value of the dependent variable. Models described in this chapter illustrate each of these situations.[13]

A.

A more detailed understanding of the basic mechanics of regression can be obtained from a consideration of a rate-making proceeding involving Western Union,[14] in which the Federal Communications Commission sought to determine Western Union's cost of equity as a step in determining its total cost of capital.[15] Although cost of equity traditionally is determined by the earnings-price ratio of a company's common stock, an expert for Western Union argued that its earnings had been abnormally depressed, so that the earnings-price ratio yielded manifestly absurd results.[16] The expert proposed to estimate cost of equity for Western Union by examining cost of equity for other regulated utility groups and adjusting for differences in risk.[17] The risk adjustment was made by using an index of

---

sion equation based on the sample is thus an estimate of the "true" regression equation which would describe the population. See notes 30 & 31 *infra*.

[12]Squared differences are used because, in an important class of cases, it can be shown that an estimate based on least squares estimation will be more precise than estimates computed on any other basis. WONNACOTT 21–22.

[13]See, e.g., the CAB models, pp. 240–43 *infra* (coefficient of primary concern); natural-gas models, pp. 226–32 *infra* (dependent variable of primary concern).

[14]In re Western Union Tel. Co. , No. 18935 (F.C.C., filed Aug. 12, 1970).

[15]The rate of return allowed to Western Union would at least equal its cost of capital.

[16]Western Union Exhibit No. 7, at 16, In re Western Union Tel. Co., No. 18935 (F.C.C., filed Aug. 12, 1970) (testimony of David A. Kosh).

[17]*Id.*

variability of earnings.[18] Research produced the statistics of cost of equity and earnings variability shown in the footnote.[19]

Before determining the optimal method of evaluating these statistics, a decision maker must accept them as an appropriate basis for estimating cost of equity. There must be some underlying theory which supports the notion that variability of earnings is indeed an appropriate measure of risk, and that risk is a relevant factor for adjusting the cost of equity. There must also be a justification for omitting other factors seemingly relevant to a determination of cost of equity, and this involves a demonstration that the particular industries selected are comparable to Western Union except for those factors which are accounted for by the difference in variability of earnings.[20]

Assuming such demonstration is made, and a decision maker accepts the expert's argument that the statistics are appropriate, how should they be evaluated? Confronted with this problem,

[18]Variability was defined as the standard deviation around the 1957–60 trend in earnings (to avoid treating simple growth in earnings as variability) divided by the mean of earnings (to eliminate the factor of absolute size of earnings per share). *Id.* at 40–41.

[19]

Utility Group	Cost of Equity	Variability of Rate Earned on Book
AT&T	9.9%	3.6%
Electrics	10.4%	7.1%
Independent Telephones	10.4%	10.6%
Gas Pipelines	11.4%	11.9%
Gas Distribution	12.2%	12.9%
Water Utilities	10.0%	17.1%
Truckers	16.5%	44.0%
Airlines	18.9%	76.0%
WESTERN UNION	?	27.0%

Id., Attachment No. 1, at 11. Kosh has used a similar approach in other proceedings, among them the proceedings before the CAB relating to fair rate of return. Exhibit JC-K, Domestic Passenger Fare Investigation Phase 8, No. 21866-8 (C.A.B., Aug. 3, 1970) (testimony of David A. Kosh). A similar approach used by Kosh in an earlier proceeding involving Western Union was criticized by the FCC. Western Union Tel. Co., 27 F.C.C.2d 515, 524–30 (1971).

[20]Kosh was in fact criticized by a rebuttal witness who argued that two of the utility groups, truckers and airlines, did not enjoy a territorial monopoly and consequently were subject to more intense competition than was Western Union. Department of Defense Exhibit No. 12, at 17, In re Western Union Tel. Co., No. 18935 (F.C.C., filed Aug. 12, 1970) (testimony of Robert R. Nathan). Exclusion of these two groups vitiated Kosh's conclusions. *Id.* at 17–19.

most lawyers would resort to an "intuitive" method. One possible intuitive approach would begin with the observation that the cost for Western Union should lie somewhere between the cost for industry groups immediately below and immediately above the company in terms of risk: the 10 percent cost for water utilities, which have a variability of 17.1 percent, and the 16.5 percent cost for truckers, which have a variability of 44.0 percent. A straight-line interpolation between these two groups would yield a cost for Western Union of about 12.4 percent.

Such an approach, however, is open to objections. First, the results are highly sensitive to the particular industries used as points of departure. For example, if for some reason the use of electrics instead of water utilities could be justified, the straight-line interpolation would yield a cost for Western Union of 13.7 instead of 12.4 percent. Second, if there is in fact a discernible relation between cost and variability, it seems irrational to discard most of the data describing that relation (the data on other industry groups) and to depend solely on two points of data. Third, there is no particular rationale for a straight line as opposed to other modes of interpolation.

Another intuitive approach would use a ratio of cost to variability derived from other industries and apply that ratio to Western Union's variability to estimate its cost. But it is unclear which ratio should be used. The ratio of the industry closest in variability to Western Union (water utilities) would yield a cost of about 15.8 percent for Western Union. The use of the average ratio of all the industry groups would yield a cost of about 28.1 percent.[21] This difference highlights the difficulty with this approach. An estimate based on a ratio for another industry group, or on the average for all groups, is appropriate only if it is reasonable to assume that there is a constant relation between cost and variability. Yet the statistics themselves belie that assumption, since the ratios vary from about 25 percent for airlines to 275 percent for AT&T.

These examples illustrate the point that intuitive methods

[21]The use of an average ratio of variability to cost instead of an average ratio of cost to variability yields a cost of equity for Western Union of about 17.2 percent instead of 28.1 percent, which further illustrates the arbitrary differences that are obtainable with different intuitive methods.

frequently require questionable assumptions, including the elimination of data, to reduce the numbers to manageable terms. In view of the almost arbitrary quality of these assumptions, any choice between significantly different intuitive methods of estimation is bound to produce disputes that cannot easily or rationally be resolved. More broadly, it might be argued that the statistics do not demonstrate a sufficiently close relationship between cost of equity and variability to justify any inference; after all, widely differing degrees of earnings variability are all associated with a 10 percent cost of equity. On the other hand, there is evidently some increase in cost of equity as variability increases. In sum, any inference must at best be uncertain, but the degree of uncertainty cannot be appraised intuitively.

Regression analysis provides a superior methodology for dealing with these problems. Given the statistics used by the expert, the basic regression decision is the choice of the form of equation that would best describe the data. One possibility is a linear equation, the form most frequently encountered. A regression in linear form assumes that a given quantity of change in the independent variable (variability) is always associated with the same given quantity of change in the dependent variable (cost). Another possibility is a regression in multiplicative or log linear form, which assumes that a given proportionate change in the independent variable is always associated with a given proportionate change in the dependent variable. These are not the only possibilities, but they are the ones most commonly encountered in practice.[22] Applied to the statistics used by the expert,[23] the linear regression equation yields a cost of equity for Western Union of 13.00 percent,[24] while the log linear equation yields a cost of 13.78 percent.[25]

The choice between forms of regression equation is determined by considerations of economic theory and by the respec-

---

[22]For a discussion of some characteristics of log linear and other nonlinear equations, see EZEKIEL & FOX 70–80.

[23]The computations in this section were performed by Thomas Shemo.

[24]The linear regression equation is

$$Y \text{ (cost)} = 9.459 + 0.1312\,X \text{ (variability)}.$$

[25]The log linear regression equation is:

$$\log Y \text{ (cost)} = 1.882 + 0.2268 \log X \text{ (variability)}.$$

tive precision of each of the regression estimates. The basic measure of precision of the equation as a whole is the correlation between the observed values of the dependent variable and the estimated values generated by the regression equation. This correlation is frequently referred to as the "fit" of the equation, and its measure, the coefficient of determination,[26] is denoted R^2. If the regression equation yielded estimates which coincided exactly with the actual values of the dependent variable, all variability would be "explained" by the regression estimate. In that circumstance, R^2 would equal one. At the other hypothetical extreme, if the regression estimate explained none of the variation in the values of the dependent variable, R^2 would equal zero. An R^2 of 0.90, for example, means that 90 percent of total variability of the dependent variable has been explained or accounted for by the regression estimate. R^2 is thus a measure of the explanatory power of the regression equation.[27]

[26]More precisely,

$$R^2 = \frac{\Sigma \hat{y}^2}{\Sigma y^2} \, ,$$

where $\hat{y}$ is the difference between the computed value of the dependent variable and the mean of the values of the dependent variable in the sample and y is the difference between the actual and mean values. "Σ" directs the summing of these squared differences over the range of the data. The square root of the coefficient of determination is known as the correlation coefficient and is occasionally used instead instead of R^2. *See* JOHNSTON 29–32.

[27]Thus, a low coefficient means that forces reflected in the regressors are not the predominant influence on the dependent variable. However, low correlations are rare in legal proceedings. Expert witnesses usually introduce regressions with relatively high coefficients of determination and argue that the close correlation demonstrates that the independent variables in fact explain the movement of the dependent variable. Their opponents often reply that the correlation is spurious with explanatory variables exhibiting a common response to propelling forces not included in the regression model. See, e.g., note 57 *infra*. High R^2 supports equally the existence of causation or mere coincidence of trends, so that the interpretation of correlation depends on the respective theoretical strengths of the rival hypotheses.

Spurious correlation may also arise in two other ways. First, if the number of observations is small relative to the number of explanatory variables, it is always possible to achieve a good fit, even though the apparent correlation would diminish or disappear if a larger body of data were included. Thus, a straight line may always be drawn perfectly through any two points of data, and on the average may be drawn with smaller deviation through three points than through ten. The excess of the number of observations over the number of explanatory variables is known as degrees of freedom; when the number of

In Western Union, R^2 of the linear equation was 0.92, while that of the multiplicative equation was 0.81.[28] Although these values are close, the higher R^2 for the linear equation, all other things being equal, provides support for choosing that mode of analysis on the ground that the linear equation is better able to explain the relationship between cost and variability. The expert witness nevertheless used the multiplicative form without discussion and without indication that the linear form would lead to a lower estimate of the cost of equity for Western Union. Since the linear form generated a slightly better fit, the expert at least should have supported his choice with some economic theory indicating that the relationship between variability and cost was more likely to be multiplicative than linear. In any event, the high values of R^2 for both forms of equation indicate that despite the lack of perfect correlation between variability and cost which was intuitively apparent from the data, the relationship between these factors is sufficient to justify an estimate of Western Union's cost based on its variability.

However, the absence of a perfect relationship between cost and variability implies that the regression estimate of Western Union's cost will have some uncertainty attached to it, which in statistical terms means that a different estimate may be obtained from a different sample of data.[29] Statisticians reflect this uncer-

---

degrees of freedom is low, the estimate of R^2 must be adjusted downward, and is known as adjusted R^2 ($\bar{R}^2$). See EZEKIEL & FOX 300–05.

Second, although the problem is seldom discussed, the selection of the explanatory variable producing the highest correlation from a large number of candidates will, as a matter of random combination, yield a relation which appears statistically significant by the usual tests even though there may be no relation between the explanatory and dependent variables. The ability of computers to try all possible combinations of variables from a large group has increased the danger of this "selection effect." For example, in a regression study introduced in a rate-making proceeding, an expert used a computer to select, out of some fifty candidates, the seven explanatory variables which produced the best fit. He obtained an R^2 of .84, which he described as "very high" without discussing the correlation-producing effect of his procedure. Long Island Lighting Company Exhibit 25, App. 4, at 9, Long Island Lighting Co., 90 P.U.R.3d 93 (N.Y.P.S.C. 1971) (testimony of Herman G. Roseman); cf. chapter 3 n.36 (discussion of selection effect in a different context).

[28]R^2 for a log linear equation is not exactly comparable to R^2 for a linear equation due to the change in scale arising from the transformation to logarithms. See generally RAO & MILLER 109–11.

[29]It should be remembered that statistical imprecision is only one element of uncertainty surrounding regression results and that in most adversary proceedings the actual variation in result produced by methodologies of competing witnesses far outstrips the potential sampling variation.

tainty in numerical terms by using an index known as the standard error to measure the sampling variation of the regression estimates.[30] If the explanatory variables in the regression equation account for all major forces acting on the dependent variable, so that the unexplained variation is the product of many small forces, statistical theory makes it possible to compute standard errors and to translate them into confidence intervals.[31] These

[30]The extent of the variation depends on the fit of the regression and the size of the sample; a better fit and a larger sample will result in less variation. Each coefficient and each computed value of the dependent variable has associated with it a standard deviation which measures the extent of such variation. Since the amount of variation is usually unknown, see note 11 *supra,* it must be estimated from the sample of data by the measure known as the standard error, denoted S.E. This is computed from, and should not be confused with, the frequently encountered "standard error of the estimate" (S.E.E. or s). See WONNACOTT 19, 30–32. S.E.E. is computed as the square root of the average squared difference between the mean observed and regression values of the dependent variable. See *id.* at 24. The standard error of a regression estimate of a dependent variable is smallest when the explanatory variable is at its mean value, and increases as the value of the explanatory variable moves toward the extremes of the range of observed data. See *id.* at 30–32. However, the standard errors of the coefficients remain constant. *Id.* at 24–27.

A source of uncertainty more significant than this sampling variation arises when a prediction is sought outside the observed range of data. In such a case, there can be no statistical assurance that the regression relation will continue in this unobserved region, a fact which has contributed to the uncertainty of estimation in some regulatory contexts. *See, e.g.,* Chief Examiner's Initial Decision at 1-13, Postal Rate & Fee Increases 1971, No. R71-1 (Postal Rate Comm'n, June 28, 1972).

[31]Confidence interval analysis is dependent on certain assumptions about the "errors" of the regression estimate. Errors are the differences between the values generated by the true or population regression equation and the observed values of the dependent variable. The technical conditions for confidence-interval analysis are the following:

1. The errors of overestimation are matched by those of underestimation, so that their average is zero; when this condition is not satisfied, the regression estimates are said to be biased.
2. There is no correlation between successive error terms; when there is correlation, the errors are said to be autocorrelated or serially correlated.
3. The average size of the errors, as measured by their variance, remains constant throughout the range of data; when errors increase or decrease systematically, they are said to be heteroscedastic.

Since the population regression equation is unknown, the differences between the values generated by the sample regression equation and the observed values of the dependent variable, known as residuals, are used for the purpose of testing for the satisfaction of some of the requisite conditions. The Durban-Watson test uses the Von Neumann statistic to test for autocorrelation in the residuals. See WONNACOTT 142–43. Testing for a correlation between

permit an assertion, with a specified level of confidence,[32] that the true value of a coefficient or dependent variable lies within a certain range of the value estimated by the regression equation. The larger an estimate's standard error, the less precise that estimate will be; this will be reflected in a wider confidence interval for any given level of probability.[33]

Confidence interval analysis generally is used to indicate whether a regression estimate is significantly different from another estimate or hypothetical value. If, for example, a reasonable confidence interval about an estimated coefficient includes zero, statisticians would conclude that the data did not show the explanatory variable associated with that coefficient to have had an influence on the dependent variable. Similarly, if an estimate of a dependent variable is not significantly different from an observed value which has been questioned, the estimate is not decisive evidence against the observed value, and a decision maker might prefer to choose the observed value, notwithstanding the regression estimate.[34] Application of confidence interval analysis to *Western Union*, although not involv-

---

the residuals and the explanatory variable will detect heteroscedasticity. See RAO & MILLER 116–21. Detection of bias through analysis of residuals is more difficult. See *id.* at 115. See generally *id.* at 112–26.

[32]This confidence is expressed as the probability that the estimate would be no further from the true value than the distance specified by the interval. Statisticians frequently use a 0.95 or 0.99 level of probability for this purpose and compute intervals accordingly, although it may be argued that in some contexts a narrower interval reflecting a lower probability would more correctly correspond to the burden of proof. However, a change in the size of intervals associated with lower levels of confidence would not have made a difference in most adversary proceedings in which econometric models have been used.

[33]The translation of standard errors into confidence intervals is made by using the so-called Student's or *t* distribution, which describes the probability of an estimate being any given number of standard errors from the true value. These probabilities are a function of the number of degrees of freedom. See note 27 *supra*. Thus, if there are six degrees of freedom, there is a .95 probability that an estimate will lie within 2.447 standard errors of the true value. A commonly computed statistic, known as the *t* value, is the value of a coefficient divided by its standard error; this is used for testing whether the coefficient is significantly different from zero. See generally JOHNSTON 21–24.

[34]For example, if the cost of equity for Western Union computed on the basis of the earnings-price ratio of the company's stock were not significantly different from the cost of equity estimated by a regression model, the FCC might properly choose the former.

ing either of the above situations, will illustrate these techniques, indicate the precision of the regression estimates, and highlight the significance of the differing assumptions of the regression and intuitive methods.

In *Western Union*, the standard error of the linear estimate is 1.15. Assuming the linear model is correct and that the necessary assumptions are fulfilled, one can say with 95 percent confidence that the true value of Western Union's cost lies in the interval 13.00 percent plus or minus 2.82 percent.[35] Such an estimate is sufficiently precise to justify the selection of 13.00 percent as the cost of equity. The same confidence interval technique indicates that there is a substantial probability (approximately 30 percent) that Western Union's cost of equity is as low as the 12.4 percent estimate, based on simple interpolation between the two nearest industry groups, but less than a 1 percent probability that Western Union's cost of equity is as great as 28.1 percent, the estimate obtained by using an average ratio of cost to variability.

Compared to the linear model, one intuitive method yields a slightly low estimate of Western Union's cost of equity, while the other yields an estimate which is definitely too high. If there were some other basis for choosing the 12.4 percent estimate,[36] one could not say that the statistical result precluded that choice, since the two estimates are within a reasonable confidence interval. But the 28.1 percent estimate would clearly be precluded if the statistical methodology were accepted.

The reason for the differences in these estimates illustrates the advantage of using regression analysis in this context. The simple linear interpolation between the two industry groups immediately above and below Western Union in earnings variability is equivalent to a linear regression estimate using only two data points. The estimate based on those points is somewhat low because they are not fully representative of all the data; the linear regression estimate, by contrast, reflects all the available data. The second intuitive method, the use of a ratio of cost to variability, is equivalent to a special case of multiplicative regression, in which a proportionate change in

[35]The corresponding 95 percent confidence interval for the multiplicative model is 13.78 ± 2.96 percent.

[36]See pp. 243–44 *infra*.

variability is matched by an equal proportionate change in cost of equity. The intuitive-ratio estimate is improbably high, which reflects the fact that the assumption of a constant ratio is untrue; a multiplicative regression is able to describe a relationship in which these ratios do vary. If the assumptions of the intuitive methods were actually borne out by the data, the linear and multiplicative regression estimates would equal their corresponding intuitive estimates; the advantage of regression lies in its ability to describe all the existing data without being constrained by the same simplifying assumptions that intuitive methods tend to require.

B.

Most econometric models introduced in regulatory proceedings are more complex than the simple two-variable regression used by the expert in *Western Union*. Such models seek greater precision in description of economic relationships by taking into account multiple explanatory factors, which are frequently analyzed with groups of equations. The regression technique for dealing with multivariate relationships is known as multiple regression. Its basic mathematical principles are essentially the same as those of simple regression; in particular, the least-squares technique is used in computing the coefficients of the explanatory variables, and confidence interval analysis is used to test the precision of the regression estimates. The utility of multiple regression arises from the impossibility of intuitive appraisal of the masses of data usually encompassed by complex multivariate models, so that the thorough analysis of such data requires a statistical technique.

In re Cargill[37] provides an example of the successful use of a relatively simple multiple-regression model. *Cargill* was an administrative proceeding before the Commodity Exchange Authority involving charges of manipulation of the price of wheat futures and the cash price of wheat in violation of the Commodity Exchange Act.[38] Allegedly in response to manipulation, both the futures and cash price on the Chicago Board of Trade rose

[37]No. 120 (C.E.A., Aug. 13, 1970), *aff'd sub nom.* Cargill, Inc. v. Hardin, 452 F.2d 1154 (8th Cir. 1971), *cert. denied*, 406 U.S. 932 (1972).
[38]7 U.S.C. §§9, 13 (1970).

dramatically to $2.285 (a total increase of 18.5 cents) on May 20 and 21, 1963, the last two days for futures trading in the 1962–63 season. The defense contended that no manipulation had occurred, but that since wheat prices had been artificially depressed, the dramatic price rise was attributable to normal supply-and-demand factors. The Department of Agriculture sponsored an econometric study to rebut this defense.

In this staff study, the cash price for wheat was regressed on three explanatory variables relating to basic supply-and-demand factors in order to determine the expected market price for wheat for the time in question. Data from a fourteen-year period were analyzed with two sets of linear regression equations to determine an annual average cash price and a May average cash price for Chicago.[39] The study of annual prices generated a 1963 average price estimate of $2.067, with a standard error of $0.035, which the expert expressed as a price in the range of $2.03–$2.10.[40] The study of May prices generated a May, 1963, average price of $2.136, with a standard error of $0.013, which the expert witness expressed as a price in the range of $2.10–$2.17.[41] The actual May average price was $2.13.

These findings were attacked by the respondents in extensive cross-examination.[42] Without discussing the defense objections, the presiding judicial officer accepted the econometric findings, apparently as evidence that the average price in May was not artificially depressed.[43] The Court of Appeals, citing the regression study in support of this point, sustained the administrative findings.[44]

[39]The data appear in complainant's Exhibit 48, and the regressions in Exhibit 49. Due to a clerical error, the data and regressions had to be recomputed; the corrections appear in Exhibits 48A and 49A, respectively.

[40]The R^2 of the equations was 0.941. Complainant's Exhibit 29, In re Cargill, No. 120 (C.E.A., Aug. 13, 1970); see In re Cargill, *id*., at ¶41.

[41]The R^2 of the equation was 0.989. Complainant's Exhibit 49A, In re Cargill, No. 120 (C.E.A., Aug. 13, 1970); In re Cargill, *id*., at ¶41.

[42]Cross-examination disclosed, inter alia, that the expert had avoided use of certain statistics because they produced a poor fit, Record, vol. 6, at 847–48, In re Cargill, No. 120 (C.E.A., Aug. 13, 1970), and highlighted the fact that the study was not designed to estimate the economic value of wheat on a particular day at a particular location. *Id*. at 849.

[43]In re Cargill, No. 120, at ¶41 (C.E.A., Aug. 13, 1970).

[44]Cargill, Inc. v. Hardin, 452 F.2d 1154, 1168–69 (8th Cir. 1971), *cert. denied*, 406 U.S. 932 (1972).

Regression analysis was successfully used in *Cargill* to demonstrate that an observed value, i.e., wheat prices in 1963, was consistent with the data of earlier years. Statistical techniques thus added credibility to a single observation by supporting it with additional data.[45] In this situation, the decision maker may have been disposed to accept econometric evidence because the regression estimate confirmed an actually observed value. One would anticipate a greater reluctance to accept such evidence in cases like *Western Union*, where the statistical evidence contradicts observed relationships, or in cases involving economic prediction where there is no confirming data. In such instances, a statistical projection—particularly one that conflicts with the a priori notions of the decision maker—is likely to be viewed with caution or skepticism. And such doubts are likely to be reinforced rather than dispelled by adversary proceedings as they are now conducted.

The process of adversary proceedings, however, does not inevitably have to deepen doubts about a study and result in its rejection. Although any study may be criticized, the opportunity for meticulous analysis in formal proceedings could be an occasion for eliminating areas of doubt, for improving the quality of studies and thus the chance for ultimate acceptance. Much depends on the procedural setting. An examination of certain cases suggests procedural protocols which would improve the adversary and decision making processes with respect to models and thereby enable decision makers to utilize regression techniques more effectively.

III

A.

In area rate proceedings to fix ceiling prices for natural gas at the wellhead (the price paid to gas producers), the staff of the Federal Power Commission made a sustained effort to introduce econometric evidence based on complex regression

[45]An analogous use of regression was made by Commissioner Jones in a proceeding before the New York Public Service Commission involving New York Telephone. In an effort to obtain a more accurate estimate of New York

models. The purpose of that effort was to estimate the effect of ceiling prices on exploratory drilling, in accordance with Mr. Justice Jackson's concurring opinion in *Colorado Interstate Gas Co. v. FPC*[46] that the wellhead price for gas should be just high enough "to obtain for the public service the needed amount of gas."[47] Such models were introduced on three separate occasions;[48] in each case, crucial economic assumptions of the models were challenged by the experts for the producers and ultimately rejected by the Commission. This meant that the extensive efforts of the staff were wasted; the Commission was left without a staff analysis to aid it in its pricing decision. The first protocol is designed to decrease the danger of such occurrences.

The FPC staff introduced its first regression study in the rate proceeding involving the Permian Basin Area.[49] Harold H. Wein, Chief Economist of the FPC, presented a complex econometric model using separate supply, demand, and price equations which purported to show that an increase in the wellhead price to be set by the Commission for new contracts of gas would decrease exploration for hydrocarbons.[50] This was a surprising conclusion, and producers subjected the model to ex-

---

Telephone's current earnings-price ratio, he regressed the common stock dividend-price ratio of New York's parent, AT&T, on Moody's average utility bond yield and found a close correlation. $R^2 = 0.91$. Concurring Statement of Comm'r Jones at 10, In re New York Tel. Co., Nos. 25612, 26080 (N.Y.P.S.C., Jan. 17, 1972). Substituting Moody's average bond yield on December 31, 1971, as fairly representative of near term future conditions yielded a dividend-price ratio of 5.22 percent for AT&T. This figure became a point of departure for the Commissioner's rate-making proposals. *Id.* at 9–12.

[46]324 U.S. 581 (1945).

[47]*Id.* at 612.

[48]In subsequent FPC area rate proceedings, no econometric models were introduced, in part because of shortage of qualified staff and in part because of the lesser importance of those proceedings.

[49]Permian Basin Area Rate Proceeding, 34 F.P.C. 159 (1965), *aff'd sub nom.* Skelly Oil Co. v. FPC, 375 F.2d 6 (10th Cir. 1967), *aff'd sub nom.* Permian Basin Area Rate Cases, 390 U.S. 747 (1968).

[50]Statement Relating to Staff Exhibits at 235–38, *id.* (statement of Harold H. Wein). The demand equation indicated that an increase in the wellhead price of new contracts would decrease consumption of gas, and this in turn would cause a decrease in gas production. The supply equation indicated a direct positive effect on exploration of the price increase, which would, however, be more than offset by the negative effect of the decrease in gas production. Thus, the model indicated that increasing the ceiling price on new contracts would in fact decrease exploration for hydrocarbons. *Id.*

tensive criticism. The hearing examiner never reached most of the objections, because he rejected the model, primarily on the ground that it presupposed that producers could not drill directionally, that is, for gas or oil as they chose, but only for hydrocarbons in general: "Since the directional thesis has been found to be a valid working hypothesis, the results of the econometric study are not relevant or material to the problem."[51] The Commission, though commenting favorably on the usefulness of econometric techniques in general, affirmed the examiner's directionality point and declined to make any estimate of the effect that the price it had selected would have on supply.[52]

In the *Southern Louisiana Area Rate Proceedings*,[53] the second to come before the Commission, staff economist J. Harvey Edonston introduced a supply-and-demand model similar to that introduced by Wein.[54] To meet the directionality point, the model was modified by changing the dependent variable in the supply equation from the number of exploratory hydrocarbon wells to the number of exploratory gas wells. Certain other changes were also made, but the Edmonston model, like the Wein model, predicted that exploration for gas would decline if prices were raised.

Amerada Petroleum Corporation leveled a "devastating"[55] attack upon the model. Its chief rebuttal witness, Professor Paul Cootner of MIT, raised a long string of objections focusing on two themes: the failure to include profitability as an explanatory variable in the supply equation, and the improper estimation of demand through the use of cross-section data[56] and through fail-

[51]Permian Basin Area Rate Proceeding, 34 F.P.C. 306, 332 (1964) (initial decision of the hearing examiner).

[52]Permian Basin Area Rate Proceeding, 34 F.P.C. 159, 187 (1965). In its affirmance of the Commission and the Court of Appeals, Permian Basin Area Rate Cases, 390 U.S. 747 (1968), the Supreme Court did not discuss the model.

[53]Southern Louisiana Area Rate Proceeding, 40 F.P.C. 530 (1968), *modified*, 41 F.P.C. 301 (1969), *aff'd*, 428 F.2d 407 (5th Cir.), *cert. denied*, 400 U.S. 950 (1970).

[54]Staff Exhibit 38A (witness J. Harvey Edmonston). The model is also described in Kline, *A Layman's Guide to the Wein-Edmonston Econometric Study of Natural Gas Supply and Demand*, Mar. 12, 1964 (issued by Office of Econometrics, FPC).

[55]Southern Louisiana Area Rate Proceeding, 40 F.P.C. 703, 857 (1966) (initial decision of the hearing examiner).

[56]There are two basic types of data collections. Time-series data are obser-

ure to include other variables in the cross-section analysis.[57] This long, withering, and effective attack persuaded the hearing examiner that "with all of its suggested defects, inadequacies, and faults," the "econometric presentation here made by the Staff has not yet reached the level where it can safely be relied upon as a basis for the Commission's critical conclusions in this case."[58] The Commission affirmed this finding by the examiner "for the reasons stated by him."[59] But it encouraged further econometric efforts, stating that "[s]hould the industry as well as the Staff find it possible to pursue similarly innovative analytical efforts in the years ahead, more reliable results may well be achieved and the regulatory process will be benefitted."[60] On appeal, the court agreed that the econometric studies were defective for the reasons set out in the examiner's opinion, but it criticized the Commission for not dealing with the supply problem in a sufficiently specific manner.[61] Yet with the rejec-

---

vations of variables in a single industry or location made over a period of time. Cross-section data, on the other hand, are observations of variables in several different industries or locations made in a single time period.

[57]Amerada Petroleum Corp. Exhibit No. 156, at 25–35, 69–113, Southern Louisiana Area Rate Proceeding, 40 F.P.C. 530 (1968) (prepared rebuttal testimony of Paul H. Cootner). In addition, Cootner pointed out the existence in the Edmonston model of spurious correlation, see note 27 *supra*, a common problem in models built on time-series data. The exploratory gas wells equation showed an extraordinary 0.999 correlation over a twenty-four–year period between the explanatory factors and the number of exploratory gas wells. Staff Exhibit 38A, at 6, Southern Louisiana Area Rate Proceeding, 40 F.P.C. 530 (1968) (Edmonston testimony). Professor Cootner argued that this high correlation was primarily due to the fact that during most of the period the values of a number of the explanatory factors (one of which was "time") were rising or declining fairly steadily, so that most of the correlation could be attributed to a coincidence of trends rather than to causation. In fact, a "time" variable alone produced a correlation with exploratory wells of 0.873. Amerada Petroleum Corp. Exhibit No. 156, *supra* at 51.

[58]40 F.P.C. at 871–72.

[59]*Id.* at 625.

[60]*Id.* at 626.

[61]Southern Louisiana Area Rate Cases, 428 F.2d 407, 436 n.91 (5th Cir.), *cert. denied*, 400 U.S. 950 (1970). The court concluded that the Commission should

> make findings, as specifically as possible, as to how the rate it has set will affect the industry's tendency to meet [the targeted] level of service. This last step means estimating the gas supply that the rate will bring forth. These are difficult matters to predict, but that is more reason why a reviewing court should not be required to guess at them.

Id. at 444.

tion of the Edmonston model, and in the absence of any substitute, the Commission might have been hard pressed to estimate future supply in a way that would have satisfied the Court of Appeals.

The third occasion for the introduction of a gas model arose when the *Southern Louisiana* case was reopened by the Commission while its first decision was pending in the Court of Appeals.[62] The FPC staff, through Professor Daniel J. Khazzoom of McGill University, sponsored a new model.[63] Unlike the Wein and Edmonston models, the Khazzoom model predicted that higher ceiling prices would increase discoveries of gas. The model was used to test the effect of a proposed settlement of the case which provided for a rate increase on future new discoveries. It showed that if the proposed Southern Louisiana price increase were applied across the board to all twenty-one pricing districts, by 1975, new discoveries of gas would rise to about 30 percent of projected production.[64] This would be sufficient at least to replace the gas being used, since extensions of previously discovered gas pools and upward revisions of former estimates increased reserves each year by approximately twice the amount of new gas discoveries.[65] But the usefulness of the model was impaired because Khazzoom would not say unequivocally that it could be applied validly to estimate the effect of a price increase in a single area, southern Louisiana, which was the issue before the Commission.[66]

The producers used four expert witnesses to generate a medley of objections.[67] It is instructive to gain a sense of the breadth and range of their many points: the model, it was argued, was in a highly reduced form, which merely related the

[62]See *id.* at 421.

[63]Staff Exhibit No. 46, Southern Louisiana Area Rate Proceeding, 46 F.P.C. 86 (1971) (testimony of Daniel J. Khazzoom). For a published description of the model, see Khazzoom, *The FPC Staff's Econometric Model of Natural Gas Supply in the United States*, 2 BELL J. ECON. & MGMT. SCI. 51 (1971).

[64]Staff Exhibit No. 46, *supra* note 63, at 193 figure XIII.5, 201–03.

[65]Initial Brief of FPC Staff at 43, n.1, Southern Louisiana Rate Proceeding, 46 F.P.C. 86 (1971).

[66]46 F.P.C. at 122–23.

[67]The testimony of these witnesses is summarized in Bernstein, *Producer's Rebuttal to Staff Witness Khazzoom's Econometric Model of U.S. Gas Supply*, Feb. 23, 1971 (unpublished memorandum of National Economic Research Associated, Inc., New York City).

variables without explaining investment behavior in the decision to drill for gas; it failed to include relevant variables such
as the cost of capital; essential data on flowing gas prices and in-
trastate gas sales was omitted; it assumed that a given increase
in the ceiling price in each district would bring forth the same
increase in the level of new discoveries in each district; pooling
of cross-section and time-series data[68] was meaningless; use of
the lagged discoveries as an independent variable was not appropriate; the model should have included extensions and
revisions, since these were major elements of supply; the BLS
wholesale price index should not have been used as a deflator;[69]
the relationships being measured were not consistent but had
varied throughout the period.

For the third time, the Commission was hesitant to embrace
the econometric findings: "the influence of price on supply
must be viewed as a matter for the application of informed judgment," due to the large number of factors, each difficult to
forecast, which were relevant to the problem; but it was not "a
subject susceptible to precise statistical measurement."[70] On
the basis of a simple multiplicative regression of exploratory gas
footage on gas price introduced by J. Rhoads Foster, a producer
witness,[71] the Commission did conclude that "there is a strong
positive relationship between price and supply...."[72] However, it rejected the more complex and extensive Khazzoom model
and refused to "even suggest that Dr. Khazzoom's nationwide
projections from the staff's econometric model confirm the reasonableness of the settlement prices in the Southern Louisiana
Area."[73] The most that the Commission was willing to say was
that the evidence of supply-price relationships furnished by the
Khazzoom model was "consistent with our conclusion based
upon other evidence in the record respecting the necessity of
price increases."[74] After commenting that the econometric

[68]See note 56 *supra.*

[69]A deflator is a number or set of numbers by which a variable is divided so
as to remove the effect of certain extraneous factors.

[70]46 F.P.C. at 121.

[71]Industry Exhibit No. 24, Southern Louisiana Area Rate Proceeding, 46
F.P.C. 86 (1971).

[72]46 F.P.C. at 121.

[73]*Id.* at 123.

[74]*Id.*

method was an "instructive experimental effort," the Commission summed up by observing that "there exists a positive relationship between gas contract price levels and exploratory efforts," but that "no reliable quantitative forecasts may be made by [*sic*] increments of additional gas supply resulting from specific increased gas prices...."[75]

The FPC's reluctance to accept basic assumptions of each of the three natural gas models led to the rejection of the model, the waste of staff energy, and, in the first two cases, the lack of any precise quantitative analysis to aid the decision maker. In the Wein model, the crucial assumption was that the producers could not drill directionally; in the Edmonston model, the crucial assumption was the appropriateness of cross-section data on prices and consumption.[76] To accept the Khazzoom model, the Commission would have had to believe not only that cross-section data were appropriate for prediction of future national trends, but also that the national relationships would hold true for the individual pricing district that was the focus of the Commission's attention in the proceeding.

In contrast to its rejection of Khazzoom's extensive model, the Commission's citation of Foster's simple model is instructive. Foster's model analyzed data for seven Southwestern states for the period 1950–69, and showed, with high correlation, that every 1 percent increase in price had been paralleled on the average by a 1.5 percent increase in exploratory gas footage.[77] The staff criticized this simple model,[78] and the Commission said it did not "accept fully" Foster's work,[79] but Khazzoom's more complex formulation was in fact less useful, because it required the Commission, in appraising data of obvious relevance and importance, also to accept debatable economic theories.

This experience suggests, as the first protocol, that *a decision maker should (1) specify the data of such relevance*

[75] *Id.* at 123–24.

[76] See 40 F.P.C. at 861–65.

[77] Industry Exhibit No. 24, *supra* note 71, at 000 n.1. R^2 equalled 0.88. See *id.*

[78] Rebuttal Testimony of Frederick W. Lawrence, Southern Louisiana Area Rate Proceeding, 40 F.P.C. 530 (1971).

[79] Southern Louisiana Area Rate Proceeding, 46 F.P.C. 86, 122 (1971).

and importance that he finds merits econometric analysis, and (2) require that econometric presentations begin with those data and incorporate other data on a separate basis only when necessary for purposes of accuracy or refinement.

Following this protocol, a decision maker might first receive submissions from the parties on the appropriate data base and then designate the data he deems appropriate for econometric analysis.[80] A proponent of a model would then introduce his analysis of the designated data and, if he deemed it necessary, also present more complex models which encompassed other data; generally, these more complex models would represent a reinforcement or refinement of the initial analysis.[81]

This protocol should be helpful in various respects. First, by predesignating data for econometric analysis, the decision maker would have the benefit of analyses focused specifically on the information of paramount interest to him. In particular, the generation of alternative models covering the same data would provide the decision maker with a range of choice. If, for example, the time-series data used in the Foster study had been predesignated for analysis, the Commission probably would have had the benefit of various treatments of that data, graduated in complexity, which might have elucidated the relation between that basic information and other significant factors not included in the Foster model, which dissuaded the Commission from fully accepting Foster's results.[82] Second, by requiring a separate analysis of the data of greatest interest, the

[80]The data to be designated may be described with varying degrees of specificity, depending on the state of data available at the time of the preliminary submission, the specificity demanded by the parties, and the confidence of the decision maker. To the extent that the specification is vague, a decision maker should be flexible in accepting models of the designated data in satisfaction of the first protocol if they are built on reasonable variations of those data. A stricter attitude would result in an excessive burden on parties attempting to comply with the protocol or in wasteful argumentation about the interpretation of the designation. Generally, a more specific predesignation, when not premature, would advance the purposes of the first protocol.

[81]Of course, the fact of predesignation of data should not create any barrier to the introduction of models incorporating nondesignated data, except possibly if the relevance of such data were rejected in the designation proceeding. A decision maker should also be free to order resubmission of models based on a new designation when a party's analysis of nondesignated data suggests that a redesignation would be desirable.

[82]See Southern Louisiana Area Rate Proceeding, 46 F.P.C. 86, 122 (1971).

decision maker would at least be assured of econometric guidance with respect to that data, in the event that more complex models encompassing other data could not be accepted. Third, the predesignation of an appropriate core of data and the resolution of disputed economic points arising in the context of a designation hearing should have a significant impact in simplifying the later proceedings in which the models are introduced and defended.[83]

From the point of view of the econometrician, the protocol should be helpful by preventing premature rejection of his efforts due to a wrong choice of data. The protocol may also be viewed simply as a rule of good legal exposition, since the technique of leading up to a complex model through simpler formulations that produce consistent results should facilitate understanding, help place the need for complexity in perspective, and increase the chance for acceptance of sound econometric conclusions.[84]

[83]There are precedents for predesignation of data and methods of statistical analysis in rate-making proceedings. For example, the Interstate Commerce Commission designates traffic and cost data to be produced, on a probability sample basis, by major motor-carrier rate bureaus in connection with filings for general rate increases exceeding $1 million. See New Procedures in Motor Carrier Revenue Proceedings, 340 I.C.C. 1 (1971). The ICC has also specified the statistical methodology to be employed in connection with such probability samples. ICC, Bureau of Economics, Guidelines for Presenting Sample Studies (Jan. 2, 1968). The Postal Rate Commission has announced that it will institute a rule-making proceeding to determine "what cost and revenue data should be obtained for use in future proceedings." Opinion and Recommended Decision at 1–265, 1–276, Postal Rate & Fee Increases 1971, No. R71–1 (Postal Rate Comm'n, June 28, 1972).

[84]A progression to complexity analogous to that suggested by the first protocol has been used in statistical presentations in adversary proceedings. For example, in an attack on the bail system in New York as violative of the equal-protection clauses of the federal and state constitutions, the New York Legal Aid Society based its case on a statistical study of a sample of criminal cases in which the dependent variable was the outcome of the case and the independent variables were pretrial status (incarceration or release on bail), seriousness of the charge, type of offense, weight of the evidence, aggravated circumstances, prior criminal record, and personal history. Statistical analysis was first used to show that each factor separately did not explain or account for the higher rate of conviction or length of prison sentence given when the defendant was not released on bail. The analysis was then extended to show that such disparity was not explained when certain of these factors were considered in combination. See Brief for Plaintiff at 13–29, A36–40, Bellamy v. The Judges, 41 App. Div. 2d 196, 342 N.Y.S.2d 137 (1973), *aff'd without opinion*, 32 N.Y.2d 886, 346 N.Y.S.2d 812 (1973).

B.

The attack on the gas models involved a veritable fusillade of objections and asserted defects. In each proceeding, cross-examination and rebuttal testimony ran into hundreds of pages. The problems faced by a hearing examiner without extensive technical training, in attempting to resolve these objections, are perhaps the most significant barrier to the effective utilization of regression studies, for the volume, technical character, and difficulty of objections has tended to force decision makers into a dubitante position. No single substantive solution for this problem can be expected, because each criticism must be evaluated on its own statistical and economic merits. There is, however, a procedural approach which should be helpful, and which may be illustrated by examining the handling of a technical problem known as heteroscedasticity in proceedings before the Securities and Exchange Commission involving a challenge to minimum commission rates on stock exchanges.[85]

In defending its minimum commission structure before the Securities and Exchange Commission, the New York Stock Exchange presented a regression study to demonstrate that costs did not rise proportionately with size of a brokerage firm (that is, with number of transactions).[86] Using 1966 cost and transaction data for a large number of firms, the Exchange regressed total expenses on number of transactions and number of transactions squared. The coefficient of the quadratic term (transactions squared) was negative and statistically significant, thus indicating that the cost per transaction declined as the number of transactions increased.[87] This being so, argued the Exchange, there were economies of scale in the brokerage industry, and fixed minimum commissions were therefore necessary to prevent cutthroat commission competition in which the larger firms, having a cost advantage, would drive out smaller firms.[88]

---

[85]SEC Rate Structure Investigation of National Securities Exchanges, No. 4–144 (S.E.C., filed May 28, 1968).

[86]Freund Exhibit No. 1, at 56–63, *id.* (study entitled "Economic Effects of Negotiated Commission Rates on the Brokerage Industry, the Market for Corporate Securities, and the Investing Public").

[87]*Id.* at 61.

[88]*Id.* at 63.

In the economic reply submission of the Antitrust Division of the Department of Justice, Dr. Michael Mann pointed out that since the Exchange had used total firm costs as the dependent variable and total commissions as the explanatory variable, the entire scale of the equation would grow with increasing firm size, thus increasing the size of the regression errors.[89] This correlation between the size of errors and the size of explanatory variable is the technical defect known as heteroscedasticity; when it is present, the usual statistical tests of precision are no longer reliable. Mann's theoretical point was undeniable, but his argument would have been inconsequential in the absence of a demonstration that the negative coefficient of the quadratic term would not be statistically significant if heteroscedasticity were eliminated.

To show the significance of his objection, Mann proposed to eliminate heteroscedasticity from the Exchange's model by using a dependent variable that did not necessarily grow with firm size. For this purpose, he chose average cost per transaction. The coefficient of the explanatory variable was positive, indicating diseconomies of scale, though not statistically significant.[90] On this basis Mann concluded that the Exchange's equation was more consistent with the hypothesis that average costs became nearly constant after a certain level of output was reached, there being no economies of scale.[91]

The Exchange implicitly recognized the correctness of Mann's criticisms by not defending its original formulation with respect to this issue. Instead, it used a new witness, Louis Guth, to respond to Dr. Mann.[92] Guth admitted that the data used by

[89]Mann Exhibit No. 1, at 33–38, SEC Rate Structure Investigation of National Securities Exchanges, No. 4-144 (S.E.C., filed May 28, 1968). For a definition of "error," see note 31 *supra*.

[90]The coefficients were computed after dividing both sides of the Exchange's equation by number of transactions. *Id*. at 36–37.

[91]*Id*. at 38. After correcting the Exchange on this matter, Mann argued that number of transactions was an inadequate measure of output for the brokerage industry and, using 1965 and 1966 data, recomputed a new regression with total expenses divided by total commissions (that is, cost per dollar of commission) as the dependent variable and total commissions as the independent variable. The outstanding fact about these equations was the low value of R^2. In 1965, only 1 percent of the variance in average cost was explained by size; in 1966, only 2 percent. Mann concluded that "size is a very unimportant variable in explaining average costs, so that economies of scale are unimportant in the brokerage industry." *Id*. at 41.

[92]See Guth Exhibit No. 1, SEC Rate Structure Investigation of National Securities Exchanges, No. 4-144 (S.E.C., filed May 28, 1968).

the Exchange were heteroscedastic, but he argued that the Exchange's original conclusion that they exhibited economies of scale was correct, even when the problem of heteroscedasticity was avoided or explicitly taken into account.[93] Guth computed a new equation, this time in log linear form, in which total cost was regressed on the total number of transactions. There was a theoretical basis for believing that this form would not exhibit heteroscedasticity.[94] Moreover, Guth tested the equation and found no significant correlation between the errors and the explanatory variable, thus confirming the absence of heteroscedasticity.[95] Since the coefficient of the transactions term was less than one, the equation indicated that costs increased at a decreasing rate as the number of transactions increased.[96] Thus, the data exhibited economies of scale.

Guth also presented a second line of argument, in which he scrutinized and then modified Mann's model. Guth first argued theoretically, and then demonstrated numerically, that Mann's deflation of total costs by number of transactions in effect overcompensated for heteroscedasticity and created a new correlation (this time negative) between the regression errors and the explanatory variable.[97] Guth recomputed Mann's equation after substituting a deflator which minimized the correlation between the errors and the explanatory variable. He found that the coefficient of the quadratic term was negative and statistically significant, thus again demonstrating economies of scale.[98] The Department of Justice did not challenge Guth's models.[99]

---

[93]*Id.* at 22.

[94]The reason is that in a multiplicative equation the error term represents the ratio of the computed and actual values of the dependent variable. There is no a priori reason to believe that this ratio would change as total cost increased, as distinguished from the linear situation where the error is the absolute difference between the computed and actual values. *Id.* at 29–30.

[95]*Id.* at 30.

[96]*Id.*

[97]*Id.* at 31–35, 40 (Table 7).

[98]*Id.* at 38 (Table 5).

[99]The existence of economies of scale in nationwide retail brokerage firms was subsequently shown in studies introduced by the Antitrust Division of the Department of Justice at the trial in Thill v. New York Stock Exchange, Civil No. 63-C-264 (E.D. Wis., Oct. 8, 1963), a judicial challenge to the Exchange's minimum commission rules. See, e.g., Government Exhibit No. 1456, at 51–53 & app. Table A, *id.* (Friend & Blume study, *The Consequences of Competitive Commissions on the New York Stock Exchange*).

The battle over heteroscedasticity waged before the SEC stands in contrast to the clash of econometricians in most administrative proceedings. Experts for the Stock Exchange and the Justice Department quantified their objections and produced competing models, thereby demonstrating the significance of their objections and providing alternative methods of analysis.[100] The narrow point of this example is that not every defect is significant in the sense that it alters the conclusions to be drawn from a model. The original Exchange model was heteroscedastic, but its conclusion that the data showed economies of scale was corroborated by Guth's alternative models, which avoided that defect. Consequently, wherever possible, objections should be accompanied by calculations which will enable the decision maker to appraise their importance.

The SEC example also yields a larger point. When parties express criticisms by introducing alternative models, the process need not necessarily be a seesaw battle of conflicting econometric demonstrations. As in the SEC case, there may instead be a progression toward greater refinement and correctness in statistical methodology which will not only be apparent to the decision maker, but which may also achieve results meriting at least tacit agreement among the experts.

This experience suggests as the second protocol that *(1) a party objecting to an econometric model introduced by another party should demonstrate the numerical significance of his objections whenever possible, and (2) a party objecting to a model of data designated by the decision maker for econometric analysis should produce a superior alternative analysis of those data.*

In criticizing models it is possible to speculate endlessly that different data, forms of equation, or explanatory variables would yield significantly different and superior results. Compelling definite calculations will bring such easy speculation down to earth. This requirement should not prove burdensome

[100]The Antitrust Division of the Department of Justice also used a regression study in an SEC proceeding under the Public Utility Holding Company Act in opposing the application of American Electric Power Co. to acquire Columbus & South Ohio Electric Co. The study purported to show that competition in electricity was significant for commerce because the cost of electricity would influence significant production decisions, including plant location. Department of Justice Exhibit No. 221, at 6, American Elec. Power Co., No. 70-4596 (S.E.C., filed Mar. 29, 1968) (testimony of John W. Wilson).

to rebuttal witnesses, although it might be unfair to compel a party to develop a full-scale model incorporating data unilaterally selected by another party.[101] However, where data have been designated by the decision maker as appropriate for econometric analysis, it seems reasonable to require each party to present his method or to suffer the selection by default of another method.[102] Of course, presentation of a model as a description of designated data would not be equivalent to sponsorship of that model's statistical projection as a prediction of the future. If a party believed—as the FPC did in *Southern Louisiana*[103]—that sound econometric prediction simply was not possible, he would be free to argue that the best available description of the past was still not sufficiently reliable to support an agency prediction. The second protocol would permit a party to make such an argument without presenting his own model, but it compels him to bear the risk that should the

[101]An illustration of the distinction between quantification of objections and production of alternative models may be found in the first *Southern Louisiana* proceeding. Professor Cootner, Amerada's rebuttal expert, quantified his objections to the staff model by computing alternative equations showing materially different results. See, e.g., Amerada Petroleum Corp., Exhibit No. 156, at 99–101, Southern Louisiana Area Rate Proceeding, 40 F.P.C. 530 (1968). He did not claim his equations were correct models, but only that they illustrated defects in Edmonston's model. Id. The staff argued that his criticisms were hypothetical because he had failed to produce a model of his own. Rejecting this argument, the hearing examiner found that the "Staff contention that it was necessary for Dr. Cootner to develop an econometric model of his own, to support his criticisms, is entirely unpersuasive." Southern Louisiana Area Rate Proceeding, 40 F.P.C. 703, 857–58 (1968). This decision was correct from the point of view of the first two protocols, since the examiner, like Cootner, was persuaded that the data covered by Edmonston's model were not appropriate to the problem and presumably would not have designated such data for analysis. Hence, it would have been unfair to compel Cootner to develop models based on such data.

[102]Reasoning similar to that underlying this part of the protocol was used in United States v. United Shoe Mach. Corp., 110 F. Supp. 295 (D. Mass. 1953), *aff'd per curiam*, 347 U.S. 521 (1954), where Judge Wyzanski rejected United's criticism of the Government's sample data on the shoe industry, commenting that

> in criticizing this sample, United has not suggested, much less offered, a preferable sample. If antitrust trials are to be kept manageable, samples must be used, and a sample which is in general reasonable should not be rejected in the absence of the offer of a better sample.

Id. at 305–06.

[103]Southern Louisiana Area Rate Proceeding, 46 F.P.C. 86, 121–22 (1971).

decision maker decide that a description of the past is an appropriate basis for prediction, it is his opponent's description which will be adopted.

Although this protocol could prove useful in both judicial and administrative proceedings, the regulatory context presents a special reason for requiring econometric submissions from all parties. In the first *Southern Louisiana* case, the FPC noted that more reliable results might be achieved in future proceedings if the industry also would present econometric studies.[104] In affirming, the Court of Appeals sounded a similar theme when it noted that the producers, "possessed of most of the information essential to effective regulation," did not help the Commission in estimating supply.[105] Thus, econometric participation by regulated industries which have more information and greater resources than an agency staff would appear to be important in the development of econometric methods. The proposed protocol, though not the only way, is one good way of compelling such participation.

C.

When models are introduced, the decision maker is faced with the problem of determining the conclusions that may properly be drawn from them. If the first two protocols are followed, the issue of the proper use of econometric models may be particularly troublesome, because the introduction of competing models may increase the temptation to give some weight to each. In one proceeding before the Civil Aeronautics Board, the parties followed procedures similar to those suggested by the first two protocols; consequently, that case is a good springboard for the development of the third protocol, dealing with the proper use of regression estimates.

In setting airline fares, the CAB is required by statute to consider, inter alia, "the effect of such rates upon the movement of traffic."[106] In an industrywide rate proceeding,[107] the Board's

[104]Southern Louisiana Area Rate Proceeding, 40 F.P.C. 530, 626 (1968).

[105]Southern Louisiana Area Rate Cases, 428 F.2d 407, 440 (5th Cir.), *cert. denied*, 400 U.S. 950 (1970).

[106]Civil Aeronautics Act, 49 U.S.C. §482(e)(1) (1970).

[107]Domestic Passenger Fare Investigation Phase 7, No. 21866-7 (C.A.B., Apr. 9, 1971) [hereinafter cited as CAB Fare Case].

Bureau of Economics, through its economist Wayne Watkins, introduced two econometric studies designed to show the price elasticity of air traffic, that is, the change in traffic associated with a change in fare level. A specification of this relation was deemed essential, because any fare increase would have to be based on some estimate of the carriers' need for increased revenues, but the anticipated revenue increase arising from a fare increase would have to be discounted by any adverse impact of the fare change on airline ticket sales.[108]

The first study was a time-series regression over the period 1946–69 using a measure of fares and other variables to explain changes in traffic. The fare elasticity, the coefficient of the fare variable, was shown to be −1.249;[109] this meant that for every 1 percent increase in fares, air travel declined by almost 1.25 percent. The results of this study were confirmed by Watkins' second model, a cross-section analysis of traffic in a recent twelve-month period between the 298 most heavily traveled domestic city pairs.[110] The coefficient of the fare variable was −1.274, a figure close to the time-series result.[111]

[108]*Id.* at 54. The dependent variable, the change from the preceding year in the logarithm of revenue passenger miles per capita, was regressed on the change from the preceding year in the logarithms of fares per revenue passenger mile, deflated by the consumer-price index, and disposable personal income per capita in constant (1958) dollars, and the logarithm of time, beginning in 1937.

[109]Staff Exhibit BC-T-4, at 1–3, CAB Fare Case (testimony of Wayne S. Watkins).

[110]Note that by presenting separate time-series and cross-section studies, the Bureau avoided the pooling of data for which Khazzoom's model was criticized. See p. 1460 *supra*. This is the approach an expert might have followed if the Board had designated time-series data for econometric analysis in accordance with the first protocol. The value of the Bureau's approach is indicated by the belief of two dissenting members of the Board that "there is substantial reason to believe that fare elasticity may really be greater than −.7" because the Board's two elasticity studies, although very different in design, both led to an elasticity in the vicinity of −1.25. CAB Fare Case 18 (members Minetti and Murphy, concurring in part and dissenting in part). "This mutual confirmation of the results goes far in our minds to offset the criticisms leveled against each of the studies separately." *Id.*

[111]CAB Fare case 59–62. For each city pair, the logarithms of the number of arriving and departing passengers over a two-month period was regressed on the logarithms of average fare per mile, average number of business day telephone messages (a proxy for community of interest between each city pair), the product of the aggregate effective buying incomes in the two cities of each pair, distance between the cities, and elapsed travel time per mile. See Staff Exhibit BC-7058, CAB Fare Case.

The air carriers attacked these studies, introduced competing models, and claimed that the elasticity was much smaller than the Bureau's results indicated.[112] TWA's time-series regression eliminated what TWA considered to be "nonrepresentative years" and employed variables somewhat different from those used by the Bureau.[113] The study generated a fare elasticity of −0.566 for the period 1954–69.[114] United, the other airline submitting its own study, found, on the basis of a time-series regression based on quarterly data for the previous four years, that fare elasticity was −0.583.[115] At some point in the proceedings, without explanation, the Bureau retreated to the position that the effect on traffic of its proposed fare increase of 7.75 percent over a 1970 fare level should be measured by a coefficient of elasticity between −0.7 and −0.566, although it adhered to the elasticities shown by its econometric studies with respect to the greater fare increases sought by the carriers.[116]

After an extensive recitation of the competing models and opposing arguments, the Board decided not to accept any model in toto, observing that "considerable doubt is cast on each of the studies."[117] Nevertheless, the Board found that the studies "can form the basis for a reasonable judgment on the issue,"[118] and provided "strong indication" that "fare elasticity [was] significantly below zero."[119] The Board concluded that fare elasticity was −0.7, which it justified (1) as within the range of elasticities of the various studies, (2) as close to the elasticity proposed by the Bureau for a 7.75 percent fare increase, and (3)

[112]CAB Fare Case 56–64.

[113]*Id.* at 56.

[114]*Id.*

[115]United developed a times-series regression based on quarterly data from the first quarter of 1963 through the first quarter of 1970. Although United appears to have used the same variables as the Bureau, United computed elasticities for each four-year period contained within the seven-year time span, arguing that these periods were related to types of fare changes. In the last period (second quarter 1966 to first quarter 1970), which began with the introduction of several discount fares and ended with two general fare increases, the resulting fare elasticity was −0.583, as stated in the text. *Id.* at 56–57.

[116]*Id.* at 57.

[117]*Id.* at 65.

[118]*Id.*

[119]*Id.* at 69.

on the basis of the standard error in the Bureau's time-series analysis, which indicated that there was only one chance in forty that the "true" value of fare elasticity was closer to zero than to −0.7.[120]

The Board's second and third reasons seem to be make-weights. The fact that the Bureau supported the −0.7 elasticity figure is unpersuasive, because the Bureau, without giving reasons, contradicted the studies of its own experts. The fact that the "true" value of fare elasticity was, on the basis of the econometric studies, unlikely to be less[121] than −0.7 is almost beside the point, since the major issue was the Board's failure to choose the −1.2 figure indicated by those very studies.

The first reason given by the Board seems more substantial; it is, moreover, of particular importance, because it is likely to represent the manner in which decision makers will be tempted to deal with conflicting regression studies. The choice of an estimate within the range of elasticities of the various studies implies that the Board was not choosing a result dictated by any particular model, but rather a number which was justified because it fell between the elasticities shown by the various models or, at best, within reasonable confidence limits of the various regression estimates. As such, the decision was a compromise.

Reasonable as it may seem, a compromise between the results of conflicting econometric studies is not an appropriate way of resolving doubts about those studies. Every model is based on assumptions about data and methodology reflected in the regression results, and statisticians using such models would use only those results for their estimates.[122] The choice of a value that lies between the estimates of two different models, though it might appear to a layman's rough sense of compromise to be supported by the results of each, is in reality consistent with the assumptions of neither, so that the compromise would lack any evidentiary support. In the CAB case, the Board's doubts about the validity of a model demonstrating an

[120]*Id.*

[121]For convenience, comparisons of elasticities will be made in terms of their absolute values.

[122]Conversation with Herbert Robbins, Professor of Statistics, Columbia University, New York City, Apr. 20, 1973.

elasticity of −1.2 were not evidence to support a finding of a definite lesser figure such as −0.7; the Board's failure to articulate a rationale for its choice of −0.7 suggests that personal judgment rather than hard evidence formed the basis for its decision.

Nor would the Board's choice of a compromise figure be any more appropriate because that figure was within a reasonable confidence interval of the results of each of several different studies. Doubts which the Board might have entertained about the correctness or relevance of regression methodology are unrelated to the size of confidence intervals, which measure only sampling variation and which are calculated on the assumption that the regression methodology is correct.[123] Moreover, if the regression analysis is correct, the regression estimate is superior to any other, because it has the greatest probability of being the true value; the probable correctness of another value diminishes with its distance from the regression estimate. There is no basis in the regression for picking a less likely estimate over the regression estimate, and consequently the choice of a number within a "reasonable confidence interval," like the compromise between models, is not supported by any of the models on which it is purportedly based.[124]

The third protocol, based on the preceding analysis, provides that *in any case in which the decision maker resorts to significant use of econometric findings, he should select the model that most usefully describes the data and should base his findings on that model.*

From its decision, it appears that the CAB had believed that elasticity of demand for air travel was in fact somewhat less than the elasticity estimated by the Bureau. A reason for this was the Board's belief that the Bureau's time-series study improperly included periods of discount fares and periods in which railroads were more viable long-distance competitors.[125] Given

[123]See note 31 *supra*.

[124]In addition to lacking evidentiary support, a compromise estimate teaches nothing as a precedent. An unexplained choice of a compromise figure denies to future litigants the knowledge of those econometric techniques which a decision maker found acceptable. A thoroughly enlightening critique of the various formulations would help, but this laborious effort is unlikely to be made when the end result is a compromise that need not be tied to specific criticisms.

[125]CAB Fare Case 65–66.

these objections, the Bureau should simply have prepared regressions on the basis of more appropriate and recent data. In fact, TWA supplied studies for more recent years which showed approximately a −0.7 elasticity, the figure ultimately selected by the Board.[126] A decision on the basis of the TWA study, as distinguished from the Board's actual decision, could have been explained and defended, and would have been an enlightening precedent for future rate making.

D.

The effect of the third protocol is to preclude a decision maker from reflecting doubts over the merits of competing econometric models by offering compromise estimates of statistical projections. While in some circumstances revised models may be helpful, frequencly it will not be possible to lay all doubts to rest. The meaning of the past may be legitimately subject to varying interpretations, and even when the decision maker choses the best model, the existence of other analyses which generate different results may be grounds for skepticism. If predictions are involved, the relevance of the past to the future may be uncertain, and the choice of a particular model as a description of the past does not assure the validity of that description for the future. Finally, doubt may be generated by expert testimony not based on econometric studies which conflicts with the preferred econometric results. The proper manner by which the decision maker faced with doubts should arrive at findings is the subject of the fourth protocol.

A "compromise" is one way to make findings, but that approach should be rejected under the reasoning of the third protocol.[127] The same reasoning compels a rejection of the subjective discounting of the results of a single model. Another possible source for a precise estimate would be subjective expert testimony not based on econometric findings. Experts making subjective estimates usually support their diverse views with different pieces of the statistical picture. Like the intuitive

---

[126]TWA showed that for the period 1954–69, the Watkins model would yield an elasticity of −0.8 with a standard error of 0.26. TWA Exhibit 7077, CAB Fare Case.

[127]See pp. 243–44 *supra*.

methods that might have been used in *Western Union*,[128] such statistical fragments are usually econometric models of a naïve type. Whatever the merits of dependence on such subjective estimates when more detailed econometric studies are unavailable, if the decision maker has already rejected any econometric analysis of the crucial data, it would seem implausible to credit an expert's estimate based on an oversimplified model of some or all of those data.

The other possible sources for expert opinion would be data not included in the econometric model or qualitative knowledge. However, if the numerical data of most immediate relevance to the decision are too uncertain to support a precise estimate, it seems extremely unlikely that the lacking accuracy could convincingly be furnished by subjective incorporation of more peripheral numerical information or by judgment based on qualitative knowledge. At most, these sources of information enable a decision maker to adjust econometric projections on a qualitative basis. Thus, an expert might properly argue in the CAB proceeding that future elasticity of demand for air travel would be less than the −1.2 figure projected by the Bureau on the ground that future deterioration in rail service would reduce nonairline travel options. But a general observation that rail service will deteriorate cannot support an opinion that future elasticity of demand for air travel will be some definite figure less than −1.2, for there is no way of reasoning from the generality of such an observation to the precision of a point estimate. The preferred method for dealing with qualitative factors or additional relevant data is the construction of a new or revised model, but when this is impossible, a precise estimate at variance with the results of the regression analysis cannot rationally be made.

Hence the remaining possibility is that the decision maker should react to doubts about statistical projections by declining to offer any precise estimate. This occurred when the FPC rejected the staff's econometric model in the second *Southern Louisiana* proceeding. The Commission cited another regression study for the proposition that there was a positive correlation between gas supply and price, but it declined to make any numerical prediction of the effect of the price increases.[129] A

---

[128]See pp. 216–18 *supra*.
[129]See pp. 228–30 *supra*.

similar conclusion was reached in the first proceeding before the Postal Service Rate Commission concerning rate increases proposed by the Postal Service.[130] There, Chief Examiner Wenner's doubt about the accuracy and reliability of the econometric elasticity studies introduced was one reason for his refusal to vary rate increase in accordance with the estimated demand elasticities of the various classes of service.[131] In each of these cases, the unwillingness to accept econometric studies for more than general qualitative results led to findings on a general qualitative basis. If this approach is adopted, it follows as the fourth protocol that *a finding resting in substantial part on data which have been analyzed econometrically should be no more precise than the finding which the decision maker is prepared to accept on the basis of the econometric analysis.*

IV

The substance of the foregoing protocols suggests that (1) the decision maker should designate data for econometric analysis and require the parties to analyze those data separately from other data; (2) the parties' objections to econometric methods should be reflected in alternative models covering the designated data, and in any case quantified whenever possible; (3) if substantial use is made of data analyzed econometrically, the

---

[130]Postal Rate and Fare Increases 1971, No. & 71-1 (Postal Rate Comm'n, June 28, 1972).

[131]In its submission, the Postal Service proposed to distribute institutional costs in accordance with the so-called Inverse Elasticity Rule. This rule provides that institutional costs be distributed to classes of service in inverse proportion to their elasticity of demand. The theory of this allocation was to maximize revenues by imposing the largest rate increases on those classes of service for which the demand is least elastic. Application of this theory depends on the existence of varying elasticities of demand among the different classes of service.

In the Postal Commission proceeding, a number of elaborate regression studies were introduced to demonstrate such elasticities for nonmonopoly classes of mail. Wenner found, inter alia, that all the demand elasticities studies "were subject to serious and valid criticisms." He therefore concluded that until it was established that one or more of the classes of mail was subject to substantial elasticity of demand, the inverse elasticity rule should not be used as a major guide in distributing institutional costs. Chief Examiner's Initial Decision at 1–12, 13, *id.*

decision should include findings designating a particular model and a projection on the basis of that model; and (4) doubts or uncertainties about the accuracy of the statistical projection should lead to a projection on a less definite basis.

It is important to recognize that although these protocols emphasize the hardminded use of objective studies, they do not eliminate subjectivity from the process of projections. While certain statistical tests are available, subjective judgment must be exercised in constructing an econometric model and in choosing between various alternative techniques. Subjective judgment frequently must also be exercised in projecting the future course of explanatory variables not within regulatory control, if such variables are part of the model.

But subjectivity in constructing models and in projecting explanatory factors has quite different implications from subjectivity exercised at or near the point of ultimate decision. Variations in subjective choices at an early stage are likely to be far less significant to the results than those at a later stage, since early subjective judgments may have minor or even mutually canceling effects. Moreover, while subjectivity at an early stage will most likely not contradict objective evidence but only fill a gap caused by the absence of such evidence, subjective judgment near the conclusion of agency proceedings will usually involve rejection of the more objective evidence provided by a model. And, finally, subjective judgment at a preliminary stage will frequently concern matters—such as estimates of future population growth—on which information compiled by public or private organizations without reference to the particular proceedings can be used to check the expert's opinion. The effect of the protocols suggested in this article is thus not to eliminate subjectivity from agency judgment but to drive it back from the ultimate conclusion into preliminary questions involved in constructing a model.

However, the emphasis of the protocols is on objective analysis. A decision maker unable to accept such analysis might well conclude that although his decision requires precise numerical findings, the past offers at best only a general guide. In such cases, the effect of the protocols would be to expose the extent to which decisions which are presently required of agencies rest only on agency discretion.

Chapter 8

COMPENSATION FOR WRONGFUL DEATH

THE DEATH OF A CHILD is a calamity of such magnitude that one might suppose the anguish of this loss would afford a basis for compensation, much as compensation for anguish is allowed in law for other emotional hurts of a much less painful nature. But generally the rule is otherwise. Wrongful death statutes in most states (applicable to both children and adults) limit recovery to the "pecuniary loss" suffered by the beneficiaries. And while the method of computing that loss may be more or less generous, depending on the jurisdiction, the essential point is that in states having such pecuniary statutes there may be no recovery—at least in theory—for sorrow, grief, or the loss of companionship occasioned by death. The issue is presented in sharpest form when the death of a child is involved. States with strict pecuniary laws solemnly require juries and judges to engage in the fanciful enterprise of "estimating" the present value of the child's wages over the period the parents may expect to receive them, less the cost of his or her support, while firmly disregarding the real albeit intangible injuries.[1]

---

[1]For discussions of these rules in cases involving the death of children, see Decof, *Damages in Actions for Wrongful Death of Children*, 47 NOTRE DAME LAWYER 197 (1971); SPEISER, RECOVERY FOR WRONGFUL DEATH, §§ 4:16-4:28 (1966); Note, *Wrongful Death Damages: Recovery of Investment in Society and Companionship of a Child*, 27 OHIO STATE L.J. 355 (1966).

It is not surprising that the pecuniary rule, at least as it requires a computation of "child-labor" wages, has been condemned as barbaric[2] and defended principally with silence. While its impact has been mitigated by presumptions of substantial loss and by more liberal conceptions of what may be pecuniary, the essential notion that no compensation should be allowed for the anguish of the survivors has remained remarkably vital, with only a minority of states expressly recognizing such injuries as compensable.[3]

Two related concerns may have inhibited reform. First, there is probably "a lively fear [that] the overenthusiasm of sympathetic juries" would lead to excessive awards and increased insurance premiums.[4] Second, there is the objection that any award would be arbitrary because no amount could in fact compensate the survivors for their loss of companionship and emotional hurt.[5] The specter of enormous, arbitrary judgments for emotional hurt has undoubtedly been a powerful deterrent to change. But the validity of the first concern and the assumptions underlying the second need not go unquestioned. Since a number of states have statutes that do not expressly limit recovery to pecuniary loss, and a few—most notably Florida and Arkansas—expressly permit recovery for emotional

---

On the development of pecuniary loss rule in wrongful death cases generally, see Note, *Blind Imitation of the Past: An Analysis of Pecuniary Damages in Wrongful Death Actions*, 49 DENVER L.J. 99 (1972); PROSSER, LAW OF TORTS, ch. 24 (4th ed. 1971); Smedley, *Wrongful Death—Bases of the Common Law Rules*, 13 VAND. L. REV. 605 (1960).

[2]See, e.g., Wycko v. Gnodtke, 361 Mich. 331, 337, 105 N.W.2d 118, 121 (1960); Gary v. Schwartz, 72 Misc.2d 332, 343, 339 N.Y.S.2d 39, 50 (Sup. Ct. 1972).

[3]Statutes expressly allowing recovery for the survivors' anguish and loss of comfort are: (1) ARK. STAT. ANN. § 27-909 (1962); (2) FLA. STAT. ANN. § 768.03 (1964); (3) HAWAII REV. STAT. § 663-3 (Supp. 1973); (4) KAN. STAT. ANN. § 60-1904 (1964); (5) KY. REV. STAT. § 411.135 (1970); (6) ME. REV. STAT. ANN. tit. 18, § 2552 (Supp. 1973); (7) MD. ANN. CODE art. 67, § 4 (Supp. 1973); (8) NEV. REV. STAT. § 41.090 (1973); (9) VA. CODE ANN. § 8-636 (Supp. 1973); (10) WASH. REV. CODE ANN. § 24.010 (Supp. 1973); (11) W.VA. CODE ANN. § 55-7-6 (Supp. 1973); (12) WIS. STAT. ANN. § 895.04 (Supp. 1973).

[4]PROSSER, LAW OF TORTS 907 (4th ed. 1971); NEW YORK LAW REVISION COMMISSION, 1935 REPORTS, RECOMMENDATIONS AND STUDIES 215, 218 (1935).

[5]Comment, *Damages for the Wrongful Death of Children*, 22 U. CHI. L. REV. 549–50 (1955).

injury in wrongful death cases, it is possible to compare the distribution of awards in these various classes of states to assess the impact of statutory differences. This chapter reports the findings of such a study with respect to minors. The purpose of the investigation was to assess the probable effect of liberalizing a wrongful death statute to make express provision for emotional injury; the results of analysis indicate that certain commonly held conceptions concerning the risks of change may well be wrong. The occasion demonstrates that the diversity of state laws and conditions is a rich—although largely neglected—source of statistical knowledge with which to test the impact of proposed legal reforms.

I

The data consist of the final judgments after all appeals in 192 reported wrongful death cases involving minors. These cases were drawn from ten states in the period 1940–72.[6] Of these states, four had statutes that limited recovery to "pecuniary injury," "pecuniary loss," or similar provisions ("pecuniary loss" statutes);[7] four had statutes (patterned after Lord Campbell's Act) sufficiently general in their terms to permit recovery for the emotional hurt of the survivors, but not expressly sanctioning such recovery ("general loss" statutes);[8] and two had statutes

[6]Nine of the states selected were those having the largest volume of reported litigation, as shown in Korpela, *Excessiveness and Adequacy of Damages for Personal Injuries Resulting in Death of Minor*, 49 A.L.R.3d 934 (1973). Arkansas was added to these states because it was the only other state expressly providing for recovery for emotional hurt that had a statute old enough to have generated a substantial volume of reported litigation.

[7]ILL. REV. STAT. ch. 70, § 2 (1969) ("pecuniary injuries"); MICH. COMP. LAWS § 600-2922 (1968) ("pecuniary injury"); N.Y. EST., POWERS & TRUSTS LAW § 5-4.3 (McKinney 1967) ("pecuniary injuries"); PA. STAT. tit. 12, § 1604 (1953)("[Such] other expenses caused by the injury which resulted in death as could have been recovered in an action by the injured person during his lifetime".)

[8]LA. CIV. CODE ANN. art. 2315 (West 1971) ("all other damages"): MISS. CODE ANN. § 1453 (1942) ("just" damages); TEX. REV. CIV. STAT. ANN. art. 4671–73 (1953) (damages "proportionate to the injury"); CAL. CIV. PRO. CODE § 377 (West 1973) ("such damage as under all the circumstances of the case may be just . . ."). These general loss statutes are less liberal than one might

that expressly sanctioned recovery for such emotional hurt ("all-inclusive loss" statutes).[9] In almost all cases, the amount of award was an important issue either before the trial judge or on appeal. There were zero awards in three New York cases,[10] and thirteen awards in excess of $50,000. The top four were two awards of $100,000 in Arkansas and Florida,[11] $252,000 in a New York case,[12] and an extraordinary $1.8 million in another Florida case.[13]

In considering the probable consequences of reform, the effect of rare, very large awards may become confused with and distort the statistics evidencing a broader and more moderate increase. Since these consequences are distinct in the sense that they raise specific legislative issues, we attempt to separate them by using what are known as nonparametric techniques. These techniques are based on the ordering of the data (in this case, the awards by size), but not on their exact values.[14] The principal statistic used in this investigation is the median award, which is calculated by arranging all awards in order of size and taking the middle award if the number of cases is odd, or the average of two middle values if the number is even. We also use nonparametric analyses based on the values of the ranks of the awards rather than their amounts. It can readily be

---

suppose from their text, because they were modeled on Lord Campbell's Act, which had been interpreted to be limited to pecuniary loss. The correctness of that interpretation has been questioned. Note, *Blind Imitation of the Past: An Analysis of Pecuniary Damages in Wrongful Death Actions*, 49 DENVER L.J. 99, 101–03 (1972). The general loss statutes were analyzed separately from the pecuniary loss statutes because the courts in general loss states might well view themselves as free to soften or abandon a restriction to pecuniary losses that was not expressly required by the legislature.

[9]FLA. STAT. ANN. § 768.03 (1964); ARK. STAT. ANN. § 27-909 (1962).

[10]Schreck v. State, 35 Misc. 2d 929, 231 N.Y.S.2d 563 (Ct. Cl. 1962) (for death of three boys).

[11]McLeod v. Young, 257 So. 2d 605 (Fla. Dist. Ct. App.), *cert. denied*, 263 So. 2d 230 (Fla. 1972); Spiller v. Thomas M. Lowe & Assoc., Inc., 328 F. Supp. 54 (W.D. Ark. 1971), *aff'd*, 466 F.2d 903 (8th Cir. 1972) (applying Arkansas law).

[12]Hart v. Forchelli, 445 F.2d 1018 (2d Cir.), *cert. denied*, 404 U.S. 940 (1971) (applying New York law).

[13]Compania Dominicana de Aviacion v. Knapp, 251 So. 2d 18 (Fla. Dist. Ct. App.), *cert. denied*, 256 So.2d 6 (Fla. 1971).

[14]See, e.g., BRADLEY, DISTRIBUTION-FREE STATISTICAL TESTS (1968); GIBBONS, NON-PARAMETRIC STATISTICAL INFERENCE (1971); NOETHER, ELEMENTS OF NONPARAMETRIC STATISTICS (1967); SIEGAL, NONPARAMETRIC STATISTICS FOR THE BEHAVIORAL SCIENCES (1956).

TABLE 16. Median Awards for Successive Time Periods (1941-72)

	NUMBER OF CASES	MEDIAN AWARD
1941-42	16	$ 7,250
1943-48	32	8,250
1949-54	21	8,500
1955-60	36	15,000
1961-66	51	15,000
1967-72	36	25,000

seen that such statistics are unaffected by extreme values, whereas more familiar parametric statistics (such as the mean) and parametric statistical tests would be so affected. The problem of the exceptional award is dealt with separately.

A.

As indicated, the data represent awards over a thirty-two-year period. During this period, the general level of awards has increased, presumably because of continuing inflation and other factors. The increase is shown clearly by the data in Table 16, which includes the median awards in successive time intervals.

In order to put older and more recent cases on a comparable basis, it is necessary to remove the effects of this trend toward higher awards over time. The average annual rate of increase in awards is 5.25 percent. To remove the trend effect, the 192 awards were adjusted to a 1973 base by increasing each award 5.25 percent per annum from the year it was made. All subsequent analyses deal with these time-adjusted amounts, unless otherwise noted.[15] The effect of this adjustment may be

[15]This figure was calculated using a least-squares regression equation relating the logarithm of amounts of award to the year of the award. The three $0 awards and the extreme $1.8 million award were excluded from the computations. Introduction of other variables, such as age of the deceased, had little or no effect on the calculated rate of increase. For a description of the statistical method used, see CROXTON, COWDEN & KLEIN, APPLIED GENERAL STATISTICS, 256-60 (3d ed. 1967). The 5.25 computed rate of increase is interesting because a similar calculation for the Consumer Price Index from 1961 to 1973 shows an annual rate of increase of 2.75 percent. Thus, awards for the death of children have increased at a substantially greater rate than the rate of inflation.

TABLE 17. Median and Mean Time-Adjusted Awards by Type of Statute

	PECUNIARY LOSS	GENERAL LOSS	ALL-INCLUSIVE LOSS
Median	$24,845	$28,585	$ 44,060
Mean	33,450	36,360	117,880[16]

seen by comparing medians. The median value of the 192 time-adjusted awards is $28,355, while the median award in actual money is $12,500. Besides improving comparability, the time-adjusted figures give a more realistic picture because they permit making assessments in terms of current dollars.

B.

Awards in the various classes of states may be compared in several ways.

First, the median time-adjusted award in the pecuniary loss states is $24,845; in the general loss states it is $28,585, and in the all-inclusive loss states it is $44,060. These results and the means for each group of states are shown in Table 17.

Are these chance differences that would vanish if considerably more evidence were available? An answer is given by the so-called median test, which examines the hypothesis that several samples come from populations with a common median.[17] As applied to the data, the test indicates that the probability of a disparity as large as that observed, if the data were from populations with the same median, is about 0.07. This suggests a genu-

[16]The difference between the median and the mean awards in the all-inclusive loss states illustrates the distorting effect of a single outlying award. If the single $1.8 million Florida award is excluded, the mean award in this class of states drops to $48,399, a figure close to the median.

[17]For a discussion of this test, see GIBBONS, NONPARAMETRIC STATISTICAL INFERENCE 164–67 (1971). The essence of the test is as follows: the overall median of the 192 time-adjusted observations is $28,355. Of the 78 awards in pecuniary states, 33, or 42.3 percent, exceed this figure; of the 86 awards in nonpecuniary states, 44, or 51.2 percent, exceed it; and of the 28 awards in emotional anguish states, 19, or 67.9 percent, exceed it. The deviations of these percentages from 50 percent lead to a χ^2 value of 5.46 with 2 degrees of freedom.

TABLE 18. Distribution of Amount of Time-Adjusted Awards by Type of Statute

	PECUNIARY LOSS		GENERAL LOSS		ALL-INCLUSIVE LOSS	
	N	%	N	%	N	%
Under $10,000	16	20.5	7	8.2	1	3.6
$10,000–19,999	16	20.5	15	17.4	7	25.0
$20,000–29,999	14	17.9	23	26.7	1	3.6
$30,000–49,999	18	23.1	24	27.9	7	25.0
$50,000 & over	14	17.9	17	19.8	12	42.9

ine difference in awards under the three different types of statute.

Next, Table 18 compares the full distribution of awards under each type of statute. Note the shift in awards toward the higher end of the spectrum as one moves from the pecuniary loss statutes to the all-inclusive loss statutes. Could differences as large as these occur by chance if amount of award were independent of type of statute? A standard statistical test of significance (chi-square) indicates that the probability of differences as large as those observed is just under 0.01, which suggests that amount of award is not unrelated to type of statute.[18]

That these differences in distributions are statistically significant does not necessarily imply that type of statute is an important determinant of amount of award. The facts of particular cases or the rules or practices of particular jurisdictions or states may influence courts and juries far more than the confines of the statute.

While it is not possible completely to disentangle such effects and estimate the separate contribution of each factor or group of factors, statistical methodology can shed some light on this question. One technique is to measure the total variation over all awards and then to determine the proportion of that total which is attributable to variations in awards within groups of states with similar statutes (intraclass variation), and the proportion which is attributable to variation among groups of states with similar statutes (interclass variation). If most of the varia-

[18] χ^2 is 20.17 with 8 degrees of freedom. For a discussion of the χ^2 test, see, e.g., CROXTON, COWDEN & KLEIN, *supra* note 13, at 586–98. See also chapter 2 *supra* at 43–46.

TABLE 19. Variance in Ranks of Time-Adjusted
Awards

	INTRACLASS	INTERCLASS	TOTAL
Variance of Ranks	2,853	155	3,008
Percent of Total Variance	94.8	5.2	100.0

tion in awards is interclass, this would indicate that type of statute was a relatively important determinant of awards. Conversely, if most variation is intraclass, factors other than type of
statute would evidently be principally responsible for the variation.

To measure variation for this purpose, we rank awards from
all jurisdictions, and using the ranks in lieu of amounts, compute the intraclass, interclass, and total variance of the award
ranks. The results are shown in Table 19.[19]

The table shows that only approximately 5 percent of the total
variation in the ranks of time-adjusted awards is attributable to
interclass differences. Consequently, it is fair to conclude that
the pecuniary-loss doctrine plays only a minor role in influencing the amount of awards compared with other factors that
operate on an individual case, locality, or state basis.[20] Since in
theory one would expect type of statute to exercise a much

[19] The variance is a commonly used measure of dispersion of data. It is
defined as the average squared deviation of the data from their mean value.
The intraclass variance referred to in the text is the mean squared difference
between the rank of each award and the mean rank of awards under the statute
pursuant to which that award was made. The interclass variance is computed
from the squared differences between the mean rank of awards under each
class of statute and the grand mean rank of all awards; the average of these figures is then taken by weighting the squared differences for the three classes of
statutes by the proportions of awards under each class of statute. The total
variance is the mean squared difference between the rank of each award and
the grand mean rank of all awards. It is a mathematical fact of great utility that
the total variance is equal to the sum of the intraclass and interclass variances.

[20] The analysis of variance technique employed here was used extensively
in the report for the U.S. Commissioner of Education prepared pursuant to the
1964 Civil Rights Act of the denial of equal educational oportunities in the
public schools by reason of race (Coleman Report). COLEMAN ET AL., EQUALI-
TY OF EDUCATIONAL OPPORTUNITY (U.S. Dep't of Health, Education and
Welfare 1966). A critical finding of the study was that school-to-school variations in the achievement test scores accounted for only a relatively small portion of the total variation in achievement scores, leaving the balance of
variation attributable to factors operating within schools. *Id.* at 296.

greater influence on awards, the statistics must reflect the degree to which the courts have already eroded the differences between statutes. Specifically, in the pecuniary and general loss states, the pecuniary loss doctrine has been softened to allow substantial recoveries, while in the all-inclusive loss states, restraint generally has been exercised in assessing amounts for anguish. And since the figures are based on cases involving children—in which sympathy is likely to be the greatest and probable pecuniary injury at a minimum—the differences in average awards for wrongful death cases generally should be less than those reported here.

However, two cautions should be observed in interpreting these results. First, the average increase in awards from pecuniary to all-inclusive loss states is not necessarily a typical increase, so that awards in a given locality or state, or in a given class of cases, may be affected very differently by a statutory change, even if the average increase is that depicted by the study. Second, the estimate itself may not fairly represent the average change likely to be encountered by a change in the law. Liberalization of a statute is a dramatic event that might invite an increase in awards, while the data reflect merely the cumulative deposit of fairly long-standing statutory differences.[21] One could speak with greater confidence if there were also direct evidence of the change in pattern of awards surrounding the passage of an amendment. A scattering of cases used as examples suggests, consistent with the analysis, that there would be a moderate increase.[22] However, the cases surrounding recent

[21]For example, changing from a pecuniary loss to a general loss statute today would probably invite awards for emotional distress. This would increase recoveries more than is indicated by our statistics, which reflect the more restrictive interpretations of general loss statutes patterned after the original interpretation of Lord Campbell's Act. See note 8 *supra*.

[22]Washington amended its statute in 1967 to allow recovery for emotional loss. WASH. REV. CODE ANN. §4.24.010 (Supp. 1973). Cf. the pre-amendment Northern Pacific Ry. v. Everett, 232 F.2d 488 (9th Cir. 1956) ($8,000 recovery for seventeen-year-old girl) with the postamendment Clark v. Icicle Irrigation District, 72 Wash. 2d 201, 432 P.2d 541 (1967) ($15,000 for two-year-old boy).

In Michigan, recoveries showed an increase following Wycko v. Gnodtke, 361 Mich. 331, 105 N.W.2d 118 (1960), which dramatically rejected earlier decisions and allowed recovery for loss of companionship as pecuniary. See, e.g., Rohm v. Stroud, 386 Mich. 693, 194 N.W.2d 307 (1972) ($24,000 for fourteen-year-old girl). In 1971, the *Wycko* decision was confirmed when the Michigan legislature eliminated "pecuniary" from the statute and added entitlement to damages for "loss of society" and "companionship." MICH. COMP. LAWS ANN. §600.2922(2) (Supp. 1973).

amendments are too few on which to base statistical findings, and to reach back into the more distant past would create sharp problems of comparability. Thus the cross-section analysis is probably the best statistical technique available in this context. And by the standards of plausibility supporting most legislative action, it affords fairly strong evidence of the magnitude of the average increase in awards that is likely to follow a liberalizing amendment.[23]

This conclusion refers to awards as a group and does not mean that amendment would not open the door to an occasional exceptional award. The extraordinary $1.8 million award in Florida (an all-inclusive loss state) indicates that this is a distinct possibility. Taking that award into account, one would have to say that there is at least some statistical evidence that awards far in excess of those recoverable for pecuniary losses would occur under all-inclusive loss statutes.[24] If such awards are deemed undesirable, a limit on the amount of recovery for emotional hurt would be an essential part of reform. This approach—which would avoid abridging compensation for pecuniary loss—would seem a better way of preventing "runaway" awards than allowing recovery for loss of companionship

[23]Since the median recovery in all-inclusive loss states is higher than in pecuniary loss states, it is appropriate to inquire whether the difference indicated by our sample is wide and deep enough to affect insurance rates. It appears not to be. For example, most wrongful death cases arise out of automobile accidents. While automobile insurance premium rates for base limits coverage ($10,000/$20,000) vary to match experience in different localities, the premium rate for excess limits coverage (up to $300,000) is computed as a multiple of the base rate, and this multiple is the same in most states. Higher multiples reflecting greater excess limit losses have been worked out for a few states, but the differences are not large and there does not appear to be any relationship with the type of wrongful death statute. Higher multiples are found in Florida (an all-inclusive loss state), but also in Illinois (a pecuniary loss state), and in Louisiana (a general loss state). See Morris, *Enterprise Liability and the Actuarial Process—The Insignificance of Foresight*, 70 YALE L.J. 554, 569 (1961). Thus the slight clustering of larger wrongful death awards in some jurisdictions is not sufficiently important to be reflected in the calculation of rates. Cf. Miller v. Miller, 22 N.Y.2d 12, 21 (1968). But cf., Rosenthal v. Warren, 475 F.2d 438, 441 (2d Cir. 1973).

[24]One exceptional award among twenty-eight is only weak statistical evidence of a nonnegligible rate of exceptional awards. For example, if the rate of exceptional awards was 0.01, a random sample of twenty-eight would include at least one such award 25 percent of the time; if the rate of exceptional awards were .005, a random sample of twenty-eight would include at least one such award 15 percent of the time.

and emotional hurt but limiting the total amount that could be recovered for all injuries combined.[25]

II

The objection that irrational or arbitrary judgment would have to be exercised in making awards for emotional hurt would appear to pose a deep problem, because it seems inescapable that no award in any amount can "compensate" the survivors for their loss. But I submit that the true basis for this objection is not that money and grief are incommensurate; rather, it is the assumption that since juries and judges would be freer to give rein to their predilections, variations in awards would be greater under an all-inclusive loss statute than under a pecuniary or even a general-loss statute.[26] Such variations are tacitly equated with highly subjective or arbitrary judgments, because in cases involving children—especially young children—there seems little firm objective basis for substantial variation in awards.[27]

The assumption of greater variability seems plausible, but the statistical facts do not support it. The variation in awards, as measured either by the variance of the rank of awards or by their adjusted median absolute deviation, is in fact less in all-

---

[25]Several states limit recovery for emotional loss. ME. REV. STAT. ANN. tit. 18 §2552 (Supp. 1973) ($10,000 limit); VA. CODE ANN. §8-636 (Supp. 1973) ($25,000); W. VA. CODE ANN. 55-7-6 (Supp. 1973) ($10,000). Others expressly permit recovery for nonpecuniary injuries but impose an overall limit. KAN. STAT. ANN. §60-1903 (Supp. 1973) ($50,000 limit); MASS. ANN. LAWS, ch. 229, §2 (Supp. 1972) ("not less than $5,000 nor more than $200,000").

[26]Cf. Comment, *Damages for the Wrongful Death of Children*, 22 U. CHI. L. REV. 538 (1955).

[27]Our analysis supports this impression. A multiple linear regression analysis showed that the objective variables of age and state of award accounted for only about 30 percent of the variation in the ranks of the time-adjusted awards.

A separate analysis of sex and age showed, contrary to the initial impression, that the median time-adjusted awards for males and females have not differed significantly, but that a disproportionate number of cases involved males (137 out of a total of 190). One possible explanation is that a smaller proportion of cases involving female children are pressed through trial. With respect to age, the analysis showed, as expected, a positive correlation with amount of award.

TABLE 20. **Variance of Ranks and Median Absolute Deviation of Time-Adjusted Awards**

	PECUNIARY LOSS	GENERAL LOSS	ALL-INCLUSIVE LOSS
Variance of Ranks	3,407	2,318	2,993
Median Absolute Deviation Actual	14,315	10,500	18,970
Median Absolute Deviation as a Percentage of Median	58.7	36.7	43.1

inclusive loss states than in pecuniary-loss states. Table 20 gives the comparative figures for these measures of variation.[28]

Why are award variations in the all-inclusive loss states less than in pecuniary loss states? In all-inclusive and general loss states, variations in awards, including amounts for emotional hurt or loss of companionship, have been restricted by various doctrines, among them the doctrine that results in comparable cases should be comparable.[29] But the more interesting and important question is why awards in pecuniary loss states should vary so widely. The cause is not hard to discover. An examination of a sample of small and large awards indicates that the variation arises from the intermittent application of the pecuniary loss rule: when it is applied, the awards are very small; when it is "winked at" by judge and jury bent on doing higher justice, the awards are large. For example, five of the dozen smallest awards in pecuniary loss states (under $3,000) are

[28]The median absolute deviation is calculated by (1) subtracting the median from each award, (2) taking the absolute value of each difference, (3) arraying the differences by size, and (4) taking the middle value, as in the computation of the median. The median absolute deviation is then divided by the median to adjust for the differences in scale.

[29]Stephens v. Natchitoches Parish School Bd., 238 La. 388, 137 So. 2d 116 (1962); Bush Construction Co. v. Walters, 250 Miss. 384, 164 So. 2d 900 (1964). See also SPEISER, RECOVERY FOR WRONGFUL DEATH 554–59 (1966). Although trial and appellate judges thus appraise the correctness of the jury's decision in a given case by reference to awards in other similar cases, the jury is not permitted to have this information. This seems anomalous, because the jury is denied factual data that are evidently legally relevant, and, as a practical matter, might guide its judgment and prevent it from straying into error.

recent decisions in New York; it is evident from the opinion in three of these cases that the awards would have been larger in the absence of the limitation to pecuniary injury.[30] It should come as no surprise that those whose lives the courts value so lightly are children in institutions or from disrupted or deprived families. On the other hand, the pecuniary limitation was either expressly repudiated or tacitly ignored in other recent New York cases, most notably two decisions involving awards of $52,000 and $252,000, respectively, to middle-class parents.[31] These differences cannot be justified in terms of true pecuniary injury; and the selective or intermittent judicial repeal of the pecuniary loss doctrine is the reason the variation in New York awards is among the largest of any state. Indeed, it may be large enough to raise constitutional doubts about the validity of the pecuniary loss rule as it has been applied.[32]

The variation of awards in pecuniary states is thus a reflection of the conflict between the rule limiting recovery to pecuniary loss and current notions of fair compensation. Despite the seemingly greater latitude under an all-inclusive loss statute, the statistics indicate that the goal of rational uniformity would be promoted by removing the conflict between rule and impulse which is currently forced on decision makers in pecuniary loss jurisdictions.

It is worth noting that our confidence in the statistical conclusions reported here is directly related to the number of states involved in the analysis. For example, if data were available from only two states, the absence of a large difference in average would be open to the interpretation that state factors other than the statute canceled part of a difference that would

[30]See, e.g., Schreck v. State, 35 Misc. 2d 929, 231 N.Y.S.2d 563 (Ct. Cl. 1962) (three awards of $0, one of $3,250, and one of $10,975, all also including funeral expenses, for deaths of five boys in state epileptic institution).

[31]Gary v. Schwartz, 43 App. Div. 2d 562, 349 N.Y.S.2d 322 (App. Div. 1973) ($53,000 for a sixteen-year-old boy who was "headed for a dental career"): Hart v. Forchelli, 445 F.2d 1018 (2d Cir.), *cert. denied*, 404 U.S. 940 (1971) ($252,000 for an eighteen-year-old boy with "tentative plans to become an attorney").

[32]The importance of the right to recover for wrongful death, see, e.g., Rosenthal v. Warren, 475 F.2d 438 (2d Cir. 1973), suggests that discriminatory judicial enforcement may raise due-process and equal-protection questions. Cf. Gunther, *In Search of an Evolving Doctrine in a Changing Court: A Model for a Newer Equal Protection*, 86 HARV. L. REV. 1 (1972).

otherwise have appeared if all other conditions were identical except for the statute. But when data sources are multiplied, and large award differences do not correlate with statutory differences, it becomes increasingly implausible that state differences would so neatly obscure the true pattern. It is for reasons of this sort that the multiplicity and diversity of state conditions create the opportunity to assess the probable impact of this and other reforms in the law.

Chapter 9

GUILTY PLEAS

IF INSISTENCE ON A TRIAL would cost nothing, presumably few of the accused would plead guilty and forgo the chance for dismissal or acquittal. In most cases it is pressure—the promise of leniency in sentencing, a reduced charge, or the desire to avoid pretrial detention—that induces guilty pleas. Some such pressure is generally viewed as an acceptable and indeed essential tool for managing criminal-court calendars,[1] but the propriety of various inducement techniques has been widely debated, and it has been said that "[f]ew practices in the system of criminal justice create a greater sense of unease and suspicion than the negotiated plea of guilty."[2]

In assessing plea-bargaining practices, a fundamental question is the extent to which results in criminal proceedings are being changed by the substitution of guilty pleas for trials. Public attention has focused on one aspect of this problem: the extent to which plea bargaining has permitted defendants to escape the just consequences of their crimes by pleading guilty to reduced charges. The variance between the offense charged and the offense accepted on a plea provides highly visible and

[1]The Supreme Court has specifically approved plea bargaining as a means of managing overloaded criminal dockets. See Santobello v. New York, 404 U.S. 257, 260–61 (1971).

[2]THE PRESIDENT'S COMM'N ON LAW ENFORCEMENT AND THE ADMINISTRATION OF JUSTICE, TASK FORCE REPORT: THE COURTS 9 (1967).

dramatic evidence of the extent to which the state's interest has been compromised. The fairness of bargaining practices, however, also depends on the likelihood of a conviction had no bargain been offered. If the case against the accused is weak, his confession of guilt can be obtained only by inducements that may taint the trustworthiness of his admission. More fundamentally, when strong pressure is necessary to compel a confession in a weak case, the prosecutor's zeal to obtain a conviction by "consent" collides with the defendant's privilege against self-incrimination.[3] The strength of the cases in which guilty pleas are obtained is thus an important element in assessing the significance and propriety of inducement practices; it is, however, a far less visible element in the fairness equation than the compromise on the charge or on the sentence.

In the two leading cases sustaining the constitutionality of plea bargaining—*Brady* v. *United States*[4] and *Santobello* v. *New York*[5]—the Supreme Court's arguments for the practice manifest an assumption that those who are induced to plead guilty would, in any event, be convicted. In *Brady*, the Court argued that plea bargaining provides advantages for both the defendant and the state.[6] The Court observed that "[f]or a defendant who sees slight possibility of acquittal, the advantages of pleading guilty and limiting the probable penalty are obvious . . .."[7] For the state, a plea conserves scarce judicial and prosecutorial resources "for those cases in which . . . there is substantial doubt that the State can sustain its burden of proof."[8] In *Santobello*, the Court noted that, among the virtues of the process, a guilty plea "enhances whatever may be the rehabilitative prospects of the guilty when they are ultimately imprisoned."[9] Neither *Brady* nor *Santobello*, however, dealt with the constitu-

---

[3]Inducement based on the threat of differential sentencing has been held in some cases to raise constitutional issues as to the voluntariness of the plea. See Scott v. United States, 419 F.2d 264 (D.C. Cir. 1969); Euziere v. United States, 249 F.2d 293 (10th Cir. 1957); Note, *The Unconstitutionality of Plea Bargaining*, 83 HARV. L. REV. 1387 (1970).

[4]397 U.S. 742 (1970).

[5]404 U.S. 257 (1971).

[6]Brady v. United States, 397 U.S. 742, 752 (1970).

[7]*Id.*

[8]*Id.*

[9]Santobello v. New York, 404 U.S. 257, 261 (1971).

tional propriety of plea bargaining when the prosecutor's case is weak.

This omission is striking. Unquestionably, prosecutors use compromises to obtain convictions in apparently weak cases.[10] This does not necessarily mean that convictions in such cases would not be forthcoming, but only that they may be less predictable. But the failure of the Court to discuss the "weak-case" problem becomes significant if in a substantial number of guilty-plea cases convictions would not have been obtained in the absence of plea bargaining.

The purpose of this chapter is to examine certain statistical evidence bearing on this question. On the basis of the analysis that follows, I conclude that the pressure on defendants to plead guilty in the federal courts has induced a high rate of conviction by "consent" in cases in which no conviction would have been obtained if there had been a contest. If this conclusion is correct, it suggests that in assessing plea-bargaining practices the weak-case problem cannot be ignored, and that more particularized judgments about the relation between the strength of the inducement and the prosecutor's case may be necessary to satisfy constitutional and ethical standards relating to pleas.

I

The most appropriate measure of the strength of a guilty-plea case is the probability of conviction had there been no plea.[11] I thus pose the following question: what proportion of those pleading guilty in the federal courts would not have been convicted if they had contested their cases? This proportion, which I shall call the "implicit rate of nonconviction," cannot be di-

[10]See, e.g., NEWMAN, CONVICTION: THE DETERMINATION OF GUILT OR INNOCENCE WITHOUT TRIAL 67–75 (1966).

[11] For conceptual purposes, the strength of a case is measured at the outset (i.e., at arraignment), and subsequent developments, such as the denial of motions to dismiss or to suppress evidence, are not considered. A plea of guilty entered after an initial plea of not guilty, however, is counted as a guilty-plea case.

rectly observed, but it can be estimated for groups of defendants on the basis of certain plausible assumptions.

To illustrate the estimation technique, assume there are two
federal district courts disposing of equal numbers of defendants. Assume further that the proportions of various crimes
charged in each district are similar, and that the likelihood that
a defendant who contests his case will be convicted (the "conviction probability") depends primarily on the crime charged.[12]
Thus, over time, the numbers of defendants convicted and not
convicted in each district after a contest would be equal if there
were no guilty pleas. Now assume that in the first district prosecutors routinely announce that they will seek maximum sen-
tences for defendants who contest their cases; as a result, 60
percent of defendants plead guilty. In the second district, prosecutors make no such threat, and only 40 percent of defendants
plead guilty.

If all guilty-plea defendants would have been convicted had
they contested their cases, one would expect that, over time, the
number of nonconvictions in the two districts would be the
same. If there are substantially fewer nonconvictions in the first
district than in the second, the difference must stem from the
fact that some of the additional defendants pleading guilty in
the first district would not have been convicted if they had contested their cases. The number of such potential nonconvictions
divided by the number of additional defendants pleading guilty
in the first district is the implicit rate of nonconviction for that
group of defendants.[13]

[12]As used in this article, the conviction probability in a district, or for a
group of cases, is the average rate of conviction in that district or for that group
of cases if there were no guilty pleas.

[13]A numerical example may help here. Suppose there are two districts, *A*
and *B*, and that in the absence of guilty pleas each district would show a 60
percent conviction rate. The nonconviction rate would then be 40 percent. If
1,000 cases were brought anually in each district and there were no guilty
pleas, on the average 600 defendants would be convicted and 400 set free. If
prosecutors in *A* dispose of 300 cases after plea bargains, the rate of nonconviction could be affected in various ways If 400 defendants still go free in *A*, it
is a plausible inference that none of the 300 plea bargainers would have been
set free in the absence of pleas. If, however, only 200 defendants now go free,
it seems likely that some of the defendants pleading guilty would have gone
free had there been no pleas. The implicit rate of nonconviction in *A* computed after plea bargaining is $(400 - 200)/(300 - 0) = {}^2/_3$. That is, of the 300
plea bargainers, we would expect that 200 would not have been convicted if
all 300 had gone to trial.

In estimating the implicit rate of nonconviction in the real situation, several complicating factors must be considered. First, the number of criminal cases disposed of over a given time will vary among the districts. This, however, is not significant, since nonconvictions and guilty pleas can be expressed as percentages of total defendants disposed of, thus making irrelevant the absolute number of such cases.[14] Second, conviction probabilities are unlikely to be the same in two districts. Whether such differences would create an important barrier to the use of the proposed model depends on their pattern and size. The influence of variations in conviction probabilities that are uncorrelated with percentages of guilty pleas can be mitigated without distorting the estimate by taking averages of aggregate data instead of comparing a single pair of districts. If, on the average, aggregate data from high-rate guilty-plea districts show lower nonconviction rates than aggregate data from low-rate districts, the correlation would provide support for the hypothesis that the difference has been caused by the proportion of nonconviction cases siphoned off in pleas.

On the other hand, there may be a correlation between percentages of guilty pleas and nonconviction probabilities. If the correlation is negative, the proposed model would lead to an overestimate of the implicit nonconviction rate, and if positive, to an underestimate. As we shall see, there are reasons for be-

---

An implicit nonconviction rate estimated in this way is, of course, subject to bias. First, nonconviction probabilities in the various districts may not be the same, because of differences in the mix of criminal cases. As will be discussed below, see p. 276 *infra*, there is reason to believe this possibility is not a major source of error. Second, it may be that prosecutors or judges in A have more time to deal with contested cases once 300 cases are disposed of through plea bargaining. If so, this additional time itself may increase the likelihood of conviction. There is, however, reason to believe that this possible effect is not a factor that would influence the estimate. See pp. 277–78 *infra*. Finally, the estimation technique that must be used in the real world—where there is no district that is without guilty pleas—provides an unreliable predictor of the implicit rate of nonconviction outside the range between the district with the lowest rate of guilty pleas and that with the highest. See JOHNSTON, ECONOMETRIC METHODS 38–43 (1972). For example, if the lowest rate of guilty pleas is 35 percent of all defendants, and the highest 80 percent, the estimated implicit rate of nonconviction is most accurate for the range 35–80 percent; we have no certain idea about what would happen if pleas dropped to 20 percent of all defendants in a district. I shall refer to the defendants in the group for which the implicit rate of nonconviction can be most accurately estimated as the "marginal defendants." See note 22 *infra*.

[14]See note 21 *infra*.

lieving that a negative correlation sufficient to disturb our conclusion based on the estimated implicit nonconviction rate does not exist.[15]

Instead of dividing districts into two groups and aggregating figures, I obtain averages in a slightly different way. The estimate of the average implicit rate of nonconviction is based on a hypothesis that may be described thus: within a certain range of variation in guilty pleas, for each percentage point increase in such pleas, there will be a fractional percentage point decrease in nonconvictions. This relation may be represented by plotting each district as a point on a graph in which the horizontal axis is the percentage of guilty pleas, and the vertical axis the percentage of nonconvictions.[16] If the hypothesis is correct, the points representing the various districts should fall on a line. The slope of that line is the difference in nonconviction rates divided by the difference in guilty-plea rates for each pair of districts that lies on it. This ratio is the average implicit rate of nonconviction among those marginally pleading guilty in such districts.

If variations in guilty-plea rates were the only factor explaining variations in nonconviction rates, all district points would fall exactly on a line and the slope of that line would have the interpretation given above. Other factors affecting nonconviction rates would disturb this perfect relationship by scattering the district points about the line, whose slope may then be thought of as representing the average ratio of the differences in nonconviction and guilty-plea rates over all pairs of districts.[17] The degree of linear correlation between the two rates, i.e., how closely the district points approximate a line, tells us the extent to which variations in guilty-plea rates account for variations in nonconviction rates, and thus furnishes an indication of the correctness of the model. This can be assessed either by inspection of a point diagram or by computation of a coefficient of correlation. The coefficient of correlation may also be used to

[15]See pp. 275–79 *infra.*

[16]The percentage of guilty pleas is defined as the total number of defendants pleading guilty in a given year divided by the total number of defendants whose cases were terminated in that year. The percentage of nonconvictions is defined in a similar way.

[17]The line may conveniently be thought of in these terms, although the "least-squares" criterion by which it is estimated, see note 21 *infra,* will not make its slope necessarily correspond exactly to the average.

Figure 1. Current District Data

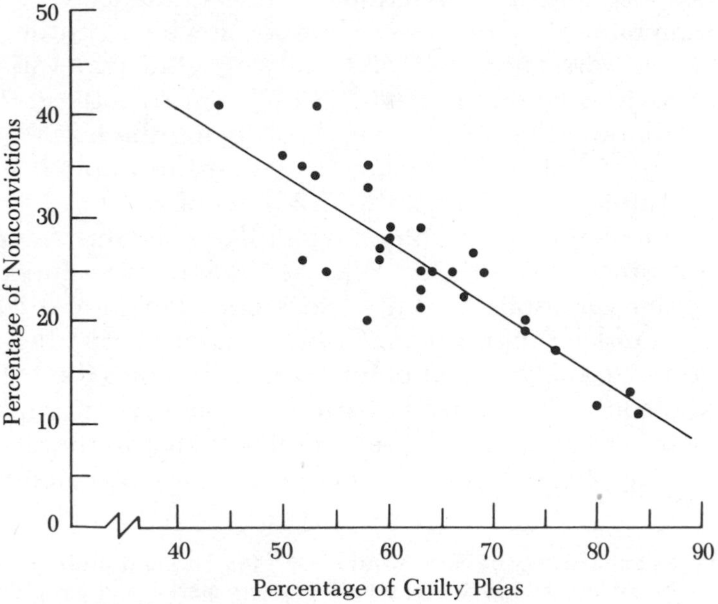

compute the precision of the estimate for the implicit nonconviction rate, i.e., how much the estimate would be likely to vary if other samples of data from the same source were subjected to a similar analysis.[18]

The data used for this purpose are the guilty-plea and nonconviction statistics for the twenty-nine federal district courts that terminated the largest aggregate number of cases in the period 1970–74. The data for each district have been aggregated for this period in order to provide larger numbers, and hence greater stability.[19] Figure 1 shows the plot of the district points.

[18]If there were a perfect correlation between guilty plea and nonconviction rates, any sample of data from the same source would show the same relationship between the two variables, and hence the same estimate for the implicit nonconviction rate. To the extent that nonconviction rates are influenced by factors other than guilty plea rates, so that the correlation is not perfect, different samples may be expected to produce different estimates, the extent of variation depending on the degree of correlation. This sampling variation is generally expressed in terms of the so-called standard error. See generally chapter 7 at pp. 218–23 *supra*.

[19]The figures are shown in Appendix 1, p. 283 *infra*. The category "guilty pleas" includes pleas of nolo contendere.

The points do not fall on a perfect line, indicating, as one would expect, that nonconviction rates are influenced by factors other than rates of guilty pleas. There is, however, a strong negative linear correlation (−0.869) between the two variables, which provides confirming evidence on our hypothesis.[20] The slope of the line that fits the data best (using the least-squares technique)[21] is −0.672, which means that the implicit rate of nonconviction is approximately 67.2 percent.

To which defendants pleading guilty may this figure be applied? Since the estimate represents a relationship determined from variations in guilty pleas between 44 and 84 percent, it would be highly speculative to assume that the same rate applies to the group of defendants making up the basic 44 percent pleading guilty in all districts and concerning whom we have no information. The 67 percent figure should therefore be viewed as applicable only to a marginal group of defendants[22]

[20]A perfect negative correlation would be −1.00. This and subsequent computations based on data in the appendices were performed by Calculogic Corp., New York, New York.

[21]The least-squares line is that line through the data that minimizes the sum of the squared distances, measured in a direction parallel to the ordinate axis, from each data point to the line. See chapter 7 at pp. 214–24 *supra*. The standard error of the 67.2 percent estimate given in the text is 7.3 percentage points. The least-squares computation was made here on an unweighted basis, each district counting as a single point without regard to the number of defendants. If a weighted basis were used, the slope of the least-squares line would not be significantly changed, but the correlation would be closer than that determined on an unweighted basis, because the districts with the largest number of defendants lie quite near the least-squares line and at its extremities.

[22]The defendants in the group for which the implicit nonconviction rate is estimated will be referred to as the "marginal" defendants. The remaining guilty-plea defendants comprise the "core" group. When comparing two districts, it is convenient to define the core group in the high-rate plea district as consisting of defendants whose conviction probabilities are the same as those guilty-plea defendants in the low-rate plea district. Thus, if we compare a district having a 60 percent guilty-plea rate with a district with a 35 percent rate, the core group in the former district would be the 35 percent of defendants pleading guilty whose risk of conviction was similar to the risk of the guilty-plea defendants in the low-rate district. The remaining 25 percent of defendants pleading guilty would constitute the marginal group. When a comparison is made among several districts, core groups for each district are determined by the guilty-plea group in the lowest-plea-rate district.

It should generally be possible to select a core group of pleas in high-rate plea districts that satisfies the condition of being equal in strength to the group of pleas in the low-rate district. If defendants in two districts have equal conviction probabilities, and equal proportions of them plead guilty, it is likely that plea-inducement practices would also be similar and, con-

whose pleas bring the total pleas in a district above the 44 percent level. This marginal group is nonexistent in the Northern District of California, which has a 44 percent rate of guilty pleas, but is highly important in the Southern District of Texas, which has an 84 percent rate of guilty pleas.[23]

The correctness of our model may be further tested by applying the estimation technique to changes in guilty-plea rates over time. Since temporal variations occur quite slowly, it is useful to confine consideration to periods when substantial changes in rates of guilty pleas were taking place. Federal data for this purpose are available in the Annual Reports of the Attorney General[24] going back to 1908. Looking at the aggregate fig-

---

sequently, that cases of equal strength would be siphoned off in pleas If one district has a much larger proportion of pleas because inducement practices differ, it is relatively easy to select a subgroup from the higher-rate plea district that would match the guilty-plea group in the lower-rate district. Obviously, it is not possible to determine whether a particular defendant belongs to the core or to the marginal group.

[23]The estimated implicit rate of nonconviction is most precise for those districts in which plea rates are near the average of all districts. See JOHNSTON, *supra* note 13, at 38–43.

Estimates of the implicit nonconviction rate are in a sense hypothetical, because the technique of estimation assumes that additional cases now disposed of by pleas could be added to trial calendars without loss of prosecutorial efficiency. To the extent that the added caseload would diminish the prosecutor's efficiency, the implicit rate could be said to be higher than the figure we have estimated. It is reasonable, however, to make no allowance for this factor, since a change in plea-inducement practices that reduced the proportion of pleas might be accompanied by successful efforts to accommodate the larger number of trials.

It is more difficult to collect recent data on which to base similar estimates for the state courts. However, in the 1930s, the U.S. Census Bureau collected judicial statistics for selected state courts. For the years 1935 and 1936, nonconviction and guilty plea data for major offenses were collected for twenty-nine states. See [1935] U.S. BUREAU OF THE CENSUS, JUDICIAL CRIMINAL STATISTICS 11 (Table 5); *id.* at 14 (Table 10); [1936] *id.* at 9 (Table 4); *id.* at 12 (Table 9). Appendix 3, *infra*, shows the aggregated data for these two years. The percentage of guilty pleas ranged from 93.9 percent (Rhode Island) to 40.9 percent (Pennsylvania). The percentage of nonconvictions ranged from 43.1 percent (Indiana) to 4.7 percent (Rhode Island). The correlation between percentage of guilty pleas and percentage of nonconvictions is −0.795, which is both statistically significant and in accord with the federal pattern. The correlation is slightly lower than that shown for the federal courts. This is to be expected, since variations in court practices other than those affecting plea rates were likely to be greater among state courts than among federal district courts. The slope of the least-squares line is −0.553 with a standard error of 0.087, which indicates a 55.3 percent implicit rate of nonconviction for guilty pleas in excess of 40.9 percent.

[24]See sources cited in Appendix 2, *infra*.

ures for all federal courts since that time, we find two periods in which there were substantial movements in plea percentages. From 1908 to about 1928, guilty pleas in the aggregate rose from a low of 30 percent to about 70 percent.[25] This increase coincided with a rapid expansion in federal caseload.[26] From 1954 to 1974, guilty pleas declined from approximately 83 percent to their current 61 percent level.[27] This decline may be attributable coincidently to the availability of court-appointed counsel,[28] more liberal bail,[29] and perhaps also to a growing resistance by defendants to any cooperation with the criminal-justice system.

If the hypothesis of the model is applicable to the 1908–28 period, one would expect the percentage of nonconvictions to decline as the percentage of guilty pleas increases. This is the case; there is a strong negative linear correlation (-0.812) between the two rates. Figure 2 shows the plot of the points for each year. While the correlation is similar to that found for the various districts for the 1970–74 period, the slope of the least-squares line is -0.265, which means that the implicit nonconviction rate was only 26.5 percent, or less than half its current estimate.[30]

The 1954–74 data show a similar pattern, except in reverse with respect to time. During this period, the percentage of guilty pleas declined, while the percentage of nonconvictions rose. The negative linear correlation is very strong (-0.977), and the slope of the least-squares line is -0.791, which is higher than the district estimate based on current data.[31] Figure 3 shows the points for these years.

[25]See Appendix 2, *infra*.

[26]There were 12,942 cases terminated in 1908, and 88,336 in 1928. See Appendix 2, *infra*. The latter high figures may be attributed to cases arising from enforcement of the prohibition laws.

[27]See Appendix 2, *infra*.

[28]Although the right to counsel when entering a guilty plea could not be doubted after Walker v. Johnston, 312 U.S. 275, 286 (1941), indigent defendants were frequently deemed to have waived counsel at arraignment in the absence of effective machinery for the assignment and compensation of counsel. See 8A MOORE, FEDERAL PRACTICE ¶ 44.02 (2d ed. 1975). It was not until the Criminal Justice Act of 1964, 18 U.S.C. §3006A (1970), that Congress made provision for the assignment and compensation of counsel in all federal district courts.

[29]Bail Reform Act of 1966, 18 U.S.C. §3146 (1970).

[30]The standard error of this estimate is 4.5 percentage points.

[31]The standard error of this estimate is 4.3 percentage points.

Figure 2. 1908-28 Aggregate Data

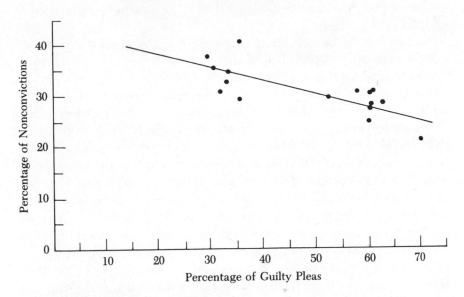

All three groups of data thus display a negative linear relation between the rate of guilty pleas and the rate of nonconvictions. This pattern is consistent with our hypothetical model.

Figure 3. 1954-74 Aggregate Data

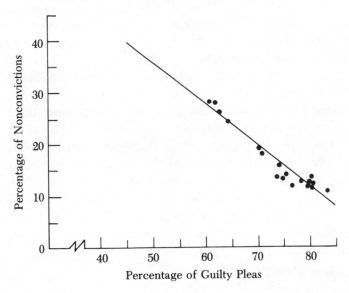

Differences among the estimates do not contradict the hypothesis that the rates are causally related, but rather suggest two additional findings.

Other factors being equal, one would expect that the proportion of defendants pleading guilty would reflect the degree of pressure against them. Given variations in pressure, it would be plausible to find variations in implicit nonconviction rates as well, since it is probable that those who plead guilty when relatively little pressure is applied are more likely to be convicted than those who plead only under greater pressure. The variations in estimated implicit nonconviction rates are consistent with this expectation. The estimate is lowest (26.5 percent) for data in the 1908–28 period, which includes a time when the proportion of guilty pleas was near the 30 percent level; it is higher (67.2 percent) for current district data, for which the proportion of pleas is generally above the 50 percent level; and it is highest (79.1 percent) for data based on the 1954–74 period, which includes a time in the early 1950s when the proportion of pleas was over 80 percent.

Differences between the earlier and current eras and between time-series and cross-sectional data preclude any conclusions based on the exact numerical differences between the estimates for these periods. The relation between them, however, is consistent with the notion that as the proportion of guilty pleas increases, weaker cases for the government are swept into the conviction category. This relationship further suggests, as might be expected, that the cases against the core group of guilty-plea defendants are likely to be stronger than against those in the marginal group.

Comparison of actual and implicit nonconviction rates suggests a second finding, one that relates to the strength of the government's case against the marginal guilty-plea defendant. The data are shown in Table 21.

It will be observed that in the 1908–28 period, the implicit nonconviction rate was far below the actual nonconviction rate in contested cases, thus demonstrating that, at that time, stronger than average cases were being siphoned off in pleas. In the current period, the two rates are about equal, which would indicate that the marginal guilty-plea cases are neither weaker nor stronger than those being tried. The current high implicit

TABLE 21

	AGGREGATE DATA		DISTRICT DATA
	1908–28	*1954–74*	*1970–74*
Average Percentages of Nonconvictions in Contested Cases[32]	62	63	70
Implicit Nonconviction Rate for the Marginal Guilty-Plea Group	26	79	67

rate of nonconviction for the marginal group may, therefore, be a product of two related forces: the need to secure pleas in a larger number of cases, and a decline in the discrimination with which such cases are selected.[33]

II

The estimate for the implicit nonconviction rate based on 1970–74 district data was computed on the assumption that there was no correlation between the proportion of guilty pleas in a district and the probability of conviction in that district. This assumption is supported by the fact that there is no statistically significant correlation (0.09) between the proportion of guilty pleas in a district and the proportion of nonconvictions in *contested cases* in that same district.[34] While the results in con-

[32]These figures are unweighted averages computed in each case from the average of the nonconviction figures shown in the relevant appendix, divided by the average proportion of contested cases (i.e., the complement of average proportion of guilty pleas).

[33]The fact that the implicit rate of nonconviction substantially exceeded the actual rate in the 1954–74 period may possibly reflect the fact that prosecutors extensively used plea bargains to secure convictions in their weaker cases. Admittedly this is speculative, since no reason is apparent why such a practice, if it existed, would have been statistically manifest at that period and not in the current data.

[34]Computed from Percentage of Guilty Pleas and Percentage of Nonconvictions in Contested Cases shown in Appendix 1, *infra*.

tested cases cannot be taken as necessarily representative of the underlying conviction probabilities, it would be a remarkable fortuity if there were a correlation between the rate of guilty pleas and the underlying conviction probabilities in the various districts which was concealed by the siphoning off of cases in pleas. The far more plausible hypothesis is that no significant correlation exists.

Other evidence supports this conclusion. In the district study, the major possible cause of variations in conviction probabilities would be differences in types of crimes. But district data indicate that types of crime among the various districts are much the same, with narcotics violations generally heading the list.[35] The most significant exception to this general pattern are immigration cases, which show a decided tendency to cluster in large numbers in southern and western Texas and in southern and eastern California. If criminal immigration charges were easy to prove, the high guilty-plea rates in these districts might be attributed to the presence of relatively large numbers of strong Government cases. The elimination of immigration cases would not, however, significantly affect our estimate. For example, in the Western District of Texas, which has the largest number of such cases, guilty pleas account for 84 percent of all cases, and nonconvictions for 11 percent. Removal of immigration cases would shift these figures to 82 percent and 12 percent, respectively.[36] These adjustments would make virtually no change in the slope of the least-squares line, because both the point corresponding to the adjusted figures and the original point lie almost exactly on that line. The example suggests that the estimate of the implicit nonconviction rate is relatively insensitive to possible clustering of cases with atypical conviction probabilities in some jurisdictions.

[35]For a district-by-district breakdown of types of cases commenced, see [1974] DIRECTOR OF THE ADMINISTRATIVE OFFICE OF THE UNITED STATES COURTS, ANNUAL REPORT 464–69 (Table D3).

[36]See *id.* at 464–69 (Table D3); *id.* at 474–78 (Table D5). These are approximate calculations based on the assumptions that (1) immigration cases commenced in 1974 as a percentage of all cases commenced in 1974 were the same as aggregate immigration cases terminated in the period 1970–74 as a percentage of all cases terminated in that period, and (2) the proportions of guilty pleas and nonconvictions in such cases were the same in the Western District of Texas as for all such cases. These assumptions appear to be sufficiently accurate for purposes of these indicative calculations.

A negative correlation might also be created between the conviction probability and the proportion of persons pleading guilty in a district if prosecutors were less effective in low-rate guilty-plea districts, because of the greater burden of contested cases or because of lesser professional competence.[37] The evidence suggests that this is unlikely to be true, however. In the two districts with the lowest rates of guilty pleas, the Southern District of New York and the Northern District of California, caseloads per prosecutor are no greater than in districts with the highest rates of pleas.[38] As for competence, this too is an unlikely explanation, since the staffs of the United States Attorneys' offices in northern California and southern New York are generally acknowledged to be among the most experienced and competent in the country. Another possible hypothesis is that conviction probabilities are smaller in low-rate guilty plea districts because judges there are under greater pressure to clear their dockets by dismissals. Again, data from the various federal districts do not substantiate this hypothesis, since the highest-rate guilty-plea districts have a slightly heavier burden of contested criminal cases per judge than the lowest-rate districts.[39] The pattern is even more striking when total caseload is considered. (This is a relevant comparative index of prosecutorial burden

[37]Even if we assume that there is a lighter criminal docket in high-rate guilty-plea districts, and that the nonconviction probabilities in those districts are low because prosecutors have more time to deal effectively with each contested case, our model would still not overestimate the implicit rate of non-conviction, unless we could plausibly make the unlikely further assumption that the prosecutorial advantage would not be impaired by an increase in the caseload burden in such districts if plea rates were reduced to the level of low-rate guilty plea districts.

[38]The average number of defendants in contested cases terminated in the period 1970–74 per assistant U.S. Attorney assigned to criminal cases as of April 8, 1975 were: Northern District of California, 35; Southern District of New York, 16; Southern District of Texas, 32; and Western District of Texas, 57. In these computations, the numbers of defendants terminated in contested cases were taken from Appendix 1, *infra*, and the numbers of Assistant U.S. Attorneys assigned to criminal cases were received by telephone from the various districts on April 8, 1975.

[39]The average numbers of defendants in contested cases terminated in the period 1970–74 per judge were: Northern District of California, 55; Southern District of New York, 39; Southern District of Texas, 60; Western District of Texas, 67. In these computations, the numbers of defendants terminated in contested cases are taken from Appendix 1, *infra*; the number of judges from the listing in volume 380 of the Federal Supplement reporter.

because negotiated guilty plea cases also take time.) For example, the Western District of Texas, with a guilty-plea rate of 84.2 percent during the 1970–74 period, had only four judges to dispose of an annual average of almost 2,700 defendants, or 670 defendants per judge.[40] In contrast, the Southern District of New York, which had only a 49.7 percent guilty-plea rate, terminated approximately the same average number of criminal defendants per year, but was able to distribute this work among 25 district judges. As a result, the annual average burden was less than 96 defendants per judge, approximately one-sixth the caseload of western Texas.[41]

Congested calendars, such as that of the Western District of Texas, have commonly been viewed as the major source of prosecutorial and judicial pressure on defendants to forgo trial. Districts with congested calendars generally have longer average periods of pretrial detention. The effect of both of these factors may be reflected in higher guilty plea rates. The fact that the highest-rate guilty-plea districts have heavier caseloads than the lowest-rate districts supports the conclusion that calendar congestion may be an important factor in inducing guilty pleas. The significant implicit rate of nonconviction in the marginal guilty-plea group may be viewed as the price paid in the high-rate guilty-plea districts for their "solution" of the caseload problem.

A somewhat different situation exists with respect to the analysis of the time data. These data showed high implicit rates of nonconviction, thus confirming the results of the district data. It was suggested that differences in estimated implicit rates for the three epochs indicated that the core group of guilty pleas defined by the district data might have a lower implicit nonconviction rate than the marginal group.[42] In reaching these conclusions, it was assumed that, within each epoch, changes in nonconviction probabilities did not correlate with changes in guilty plea rates. In contrast, if it is assumed that the results in contested cases fairly reflect underlying nonconviction proba-

[40]The caseload figure is from Appendix 1, *infra*; the number of judges from the listing in volume 380 of the Federal Supplement reporter.

[41]*Id.*

[42]See p. 274 *supra*.

bilities, as they may in the current data, it follows that marginal guilty-plea cases in each year would be similar in strength to the cases remaining for a contest. Thus, the average implicit nonconviction rates would be 63 percent for the 1908–28 period and 61 percent for the 1954–74 period.[43] The rates are still substantial, which is consistent with the analysis of the district data. But under this alternative hypothesis, differences among the three periods essentially vanish, and no valid inference could be drawn from the time data about the relationship between the core and marginal groups defined by the 1970–74 district data.

However, the pattern of the 1908–28 data argues against this alternative interpretation for that period.[44] The interpretation is based on the supposition that increases in guilty-plea rates are a consequence of a decline in nonconviction probabilities. But during the 1908–28 period, the rate of guilty pleas and the rate of nonconvictions in contested cases showed parallel increases over time. This pattern is consistent with our original conclusion that during this period stronger than average cases were being siphoned off in guilty pleas. In contrast, the parallel movement could not be explained except by the assumption that the trends in plea rates and in nonconviction rates were coincident rather than causally related.

The pattern is different with respect to the 1954–74 data. The rate of nonconvictions in contested cases showed an upward trend in this period as guilty plea rates declined.[45] It was implicitly assumed that the decline in guilty pleas caused an increase in nonconviction rates as weaker than average cases were returned to be contested matters. The very high correlation displayed by the data strongly supports this assumption. The alternative hypothesis—that nonconviction rates declined from independent causes, and that this decline led to a corresponding decline in plea rates as defendants took advantage of greater opportunities for acquittal—seems too imperfect a causal chain to create the very tight linear relationship displayed by the data.

[43]See Figure 1, *supra.*
[44]See Appendix 2, *infra.*
[45]See *id.*

III

The foregoing analysis indicates that the inducement of guilty pleas is not merely a way of shortening the criminal process. Instead, pressures to plead guilty have been used to secure convictions that could not otherwise be obtained. In the highest-rate guilty-plea districts, the marginal defendants covered by our analysis constitute approximately one half the total group pleading guilty.[46] Assuming (unrealistically) that no other guilty-plea defendants would have escaped conviction, the 67 percent implicit nonconviction rate for the marginal group means that at least one third of all defendants pleading guilty in high-rate districts would ultimately have escaped conviction if they had refused to consent. Clearly, plea bargaining in such districts raises difficult ethical and constitutional issues that the Supreme Court ignored in its *Brady* opinion.

In *Brady*, the Court observed that it would have "serious doubts" about the case, "if the encouragement of guilty pleas by offers of leniency substantially increased the likelihood that defendants, advised by competent counsel, would falsely condemn themselves."[47] But the Court's expectation was "that courts will satisfy themselves that pleas of guilty are voluntarily and intelligently made by competent defendants with adequate advice of counsel and that there is nothing to question the accuracy and reliability of the defendants admissions that they committed the crimes with which they are charged."[48]

While our analysis does not touch directly on the innocence of those pleading guilty, the results have a bearing on this issue. It may be that most or even all of those "erroneously" pleading guilty may nevertheless be guilty. But since this group is large in the high-rate districts, one would have to assume that the plea-bargaining process was a far more accurate method of determining guilt than the trial process. This is unlikely to be true if the prosecutor's evidence would be admissible at trial. The prosecutor's conclusion that defendant is guilty is no substitute for the scrutiny of a trial, because it rests on a partisan's view of the evidence. A judge's view of a guilty plea case may be more

[46]See p. 271 *supra.*
[47]Brady v. United States, 397 U.S. 742, 758 (1970).
[48]*Id.*

dispassionate, but it depends on a relatively brief and one-sided review of the prosecutor's evidence in which the court need only satisfy itself that the plea has a "factual basis."[49] The only greater assurance of reliability in the plea-bargaining process is the defendant's confession extracted from him as the price of the bargain. But this is no longer a trustworthy source if the inducement is strong.[50]

Undoubtedly, in many cases in which formal proof might fail, the truth would be better served by the administrative process. But even assuming that in most such cases those pleading guilty are in fact guilty, statistical findings demonstrate that current guilty-plea practices raise important questions of candor and consistency. While our formal adversary system is hedged with protections proclaimed to be vital for the accused—including the privilege against self-incrimination and the requirement of proof beyond a reasonable doubt —it appears that informal, and less visible, administrative practices have been used to induce convictions by "consent" in a significant number of cases in which the protections of the formal system would have precluded a condemnation.

[49]FED. R. CRIM. P. 11.

[50]A physician working in a pretrial detention facility forcefully made this point in a letter to the *New York Times:*

> Consider a man arrested and indicted for murder, often, as you point out, on insufficient evidence. He is represented by a lawyer appointed by the court, whom he neither knows nor necessarily trusts and who is himself often harried and overworked. He is pressured by the District Attorney, and often by his own lawyer, to plead guilty to a lesser charge. He knows that if he does, he may get probation, or parole after three years; if he does not, he may get a life sentence.
>
> If he says he is guilty, he may be immediately released, but if he says he is innocent, he may go to jail for life. Given this choice, the question of his actual guilt or innocence becomes academic. Unless he had complete faith in the justice of the criminal-justice system, it is very possible that he will take the course of least risk, whether he is in fact guilty or not.
>
> As a physician working in pretrial detention facilities, I met many men facing similar "choices."
>
> Often, indicted for a lesser offense and having waited many months in jail for a trial, they were offered immediate release for "time served" if they pleaded guilty, versus a longer wait for trial which could result in a longer sentence, if they insisted on their innocence. Does a guilty plea under such circumstances have any relation to a defendant's actual guilt or innocence?

Moltz, *Plea Bargains vs. The Innocent*, N.Y. TIMES, Feb. 27, 1975, at 34, cols. 3–4.

Obviously, the techniques by which pleas are induced will inevitably reflect some workaday compromises between procedural meticulousness and the need to dispose of a far larger number of cases than could ever be tried. Arguably, informal plea-inducement practices can legitimately be used to some extent to achieve substantial justice in cases in which justice might otherwise be frustrated by the requirements of the formal system. The zero implicit rate of nonconviction assumed in *Brady* is in fact a hypothetical ideal that is unlikely to be achieved unless the proportion of guilty pleas is very small.

Nevertheless it is difficult to justify practices by which so many convictions in the high-rate guilty-plea districts are obtained without sufficient evidence to satisfy the state's burden of proof.[51] It is doubtful that the necessities of the system compel this result. Plea bargaining itself does not invariably produce high implicit rates of nonconviction, since a substantially lower implicit rate appears to have existed shortly after the turn of the century, and since equally low rates may exist today in districts with plea rates near historical levels. The need to dispose of a very large proportion of criminal cases without a trial may drive up the implicit rate, but this is a better argument for adding prosecutors and judges in the high-rate guilty-plea districts than it is for the status quo in plea bargaining. Since it appears that a prosecutor's stronger cases tended to be selected for guilty pleas in the historical period, while weaker cases are selected with greater frequency today, a refocusing of plea bargaining on stronger cases might improve the statistical picture without adding materially (if at all) to the number of trials.

Statistical evidence cannot tell us the probable outcome of a contest in a particular case, or even in a class of cases in which guilty pleas were secured by inducement. More detailed knowledge of plea-inducement practices is necessary both to verify the assumptions of the statistical estimates and to assess the probable impact of more stringent controls on bargaining. Nevertheless, the finding of a high implicit rate of nonconviction should be sufficient to lead us to re-examine and compare inducement practices in the various federal districts, and to

[51]Most nonconvictions are dismissals, see Appendix 1, *infra*, and these are frequently at the instance of the prosecutor who finds his case too weak to proceed. Consequently, many of the cases against marginal-guilty-plea defendants would have been dismissed at the instance of the prosecutors if no pleas had been offered, and would not have been tested in court.

assess from a new perspective the ethical and constitutional implications of this administrative mode for securing convictions.

Appendix 1

Disposition of Defendants in Twenty-nine Federal District Courts

District	Defendants Terminated	Guilty Pleas	Dismissals	Acquittals
E.D.N.Y.	6582	3962	1633	303
S.D.N.Y.	9874	4908	2931	584
D.N.J.	4221	2448	1254	227
E.D.Pa.	4817	2547	1350	275
D.Md.	3645	2423	722	88
E.D.N.C.	1841	1186	371	83
E.D.Va.	4591	2365	884	290
N.D.Ala.	2499	1991	253	51
M.D.Fla.	3843	2323	917	190
S.D.Fla.	4949	2930	944	365
N.D.Ga.	4245	2690	779	213
M.D.Ga.	2108	1318	284	166
S.D.Ga.	1957	1435	327	61
E.D.La.	3614	1963	776	123
W.D.La.	1976	1365	427	75
N.D.Tex.	3577	2599	590	74
S.D.Tex.	12286	10222	1413	142
W.D.Tex.	10743	9048	1128	77
E.D.Mich.	6418	3378	2366	239
N.D.Ohio	4687	3199	1140	103
S.D.Ohio	2055	1292	537	57
E.D.Tenn.	1867	1077	233	158
N.D.Ill.	5672	3565	1167	241
D.Ariz.	7110	4141	2122	191
N.D.Cal.	5416	2407	1785	441
E.D.Cal.	4170	3178	626	86
C.D.Cal.	10810	6367	2265	515
S.D.Cal.	12127	8010	2683	286
D.Mass.	2840	1482	829	157

Source: [1974] DIRECTOR OF THE ADMINISTRATIVE OFFICE OF THE U.S. COURTS, ANNUAL REPORT 278–80 (Table 72); *id.* at 459–61 (Table D–1); *id.* at 482–87 (Table D–7); [1973] *id.* at 193–95 (Table 43); *id.* at 390–94 (Table D–1); *id.* at 416–21 (Table D–7); [1972] *id.* at 138–41 (Table 33); *id.* at 360–63 (Table D–1); *id.* at 394–99 (Table D–7); [1971] *id.* at 151–61 (Table 26); *id.* at 317–19 (Table D–1); *id.* at 359–71 (Table D–7); [1970] *id.* at 146 (Table 37); *id.* at 264–66 (Table D–1).

In those situations in which a defendant is disposed of in two or more criminal cases, e.g., by conviction on one indictment and by dismissal of another indictment, only the conviction is recorded. Thus only a single conviction is recorded in the common situation in which a defendant is convicted on certain charges (counts) while the other charges (counts) are dismissed. See, e.g., [1974] *id.* at 472 (note) (Table D–4).

PERCENTAGE OF GUILTY PLEAS[1]	PERCENTAGE OF NON-CONVICTIONS[2]	PERCENTAGE OF NONCONVICTIONS IN CONTESTED CASES[3]
60.2	29.4	74
49.7	35.6	71
58.0	35.1	84
52.9	33.7	72
66.5	22.2	66
64.4	24.6	69
51.5	25.6	53
79.7	12.2	60
60.4	28.9	73
59.2	26.5	65
63.4	23.4	64
62.5	21.3	57
73.3	19.8	74
54.3	24.9	54
69.1	25.4	82
72.7	18.6	68
83.2	12.7	76
84.2	11.2	71
52.6	40.6	86
68.3	26.5	84
62.9	28.9	78
57.7	20.4	48
62.9	24.8	67
58.2	32.5	78
44.4	41.1	74
76.2	17.1	72
58.9	25.7	63
66.1	24.5	72
52.2	34.7	73

[1] Guilty Pleas divided by Defendants Terminated.

[2] Dismissals plus Acquittals divided by Defendants Terminated.

[3] Percentage of Nonconvictions divided by the complement of Percentage of Guilty Pleas.

Appendix 2

Disposition of Defendants in Federal District Courts (Excluding the District of Columbia) (Fiscal Years 1908–74[1])

Year	Defendants/ Cases Terminated[2]	Percentage of Guilty Pleas[2]	Percentage of Non-convictions[3]	Percentage of Nonconvictions in Contested Cases[3]
1908	12942	33.7	35.0	53
1909	11705	35.7	41.2	64
1910	15371	29.5	38.5	55
1911	14700	30.1	36.1	52
1912	15741	33.6	35.5	54
1913	16757	37.9	31.5	51
1914	18128	32.9	33.3	50
1915	19120	35.2	29.5	46
1916	20432	49.8	30.8	62
1917	17671	52.6	29.9	63
1918	30949	61.2	24.9	64
1919	35734	61.0	27.8	72
1920	34230	57.4	30.9	73
1921	47299	60.3	30.7	78
1922	53155	59.4	30.8	76
1923	68152	61.2	28.5	74
1924	73488	62.8	28.4	77
1926	76536	63.0	29.2	79
1927	67279	61.3	28.1	73
1928	88336	69.9	21.5	72
1929	85328	68.6	21.1	68
1930	82609	73.7	17.9	69
1931	91701	77.2	15.6	69
1932	96949	79.5	13.7	67
1934	45577	60.3	31.4	79
1936	52777	70.5	20.9	71
1937	52393	71.1	19.9	69
1945	41653	73.9	18.0	70
1946	36482	75.0	18.0	73
1947	36635	79.5	15.0	74
1948	34242	81.2	14.1	76
1949	36264	83.9	11.5	72
1950	37675	84.2	11.0	70
1951	41066	85.8	9.9	70
1952	38622	84.7	9.9	65
1953	37762	82.9	11.3	67
1954	42989	82.7	11.2	65
1955	38990	79.5	13.1	65
1957	29725	80.2	11.6	59
1958	30469	79.6	12.0	59
1959	30729	80.6	12.0	62

Year	Defendants/ Cases Terminated[2]	Percentage of Guilty Pleas[2]	Percentage of Non- convictions[3]	Percentage of Nonconvictions in Contested Cases[3]
1960	30512	79.4	12.4	60
1961	32671	76.0	12.3	52
1962	33110	74.4	13.8	54
1963	34845	74.3	14.4	57
1964	33381	78.7	12.6	59
1966	31975	75.4	14.5	59
1967	31535	73.3	16.4	62
1968	31843	69.2	19.3	63
1969	32796	70.5	18.2	62
1970	36356	66.3	22.4	67
1971	44615	61.7	28.0	73
1972	52506	64.1	24.6	69
1973	46724	62.0	25.1	66
1974	48154	60.5	27.9	71

Sources: [1974] DIRECTOR OF THE ADMINISTRATIVE OFFICE OF THE U.S. COURTS, ANNUAL REPORT 470 (Table D–4); [1973] *id.* at 402; [1972] *id.* at 381; [1971] *id.* at 340 (data for 1971); *id.* at 337 (data for 1970); [1969] *id.* at 273; [1968] ADMINISTRATIVE OFFICE OF THE U.S. COURTS. FEDERAL OFFENDERS IN THE U.S. DISTRICT COURTS 7 (Figure B); [1967] DIRECTOR OF THE OFFICE OF ADMINISTRATION OF THE U.S. COURTS, ANNUAL REPORT 260 (Table D–4); [1966] *id.* at 220; [1964] *id.* at 256; [1963] *id.* at 240; [1962] *id.* at 234; [1961] *id.* at 280; [1960] *id.* at 304; [1959] *id.* at 236; [1958] *id.* at 208; [1957] *id.* at 220; [1955] *id.* at 208; [1954] *id.* at 194; [1953] *id.* at 184; [1952] *id.* at 162; [1951] *id.* at 166; [1950] *id.* at 178; [1949] *id.* at 164; [1948] *id.* at 170; [1947] *id.* at 144; [1946] *id.* at 118; [1945] *id.* at 112; [1937] U.S. DEP'T OF JUSTICE, ANNUAL REPORT OF THE ATTORNEY GENERAL 178 (Table 2B); [1936] *id.* at 168; [1934] *id.* at 170 (Exhibit No. 2); [1932] *id.* at 146; [1931] *id.* at 140; [1930] *id.* at 106; [1929] *id.* at 90; [1928] *id.* at 88; [1927] *id.* at 80; [1926] *id.* at 129; [1925] *id.* at 135; [1924] *id.* at 117; [1923] *id.* at 108; (Summary of Business, Revenues and Expenditures of the Dep't of Justice and the Courts of the U.S.); [1922] *id.* at 109 (Exhibit No. 2); [1921] *id.* at 151; [1920] *id.* at 201; [1919] *id.* at 120; [1918] *id.* at 156; [1917] *id.* at 125; [1916] *id.* at 103; [1915] *id.* at 87; [1914] *id.* at 89; [1913] *id.* at 79 (Appendix 2); [1912] *id.* at 110 (Appendix); [1911] *id.* at 98; [1910] *id.* at 95; [1909] *id.* at 152 (Exhibit 9); [1908] *id.* at 185 (Exhibit 7).

[1]The following omissions are noted: The years 1938–44 are not reported because comparable data were not published for that period. The years 1925, 1933, and 1965 are not included because the Annual Reports for those years were not available at the time the data were collected. The years 1933 and 1956 were eliminated because the reported results were so far out of line with the remaining data as to suggest the possibility of reporting error. The rejection of such data is an accepted statistical technique. See, e.g., G. SNEDECOR & W. COCHRAN, STATISTICAL METHODS 137 (6th ed. 1967).

[2]The earliest Attorney General reports aggregate figures for the courts of appeal and the district courts. See, e.g., [1910] U.S. DEP'T OF JUSTICE ANNUAL REPORT OF THE ATTORNEY GENERAL. Since the data for those years show total cases terminated as exceeding the sum of the conviction, acquittal and dismissal figures, appeals may have been reflected simply as terminations. To eliminate this possible contamination, the total of the component figures has been used as the total termination figure.

A second defect in the data is that the Attorney General reports reflect cases terminated, while the Annual Reports of the Administrative Office reflect defendants terminated. No adjustment has been attempted to correct for this difference since it would not appear to affect the analysis used in the article.

[3]Computed as in Appendix 1.

Appendix 3

Disposition of Defendants Charged with Major Offenses in Courts of Twenty-nine States (Aggregate Data, 1935–36)

STATE	DEFENDANTS TERMINATED	GUILTY PLEAS	NON-CONVICTIONS	PERCENTAGE OF GUILTY PLEAS[1]	PERCENTAGE OF NON-CONVICTIONS[1]
Ind.	10870	4686	4685	43.1	43.1
N.M.	1811	925	702	51.0	38.7
Me.	945	567	315	60.0	33.3
Ill.	6326	2939	2325	46.4	36.7
Colo.	2987	1668	969	55.8	32.4
Pa.	45086	18477	14192	40.9	31.4
Ore.	1829	1309	398	71.5	21.7
N.J.	12426	7472	3431	60.1	27.6
Mont.	1159	717	339	61.8	29.2
Utah	706	331	215	46.8	30.4
Ariz.	1614	965	457	59.7	28.3
Kan.	3952	2516	1023	63.6	25.8
D.C.	3530	2089	934	59.1	26.4
Vt.	1036	702	268	67.7	25.8
La.	3461	2354	898	68.0	25.9
Ohio	12323	7727	3158	62.7	25.6
N.D.	834	591	175	70.8	20.9
Wyo.	629	421	153	66.9	24.3
Wash.	3222	2095	705	65.0	21.8
Cal.	14437	9322	2888	64.5	20.0
N.H.	811	569	157	70.1	19.3
Wis.	6422	4395	1384	68.4	21.5
Idaho	902	640	169	70.9	18.7
Neb.	2409	1631	434	67.7	18.0
Mich.	5317	3815	858	71.7	16.1
Conn.	1881	1449	292	77.0	15.5
Minn.	4075	3348	515	82.1	12.6
S.D.	1079	510	135	47.2	12.5
R.I.	1188	1161	59	93.9	4.7

Source: [1936] U.S. BUREAU OF THE CENSUS, JUDICIAL CRIMINAL STATISTICS 9 (Table 4) (all defendants disposed of); *id.* at 11 (Table 5) (nonconvictions); *id.* at 12 (Table 9) (guilty pleas). [1935] *id.* at 11 (Table 5) (all defendants disposed of); *id.* at 12 (Table 7) (nonconvictions); *id.* at 14 (Table 10) (guilty pleas).

[1]Computed as in Appendix 1.

THE CONTINUING DEBATE OVER MATHEMATICS IN THE LAW OF EVIDENCE

The use of Baye's theorem discussed in Chapter 3, at pp. 91–94, first appeared in an article by the author and William B. Fairley, entitled *A Bayesian Approach to Identification Evidence*, 83 HARV. L. REV. 489 (1970). Professor Laurence B. Tribe of Harvard criticized this proposal in *Trial by Mathematics: Precision and Ritual in the Legal Process*, 84 HARV. L. REV. 1329 (1971). The authors' reply and Professor Tribe's rejoinder, 84 HARV. L. REV. 1801 (1971), are reprinted below.

A Comment on "Trial by Mathematics"

Michael O. Finkelstein
& William B. Fairley

IN AN ARTICLE PUBLISHED last year in this *Review*,[1] we proposed the use of Bayes's theorem as an aid to evaluating certain types of statistical identification evidence. Professor Laurence H. Tribe, in *Trial by Mathematics: Precision and Ritual in the Legal Process*,[2] attacked this proposal; after a lengthy analysis, he concluded that use of a Bayesian approach, or any similar technique, would be fundamentally unsound in the trial context. We feel compelled to comment because Professor

---

[1] Finkelstein & Fairley, *A Bayesian Approach to Identification Evidence*, 83 HARV. L. REV. 489 (1970) [hereinafter cited as Finkelstein & Fairley].

[2] HARV. L. REV. 1329 (1971) [hereinafter cited as Tribe].

Tribe supposes a use of Bayes's theorem which goes beyond anything we would think suitable, and thus finds difficulties that would not exist if the technique were confined to its proper setting. Unfortunately, he uses these difficulties not to argue for limitation, but to support his claim that any use of Bayesian techniques in the trial context should be precluded.

We illustrated our theme with a simple hypothetical:[3]

> [A] woman's body is found in a ditch in an urban area. There is evidence that the deceased had a violent quarrel with her boyfriend the night before. He is known to have struck her on other occasions. Investigators find the murder weapon, a knife which has on the handle [an incriminating] latent [right hand] palm print similar to defendant's print. The information in the print is limited so that [a fingerprint] expert can say only that such prints appear in no more than one case in a thousand [in the general population].

Did the defendant leave the print? The evidence of his relationship to the deceased suggests that the print may be his, although this evidence alone is far from conclusive. The one-in-a-thousand statistic greatly strengthens our belief that the print is the defendant's, but the evidentiary force of this statistic is not intuitively obvious. Bayes's theorem is a mathematical technique for combining the evidence apart from the palm print with the statistical palm print information to generate a final estimate of the probability that the print belonged to the defendant.[4] We argued that use of Bayes's theorem in a trial setting would be helpful to enable jurors to assess more precisely the significance of the one-in-a-thousand statistic.

I

In accordance with general usage, we described the force of the nonstatistical evidence as the "prior probability" or "prior" (i.e., prior to the statistical evidence) and of the combined evidence as the "posterior probability." We suggested that a statis-

---

[3]Finkelstein & Fairley 496.

[4]For discussion of the mathematical basis for Bayes's theorem, see *id.* at 498–500.

tician, testifying as an expert, could "suggest a range of hypothetical prior probabilities, specifying the posterior probability associated with each prior. Each juror could then pick the prior estimate that most closely matched his own view of the evidence."[5] Professor Tribe objects that the average juror would have great difficulty in making a prior estimate;[6] he says by way of illustration, that it might be "pure chance whether a particular juror converts his mental state of partial certainty to a figure like .33, .43, or somewhere in between."[7]

But we analyzed the problem of estimating prior probabilities in our article; there we pointed out that while there would be variations in jurors' estimates of the prior, in most cases the statistical evidence would be sufficiently strong so that variations in the prior would lead to insignificant differences in the result.[8] As we demonstrated in our article, using the one-in-a-thousand statistic,[9] when the prior probability increases from .25 to .50—a range of variation much larger than that suggested by Professor Tribe—the posterior probability only increases from .997 to .999. The difference of .002 is surely not great enough to lead to different outcomes in any significant number of cases.

Of course, if the statistical evidence is very weak (e.g., the print appears in one person out of two rather than one out of every thousand), then precision in the prior becomes more important.[10] But no one would engage in a statistical analysis of a print when half the population had similar prints. The most common use of Bayesian methods arises when the identifying trace is rare—usually much more rare than a frequency of one in a thousand—and in that circumstance exact specification of the prior is unimportant.[11] What is important is whether jurors,

---

[5]*Id.* at 502.

[6]Tribe 1358–59.

[7]*Id.* at 1358.

[8]Finkelstein & Fairley 505.

[9]See the bottom line of our table of posterior probabilities, Table I, *id.* at 500.

[10]If the characteristics of the print found are present in the prints of one person out of two in the general population, then when the prior increases from .25 to .50, the posterior probability increases from .400 to .666. See the top line of Table I, *id.*

[11]Exact specification of the prior in such cases is in fact so unimportant that we suggested that it could be dispensed with entirely. *Id.* at 502 n.32.

In the unusual case in which identification is sought on the basis of a trace

evaluating only the nonstatistical evidence, believe that the defendant is far more likely to have left the print than someone chosen at random from the population.

II

In our article we assumed that if the defendant had in fact used the knife and left the print that was found, then that print would perfectly match a sample print of the defendant's taken at the time of trial;[12] thus we excluded for simplicity the problem of "source variations" that occurs when two prints from the same source vary in their characteristics.[13] Professor Tribe does not object to the assumption in our hypothetical that the probability of source variations was zero;[14] however, he argues that, "moved by the greater ease of applying Bayes's Theorem,"[15] we overlooked in the probability factor for source variations[16] the additional possibilities that a print would not have been left on the knife because the guilty party would have worn gloves or wiped the print off.[17] However, these possibilities were not overlooked—they were expressly excluded, for we computed our probability factors "assuming that a right-hand palm print was left by the person who used the knife."[18]

Given the assumption that a print was found, the issue raised by Professor Tribe's objection is whether the finding of a print is itself significant evidence in a sufficient number of cases to make it unrealistic to exclude it in an illustration. We can imagine cases in which the fact that a print has been found is it-

---

with relatively high frequency, a more precise means of estimating the prior becomes essential. The use of blood tests as affirmative evidence in paternity suits is an example of a situation in which Bayesian analysis can be used even though the trace is relatively common, because the method of estimating the prior is more precise. See *id.* at 506–09.

[12]*Id.* at 498.

[13]See *id.* at 509–11.

[14]In the case of palm prints or fingerprints, the assumption that source variations will not be significant is not at all unrealistic.

[15]Tribe 1362.

[16]This was the factor denoted $P(H|G)$. Finkelstein & Fairley 498.

[17]Tribe 1362.

[18]Finkelstein & Fairley 498 n.22.

self important evidence—e.g., the print is from a right-hand palm and the defendant either lacks a right hand or is convincingly left-handed. But we excluded the probability of finding a print and "assumed that the leaving of a print is not per se evidence either for or against the defendant,"[19] because in the common run of cases the finding of a trace itself (apart from the information it contains) will not be of evidentiary significance. Professor Tribe does not say why the fact that a print has been found is itself important; we see no reason why our assumptions are either unreasonable or unrealistic. In the unusual case where the appearance of a trace *is* per se evidentiary, that factor would probably have to be considered separately and not mixed with the Bayesian analysis, as Professor Tribe suggests to show how complicated matters can become.[20]

III

Professor Tribe also argues that we overlooked the fact that identifying the print on the knife as the defendant's is not dispositive of guilt because the murderer could have framed the defendant by planting his knife at the scene of the crime.[21] However, this argument misconceives the thrust of our article. We are well aware that in any case in which identification of the defendant is sought on the basis of some evidentiary trace, two distinct issues are presented: (1) is the defendant the source of the trace? and (2) did he commit the offense? Though in some unusual cases the trace may be so intimately tied to the criminal act that linking it to the defendant would be virtually conclusive evidence of his guilt, in most cases a finding that the defendant was in fact the source of the trace would be significant evidence, but not dispositive.

The purpose of Bayesian techniques, as we propose them, is to assist the fact finder in interpreting statistical evidence to decide only the issue of whether a certain trace comes from the accused. The fingerprint expert will testify that the print on the

[19]*Id.*
[20]Tribe 1363–64.
[21]*Id. at 1362–63* & n.110, 1365–66.

knife is similar to the defendant's print and that such prints occur with a frequency of one in a thousand in the general population. The expert statistician will then use Bayes's theorem to help jurors evaluate that statistic so that they can act more rationally in deciding whether the print came from the defendant. Neither the fingerprint expert nor the statistician could possibly testify as to the guilt of the accused, for this would be a matter wholly outside his competence. When a fingerprint expert, a chemist, or a handwriting expert makes an identification of a trace element, with or without quantification, his testimony is not ruled inadmissible because he does not testify as to the ultimate issue of guilt; we see no reason for treating the statistician differently. When we referred to "guilt" or "prior probability of guilt" in various contexts, we did not mean to imply that the expert would direct jurors to *posterior* probabilities of guilt, as Professor Tribe chooses to interpret it.[22] The significance of the conclusion that a trace came from the defendant—i.e., whether it indicates guilt, a frame-up, or mere chance—must be

[22]Professor Tribe discussed our hypothetical and finds it ambiguous as to whether the expert would use Bayes's theorem to direct the jurors to estimate the probability of defendant's guilt or the probability that the print came from the defendant. See *id.* at 1363 n.110. After observing that we use the phrase "prior probability of guilt," he concludes that the first interpretation was intended. *Id.*

Assuming that our hypothetical was ambiguous, what valid purpose is served by deliberately choosing the interpretation which makes the Bayesian approach unacceptable? Our analysis of People v. Risley, 214 N.Y. 75, 108 N.E. 200 (1915), which immediately followed the hypothetical, makes it clear that in the real world only one approach is even plausible. In that analysis we applied Bayes's theorem to determine the probability that a forgery was typed on the defendant's typewriter, and concluded with the observation that Bayesian analysis could demonstrate "a very high probability that defendant's machine was used." Finkelstein & Fairley 501. Nothing was said about using Bayesian techniques to prove defendant's guilt, and it is clear on the facts that a statistician would have no competence to testify on that question.

We used the phrase "prior probability of guilt" anticipating that the expert might ask jurors to estimate the prior in terms of guilt rather than identity because this might be a more natural formulation in which to evaluate the nonstatistical evidence in the case. There should be little objection to this, since if the trace seems to be related to the crime, a juror's estimate of the prior probability of guilt would not generally be larger than that of the prior probability of identity; it might well be smaller if, in the opinion of the jurors the defendant was more likely to have been the source of the trace than to have committed the crime.

left to other witnesses just as it is in every case in which an identification is made without the use of Bayesian methods.

Professor Tribe draws two conclusions from our "oversight." First, he argues that since we were "blinded" by the mathematics. even the adversary process cannot be relied on to correct "the jury's natural tendency to be similarly distracted."[23] Of course, the question whether jurors will be helped, misled, or simply confused by Bayesian techniques is an important one. A sensible approach to this question would be to test the use of Bayesian methods under controlled conditions and to compare the results with the ability of the controlled jury to handle the one-in-a-thousand statistic without the use of Bayesian methods. As we reported in our article, we in fact did this informally on a small scale and the results seemed to justify further inquiry.[24] The ability of jurors to handle Bayesian techniques might also be profitably compared with their ability to handle other types of technical evidence which are being used in trials with increasing frequency.

Second, Professor Tribe asserts that it would be impractical to take the frame-up possibility into account in the Bayesian formulas and argues that the entire enterprise is therefore defective, for he claims that trial accuracy would be enhanced only if all variables are quantified.[25] It is unnecessary to evaluate Professor Tribe's argument that we should not have any hard numbers before the jury unless everything is quantified. The whole point of our article was that jurors do in fact have one hard number before them—the one-in-a-thousand statistic. Bayesian analysis is useful because it helps them to interpret that number.[26]

[23]Tribe 1363.

[24]Finkelstein & Fairley 502–03 n.33. It should be noted that in giving this test we explicitly asked the respondents to assume that if the print was the defendant's, then he was guilty of the crime. We omitted to make this explicit in our article and this may have been the source of some confusion.

[25]Tribe 1365.

[26]Professor Tribe implies that jurors would have greater difficulty in remembering that "impressive" Bayesian results are subject to such "fuzzy imponderables" as the frame-up possibility than in understanding the one-in-a-thousand frequency statistic. *Id.* This is, of course, an empirical question, but our experience does not support Professor Tribe's view. The subjects in our informal test seemed to be well aware that identifying a trace as coming from the defendant did not necessarily mean that he was guilty. They did

Of course, one could exclude all statistics as to the frequency of evidentiary traces, and then the need for Bayesian analysis would disappear, along with a major part of current forensic science learning as to trace identifications. This would be such a retrograde step—and contrary to existing case law—that Professor Tribe frowns on the cases, but draws back from repudiating them.[27]

IV

The analysis of Bayesian methods in *Trial by Mathematics* closes with extensive arguments that they would endanger the presumption of innocence;[28] would involve the quantification of a probability of guilt which, if not "basically immoral " is at least undesirable;[29] and would further dehumanize criminal justice.[30]

Professor Tribe argues that the presumption of innocence would be endangered because "at or near the trial's start"[31] jurors would be asked "to arrive at an explicit quantitative estimate of the likely truth [of the accusation] . . ."[32] by assessing a prior; forced to do so on little evidence, they might base their estimate on prejudicial factors outside the evidence in the case, such as the fact of indictment.[33] It would of course be wholly

---

however, have difficulty in appraising the combined evidentiary significance of the one-in-a-thousand statistic and the other, non-statistical evidence.

In addition, Professor Howard Raiña conducted an informal test with lawyers and statistics students which was similar in conception to our test. He also found that both groups were unable to assess intuitively the probability of an event from the statistical evidence. See H. RAIFFA, DECISION ANALYSIS: INTRODUCTORY LECTURES ON CHOICES UNDER UNCERTAINTY 20–21 (1968). The difficulty that even well-educated persons experience in drawing inferences from statistical data suggests that Bayesian methods could profitably be used by judges and other decision makers.

[27]See Tribe 1377 n.155.
[28]*Id*. at 1368–72.
[29]*Id*. at 1372–75.
[30]*Id*. at 1375–77.
[31]*Id*. at 1368.
[32]*Id*.
[33]*Id*. at 1369.

improper for the prosecutor's expert to invite jurors to estimate their prior on anything but admitted evidence. As we stated, the expert should ask jurors for their estimate of the prior based on "the other [nonstatistical] evidence;"[34] there is no reason to think that jurors would be more lawless with such directions than with others. Because the jury, in estimating a prior, would confine itself to consideration of evidence admitted up to that point in the trial, the prosecutor will have every incentive to use Bayes's theorem near the end of his case, when jurors would have the most evidence on which to base their estimate.[35]

The exercise of estimating a prior may in fact diminish the kind of prejudice that concerns Professor Tribe. We speculated that "a juror forced to derive a quantitative measure of his suspicion on the basis of the evidence at trial is likely to consider that evidence more carefully and rationally, and to exclude impermissible elements such as appearance or popular prejudice."[36]

Professor Tribe further objects that the presumption of innocence would be endangered by the expert's suggestion to jurors that they estimate a prior. The presumption, he argues, requires jurors to withhold all judgments—even tentative ones—about the strengths and weaknesses of the prosecutor's case until the defendant's side has been heard.[37] It does not appear likely to us that focusing on the strengths of the prosecutor's evidence—something a juror is likely to do in any

[34]Finkelstein & Fairley 502.

[35]Estimation of the prior after the presentation of all the evidence in the case raises the question of the interdependence of the statistical and nonstatistical evidence—i.e., the problem that the jurors may take the statistical evidence into account in estimating the prior. and thus double-count that evidence. See Tribe 1366–68. Professor Tribe argues that the jury will be unable to make use of Bayes's theorem because the two kinds of evidence will be "hopelessly enmeshed" in the jurors' minds, *id.* at 1367, and because proper use of the method "would become completely opaque to all but the trained mathematician." *Id.* at 1368.

Whether the use of Bayes's theorem after all the evidence has been presented will in fact present serious problems of interdependence is, like the problem of possible confusion over the meaning of the Bayesian conclusion, see note 26 *supra*, an empirical question. As to the second point, however, proper use of Bayes's theorem is no more "opaque" than numerous other technical inputs into the trial process.

[36]Finkelstein & Fairley 317.

[37]Tribe 1370.

event—would interfere with the juror's ability to assess the impact of the defendant's case.[38] Nor does this suspension of judgment seem necessary to uphold the other policies Professor Tribe cites as protected by the presumption of innocence: to protect the defendant from "onerous restraints" before being found guilty; to prevent interference with community acceptance of his acquittal should that be the outcome of the trial; and to deny the existence of prosecutorial omniscience.[39]

Professor Tribe's objection that jurors would have to quantify their opinions as to guilt does not seem pertinent, since Bayesian techniques will relate to the likelihood that the trace came from the defendant, not to whether he was in fact guilty. But even if a quantitative measure of the prior probability of identity would be an "upper bound" for the strength of the jurors' suspicion of guilt, as Professor Tribe suggests,[40] what is wrong with that? The system is not infallible; it makes mistakes. Jurors convict when they have doubts. Why not recognize things as they are?

Professor Tribe agrees that "such compelled candor about its operation might have great value [for the system]."[41] Yet he says that quantification is unacceptable because it would reveal an acknowledged doubt and the system prohibits conviction when jurors have such doubts.[42] However, the standard "beyond a reasonable doubt" does not mean beyond any doubt. Jurors are commonly charged that reasonable doubt is not *no* doubt at all, but rather a doubt founded on reason and sufficient to cause a person to "hesitate to act" in a serious matter.[43] Doubts of that magnitude can be quantified, and, given the fact that jurors are allowed to convict with acknowledged doubt, there seems to be no reason why they should be denied the op-

[38]Nor does use of Bayesian methods necessarily violate Professor Tribe's requirement of a suspension of judgment until the end of the trial. A prior probability is itself a "suspension of judgment" in a sense, representing as it does a recognition that the event in question may or may not be true; it merely has the additional feature of quoting tentative odds on the likelihood of that event.

[39]See Tribe 370.

[40]See *id.* at 1372, n.138; pp. 1817–18 *infra.*

[41]Tribe 1373.

[42]*Id.* at 1374.

[43]Holland v. United States, 348 U.S. 121, 140 (1945).

portunity to use an otherwise valuable technique of weighing evidence merely because it requires them to use some quantitative measure of their uncertainty.[44]

Finally, given the narrow compass of Bayesian techniques, it seems unrealistic to argue that jurors listening to the testimony of the statistician would suddenly perceive themselves as performing no more than an automatic role and forget their humanizing function. Bayes's theorem is in fact a relatively simple tool to help explain the results of the highly complicated and technical processes which lie behind the expert's statement that the trace is similar to a source associated with the accused and that it appears with a certain frequency elsewhere. Why the Bayesian step in this process should be so deeply prejudicial to the humanity of the trial process while the large technical foundation on which is rests does not share this reproach is not apparent from the discussion in *Trial by Mathematics*.

[44]It would seem that the mere admissibility of the one-in-a-thousand statistic implies the willingness of the present judicial system to accept a quantified doubt as to the defendant's guilt. Hence, the quantification of doubt is already consistent with the respect that the present system shows for the defendant's rights, and the expressive functions of the reasonable doubt standard should continue to operate despite a different form of presentation.

A Further Critique of Mathematical Proof

Laurence H. Tribe

IN A RECENT ARTICLE in this *Review*,[1] I undertook to assess the usefulness, limitations, and possible dangers of employing mathematical methods in the legal process, both in the conduct of individual trials, and in the design of procedures for the trial system as a whole. Michael Finkelstein and William Fairley, addressing themselves exclusively to that part of my discussion of the use of mathematical methods in the conduct of trials which criticized their earlier work,[2] reply to several of my criticisms by suggesting that their intentions were far more modest than the methods of mathematical proof I examined.[3] Indeed, if the technique they advocated were as carefully confined as they had evidently intended, some of the problems I discussed would not arise.

Yet their good intentions do not diminish the force of my criticisms. I realized, in writing my article, that by investigating irrational as well as rational uses of theoretically sound methods, I would open myself to the "charge that ... I have confused the avoidable costs of using a tool badly with the inherent costs of using it well."[4] As I went on to say, however, "the costs of abusing a technique must be reckoned among the costs of using it at all to the extent that the latter creates risks of the former."[5]

---

[1]Tribe, *Trial by Mathematics. Precision and Ritual in the Legal Process*, 84 HARV. L. REV. 1329 (1971) [hereinafter cited as Tribe].

[2]Finkelstein & Fairley, *A Bayesian Approach to Identification Evidence*, 83 HARV. L. REV. 489 (1970) [hereinafter cited as Finkelstein & Fairley].

[3]See p. 291 *supra*.

[4]Tribe 1331.

[5]*Id.*

   To illustrate the ease with which the techniques proposed by Finkelstein and Fairley could be misused, I turned to the computations that they performed in their hypothetical case and argued that those computations overlooked several critical variables.[6] In the hypothetical, a palm print similar to the defendant's was found on the knife that was used to kill his girlfriend, with whom he had quarreled violently the night before. Finkelstein and Fairley proposed the use of Bayes's Theorem to inform the jury of the precise incriminating significance of the finding that similar prints appear in no more than one person in a thousand. According to their proposal, each juror would first estimate the "prior probability of guilt"[7] based on the nonmathematical evidence as to the defendant's relationship with the deceased and their previous violent quarrels; a mathematical expert would then instruct the jury as to how much the one-in-a-thousand finding increase that prior probability.[8]

I

One of my major objections to this procedure was the ease with which its significance could be mistaken. All the mathematician could realistically help the jury conclude by applying Bayes's Theorem, I argued, was the likelihood that the print on the knife belonged to the defendant—not the likelihood that the

[6]*Id.* at 13358–68.

[7]Finkelstein & Fairley 500.

[8]In my article I objected that "the lay trier will surely find it difficult at best, and sometimes impossible, to attach to $P(X)$ [the prior probability] a number that correctly represents his real prior assessment." Tribe 1358. Finkelstein and Fairley reply that "in most cases the statistical evidence would be sufficiently strong so that variations in the prior would lead to insignificant differences in the result." See Finkelstein & Fairley 305. To establish this proposition, they point to the bottom line of Table I of their article, *id.* at 500, and observe that "when the prior probability increases from .25 to .50 . . . the posterior probability only increases from .997 to .999." P. 290 *supra.*

   However, the bottom line of Table I refers only to cases in which there is a .001 probability of finding a print like the defendant's on the knife assuming that he did not use the knife to kill—something that will be true, given the possibility of frame-up, only if a similar print appears in substantially less than

defendant, rather than someone interested in framing him, had used the knife in the murder.[9] Yet this distinction, it seemed to me, could all to readily be blurred by the greater facility of quantifying the former probability than the latter.[10]

Indeed, the original article by Finkelstein and Fairley demonstrates the ease with which this distinction can be lost: they at least appeared to confuse the distinction between indentifying the print and identifying the killer. For example, they urged that Bayesian techniques be employed to quantify "the probability that defendant *used the knife*,"[11] not simply the probability that the print was his; they mistakenly argued that "defendant is a thousand times more likely to have *committed the crime* than someone selected at random from the population";[12] and they concluded that "jurors may be surprised at the strength of the *inference of guilt* flowing from the combination of their prior suspicions and the statistical evidence."[13]

---

one case out of every thousand. If, instead, one looks to the middle line of their Table I, Finkelstein & Fairley 500, which refers to cases in which there is a .1 probability of finding a print like the defendant's on the knife assuming that he did not use it to kill, one discovers that when the prior probability increases from .25 to .50, the posterior probability increases from .769 to .909, a very substantial difference indeed.

Finkelstein and Fairley now suggest that their technique should not be employed unless "the identifying trace is rare—usually much more rare than a frequency of one in a thousand...." Their original article, however, suggested that the technique would yield "significant posterior probabilities" even for "relatively high frequencies such as one in a hundred," Finkelstein & Fairley 500; stressed the utility of "evidentiary traces ... which occur quite frequently," *id*. at 501; and illustrated the use of their technique for frequencies of .5, .25, .1, .01, and .001, *id*. at 500. To be sure, limiting the original proposal to frequencies even lower than .001 would greatly diminish the significance of the objection discussed in this footnote—but it would similarly diminish the significance of the proposal itself. It leads one to wonder how the expanding set of rather imprecise limitations on the applicability of Bayesian techniques could be acceptably defined and successfully enforced. *See also* note 13 *infra;* note 16 *infra;* p. 306 *infra.*

[9]Tribe 1362–65.

[10]*Id*.

[11]Finkelstein & Fairley 498 (emphasis added).

[12]*Id*. at 497 (emphasis added).

[13]*Id*. at 517 (emphasis added). See also *id*. at 502 ("measuring probability of guilt").

Indeed, Finkelstein and Fairley explicitly used the terminology "prior probability of guilt." *Id*. at 500. They now suggest that use of this phrase was not meant to "direct jurors to *posterior* probabilities of guilt." Yet it is obvious

It now appears that Finkelstein and Fairley do regard the distinction between identification of the print and identification of the killer as important.[14] They disavow any intention to direct Bayes's Theorem to the ultimate probability that the defendant used the knife to kill his girlfriend; the only purpose of Bayesian techniques, as they now clarify their proposal, "is to assist the fact finder in interpreting statistical evidence to decide ... whether a certain trace comes from the accused."[15] But the fact remains that they originally neglected to define precisely the events under consideration, failed to make clear what possibilities were excluded by assumption, and slipped into statements that overlooked precisely those risks— such as the risk of frame-up[16]—which resist ready quantifica-

---

that if G were defined in terms of guilt for purposes of the prior probability, after application of Bayes's Theorem it would still necessarily be defined in terms of guilt in the resulting posterior probability.

They also suggest that even if G is defined to mean only that the print is the defendant's, it is proper to ask the jury to estimate $P(G)$, the prior probability of the print's indentity, by formulating their estimate in terms of guilt. This, they claim, would be a more natural way to ask the jury to evaluate the non-statistical evidence and yet, since prior probability of guilt is typically a conservative estimate of prior probability of identity, "should [meet] ... little objection." To be sure, it would not ordinarily be prejudicial to the defendant to employ a prior estimate of guilt as a conservative estimate of the probability that the print was his. See note 40 *infra*. But this proposal does nothing to reduce the risk that the jury will misunderstand the meaning of the posterior probability obtained through Bayesian techniques; indeed, asking the jury to estimate the defendant's guilt would seem to increase substantially the danger that the jury may confuse the distinction between identity and guilt at the trial's end. Additionally, asking the jury to estimate the prior probability of the print's identity in terms of guilt is still subject to all of my objections that this procedure would undermine the presumption of innocence and erode the purposes of the reasonably doubt standard. See pp. 305–09 *infra*.

[14]See pp. 292–95 *supra*.

[15]P. 292 *supra*.

[16]Another such risk is represented by the possibility "that a man about to commit murder with a knife might well choose to wear gloves, or that one who has committed murder might wipe off such prints as he happened to leave behind." Tribe 1362. Finkelstein and Fairley explain that they did not overlook the glove-wearing and erasure possibilities; rather, they "expressly excluded" such possibilities *see* p. 291 *supra*, by "assuming that a right hand palm print was left by the person who used the knife." Finkelstein & Fairley 498 n.22. But no such assumption was included in the original definitions of G as "the event that defendant used the knife," of H as "the event that a palm print similar to defendant's is found," or of $P(H|G)$ as "the probability of finding the print assuming there is identity," Finkelstein & Fairley 498. If that assumption had been included, the difficulty of quantifying the probabilities of glove-wearing or erasure would have complicated the initial estimation

tion.[17] And, by doing so, they demonstrated the temptation to focus on readily quantifable factors to the exclusion of what I have described as "soft variables "[18] a temptation to which less sophisticated users of Bayesian analysis would be even more susceptible.

II

Even if this temptation could be successfully resisted, however, and even if Bayesian techniques could as readily be confined to their proper compass as Finkelstein and Fairley would wish,

---

of "the probability that defendant used the knife, $P(G)$," *id.* at 500, no less than it otherwise complicates the computation of $P(H|G)$. See Tribe 1362–64.

Moreover, the glove-wearing and erasure possibilities are *not* in fact excluded by "assuming that a right-hand palm print was left by the person who used the knife," unless one *also* assumes that the person who once used it and left his print on it must necessarily be the person who ultimately used the knife to kill—i.e., unless one assumes that "used the knife" means "used the knife to kill." This is an assumption consistent with the original willingness of Finkelstein and Fairley to disregard the possibility of frame-up—presumably by a gloved person or by one who wiped off his own print—but hardly consistent with their present insistence that this possibility not be overlooked.

Finally, if G were to be consistently defined, not as the event that the defendant used the knife, but rather as the event that the defendant's print was found on the knife, then the probabilities of glove-wearing or erasure, as well as the probability of frame-up, would not enter into the Bayesian computation of a posterior probability of G. But they would have to be reflected instead in any assessment, given the posterior probability of G, of the probability that the defendant used the knife to kill, thus leaving the basic problem unsolved.

The "finding of a print is itself significant evidence" to use the Finkelstein-Fairley terminology, precisely because a substantial number of guilty men would have taken care not to leave one on the nurder weapon. To assume the contrary without further information is indeed both "unreasonable" and "unrealistic." *Id.*

[17]That these oversights were made seems undeniable in light of the quotations in the text, p. 301 *supra.*

Contrary to the suggestion of Finkelstein and Fairley, p. 293 n.22 *supra*, I did not find it "ambiguous . . . whether the expert would use Bayes theorem to direct the jurors to estimate the probability of defendant's guilt or the probability that the print came from the defendant." Although I considered the latter possibility, I concluded that it would require another step "to determine the probability of guilt from the knowledge of the probability that the print was the defendant's, a step that Finkelstein and Fairley clearly did not intend." Tribe 1363 n.110.

[18]Tribe 1361.

what would the use of such techniques at trial accomplish? Their use was proposed as a means of "integrating the mathematical evidence [such as the one-in-a-thousand finding] with the non-mathematical ... so that the jury would not be confronted with an impressive number that it could not intelligently combine with the rest of the evidence, and to which it would therefore be tempted to assign disproportionate weight."[19] But the use Finkelstein and Fairley would make of Bayes's Theorem confronts the jury with a number even more impressive and yet no more conclusive. Instead of learning that prints like the defendant's appear in only one case out of a thousand, the juror learns for example, that there is a 99.7 percent probability that the print was the defendant's.[20] Assuming he does not confuse this with a 99.7 percent probability of the defendant's guilt,[21] he is still left with the task of offsetting this number against "such fuzzy imponderables as the risk of frame-up."[22] There is simply no reason to suppose that a juror informed of the 99.7 percent conclusion will be better able to place it in perspective than would a juror informed only of the one-in-a-thousand finding. And, because the Bayesian conclusion is aimed closer to the ultimate issue of the defendant's guilt, there is at least some reason to fear precisely the opposite.[23]

[19]*Id.* at 1365.

[20]This would be the result if the juror estimated the prior probability as twenty-five percent. See Finkelstein & Fairley 500; Tribe 1357. If the juror estimated the prior probability as 75 percent, he would be informed that there was a 99.96 percent probability that the print was the defendant's. See Finkelstein & Fairley 500.

[21]This confusion can entail not only ignoring the risk of frame-up and similar possibilities, but also overlooking such issues as intent. *See* Tribe 1365–66.

[22]*Id.* at 1365.

[23]I have not urged, as Finkelstein and Fairley assert, that no "hard numbers" should be introduced at trial "unless everything is quantified," *id.* On the contrary, I recognized in my article that, subject to careful instructions, there may indeed be occasions on which the jury should be informed of the underlying statistical evidence. See Tribe 1355, 1377 n.155. I argued, however, that trial accuracy might well be reduced rather than enhanced if mathematical analysis were applied to this statistical evidence to obtain a quantitative value for *one* of the variables in the case, such as the probability that the print belonged to the defendant, while *other* crucial variables necessarily remained unquantified. *Id.* at 1365.

I do not, of course, exclude the possibility that testing Bayesian methods under controlled conditions, see p. 294 *supra,* might shed helpful light on the

III

In addition to defending the accuracy of the technique they proposed, Finkelstein and Fairley consider my arguments that Bayesian methods would undermine the presumption of in-nocence, erode the values served by the reasonable doubt standard, and exacerbate the dehumanization of justice.[24]

In asserting that use of Bayesian methods in criminal trials would undermine the presumption of innocence, I advanced two quite different propositions. I argued first that the Finkel-stein-Fairley proposal would create a substantial risk that the jury, invited at any given point during the trial to assess the probability of guilt in light of the evidence admitted up to that point, would make an initial assessment based in part on evi-dence not yet admitted, and perhaps never to be admitted at all. Such an assessment, if based on facts inadmissible at trial, "would undercut the many weighty policies that render some categories of evidence legally inadmissible";[25] or, if based in-stead on evidence to be admitted later in the trial would entail counting that evidence twice, thus giving it more weight than it deserves.[26]

That it would be "wholly improper . . . to invite jurors to es-timate their prior on anything but admitted evidence,"[27] as Finkelstein and Fairley argue, is, of course, true—but the point is that directing jurors to estimate a prior probability on *part* of the admitted evidence might well be *treated* as such an invita-tion. Perhaps "there is no reason to think that jurors would be *more* lawless with such directions than with others "[28] but there

---

question whether trial accuracy can be increased by the use of Bayesian anal-ysis. But I would stress that such testing must explore the impact on *the accu-racy of trial outcomes* of using Bayesian analysis to quantify only one of many relevant variables and not merely the impact of Bayesian analysis on *the ac-curacy with which that one variable can itself be quantified;* the survey con-ducted by Finkelstein and Fairley, see Finkelstein & Fairley 502–03 n.33, in-vestigated only the latter.

[24]See pp. 295–98 *supra.*

[25]Tribe 1369.

[26]*Id.*

[27]Pp. 295–96 *supra.*

[28]*Id.* (emphasis added).

is every reason to think they would be no *less* so. Unlike the situation at the trial's end, when a juror might at least find it plausible to believe that all of the evidence was before him, a juror asked to estimate a prior probability of guilt in mid-trial *knows* that there is far more in the case, and that more was known to the charging authorities, than he is being asked to weigh. Told to estimate the likelihood of the defendant's guilt based only upon several evidentiary fragments—such as the fact of violent quarrels with the deceased in the palm-print hypothetical—a juror would be hard-pressed to put this knowledge out of his mind.[29]

If, as Finkelstein and Fairley suggest,[30] the jury might not be asked to estimate a prior probability until near the end of the prosecutor's case, then the risk that the jury will reflect in its assessment facts not introduced at trial is obviously reduced. But the risk that it will count the statistical evidence twice is correspondingly increased, for the jury, having heard that evidence already, will find it impossible wholly to ignore it in estimating the prior probability.[31]

However, the core of my concern for the presumption of innocence lay elsewhere. I explained that, even if the problems discussed above were not present, merely "directing the

[29]Cf. Bruton v. United States, 391 U.S. 123 (1968) (conviction reversed because of risk that jury, even with instructions to disregard as to this petitioner evidence introduced against his codefendant, would be unable to exclude such evidence from its consideration of petitioner's guilt); Jackson v. Deenno, 378 U.S. 368 (1964) (rejecting procedure in which jury rules on voluntariness of confession because the jury, in ruling on voluntariness, will often be unable to exclude from its consideration other evidence of guilt which tends to confirm the confession; or, alternatively, if it finds the confession involuntary and hence inadmissible, the jury will often be unable to ignore knowledge of its contents when ruling on guilt).

[30]See p. 296 *supra*.

[31]That such mental gymnastics will almost certainly be beyond a jury's capacity has now been widely recognized. See, e.g., note 29 *supra*. Nor does the quite separate problem of interdependence that is posed *whenever* Bayes's Theorem is used seem to raise any significant empirical question, contrary to what Finkelstein and Fairley suggest. As I explained at greater length in my article, even if the prior could be estimated without any consideration of the statistical evidence, the proposed application of Bayes's Theorem—at any point in the trial—would entail a distorted outcome whenever some or all the evidence that underlay the prior is conditionally dependent upon the statistical evidence, a circumstance whose presence or absence cannot be feasibly determined in any given case. See Tribe 1367—68. The resulting distortion, it should be emphasized, undermines the accuracy of the proposed technique in all cases civil and criminal alike.

jury ... to assess the probability of the accused's guilt at some point before he has presented his case"[32] must inevitably conflict with a basic function of the presumption of innocence: to express respect for the accused "by the trier's willingness to listen to all ... [he] has to say before reaching any judgment, even a tentative one, as to his probable guilt."[33]

Finkelstein and Fairley reply by asserting that jurors are already likely to focus on "the strengths of the prosecutor's evidence"[34] before considering the defense. But it obviously does not follow from this assertion that jurors currently *estimate probable guilt* before hearing the defense, something the Finkelstein-Fairley technique would undeniably require them to do.[35] "Jurors cannot at the same time estimate probable guilt and suspend judgment until they have heard all the defendant has to say."[36] Insofar as this suspension of judgment is critical to fulfill the expressive function of the presumption of innocence as an affirmation of respect for the accused, one can only conclude that the proposed use of mathematics at trial would "interfere with ... the complex symbolic functions of trial procedure and its associated rhetoric,"[37] symbolic functions that Finkelstein and Fairley fail to examine.

IV

I argued next that adopting the Finkelstein-Fairley procedure would erode the values that lie behind the reasonable doubt standard by requiring society to embrace a calculated policy

[32]Tribe 1370.

[33]*Id.*

[34]P. 296–97 *supra.*

[35]See note 13 *supra.* Even if the jury were asked to estimate only the prior probability that the print was the defendant's the same objection would obtain, for the jury would be forced to prejudge, before hearing the defendant's side of the case, an important issue in the trial—perhaps the very issue that he will choose to contest.

[36]Tribe 1371. To describe the assessment of a prior probability of guilt as itself a "suspension of judgment," seems to me mere semantic confusion. To be sure, such a probability assessment acknowledges that "the event in question may or may not be true," id., but the same can be said of any probability assessment, including the final probability of guilt assessed at the trial's end.

[37]Tribe 1371.

that juries should convict even though "conscious of the magnitude of their doubts . . . [and despite] acknowledged and quantified uncertainty."[38]

To this, Finkelstein and Fairley offer two replies. They answer first that my objection "does not seem pertinent, since Bayesian techniques will relate to the likelihood that the trace came from the defendant, not to whether he was in fact guilty";[39] because opinions as to guilt will remain unquantified, juries will not be asked to convict in the face of numerically measured doubt. Yet, as I explained in my article, even if Bayesian methods are used to quantify something less than guilt, the number they yield "sets an upper bound on the probability of guilt,"[40] making all of my objections follow a fortiori. For example, if the figure of 99.7 per cent represents only the probability that the print was the defendant's leaving a margin of doubt of .3 per cent on the issue of the print's identification, it seems clear that there will be an even *larger* margin of doubt on the ultimate issue of the defendant's guilt.

But Finkelstein and Fairley go further. Even if Bayesian analysis would provide an upper bound for the probability of the defendant's guilt, they argue, it makes no difference. "The system is not infallible; it makes mistakes"—so "[w]hy not recognize things as they are?"[41]

The major problem with this argument is that it begs the question of how "things . . . are" in fact.[42] As I argued at some

[38]*Id.* at 1375 (emphasis omitted).

[39]P. 297 *supra*.

[40]Tribe 1372 n.1318. It is, of course, theoretically possible that the defendant is guilty even though he is not the source of the trace in question. But the likelihood of the converse—that he is not guilty although the trace is his—would typically be so much greater that is seems reasonable to assume that the probability of guilty will be lower than the probability that the defendant is the source of the trace. Finkelstein and Fairley apparently agree, for they seek to use the prior probability of guilt as a conservative estimate of the prior probability of trace identity.

[41]P. 297 *supra*.

[42]It also fails to respond to my argument that an undue willingness to sacrifice others and an excessive fear of unjust conviction might flow from "the explicit quantification of jury doubts in criminal trials—whether or not it would be *factually accurate* to describe the trial system as imposing criminal sanctions in the face of quantitatively measured uncertainty in particular cases." Tribe 1373 n.140.

length in my article, "the system does *not* in fact authorize the imposition of criminal punishment when the trier recognizes a quantifiable doubt as to the defendant's guilt. Instead, the system . . . insists upon as close an approximation to certainty as seems humanly attainable in the circumstances"[43]—not the unattainable goal of certainty "beyond any doubt,"[44] to be sure, but the closest approximation thereto that human knowledge will permit.[45] As I explained, the undeniable fact that

> some mistaken verdicts are inevitably returned even by jurors who regard themselves as 'certain' [in this sense] is . . . irrelevant; such unavoidable errors are in no sense *intended,* and the fact that they must occur if trials are to be conducted at all need not undermine the effort, through the symbols of trial procedure, to express society's fundamental commitment to the protection of the defendant's rights as a person . . .[46]

by "declining to put those rights in *deliberate* jeopardy."[47] It is precisely this expressive effort that would be undermined by abandoning the insistence that *any* "doubt founded on reason,"[48] of "whatever magnitude, must be resolved in favor of the accused,"[49] and replacing it with the formulation of an "'acceptable' risk of error to which the trier is willing deliberately to subject the defendant."[50]

[43]*Id.* at 1374.

[44]See p. 297 *supra.*

[45]To argue that the present system of criminal justice has already embraced the principle of convicting in the face of quantified doubt by its acceptance of such statistical evidence as the one-in-a-thousand figure, is to ignore, first, that the admissibility of such statistical evidence itself remains a highly controverted matter, see Tribe 1343–44; and second, that the introduction of a frequency statistic no more implies the existence of a quantified doubt at the end of trial than does the introduction of any other item of evidence which by itself is less than conclusive—a juror can of course feel subjectively certain of the defendant's guilt after all the evidence has been placed before him even if each individual item is not itself decisive.

[46]Tribe 1374 (footnote omitted).

[47]*Id.* (emphasis added).

[48]See p. 297 *supra.*

[49]Tribe 1374.

[50]*Id.*

V

Finally, Finkelstein and Fairley, supported in part by an informal survey they conducted, observed in their article that "jurors [using their method] may be surprised at the strength of the inference of guilt flowing from [its application] . . . ."[51] I suggested in response that techniques of proof which are so far removed from the untutored intuition "threaten to make the legal system seem even more alien and inhuman than it already does to distressingly many,"[52] and concluded that "[t]he need now is to enhance community comprehension of the trial process, not to exacerbate an already serious problem by shrouding the process in mathematical obscurity."[53]

Finkelstein and Fairley reply by characterizing my fears as "unrealistic"[54] and comparing their proposal to technical evidence generally. Yet this ignores the fact that such evidence "typically represents no more than an input into the trial process, whereas the proposed use of Bayesian methods changes the character of the trial process itself."[55] And, in any event, to say, as Finkelstein and Fairley do, that "other types of technical evidence . . . are being used in trials with increasing frequency"[56] and to note the technological complexity underlying the expert's subjective assessment of the rarity of a trace[57] is only to underscore the need to examine critically any proposed extension of the plunge into the obscure.

[51]Finkelstein & Fairley 517.

[52]Tribe 1376.

[53]*Id.* Both the survey conducted by Finkelstein and Fairley, and the informal test conducted by Professor Raiffa, see *id.* at 1375 n.148, underscore my conclusion that Bayesian methods can readily yield results that defy common intuition. These findings obviously support the power of such methods as tools of rational inquiry, see *id.*, but they simultaneously undermine the appropriateness of such techniques of proof in a system that ought to be as comprehensible as possible "to the larger community that the processes of adjudication must ultimately serve." Tribe 1376.

[54]See p. 298 *supra*.

[55]Tribe 1375.

[56]P. 294 *supra*.

[57]See p. 298 *supra*.

INDEX OF CASES

INDEX

315